Human Rights: Global Issues

Human Rights: Global Issues

Pramod Mishra

KALPAZ

Published by

Kalpaz Publications
C-30, Satyawati Nagar,
Delhi – 110052
Ph.: 011-47034999, 9811692060
www.kalpazpublications.com
E-mail: kalpaz@hotmail.com

Distribution Network
gyanbooks.com
India, USA, Canada, UK, Australia, France

ISBN: 978-81-7835-011-0 (HB)

Reprint in India, 2024
First Published, 2001

Printed at: Gyan Press, Delhi.

Human Rights: Global Issues
Author: Pramod Mishra

Contents

1 Introduction

The protection of human rights has now become one of the keystones in the arch of peace, democracy and development. The number, of procedures for guaranteeing human rights has been increasing for years, but guaranteeing human rights also means setting up jurisdictional controls to punish any violations that occur.

The link between democracy, development and human rights is meanwhile being recognized as inescapable. There can be no sustainable development without promotion democracy and, thus, respect for human rights is a matter of concern to the entire international community, for only through individual development can peace for all be ensured.

In its Vienna Declaration and Progamme of Action, the Conference recognised that all human rights were universal, indivisible and interdependent and interrelated, and the international community must treat human rights globally in a fair and equal manner, on the same footing, arid with the same emphasis. While the significance of national and regional particularities and various historical, cultural and religious backgrounds must be borne in mind, it is the duty of States, regardless of their political, economic and cultural systems, to promote ani protect all human rights and fundamental freedoms. The Conference stated that the efforts of the United Nations system towards the universal respect for, and observance of, human rights arid fundamental freedoms for all contribute to the stability and well-being necessary for peaceful and friendly relations among nations, and to improved conditions for peace and security as well as social and economic development, in conformity with the Charter of the United Nations.

The Conference deemed enhancement of international cooperation in the field of human rights as essential for the full achievement of the purposes of the United Nations. The processes of promoting and protecting human rights, it stipulated, should be conducted in conformity with the purposes and principles of the Charter and international law.

The Conference reaffirmed the right to development as a universal and inalienable, right and an integral part of fundamental human rights, with the human person as the central subject of development. Recognizing democracy, development and respect for human rights and fundamental freedoms as interdependent and mutually reinforcing, it specified that democracy is based on the freely expressed will of the people to determine their own political, economic, social and cultural systems and their-full participation in all aspects of their lives. In that context, the promotion and protection of human rights and fundamental freedoms at the national id international levels should be universal and conducted without conditions attached.

The international community should support the strengthening and promotion of democracy, development and respect for human rights and fundamental freedoms in the entire world. The Conference further determined that while development facilitates the enjoyment of all human rights, the lack of development may not be invoked to justify the abridgement of internationally recognized human rights. In order to foster human rights, priority needs to be given to national and international action to promote democracy, development and human rights, with special emphasis on measures to assist in the strengthening and building of institutions relating to human rights, strengthening of a pluralistic civil society and the protection of vulnerable groups.

Assistance provided on the request of Governments for the conduct of free and fair elections, including assistance in the human rights aspects of elections and public information about elections, is of particular importance, as is assistance for strengthening the rule of law, the promotion of freedom of expression and the administration of justice and for the real arid effective participation of the people in the decision-making processes. Essential for the promotion and achievement of stable and harmonious relations among communities and for fostering mutual understanding, tolerance and peace is human rights education, which should cover peace, democracy, development and social justice, as set forth in international and regional instruments. Governments should promote increased awareness of human rights and mutual tolerance, supporting human rights education arid undertaking effective dissemination of information in that field.

Historical Background

The concept of human rights tells a detailed story of the attempts made to define basic dignity and worth of the human beings and his or her most fundamental entitlement. The denial of human rights and fundamental freedoms not only is an individual and personal tragedy but also creates conditions of social and political unrest sowing the seeds of violence and conflict within and between Societies and Nations. Just to avoid these problems various international agencies including League of Nations, U.N.O., laid stress for the protection of human fights permanently, although the idea of human rights predates the United Nations. It can be easily appreciated that human rights and fundamental freedoms allow us to develop fully and use our human qualities, our intelligence, our talents and our conscience and to satisfy our spiritual and other needs. They are based on mankind's increasing demand for a life in which the inherent dignity and worth of each human being will receive respect and protection.

In the language of United Nations Center for human rights—"human rights could be generally defined and those rights which are inherent in our nature and without which we cannot live as human beings". The expression human rights had its on in international law relating to the development of the status of an individual in the international legal system, which was originally confined to the relation between sovereign states, who were regarded as the only person in international law. For all practical purposes, the genesis of human rights is not older than Second World War though the concept of individual having certain inalienable rights as against state had its origin in the dim post. The concept of human rights, embodying the minimum rights of an individual versus his own State is as old as political philosophy.

Human rights are those minimum rights which every individual must have against state or other public authority by virtue of his being a member of human family, irrespective of any other consideration. The concept of human rights is as old as the ancient doctrine of natural rights founded on natural law, the expression human is of recent origin. It is only natural rights which eventually led to the formation of human rights.

The concept of human rights, in its expanding comprehension, has now travelled to encompass what are called "third-generation" or "solidarity" fights. At the very beginning stands the rights of self-determination, a fight regarded as belonging to peoples rather than individuals, and which India, with its emphasis on national integrity, has rightly identified as a right applicable only to peoples under foreign domination. Then, there is the right to sovereignty over the natural wealth and resources of the country and the right to the peoples of developing countries. Both rights are found in identical language in both covenants, and therefore may be regarded as civil and political rights as well as economic, cultural and social rights.

The third-generation rights extend to the right to international peace, the right to a satisfactory environment favourable to development, and the rights of ethnic, religious and linguistic minorities. It can no longer be doubted that the concept of human rights, at one time indulgently looked upon as the impracticable dream of natural law philosophers, has became in the course of these four decades an international reality. But problems remain in the application, implementation and protection of human rights. A not inconsiderable degree of intellectual confusion prevails among political scientists and international lawyers in adequately formulating the more fundamental problems, and in performing the necessarily intellectual tasks relating to establishing and maintaining appropriate constitutive processes and public order policies.

The principal difficulty lies in the non-availability of an adequate substantive definition of human rights. The definition provided by Richard Wasserstrom reflecting the common general understanding of the concept, that "one ought to be able to claim as entitlements (that is, as human fights) those minimal things without which it is impossible to develop one's capabilities and to live life as a human being "fails as an insufficient and simplistic definition. In that context, referring to the doubt raised on whether economic, social and cultural rights can be classified as human rights, some commentators cite concerns" about definition imprecision, unenforceability, unmanageability of the concept as a whole, and the difficulty of achieving the full justiciability of the rights in question". Similar problems arise in relation to the "third-generation" rights. Described as the rights of "problem", their claim to be considered as human rights are doubted because, as Paul Sieghart points' out, they "cannot belong to any identifiable individuals". Little effort has been made to create a comprehensive map of the totality of human rights, and there has been no appreciable discussion of the detailed content of particular rights.

The importance of precise definition cannot be underestimated. For, as Bilden observes, "what we think human rights really are will inevitably influence not only our judgment as to which types of claims to recognize as human rights, but also our expectations and programs for implementation and compliance with these standards". Sometimes human rights are conceived in terms of natural law absolutes and buttressed by trans-empirical justifications, both theological and metaphysical. At other times, human rights are defined in terms of the demands made by individuals or groups at particular times within their particular communities.

Human rights may also often be confined to the particular rights which the ruling system of law in the state will protect. Human rights may, further, be defined solely by reference to a larger regional or global community context. The problem often arises because of difference in approach and perspective, for instance whether the concept of human rights is related to the Natural Law approach, the Historical approach, the Positivist approach or the Marxist approach.

In the Third World, the perspective applied to the concept and reality of human rights varies with prevailing local philosophy, culture, ideology and historical tradition. Understandably in the case of former colonies the emphasis will lie as much on civil and political rights and the "third-generation" rights, with a somewhat decisive inclination in favour of community interest, where in the context of community interest, where social and economic progress and development are regarded as of primary importance.

Credit must go to those commentators who have attempted to reconcile development with respect for human rights, especially when it cannot be doubted today that the enjoyment of human rights bears an essential connection with economic development, each being necessary to the other. Following the proposal suggested by the International Commission of Jurists, Sieghart treats of development as conceivable in two directions, the right vested in the state (that is, the "people").

The individual right to development is the right to participate in, and benefit from, the process of development intended by the state for all members of the community so that each individual may enjoy all his human rights, whether civil, political, economic, social or cultural. And a state which can demonstrate that it has fashioned such an environment for its citizens will be legitimately entitled to claim a right to development on the international plane, calling upon other states to assist it in the realization of its internal ethos.

The human rights movement has progressed to a point where in its fundamental conception it treats of members of the human race as members of a global community and, therefore, broadly entitled to a common pattern of human rights. The pervasive presence of human rights in almost all the dimensions of daily fife in most societies provides a cementing influence in the realization of the world recognizing the need in the current political climate for examining issues on a global basis, the internationalization of human rights values can be excepted to proceed apace. The process may move slowly, but the beginning of the trend is unmistakable. We have growing evidence already of reference by domestic courts to international human rights norms when construing municipal legislation.

The question of primacy between society and the individual is a perennial problem of social philosophy. If the question is considered chronologically against the backdrop of biological evolution, it is similar in the conundrum; which came first, the hen or the egg. Human beings have always been gregarious. It is well established by now that the origin of the new species was through a chance mutation in the composition of a genetic cell. This may indicate that a new species is born with the birth of an individual having a different gene than its parents. It is at the same time obvious that the further development of a new species might have taken place through a series of sexual combinations which caused further genetic alterations.

The origin of a new species appears to be both an individual and a social phenomenon. The science of biological evolution does not help in establishing the primacy of society over the individual or vice versa. There is, however, a reason, logical rather than chronological, Which justifies primacy of the individual over society. This is that the individual is a biological being, possessed of consciousness and pain, progress and regress. Society is not a biological being and it is not possessed of a consciousness of its own. It cannot as an entity have any mental experience. Its happiness and its progress can be measured only in terms of the happiness and progress of the individuals, which compose it. It is in this sense that primacy belongs to the individual.

The fact that the human individual is alone possessed of consciousness and not any combination of individuals such as a society, a nation or a class, justifies the humanist principle that man (the human individual whether male or female) is the "measure of things". The question of the comparative worth of social institutions, such as democracy versus dictatorship in politics or capitalism versus state ownership in the economic sphere, can only be decided by assessing its impact on the individuals who constitute a society or a nation.

The genesis of the concept of human rights can be traced into the emergence of classical liberalism. Classical liberalism made a passionate defense of the principles like competitive individualism, private property and market ethics, etc. It cherished the realization of Individual's liberty, his development and human progress through the functioning of the above principles. The ideas of the rule of law, limited government and individualism characterized the seventeenth and eighteenth century anti-nationalist school of political liberalism."

Human rights are not merely ideals or aspirations, nor are they some rights granted to us by the existence of particular set of laws. They are claims made by virtue of the fact that we are human beings with an inalienable right to human dignity. Therefore, we cannot delegate the authority to a group of persons to define these lights. All individuals and all peoples have these rights to self-directed development.

Now we should consider about the concept of human rights as Propounded by Justice V.R. Krishna Iyer. He has described "Human rights and fundamental freedoms are indivisible, the full realization of civil and political rights and cultural rights, is impossible. This process of realization calls for legal positivisation, not political polemics nor diplomatic clap-trap but normative formulation. But what are human rights? Religion of Man is located in the Vedas, Buddhist Texts, Bible, the Quran or the holy literature or other authentic teachers to upholds human divinity. Every human being is a divine being and has title to dignity, liberty, equality and other basic rights. We cannot understand or evaluate human rights divorced from the historical and social context. Idle ideals and empty assertions cut no ice. The status of human rights takes us to the life-style of a society. That is why the Indian constitutional approach is soaked in the social milieu and human conditions. India is plural Society and the concept of the human rights in such society has a different and unique position."

With regard to the position of human rights Scarman has said "an article that the problem is old". Today we tend to think in terms of ethic origin or skin colour when we take of a plural society. But there are other social divisions just a difficult to bridge that most unitary of Societies, the greek city state was a plural society, incorporating the rightless slave as well as the fully entitled citizen and the Roman world was a compiles plural society as any in the history of mankind, but human rights are they as prevalent or as old established as the plural society? That is another story. For most of mankind's human rights have and continue today to be, more conspicuous in the mouth of men than in their practice. Vis-a-vis woe to the conquered and the oppressed, the true facts of life, than the lipservice paid by the Universal Declaration of Human Rights.

The concept of human rights has gradually evolved over the past several centuries. It is immaterial whether you call these rights as inherent rights, fundamental rights or by some other name. These rights by themselves have no fixed content as has been rightly remarked by Justice Mathew and most of them are empty vessels into which each generation has poured its content in the light of its experience. Human fights, as conceived in the last few decades of the twentieth century, are justifiable claims on behalf of all men to corporate action. They are owed to the individual by the State as well as by the organized social and economic groups which are the center of power and authority. The concept of human rights has a dynamic nature in reference to time and space.

Human fights have existed, in however, nascent a form, ever since man as a gregarious animal has lived in communities; family, clan, tribe, village, town or nation, and now in an independent, world community. The superstitious acceptance by the ignorant masses of their object poverty, of human miseries, hunger and disease, of callous discrimination and exploitation of man-by-man, and of the age-old apathy of the elite in power in large parts of this globe, has further complicated the problem of human rights.

The U.N. Charter has provided a Constitutional basis on which the United Nations can bring about changes in the status of the individual vis-a-vis his own State. The United Nations have been deeply involved in the furtherance of the cause of human rights ever since its inception. Human Rights could thus be defined to be the rights of an individual and the interest to be protected collectively both at international and national level by the coordinated efforts with the intervention of the States in pursuance of intended objectives collective wisdom is utilized for formulating basic policies on a uniform pattern which are given recognition jointly so as to adopt and enforce them in the form of so-called human rights and in this process even if there is any conflict of interest among various nations but it occupies insignificant position and having least regard to national boundaries, common consensus is arrived at for the purpose of upliftment of mankind, in general and for improving the lot of downtrodden masses, in particular. In this context, it could be rightly said that a man is a human-being first and foremost irrespective of where he is born to live and it is indeed a welcome development.

The basic problem that arises concerning human right relates to their proper enforcement and this aspect varies today from State to State. This is indeed so because the first initial step in the direction of enforcement of human rights is very much confined to the national frontiers of the state where the individual resides. It would be certainly justified to presume that so far as the basic job of drafting the human rights is concerned, this job has been successfully accomplished by the efforts of member states of United Nations Organization but the basic problem has been the effective enforcement of human rights so as to eradicate poverty and improve standard of living of mankind, in general and the worker, in particular. It is apparent that any concept of human rights which can be acceptable to the modem liberal democratic societies must fulfil two basic assumptions.

First, the rights must be equal in an effective manner. Second, there must be an obligation on others to accept each notion of natural rights does not meet these requirements. Writing primarily in the concept of classical political philosophies Hobbe's and Locke's views on natural rights. Macpherson explains this failure in the following manner: "The inability of either doctrine to meet our requirement is due to the same basic postulate about the nature of man and society; and it is this postulate which makes it impossible that any extension or reshaping of their concepts of natural rights could produce a new acceptable theory of human rights. Both writers imputed to the nature of society a permanent conflict of interests between individuals. Hobbe's men necessarily sought power over others. Locke's national men sought unlimited property, which he assumed must be at the expense of others'. Thus classical liberalism, which lies at the heart of natural right tradition, cannot be acceptable to modem liberal democratic as it rested on the sanctification of bourgeois self-interest.

The liberal democratic concept of human rights in the second half of the twentieth century has come to mean defense of the rights of the human being against abuses of power committed by the organs of the state with the help of institutionalized means. It also involves the promotion of the establishment of human living conditions and the overall development of the human personality.

What are the main contentions of the twentieth century human rights theory? Briefly stated, they are among others; First, the validity of human rights is established by specific legislation. The inherent dignity of human being is not sufficient. Thus the whole concept has acquired a juridical character; second, within the bourgeois legal system the human rights issue receive an extended treatment by two branches of law, i.e. constitutional and International Law; third, the human rights are vested in all individuals and only in individuals, not in professional groups, Social groups, communities, tribes, races, classes, castes, nations or other entities. Furthermore, a human being enjoys his or her human rights both as an individual and a citizen; fourth, the human rights concept remains immutably valid wherever human beings lead a collective life.

The above concept of human rights has been gaining wider significance and acceptance in the western liberal democratic countries who have reached the stage of advanced capitalism. Liberal democratic theory of human rights has not been accepted both by the socialist countries as well as the developing countries.

Writing in the Holy Family, Marx and Engels stated: 'The recognition of the rights of man by the modem State has no other meaning than the recognition of slavery by the ancient state had slavery as its natural basis, the modem state has as its natural basis, civil society and the man of civil society, i.e. the individual man linked with other men only by the ties of private interest and unconscious natural necessity, the slave of labour for gain and of his own as well as other men's selfish needs. It follows that the very notion of human rights, according to Marx and Engels is linked to the competitive struggle that is the hallmark of the bourgeois society and is based on vision of society and the individual as inherently separate and antagonistic units.

Human rights are thus viewed as instruments for carrying out adversary relations between competing, primarily atomistic individuals. Central to Marxism in its concern for human beings and the idea that man, stripped of 'his human essence' when he first fell into the class of the exploited, confronts the destruction of all humanity' in him in a bourgeois society. The process of bourgeois exploitation, with its natural corollary 'greed and the war between the greedy competition' holds the entire society at the mercy of the market forces. It 'estranges man from nature; from himself, his own active functioning . . . from his universal, essence . . . it makes his essence into a mere means for his existence . . . It estranges . . . his spiritual, his human essence . . . it results in) the alienation of man from man'. Such kind of alienating, depersonalizing and dehumanizing impact of bourgeois system makes the whole context that Marx stated about communism that it is the actual phase necessary for the next stage of historical development in the process of human emancipation and recovery. Thus in a Communist Society, Marx argued in the critique of the Gotha Program working class would enjoy the right to compensation for labour.

In the early socialist stage the working class would contribute a quantity of labour and in return, would acquire a right to receive back a share of the social product exactly in proportion to its contribution in the production process. However, in the later phase of communism when subordination to the division of labour would be ended 'only then come the narrow horizon of bourgeois right be crossed in its entirety and society inscribe on its banners' from each according to his ability, to each according to his needs.

The liberal democratic theory of human has also invited criticism in the context of its application in the developing stages. Like the Marxist critique, one common theme in analysis of third world conceptions of human rights is the individualism of the human rights theory, its 'obsessive concern with the dignity of the individual, his worth, personal autonomy and property.'

Presenting a view from the periphery, Legesse argues: If Africans were the sole authors of the Universal Declaration of Human Rights, they might have ranked the rights of communities above those of individual's. What is true for Africa is also true for the Arab world. Writing of the predominantly Islamic societies Yamani criticizes the western liberal democratic tradition as it, according to him, is so overzealous in its defense of the individuals freedom, rights and dignity, that it overlooks the acts of some individuals in exercising individual centered and universalist philosophical premises of western liberal human rights concept. Legesse argues that 'any system of ideas that claims to be universal must contain critical elements in its fabric that are avowedly of African, Latin American or Asian derivation'. In a similar vein, Cranston asks: How can the governments of those parts of Asia, Africa, and South America, where industrialization has hardly begun, be social rights . . . secured by fairly simple legislation. Since these rights are largely rights against government interference, the greatest effort will be directed towards restraining the government's own executive arms. In essence, the western liberal democratic human rights concepts with its emphasis on the natural, inalienable and individualistic rights of human beings favour the empowerment of the state and its organs.

The whole idea is that if the human beings are to be empowered to become able to enjoy the human rights, the state and its organs must be correspondingly disempowered. Such an idea if considered in the non-western context leads to an 'acute' and 'real' dilemma, especially if it gets too far fetched. As Upendra Baxi argues: 'The notion of disempowerment makes sense. But should it be extended all the ways? Obviously not.

Activists to ask that new laws may be made addressing the worst forms of violations of human rights in the civil society, usually associated with the most regressive forms of social behaviour associated with a historic revival of religion, culture and ethnicity. Should there not be stricted law and state action, for example, on sati, dowry murders, sex-selective abortions through the abuse of amniocentesis techniques, nutritional sex discrimination which creates new forms of deferred female infanticide, child abuse, familial violence against women, atrocities against dalits, exploitation of bounded, migrant and contract labour? The answer is yes. The difficulty with this answer is that it empowers the state. Baxi's views held true for India as well as other developing countries where there has been wider agreement in favour of the acceptance of the inclusion of group or people's rights along with the individualistic human rights.

The third world concept of articulation between human rights and people's rights may result into the marginalisation of the sentinel character of human rights. However, one must understand that the unique social, economical and political structures of the developing countries make it imperative that a relatively autonomous 'overdeveloped' state has to play a pivotal role in maintaining human rights with the help of a relatively independent judiciary, while recognizing that the state is an instrument of the class domination, of disorganizing the sub-patterns, of fracturing their emergent unity, and disorienting the masses struggle for justice and rights. We have to retain state and its bourgeois legal system. 'To renounce this . . . altogether is . . . to enfeeble the potential of controlling the privileges class deviance, which is far more difficult to combat than the deviance of the impoverished.

The solution of the above problem lies in the radical transformation of the society, state and economy which would be accompanied with a vision of counter-law, an alternate legality which will base itself on moralities, ideologies and practices, not merely different from but superior to those of the (existing bourgeois) state law. Until that is realized with the achievement of scientific socialism, the human rights movements in the developing states must not remain observed with the condemnation of state and its relatively autonomous legal system, of course, this does not mean that the repressive laws, agencies, ideology, actions, etc. of the state are not to be combated. All of us belong to one family: mankind. Every member of our fan-lily has the same fundamental and equal rights. Each of us is entitled to have these rights respected and each of us has a responsibility to protect these rights for all others. Differences of race, sex, language and colour do not change these rights. Nor go differences of property, social origin, political ideas or religious beliefs.

Every one regardless of who they are and what they do or think, is born with human rights. It is worth mentioning here that the subject of human rights' is of universal concept of human rights is that of the respect for human personality and its absolute worth regardless of colour, race, sex, religion or other considerations. These rights are essential for the full development of the human personality and for human happiness. Woven into the wrap and woof of human history, the concept of Human Rights has been a variable and dynamic one. It has in fact varied from generation to generation and evolved with the changing times and under the constantly shifting conditions. Even within the same Society, perception of what human rights are, may vary from state to state. Human rights ought to be for all men and women, general and universal and not linked to any special positions.

What shall vary in different situations and at different points will be the extent of implementation and limitation of human rights and not the content or nature of the rights themselves. Human rights are rights both of individuals and of Society, of groups, of minorities and of majorities.

The human right signifies both rights and duties which are inter-linked. The term "Human Rights" means being argued as vital for a democratic society, but also an economic, social and cultural rights as well as the rights are essential component of sustainable development and therefore not possible without respect of human rights. Respect of human rights makes freedom meaningful. Human rights are meaningless in an environment of poverty and deprivation. Human rights are above politics. They are part and parcel of life in society and they concern humanity. Human rights necessarily signify human values in an absolute senses: but they have greater relevance to the real well-being of the individual if they are applied in the context of society.

The human rights are sign and symbol of human development and peace. The whole fabric of society depends upon human rights. Without human rights the society cannot run smoothly, and there could be many chances of crimes and disturbances in the society. The protection of human rights is a constant struggle which cannot be won unless every man and woman participate in it. In real practice the human rights is the sum of all rights necessary to ensure our rights to be human and it is the duty of all peoples and governments to create the condition headed to exercise our right to be human.

Let us conclude few basic essentials to qualify a particular right to be human rights. These essentials may be counted as follows:

1. It is a right of individual or group of individuals.
2. It can only be executed in a Society for and against state by individual or groups.
3. These rights are inalienable and human beings are entitled to them by birth.
4. It is a permanent universal and legal concept in all spheres of life.
5. These rights are meant to uphold human dignity and equality and to set forth liberty and fraternity to all without any kind of discrimination to all needy.
6. These rights are minimum requirements for survival of mankind or human beings in Societies.
7. These rights are protected and enforced by the Authority

of society or state at all levels.

In brief, "human rights comprise rights of individual or groups in a society in all spheres of life since inception up to the last, i.e. from birth to death. They may be exercised individually or collectively." No specific set of rights can be created universally. These may differ from time to time and place to place, but their applicability is universal. Hence, human rights are "those minimum set of rights of a mankind available in all spheres of life to all individual or groups of Societies individually or collectively which is expected to be permanently inalienable since berth up to last of man or society for the purposes of survival or benefit of mankind, individual or society."

Classical liberalism made a passionate defense of the principles like competitive individualism, private property and market ethics, etc. It cherished the realization of individual's liberty, his development and human progress through the functioning of the above principles. The ideas of the rule of law, limited government and individualism characterized the seventeenth and eighteenth century and anti-nationalist school of political liberalism.

Macpherson in his brilliant study of classical political liberalism refers to the assumptions, inherent in the view it takes of man, society and political society. These assumptions according to Macpherson, and 'peculiarly appropriate to a possessive market society', as 'possessive individualism'. Thus the individual is conceptualized 'as essentially the proprietor of his own person or capacities, owing nothing to society for them. Freedom is viewed as 'a function of possession'. Essentially the greatness of liberalism was its assertion of the free rational individual as the criterion of the good society.

Broadly speaking, these different variants of general political theory can be viewed as deriving their theoretical fundamentals from one of three types. The individualist-liberal theory has no difficulty accommodating the rights of life, liberty, and property, for it was built largely on the individual, but it finds some difficulty fitting in the modem ideas of economic rights, but do not find it so easy to accommodate the earlier trilogy of natural rights of life, liberty and property, which they have tended to mistrust on the ground that these are essentially bourgeois' rights.

Everyone is born with human rights regardless of who he is and to which community he belongs, and wears different culture. Everyone has a right to be protected by the state and the people. Human rights are inherent in and integral to every human beings, basic for human life and its development, and incorporated in the constitutions of every state.

The concept of human rights has gradually evolved over the past several centuries. It is immaterial whether you call these rights as inherent rights, fundamental rights of by some other name. These rights by themselves have no fixed content as has been rightly remarked by Justice Mathew" and most of them are empty vessels into which each generation has poured its content in the light of its experience. Human rights, as conceived in the last few decades of the twentieth century, are justifiable claims on behalf of all men to corporate action. They are owed to the individual by the state as well as by the organized social and economic groups which are the center of power and authority. The concept of human rights has a dynamic nature in reference to time and space.

According to religious philosophical views the basis of human rights is "Dharma" which is vitally concerned with humanity. Dharma is one word which defines and covers the totality of human experience and existence.

Dharma derived from the root, Dhr meaning to uphold, to support, to nourish, to integrate, etc., is the sum total of essential values and ideas on which the political, economic, cultural and religious expression of life are based. Dharma has another dimension when relates to the individual person who contribute society.

Source of Human Rights

There are various theories and sources of human rights. Let us first concern ourselves to the various sources of human rights. Religion is one of the old. Ancient source, not only of human rights but also to the world at large. Its ambiguity cannot be identified. All basic principles of human rights are derived from all major religions. Principles of natural justice and Law constitute another old and essential basic of all societies in all respects. Human rights are no exception to it. All universal natural law principles are human rights. These are principles of logic which still govern the conscience of society and man. Individuals thinking constitute major thought of human rights. It shall be considered later on. All codification which provide rights to Individual constitute major modem human rights at present.

Sometimes Governmental orders, circular orders and executive actions also play a vital role in the field of human rights. Marxim thoughts also define the human rights in one special society of communism. Now the sociological aspect has a key role to play in modern times. Law has been a method of social engineering. Law is meant to progress of society by social actions. It is only possible if all human rights are observed in society.

The ancient heritage of India was not only rich and great, but also mostly spiritual and ethical in nature. Indian culture and civilisation were based on certain spiritual and ethical values which may be taken as

Dharma which is not religious in true sense of the term. The term 'Dharma' etymologically means which upholds, supports and nourishes the society. It maintains stability of the social order and promotes well-being and progress of the mankind. Dharma, is thus, asserts to oneself good conscious and conscientious principles that spring from and aims at increasing one, s happiness and well-being. It relieves from ignorance, fear, disease and other evils and cherishes and moulds fellow-feeling, brotherhood and amity and other good feelings.

The Vedas and Puranas contain basic principles of Dharma, Artha, Kama and Moksha. Dharma was practically dominating other aspects of Indian life in the past. It influenced substantially social, economic and political life and seemed to have moulded and welded into a social order which was a unified configuration of ideas, ideals and practices that are mostly ethical as well as spiritual. The fundamental principles propounded in the Vedas aim at securing happiness to all, which constitute Dharma. These were all basic human rights incorporated in the Smritis and Puranas in various rules and regulations, customs and usages.

Anything which goes against these principles were rejected as invalid. Dharma as enunciated by Vyas, the author of Mahabharat, also says that when there is conflict between what is Dharma in the Vedas and provisions in the Smritis, Puranas, etc.—what is declared in the Vedas shall prevail. These principles enable us to decide what is Dharma and what is Adharma? These provisions also intend us to adopt Dharma and reject Adharma. As observed by Justice Jois, "This is similar to Art. 13 of our Constitution which provides that laws enacted by the Legislature/Rules made by the State are liable to be struck down as void if they violate the spirit of the Fundamental, Rights".

The principles of Dharma show that human rights are valuable and eternal. These are identified and are recognised in Indian civilisation from time immemorial as the basic conditions for peaceful and progressive life. These are the values included in the human rights subsequently incorporated in the Universal Declaration of Human Rights and also in various Fundamental Rights contained in Part III of the Constitution of India.

Moksha or salvation was the ultimate reality for the Indians, and it aims at not only salvation from the birth but also from ignorance and poverty of all kinds. It was closely related to spiritual and religious pursuits of the people. Dharma also is not aloof from the well-being of the people. Rather all the individuals regard moksha as the most alluring spiritual well-being to be relished and the most valuable, and ethical, metaphysical wealth created through religious activities. Thus Dharma was taken as the ultimate reality and basic to all spiritual activities of the ancient Indians.

The material attainment through Artha and Kama-two most important worldly pursuits were an integral part of Dharma and the purpose of all these achievements was the realisation of the ultimate end of life-Moksha. Individual was considered basic unit of the society and he has to be given all the facilities and conditions for attainment of excellence in all these directions. These facilities and conditions are the basic human rights. These are regarded as the instruments for achieving objectives of Dharma, Artha, Kama and Moksha. These four cardinal values (chaturbarg) constituted the ancient cultural heritage-of India. Although there were some contradictions and contentions to the basic value, these principles ultimately pre-dominated the spiritual life of Indians. Charvaka was one of the pioneers and powerful exponents of materialism. His words were sweet and alluring for

Charu means nice and Vaka means words. But he did not drift away Indians in general.

On the whole, Artha and Kama were the main aims of life according to the Charvaka's philosophy. The worldly pleasure was rather the ultimate end of or aim of materialism as advocated by this school of philosophy However, Vedas and vedic philosophy did not accept the materialism of Charvaka and as such it was mostly rejected by the vedic culture of India. It was rather criticised and condemned by most of the philosophical schools of India, as it was gross egoistic hedonism. It was also felt that such individualistic and gross material interest would destroy social structure and frame of human relations.

The pleasure seeking worldly pursuit would spoil the ethical and cultural values which are the bases of human rights. The materialistic philosophy of Charvaka was, however, refined by some thinkers. For instance, Vatsayana, the famous author of Kamasutra was called materialist alongwith a few others. He pleaded for pleasures of life and believed in the positive aspects of life of desirable happiness in a civilised manner. Charvaka laid emphasis on spiritual discipline, self-control and self-sacrifice to some extent which are the basic human rights i.e., restraint of one's pleasure for allowing others to live gracefully. The entire ancient Indian civilisation was based on a kind of realistic idealism.

The sweet reconciliation was made between secular and spiritual spheres and compromises made in between. Rather both of them were wonderfully blended into a harmonious whole. Gupta has rightly observed, "Indian life in all its respects both in daily course and more important relations was bound up with religious observation called to bring about the realisation of the ultimate truth by progressive course of mental and moral discipline. Physical body was looked upon as a scared duty. Chaturbarg or four types of principles viz., Dharma, Artha, Kama and Moksha ensure and promote a cluster of human rights like Right to Happiness, Right to Equality, Right to Religion, Right to Protection, Right to Education, Right to Social Security, Right to Humane Treatment and Right to justice, etc. All these human rights are duty-based and the society cannot guarantee such rights without reciprocal duties. These rights are discussed as follows:

Right to happiness

Human beings desire happiness at every stage and in every sphere of his/her life. Pleasure or satisfaction gives happiness and displeasure or frustration creates unhappiness. Man is apt to avoid unhappiness and seeks happiness. Hence, it is a natural human right to be happy and without happiness life becomes dull and dreamy. Right to Happiness is, therefore, essential for every individual and has been recognised as salt of life. Since it is the most important human right and comprises all rights relating to self-fulfilment and satisfaction, it is very much comprehensive.

Every human being has the capacity to fulfil his/her desires through his/her efforts and secure happiness for himself/herself and for others who are his near and dear ones to him/her. Human life is full of sorrows and sufferings and pleasure and happiness. Happiness which is beyond one's reach may create unhappiness. Some unhappiness is created by one's inadequacies and some are by various accidents and accumulated whether man made or natural.

Miseries which can be avoided create more unhappiness and miseries which cannot be avoided are tolerated easily. Individual being rational has to take decisions judiciously and discharges his/her responsibilities for achieving his pleasure and happiness. It is natural that every human activity has certain objectives which may be personal or otherwise and man performs his work as a result of the impulse of his desire, or Kama. The force behind man's every action is his/her desire or Kama whether for getting good food or cloth or wealth and for other valuables i.e., Artha for securing comfort and pleasure.

To get rid of all these man-made miseries is an eternal issue confronting mankind. By that we can ensure the realisation of right to happiness. Every human activity, good or bad is motivated by certain desire. Centuries back, Manu, has rightly said, "There is no act of man which is free from desire. Whatever man does is the result of impulse of his desire". Relating to desire we have the Kama and Artha which are at the root of desire and difficulties. Man's desire, i.e., Kama is influenced by other impulses like Krodh (Anger), Moha (Passion), Lobha (Greed), Mada (infatuation) and Matsarya (Hostility). These six impulses are considered as man's enemies and if they are uncontrolled they created selfish desire and cause injuries to others as a result of which wrongful actions/acts are done and happiness is sacrificed in the long-run.

Dharma or righteous conduct ensures happiness among the people treading the path of Dharma. The people are overpowered by sensual desires, Passion and Greed. Manu has, therefore, laid down tri-varga i.e., Dharma, Artha and Kama for promoting welfare and happiness among the people. This is the basic philosophy of Indian life and this doctrine was introduced to strike a balance between the interest of individuals and that of public. The objective was to secure right tic) happiness through supremacy of Dharma over Artha. The advocates of Dharma also observed that the fulfilment of desire was an essential aspect of human life. Without it, life was meaningless. But such desires are to be regulated by the Principles of Dharma.

As we all know, peace is the outcome of happiness and if peace is sought and found, then naturally happiness is ensured. In Mahabharat also a stateless society was contemplated where, human rights were protected by others confirming to Dharma, Kautilya, in its Arthasastra incorporated Rajadharma emphasising the right to happiness of all individuals and the righteous duties of the King. The principle of Dharma is inculcated in the hearts of every individual. The principles should also prevail in the modem democratic society which stands for the ideal "Sarve Bhavantu Sukhinah" (Let all people be happy). This doctrine was also adopted in the Constitution of India and has been reinforced through various Acts and Policy decisions of the modem Government.

Right to Equality

The very foundation of Indian culture is laid on the principles of equality, equity and other egalitarian tenets. The Right to Equality (Samanata) or Samya is regarded as an important right without which happiness is not available. The discrimination led to inequality that resulted in discontent and miseries. Vedas preach Dharma and a charter of equality is incorporated in the Rig Vedas and also in the Atharva Veda. In the Rig Veda, it has been rightly said, "No one is superior or inferior. All are brothers and all should strive for the interest of all and progress collectively". Similarly in Atharva Veda, it has been pointed out, "All have equal rights in articles of food and water". Yoke of the chariot of life is placed equally on the shoulders of all. All should live together with harmony supporting one another like spokes of a wheel of the chariot connecting its ring and the hub".

Hence Right to Equality of all human beings has been said and reiterated in so many hymns of the Vedas. All individuals are regarded as the children of God and there should be no discrimination and disparity in the human society Rig Veda and Atharva Vedas are vociferous about the equality of man which is taken as an integral part of Dharma. It is also interesting to see the Article 1 of the Universal Declaration of Human Rights, 1948 in this context, "All human beings are born free and equal in dignity and right. They are endowed with reason and conscience and should get Act towards one another in a spirit of brotherhood. It has also been reinforced in the Article 7 of the same document, "All are equal before law and are entitled without any discrimination of equal protection of the law. All are entitled to equal protection against any discrimination in violation of this Declaration and against any incitement to such discrimination.

In explaining Rajadharma, Manu says, "Just as the mother Earth gives equal support to all the living beings so also a King should give support to all without any discrimination (IX-31)." Hence it is emphasised that a King should give equal treatment to all the citizens in the same manner as a mother towards her children. Article 14 of the Constitution of India has also aptly says, "State shall not deny to any person equality before law or the equal protection of law within the territory of India. Article 14 of the Constitution is regarded as the fundamental right to equality which secures equality of the individual before law and equal protection to all on the part of the state.

The Supreme Court and High Courts of India in different states have also ensured Right to Equality of the Indian citizens through their various judgements. The latest incidence in this context is the transfer of Ex-Chief Ministers of Bihar Shri Laloo Prasad Yadav and Dr. Jagannath Mishra from Bihar Military Police Guest

House to Beur Central Jail at Patna in response to Public Interest Litigation filed before the Supreme Court of India.

Right to Education

Through ages education regarded as a means of equality and potential instrument for social change. An individual can improve to the maximum mainly through education. Therefore, the Vedas laid stress on three pious obligations as Dharma, namely 'gratitude' in which every individual has an obligation to the source of all benefits received by him including his own existence. These obligations as declared in the Vedas are:

(1) towards God (Devaruna);

(2) towards Parents (Pitruruna); and

(3) towards Rishis (Rishiruna).

These ethical obligations have been explained by Vyas in Bhagwat Gita and he had added fourth obligation, namely towards human society (Manavruna). This is very remarkable contribution of Vyas towards mankind.

Man should discharge Pitruruna by maintaining continuity of family, Devaruna by worshipping God, Rishiruna by the acquisition and dissemination of knowledge and Manavaruna by performing /involving oneself in every type of social services. All these obligations are founded on the sense of gratitude which may be taken as the most fundamental value. In every generation individuals are bound to discharge their debts towards society by performing his duties towards parents, towards God and to every individual. One should acquire knowledge by studying hard and by painstaking effort through concentration of mind and devotion. It can not be acquired by easy methods. One may obtain degrees and diplomas by malpractice in the examinations but cannot acquire genuine knowledge.

Rather by getting certificates through unfair means put him to various embarrassing and undesirable situations.

To impart knowledge is also equally regarded as an obligation towards teachers. If it has been discharged faithfully over thousands of years in this country, it has therefore been possible to conserve knowledge and desire to succeeding generation. The Great Sanskrit Poet Bhartruhari of the 1st Century has rightly observed, "Education is the special manifestation of the man, education is the treasure which can be preserved without fear or less, education secures material pleasure, happiness and fame, education is the teacher of teacher; education is the friend when one goes abroad, education is God incarnate, education secures honour at the hands of the state, not money. A man without education is equal to animal i.e., he can be truly called "Vidya Bihinah Pashuh".

Patanjali highlighted four aspects of education with necessary duties to every individual:

(i) acquire knowledge/education from parents and teachers,

(ii) study and improve knowledge on your own,

(iii) impart value-based education to every individual and to your children as parents and to others as teachers, and

(iv) use that knowledge for the benefit of the family and the society through your profession or avocation.

These four aspects of education have been emphasised not only for improving the education but also for developing the society. He also added that potential energy of an individual would be unfolded and could help an individual to lead a purposeful life. In the Hitopadesha it has been said "Education imparts humility; humility gives stability; stability enables us to secure wealth and wealth enables us to perform Dharma which in turn leads to happiness". Taittariya Upanishad explaining education has asked every individual/student to treat his parents/ teachers (Acharya) as equal to God.

Importance of education thus cannot be overestimated and it has been rightly emphasised for development of the child. Right to Education has, therefore, been guaranteed to every child. The Constitution of India says, "State shall endeavour to provide within a period of ten years from the commencement of this Constitution free and compulsory education for all children until they complete/attain the age of 14 years". However, this goal has not yet been fully realised and all attempts are being made to reach to target of Education for All by 2000 AD. The UNICEF and UN have also declared Education as an important right of the child and have been emphasising its realisation in all the countries of the world.

Right to Religion

Irrespective of the degree of our belief in God, religion has been playing an important role in human life since time immemorial. We have our religious practices and rituals according to our family background or various other factors. There are a lot of differences in the religious practices of man and for that we have to maintain tolerance and positive attitude towards all these religions. But Indians believe in God from the ancient times and they are very liberal and universal. That is why some people name it as Sanathan Dharma. Only foreigners have given it the name Hinduism as this religion prevailed in the area on the bank of river Sindhu. It is said in our ancient scriptures that, "just as the rain water comes down to Earth from the sky and reaches Ocean, we pay obeisance to God. Whatever may be its name, the destination is the same. We differ in the modes of worshipping God and we address God in various names whether it is Ishwar or Allaha.

Therefore, eminent sages and saints and sadhaks of India have been emphasising on the religious equality and harmony and the Right to Religion has been recognised as an integral part of harmony. In the Rajadharma it has been mentioned, "a King should offer protection to groups and association of believers of Vedas as also dis-believers in Veda and others. The above rule of Dharma is very unique to Indian culture and civilisation. It required the State to give equal protection not only to believers of God but also to disbelievers of God.

The broad concept of religion ensures freedom of thought, belief and faith in India. Article 18 of the Universal Declaration of Human Rights reads, "Everyone has the right to freedom of thought, conscience and religion. This Article includes freedom to change his religion or belief and freedom as that alone or in community with others and in public or private, manifest his religion or belief in teaching practice, worship and observation. The Constitution of India has also recognised freedom to religion as one of the fundamental rights. It is Article 21 which reads, "freedom of conscience, free profession, practice and propagation of religion subject to public order and health and to other professions. All these parts of business are equally entitled to freedom to conscience and the right to freely profess, practice and propagate religion". Thus secularism has been given a significant place in our religion.

Right to Protection

It is the basic responsibility of the state to ensure protection to its individuals from insecurity and oppression. The State has to see that all its citizens live happily in peace and tranquility. As already discussed in the Mahabharat, Rajadharma should emphasise such protection as an important responsibility of King or the ruler. It has been said therein, "to punish wicked to protect Good; to enrich treasury by fairmeans; to be impartial in the litigation and to protect the Kingdom-these are five yajnas (selfless duties) to be performed by a King.

The paramount duty of the state is to protect its people. It is the responsibility to protect helpless and the deceased or diseased; to protect be life and personal liberty is equally important for enabling people for leading a comfortable life and to live with dignity and happiness. It has, therefore, been included as a fundamental right under the Article 21 of the Constitution of India. It has also been declared as one of the human rights. Convention of the Right of the Child has included the Right to Survival and Right to Protection as important rights of every child. According to UN, Right to Survival includes Right to live, the highest attainable standard of health, nutrition and adequate standard of living and the Right to protection includes freedom from all forms of exploitation, abuse; inhuman or degrading treatment and neglect including Right to special protection in situations of emergency or armed conflicts.

India alongwith other countries of the World has accepted the Convention and has affirmed its commitments in its National Policy for Children since 1974. Under the Right to Protection, Child Labour has been banned in order to protect the children of India-the future citizens of the nation from economic exploitation, physical as well as psychological oppression.

Right to Social Security

All individuals are not equal and they have individual differences of all kinds. Many individuals suffer from deficiencies like poverty, disease and other difficulties. They are not able to earn their livelihood and even to get education for leading a happy life. Due to physical deformities/ diseases, old age and loss of earning capacity. They live in misery and do not have the basic human right to happiness. It has been declared as one of the duties of the individuals and assistance to enable them to give them special help lead a normal life. The Mahabharat has also declared such protection as one of the Principles of Dharma, and recently it has been declared as a Right to Social Security.

Right to Humane Treatment

Humane Treatment is pervasive and comprehensive if we will allow equality, equity, happiness and social security, it is implied that we have to be humane and considerate. Employees enjoy the Right to Humane Treatment if he has been given fair wages and decent facilities, bonus and other incentives.

Deceased employee's son or daughter is to be given preference for the appointment. This Right has been an integral part of mankind. Article 23(3) of Human Rights Declaration says, "Everyone who works has the right to just and favourable remuneration ensuring for himself and his family an existence of worthy human dignity and supplemented, if necessary, by other means of social protection". Similarly, an individual in custody or in prison deserves humane treatment. The officer in charge of prison and lock up should be aware of this basic right and ensure protection to the prisoners. Even any misconduct by them was described by Kautilya as punishable offence, who says, "Superintendent of a jail is liable to be punished for his acts of, omission and commission as follows:

(a) for putting a person in jail without disclosing the ground for his detention;
(b) for subjecting prisoner to unjust torture;
(c) for transporting the prisoner to any other place or deprive him of food and water;

(d) for causing trouble to prisoner or receiving bribes from them;

(e) for beating the prisoner resulting in his death;

(f) for having sexual intercourse with the wife of a thief or prisoner who is dead; and

(g) for having sexual intercourse with an arrested woman in lock up.

It is also interesting to note that the clever Kautilya not only laid down these offences, but also gave the punishment according to the degree or seriousness of the offences. At present such offences are found to be rampant in the society and there are frequent instances of violation of human rights by the police who are entrusted with the duty to enforce law and order.

There is specific provision in the Constitution requiring production of a prisoner or an arrested person by the police before the Magistrate within 24 hours, there are several instances which depict/reveal that it is not adhered to. Fortunately the modem Indian judiciary has been taking many laudable steps in giving justice to the suffering. The Supreme Court of India has declared that Human Rights should be a subject matter of Public Interest Litigation and in a given situation, if an individual whose-human rights are violated is not able to approach the Court, any individual/ public spirited person has right to move the Court on his behalf or on behalf of the former.

Right to Justice

It is the duty of the King or the ruler to give/offer justice to the oppressed and those who are deprived. Rajadharma included this duty as a very pious of the King. Narada Muni has said that the King should try cases with great care, should give decision according to the Law and should adhere to the opinion of the Chief justice. The King was required to decide all such cases impartially and in accordance with the relevant laws. But such justice should be rendered speedily.

Similarly, Katyayan has very aptly observed, "The King should not delay in examining the witnesses. A serious defect, namely, miscarriage of justice would result owing to delay in examination of witnesses". The King was to desist from greed and anger in deciding cases. It is therefore rightly said that, "Justice delayed is justice denied"'. Utmost care should be taken for examining the cases and giving final judgment from the view point of speed and impartiality. Article 10 of the Universal Declaration of Human Rights says, "Everyone is entitled in full equality to a fair and public hearing by an independent and impartial tribunal, in the determination of his rights and obligations and of any or all criminal charges against him".

The speedy and objective disposal of litigation has been recognised as one of the basic human rights not only in the Universal Declaration of Human Rights but also in the Constitution of India and therefore various acts have been legislated from time to time. Human Rights should be regarded as sacrosanct and maximum opportunity should be allowed in ensuring human rights to all citizens. This kind of protection has been eulogised and confirmed through multifarious Indian epics. During modern times also the Constitution fathers even have guaranteed such basic rights to all the Indian citizens and the UN, UNESCO and other International Agencies have also clearly laid guidelines on these issues.

2
Refugees and Human Rights

International arrangements exist to provide material assistance and protection to refugees who qualify for that status according to the universally accepted definition contained in the 1951 United Nations Convention Relating to the Status of Refugees. According to it, a person is a refugee if he is unable or unwilling to be in his own country for reasons of persecution or well-founded fear of it due to his "race, religion, nationality, membership of a particular social group or political opinion". There are, however, tens of millions of other uprooted people in the world today whose plight is as real but whose problems are relatively ignored by the international community and the general public.

We felt that it was important for our Commission to examine the different categories of these displaced people and raise public awareness of the humanitarian issues involved. Our analysis and conclusions have already been published in a Sectoral Report. In recent decades, the root causes of refugee problems have become much more complex. People flee for a series of reasons and it is becoming increasingly difficult to distinguish clearly between refugees and nonrefugees on the basis of the established criteria.

Many of the world's poorer countries are locked into a vicious circle of repression and opposition. Finding that the constitutional means of expressing their opinions are limited, opposition groups turn to terrorism or guerrilla warfare. In response, the government launches a military campaign to reassert its authority and to eliminate the opposition. The civilian population, especially in rural areas, are caught between these conflicting forces and many, if they are not killed, flee for their lives.

Communal violence is one of the most frightening forms of conflict. When the members of one ethnic, religious or linguistic group clash with the neighbouring members of another, atrocities are almost inevitable. Even when governments do not have discriminatory policies, their inability to protect their own minorities or a threatened social group can indirectly cause the flight of large numbers of people. Environmental disasters such as drought and famine are also uprooting more and more people every year. Deforestation, desertification, rapid urbanization and ineffective agricultural policies have all played a part in upsetting the delicate balance between man and his environment. The people most affected are the poor and powerless.

The development process is just as likely to uproot people as an environmental disaster. In many developing countries, land is being systematically appropriated in an attempt to fuel economic growth. Dams, highways, mines, energy pipelines and timber reserves all require large amounts of land. Planners politicians and businessmen often regard the traditional land users as an inconvenience and a hindrance to growth, In many cases the local inhabitants are simply told to leave their land or are forcibly evicted from it. At the same time, a growing number of people are being uprooted as a direct result of government policies to redistribute populations from over-populated to under populated regions of the country. Sometimes these policies are a response to intractable political, economic and social problems or the perceived requirements of national security.

In the developed countries elaborate methods have been established to determine population distribution and to control the movement of migrants. Few governments in the developing countries have the resources to establish such sophisticated controls. Their administrative structures are often weak and their enforcement agencies operate with a high degree of autonomy. Decision-makers are often looking for quick solutions to complex problems. Compulsory relocations appear to offer a way out.

The urbanization of the developing countries has accelerated rapidly in the last forty years. Much of the increase in the urban population is a result of massive movements of people from the countryside to the towns, prompted by indebtedness, land exhaustion, and the neglect of rural areas in official development plans. In some cases, large numbers of people from the countryside flock to cities to escape armed conflicts or guerrilla activity.

Uncontrolled urban expansion places a great strain on public services in addition to creating serious social and political problems. Confronted with these problems, many governments have found it imperative to redistribute the rural population. Throughout Africa, Asia and Latin America, governments have resorted to periodic urban removal campaigns, rounding up the unemployed and underemployed, and sending them to work in the countryside. In the rural areas themselves, people have also been uprooted. Villagization programmes have been introduced, concentrating scattered farmers into planned villages and state farms. When people are brought together, it is argued, scarce resources can be allocated more efficiently and equitably.

Serious humanitarian issues are raised by such official relocation programmes. None would deny the need for governments to take measures for containing the severe consequences of rapid urbanization and rural impoverishment. But relocation programmes have often been implemented in a coercive and poorly planned manner. What is more, they do not appear to have been particularly successful. Urban evacuees have often made their way back to the cities.

Villagization programmes have failed to produce significant increases in agricultural output. Resettlement schemes have been the cause of considerable suffering, amongst both the settlers and the local populations of the resettlement areas. Humanitarian responses to the plight of people uprooted by official relocation programmes are especially difficult to formulate. The motivations for forced relocations can often be understood, but can the methods used be endorsed? In situations where there appears to be no alternative to a controlled population movement, there is a case to be made for the involvement of external humanitarian agencies. Such a policy of constructive engagement could at least open up relocation programmes to impartial observation and ensure that they are carried out humanely and effectively. But the ambivalent attitude of many agencies to such programmes does reflect a very real dilemma: is the use of compulsion acceptable even in cases of extreme national emergency, and under what circumstances can the international community support such a policy?

The victims of mass expulsions are also inadequately protected and assisted by the international community. In recent years, a number of governments have attempted to resolve pressing political and economic problems by expelling unwanted sections of the population. Ethnic minorities, political dissidents, and migrant workers have been the most frequent targets of such exercises. The plight of all these new categories of uprooted people calls for urgent initiatives at the international level. People who are displaced within their own country are a particularly vulnerable group. Their rights are fully recognized neither in national nor international law.

We recognize the difficulty involved in regulating international law and practice in regard to matters which are essentially within the domestic jurisdiction of States. We also recognize that the internationalization of internal problems can sometimes further aggravate the situation and possibly cause more harm to the victims. It seems nonetheless feasible and desirable to elaborate internationally recognized standards of treatment for the millions who are victims of circumstances beyond their control.

In situations where direct government actions contribute to displacement of large numbers of people, it should be possible to establish a code of conduct based on humanitarian principles for the guidance of governments. The problem of refugees and displaced persons is afflicting many developing countries. There are now 25 countries in Africa, Asia and Latin America with refugee populations in excess of 80,000. In a few, the numbers run into hundreds of thousands. Most of these countries are poor. Refugee influxes and internal displacements impose in massive burden on limited government revenues and overstretched administrative structures. The burdens on ordinary people are even more significant.

Impoverished newcomers compete with their local hosts for scarce resources such as food, water and fuel. Deforestation, soil erosion and a deterioration of public services are all likely to take place when an already poor area suddenly has to support a much larger population.

Tension and conflict can easily arise between displaced people and host communities. At the international level, mass displacements can reinforce political tensions and obstruct regional co-operation. Under international law, the granting of asylum is a humanitarian, non-political act. In practice, it is not always so perceived.

Moreover, refugees are not only the victims of local and regional conflicts, but are sometimes also active participants in them. Governments are becoming increasingly reluctant to practise an 'open door' policy and to grant asylum generously. The international community has tended to perceive mass displacements as an inevitable deviation from the norm. But it is now clear that refugee movements are the product of some very profound, structural problems confronting the contemporary world. The existing legal and organizational framework of refugee protection and assistance needs adjustment to this new reality.

Within the United Nations, two agencies have specific mandates to take care of defined categories of refugees: the Office of the United Nations High Commissioner for Refugees (UNHCR) which was established to protect and assist refugees and to promote permanent solutions to refugee problems and the United Nations Relief and Work Agency (UNRWA) which was established to assist and provide relief to Palestinian refugees within a defined geographic area.

When UNHCR was founded in 1951, the number of recognized refugees was less than two million. Most of them lived in the more prosperous countries of the world. Now there are over six times as many, the vast majority of them in the poorer States. Similarly the number of Palestinian refugees has continued to increase since 1948 and the problems faced by UNRWA have become more complex. A second generation of Palestinians has now been born in refugee camps in various countries of the Middle East. Hundreds of thousands of Palestinians have, thus, grown up with the despair and deprivation of camp life. There are serious political and financial implications arising from this situation. Both UNHCR and UNRWA have had funding problems in recent years. The finances available are swallowed up by expensive relief operations and care and maintenance programmes. The intergovernmental and voluntary agencies working with refugees have, therefore, not been able to concentrate their resources on finding lasting solutions to refugee situations.

Refugee protection is weakening, as both industrialized and developing States grow tired of giving sanctuary to large numbers of distressed foreigners. A few countries have forcibly returned refugeen and asylum-seekers to their own country, in clear violation of international law. Many more have introduced measures specifically designed to deter refugees from claiming asylum. Similarly, the harassment of refugees and military attacks on their settlements are growing in scale and frequency. States cannot be forced to ratify conventions or observe international laws designed to protect refugees. Humanitarian organizations are constrained by the realities of political power.

Under certain situations they can improve the material well-being of refugees and offer them a degree of protection they might not otherwise enjoy. Exceptionally they might even help to resolve a situation which is creating refugees. But ultimately, their ability to influence the behaviour of States is quite limited. Indeed, intergovernmental organizations are often open to pressure from States in pursuit of national political or strategic interests. There are many ways in which the protection and assistance of refugees could be strengthened. The principles of refugee law must be more widely disseminated, especially amongst the government officials and security personnel who come into contact with refugees and asylum-seekers.

The specific needs of refugee women and children and of refugees who are subject to armed attacks could be recognized in United Nations declarations and special measures taken on their behalf. There is a strong case to be made for a critical re-examination of the United Nations Refugee Convention. Can it adequately meet contemporary needs and situations? Should the victims of conflict, turmoil and environmental disaster be given international legal recognition like the victims of persecution? As far as assistance is concerned, there is a need to see whether the resources available are being equitably distributed amongst the countries giving sanctuary to large numbers of refugees.

Accurate censuses of refugee populations are required and their needs more rigorously and scientifically assessed. Governments which receive large amounts of relief aid must be encouraged to implement programmes enabling refugee communities to become self-sufficient. The resilience and innovative ability of refugees is often underestimated by aid agencies. The fact is that an overwhelming majority of refugees survive without international aid. They integrate into the new society more easily on their own in the developing countries. Such 'spontaneous integration' should be encouraged and facilitated through appropriate projects which take fully into account local conditions and traditions.

In recent decades, ambitious schemes of resettlement of refugees in countries outside their region have been implemented. While the generosity of receiving countries is commendable, it is important that resettlement within the region rather than across the continents is encouraged. Instead of spending vast sums to integrate refugees in an entirely alien social environment, donors would do well to assist more generously countries within the region to assimilate them.

Most refugees would like to go home, but will not do so until the conditions which prompted them to leave have changed. In many cases, they are deterred from returning by the daunting prospect of establishing a livelihood and reintegrating into their own society. External assistance has a vital role to play in promoting the option of voluntary repatriation. The assistance currently given to returnees is often inadequate. Food aid, for example, is provided for a very limited period.

Much more ambitious programmes, designed to rehabilitate the infrastructure of returnee areas and to provide new income-earning opportunities, are called for. With aid agency personnel stationed in these areas for an adequate period of time, the security of returnees would also be reinforced. The circumstances which force people to abandon their homes and which prompt governments to uproot their citizens do not spring up overnight, They develop gradually and are, therefore, foreseeable. Yet the international community has hitherto failed to establish an effective early warning system which would enable contingency planning and anticipatory action to be taken.

We need to know much more about the dynamics of mass displacement. On the basis of that knowledge, the international community should be able to establish a means of collecting, sifting and analysing information relevant to potential refugee movements. Given the very rapid development of communications and computer technology, a new early warning facility should have a substantial forecasting potential.

At the same time, we must recognize that preventive and anticipatory action is more often obstructed by political than technical obstacles. Governments have the ultimate responsibility for the actions, or failures to act, that cause refugee movements.

In seeking change at the political and governmental levels, the role of the public cannot be over-emphasized. Throughout the world, ordinary men and women have demonstrated in recent years their concern for the victims of famine in Africa. Such concern must be directed, not simply at the collection of money for relief, but at the governments and decision-makers who shape the policies which create or aggravate refugee problems instead of solving them.

We wish to emphasize the need for elaborating international humanitarian standards and strengthening the assistance network at national and international level for those groups of uprooted persons who do not clearly fall within the category of refugees as defined by existing international instruments. We recognize that this relatively unexplored field does not lend itself easily to definitive recommendations and suggestions without a more thorough study. We urge governments, inter-governmental agencies and non-governmental organizations, as well as scholars and experts to undertake such studies and to look into practical ways and means to alleviate suffering and promote solutions to the problems. There are now tens of millions of internally and externally displaced persons and their numbers may well increase if timely action is not taken.

We are of the opinion, in so far as refugees as defined by existing instruments are concerned, that, in the field of protection:

— It is essential to elaborate further the concept and State practice relating to asylum. The international community must support this process giving positive expression to the notions of burden-sharing and human solidarity. States should be dissuaded from introducing measures designed to deter individuals from seeking asylum, Likewise, It is essential that governments deal with asylum applications quickly, thoroughly and in a context where humanitarianism prevails over political considerations. The inter- and non-governmental agencies concerned have a vital role to play in assisting governments in this regard and in exerting pressure when humanitarian principles are not fully respected.

— A set of minimum humanitarian standards applicable to refugees and asylum-seekers should be developed and the international agencies should monitor and encourage their observance by governments and local communities.

— The physical security of refugees in situations of conflict must be strengthened by governments and the international agencies should play an active supervisory role.

— International humanitarian agencies must enjoy free access to refugees and in situations of tension or conflict the possibility of stationing impartial humanitarian observers should be explored.

Regarding material assistance, we are of the opinion that.

— Available sources must be equitably distributed among the countries receiving large numbers of refugees, and objective humanitarian rather than political criteria should be applied by donors.

— Accurate censuses of refugee populations are required and their needs should be more precisely assessed.

— Emergency relief assistance should be provided for a predetermined and limited period and income-generating projects as well as assistance measures designed to promote self-sufficiency should be encouraged.

— The concept of refugee camps and rural settlement needs to be radically reviewed. Beyond the emergency period when they are required, camps have serious disadvantages. They rarely become self-sufficient. They also produce social tensions and constitute 'human islands' which isolate refugees from their local hosts while creating open-ended dependency upon external assistance.

— Criteria of material aid to refugees should be standardized in terms of nutrition, health care and other subsistence items. Donors should provide aid which corresponds to real, identified needs as well as the habits and traditions of the recipients.

During the International Year of Shelter for the Homeless 1987 attention was drawn to homelessness as a worldwide phenomenon-a billion people without adequate housing and 100 million more with no shelter at all—the U.N.'s Nairobi-based Centre for Human Settlements (HABITAT) served as focal point for the drafting of a Global Strategy for Shelter to the Year 2000.

In December 1988 the General Assembly gave its unanimous approval to the strategy 143/1811, which was launched at U.N. Headquarters in February 1989. HABITAT was named coordinator of the U.N. system's shelter programs, and the intergovernmental Commission on Human Settlements was asked to review the progress made at the national level.

Four principles guide the strategy: private as well as public resources should be encouraged and allowed to work to best advantage; women, often the family breadwinner and head of household, should be involved in shelter programs and policymaking; the links between shelter and economic development are strong and abiding; and "sustainable development" must be a consideration in all matters relating to the building of shelters. Singled out for attention are the developing countries, where an estimated third to a half of all citizens are ill housed or without shelter.

In the first stage of the Global Strategy, 1989-1991, the focus is on formulating national shelter strategies, designing new institutional arrangements, and implementing national programs. In stage 2, 1992-1994, these new institutional arrangements are expected to be put into effect and existing national programs strengthened. In the last stage, 1995-2000, it is envisioned that national programs will go into high gear, and national institutions will be on the path to sustained progress.

Meeting at its 12th (biannual) session in spring 1989, the commission adopted a set of guidelines drafted by HABITAT to aid governments in developing national shelter strategies and in assessing their performance, and it also suggested a timetable for national efforts. The 44th General Assembly "noted with satisfaction" the assistance rendered by various member states in helping other governments develop these strategies and "urged" the organizations of the U.N. system to supply financial and technical support for implementing them.

Refugees: A Continuing Challenge for Humanity

The challenge presently confronting the international community is to focus State thinking and approaches on the realities of today's movements of refugees and asylum-seekers, while ensuring that, in the process, the human values underlying international concern for refugees retain their central place and that international protection is guaranteed for those who must depend upon it.

It is also partly as a result, a very serious question for UNHCR at the present time. In any effort to redefine the parameters of refugee and asylum policy, the perspective from which the refugee problem is approached and the promises on which policy makers proceed are both fundamental. As States take their thinking more decisively forward, there is a need for injection into the national decision-making process of the perspective of NGOs working with refugees as well as that of UNHCR. These non-governmental and international perspectives complement those of States with the expertise of humanitarian organizations created to fulfill responsibilities towards a particular group of people at risk.

The promises identified in the document as the basis for developing new approaches, together with the recommended approaches to be pursued, stem directly from the protection problems facing refugees and asylum-seekers today as UNHCR experiences them, Each refugee situation generates its own, situation-specific problems. These can, though, be grouped Into two main types of problems—that is problems of an operational day-do-day character, and problems which together go to the heart of international protection efforts, threatening to compromise them on a global basis. Among the former, for example, serious violations of the physical security of refugees, their unwarranted detention or ongoing difficulties in securing their basic rights.

Clearly the arrival of large numbers of asylum-seekers and the absorption of some or all of them as refugees, even on a temporary basis, can create serious strains for host countries. This is particularly the case for the poorer communities where the ability of the people and the government to shoulder the resulting burden may be much diminished by severe socioeconomic problems.

It is also understandable in developed countries which over-burdened asylum structures, including as a result of significant arrivals of non-refugees with costly social services and with a disenchanted public opinion.

On the other hand, it needs to be emphasized time and again that being a refugee and enjoying asylum are inextricably linked, In some senses one can say that asylum is the very condition of a refugee's existence. Once a refugee leaves his or her country, the pre-requisite for all that follows is at least temporary asylum. International conventions and customary international law both reaffirm the prohibition against return of refoulement of a refugee to situations endangering life or freedom as one of the most fundamental principles of refugee protection. Irrespective of this fundamental character of asylum, incidents of expulsion or refoulement, in some instances on a large-scale, are too frequent.

Restrictive responses by many states to asylum-seekers attempting to enter their territories have increased. Due to expanded visa regimes and stricter passport requirements, entry and inter alia access to full procedures for determination of refugee status have become a function of prior authorisation, with discretion to allow entry on the basis of need considerably curtailed by enforcement mechanisms such as indiscriminate sanctioning of airlines for carrying improperly documented passengers. Here the concern is not the legitimacy of such measures, which is not contested. Rather it is their inflexibility where refugees are involved and the resulting possible denial of protection to individuals in need.

Related problems include the narrower view being taken by a number of States of their Convention responsibilities, reflected in part in their interpretation and application of the refugee definition in Article 1 of the 1951 Convention, as well as the strict adherence of a number of countries to the "country of first asylum" principle, even given the ambiquity surrounding its proper application. One result of such restrictive approaches Is a rejection rate even higher than it would or should otherwise be, This arguments the number of rejected cases, which in themselves pose a complex problem, particularly in States where, for various reasons, there are difficulties in deporting groups or categories within the rejected group.

In a number of countries, for example, because the necessary decisions on return are problematic or appropriate arrangements to enable return do not exist, human and material resources have to be directed to supporting persons whose status has been rejected. In addition, policies on admission and access to procedures, as well as public opinion in general, are coloured by this blurring of distinctions between refugees and rejected claimants in terms of treatment and entitlements. It is clear that failure to find a solution to non-refugee problems has serious consequences for refugees who are the responsibilities of UNHCR. This is particularly the case as the pressures resulting from poverty and potentially from environmentally driven migratory flows will increase to the point, perhaps, where the principle of first asylum is gravely threatened.

The diminishing accessibility of asylum an a global basis is a problem in itself. As important is the spin-off effect on the capability and willingness of countries of first asylum, often countries suffering significant socio-economic problems of their own, to assume the resulting additional burden, or even to continue to receive refugees as in the past.

If we have, perhaps, not done justice to their complexity, it must at least be acknowledged that there are no clear-cut or right explanations here. The reality is that it is becoming harder and harder to maintain a steady focus on what is the refugee problem today, on who are the victims, what are their rights and legitimate expectations and who owes what responsibilities. By a process almost of imperceptible absorption, the refugee problem has become part of the broader global issue of movements of people, with the various groups involved—including, for example, the migrant workers, the victims of poverty and the legal and illegal immigrants as well as the refugees—imprecisely delineated, one from another.

States have for some time been moving from a particular to a generalised response to the movements involved and, in the process, the elements peculiar to the situation of the refugee have diminished in significance. This development argues strongly for reassessment of refugees and asylum policies which, States, UNHCR and NGOs concerned with the refugee problem have come, not only to appreciate, but to act upon. Against this background, let me return now, briefly, to UNHCR's Note for the Executive Committee. This Note ventures the following as among the important assumptions to underlie any new approach:

— First that prevention is preferable to cure and that early warning of developing situations and their mediation can be a far more effective method to contain problems as long as humanitarian considerations are fully respected and the option of departure is not foreclosed for those who need it;

— Secondly, that a refugee movement is a grave human rights issue, not only one affecting national interests or international peace and security;

— Thirdly, that refugees and immigrants are not one and the same and any new policy must respect fundamental distinctions between the two categories of people;

— Fourthly, that the numbers of persons seeking asylum or refuge cannot, by itself, be a reason for denying protection, or according it under harsh conditions;

— Fifthly, that voluntary repatriation, local settlement or resettlement—that is, the traditional solutions for refugees all remain viable arid important responses to refugee situations.

— Sixthly, that countries of origin must assume a significant responsibility in the search for appropriate solutions including through facilitating voluntary repatriation and the return of non-refugees.

If these, among others, are accepted as the assumtions which must underlie any new approach, then certain conclusions about the general direction of this approach must follow.

From UNHCR's perspective, what is required overall is a globally based approach which will develop asylum and refugee policy so that humanitarian and human rights concerns are well integrated and balanced in relation to the development, foreign policy and immigration control considerations of States. In the development of such a comprehensive approach, there is a need to proceed most carefully and without haste, on the basis of full awareness of all the interests at stake and their implications in human terms.

Human rights promotion and protection must occupy a central place, given the close interrelationship between violations of human rights and mass exoduses of refugees, as well as between restoration of acceptable human rights situations in countries of origin and successful resolution of refugee problems through voluntary repatriation programs. Strengthened observance of civil and political rights, but equally of economic, social and cultural rights, is fundamental in addressing root causes or refugee flows. In addition, when one examines the range of causes leading to movements of asylum-seekers, together with the fact that the majority of refugees originate from arid find asylum in the developing countries, it is clear that there is an important development factor at issue.

In policies on development and through development aid there is considerable potential not only for actively promoting human rights, but also for alleviating socio-economic conditions causing people to leave, or hindering their return to their countries of origin. The manner in which regional bodies might more actively contribute to positive resolution of problems in their region should be explored both by these regional entities and by the international community generally. How to redress root causes and promote lasting solutions to regional refugee problems should be examined in this context. It needs, though, to he stressed that international burden-sharing.

While a new approach must respond in the first instance to the needs and rights of the affected persons, to have any realistic chance of being effective it must also acknowledge the legitimate concerns of all affected States. These include the protracted nature of refugee problems in many first asylum countries with their own troubled economies and their concerns about the political and security difficulties accompanying influxes and the waning international solidarity in sharing the burden. They also include, in the developed countries, increased caseloads, the backlog of claims, strained reception and integration facilities and significant expenses for material assistance.

There is the problem of abuse of the system as well as, more generally, of the large rejected caseload. Any new strategies must contain measures to deal humanely and effectively with rejected asylum seekers. The importance

UNHCR places on public information activities being made an integral part of new strategies in order to educate public opinion and encourage positive attitudes. At the same time, open debate on new approaches should precede decisions in this regard at the political level.

Protection and Resettlement of Refugees

In the absence of massive new refugee influxes, the work of UNHCR throughout 1995 and the first part of 1996, under the direction of the United Nations High Commissioner for Refugees, Sadako Ogata, was characterized by the consolidation of programmes and mechanisms launched in response to previous large-scale emergencies; by the pursuit and implementation of durable solutions, whether voluntary repatriation, local integration or resettlement; and, where circumstances have permitted, by the elaboration of preventive strategies. While refugee numbers continued to show a slight decline during the period under review, concern remained over the real, potential and perceived burden of protecting and assisting refugees.

Many Governments continue to uphold asylum as an indispensable instrument for the international protection of refugees and to demonstrate commitment to receiving and hosting refugees in cooperation with UNHCR. Others, however, have denied entry to asylum-seekers, forcibly returned them to their countries of origin or restricted their entitlement to basic rights. This has again underscored the need, on the one hand, to strengthen the institution of asylum ana on the other, to continue to promote innovative approaches that take due account of the protection needs of refugees and the legitimate concerns of countries of asylum and origin.

UNHCR has continued to make efforts to ensure that the special needs of refugee women and children are taken fully into account. A memorandum of understanding signed in March 1996 between UNHCR and UNICEF defines the beneficiary populations (refugees, returnees, internally displaced persons and affected local populations) covered by the two agencies.

The memorandum covers advocacy, promotion and strategy-formulation roles, in particular with regard to the Convention on the Rights of the Child, as well as operational, reintegration and rehabilitation activities. UNHCR has paid particular attention to the coordination of its activities with other United Nations agencies, notably within the context of Economic and Social Council resolution 1995/56 on the strengthening of the coordination of emergency humanitarian assistance of the United Nations. UNHCR also participates actively in parallel interagency consultations under the aegis of the Department of Humanitarian Affairs and the Interagency Standing Committee.

Emergency response

No new large-scale refugee emergencies occurred in 1995 on the scale experienced in recent years, giving rise to some optimism that a period of increased stability in international affairs might be in sight. Nevertheless, ongoing emergencies presented various challenges. UNHCR continued to cope with a series of crises in Bosnia and Herzegovina, peaking with the fall of the eastern Muslim enclaves in July 1995 and the forced exodus of 36,000 people.

A further major upsurge of displacement occurred in August 1995 with a mass influx of approximately 200,000 refugees from the Krajina region of Croatia into the Federal Republic of Yugoslavia. In the northern Caucasus, where the Office had envisaged phasing out its emergency operation for the displaced population from Chechnya

(Russian Federation) at the end of 1995, new developments generated an additional influx of displaced persons into the neighbouring autonomous republics and necessitated a continuation of humanitarian assistance by UNHCR.

The Office also responded to crisis situations in Guinea the United Republic of Tanzania and Uganda. In response to those situations, UNHCR has consolidated the wide range of arrangements for contingency planning and emergency preparedness and response that it has developed since 1991. These mechanisms have been complemented by external standby arrangements. External rosters have been established with the Norwegian and Danish Refugee Councils United Nations Volunteers and Rädda Barnen (the Swedish Save the Children Fund). In 1995, UNHCR entered into a new emergency standby arrangement with the Register of Engineers for Disaster Relief (REDR) (Australia), which agreed to provide engineers for emergency deployment.

Working in close coordination with the Department of Humanitarian Affairs, UNHCR has made considerable progress in the development of self-contained government service packages for exceptional emergency response. In a related initiative, steps are being taken to gauge better the traditional response resources provided by non-governmental organizations in refugee emergencies. UNHCR has begun work on the establishment of a database to which 30 key non-governmental organizations will contribute.

In recent years, the environmental impact of large-scale refugee presence has become an increasingly important preoccupation for countries of asylum. UNHCR has taken steps to ensure that humanitarian assistance is provided in an environmentally sensitive manner and in a way that is supportive of and reinforces development initiatives. At its forty-sixth session in 1995, the Executive Committee of the High Commissioner's Programme adopted a new policy on the environment that aims to reflect environmental concerns in a more comprehensive manner throughout UNHCR refugee assistance operations. To give effect to that policy, new environmental guidelines have been developed.

Voluntary repatriation is regarded by UNHCR as the preferred durable solution to refugee situations. Developments in many parts of the world have provided continued grounds for hope that voluntary return can become a reality for a large number of the world's refugees. Following the signing of the Dayton Peace Agreement in November 1995, a durable solution to the plight of the 2 million Bosnian refugees and displaced persons appeared within reach. Within the General Framework Agreement for Peace in Bosnia and Herzegovina, UNHCR has been designated the agency responsible for planning and implementing the repatriation of the many Bosnians who can now contemplate return. In March 1996, the Office submitted an operational plan in which it elaborated the conditions required for repatriation and the principles that should govern the return of refugees and displaced persons.

The Office remained concerned, however, at the pace of the implementation of the civilian component of the peace plan and at the impact this may have on repatriation. More than seven months after the signing of the Dayton Agreement, only 70,000 to 80,000 refugees and internally displaced persons had returned to their homes,

In the Great Lakes region of Africa, durable solutions continued to prove more elusive. While three quarters of a million Tutsi refugees from earlier periods had returned home, and 400,000 more recent Hutu refugees, the repatriation of the remaining 1.7 million refugees had stagnated. The Tripartite Commissions on repatriation involving Rwanda, UNHCR and Burundi, the United Republic of Tanzania or Zaire have focused on ways of enhancing repatriation through mass information campaigns, separation of intimidators from refugees and cross-border visits. However, major obstacles to large-scale repatriation of Rwandan refugees remained, including continuing intimidation in refugee camps, increased tensions and insecurity in the border region and the lack of a comprehensive political solution.

Escalating violence in Burundi was an additional cause of grave concern. In late July, over 12,000 refugees were sent back to Rwanda. The continuing deterioration of the situation in Burundi led UNHCR to step up its contingency plans and preparedness measures. In South-East Asia, the winding up of the Comprehensive Plan of Action for Indo-Chinese Refugees, which was due to terminate in June 1996, marked the closing of a chapter in a refugee situation that originated in the 1970s. In North and Central America, the decision by the Mexican authorities in late 1995 to permit the local integration of Guatemalan refugees who do not wish to repatriate has opened up a new avenue for the solution of the one remaining refugee problem in that region.

Voluntary repatriation of refugees frequently takes place in the aftermath of conflict. Invariably, peace after fratricidal communal strife is frail and in need of sustained support. The short-term rehabilitation assistance provided by UNHCR to facilitate the social and economic reintegration of the returning refugees needs to be anchored within a broader recovery and reconstruction strategy that ensures a continuity from initial recovery to sustainable development. UNHCR, therefore, has been reinforcing its operational linkages with United Nations agencies and other development partners. In Mozambique, where the voluntary repatriation of 1.7 million refugees was completed last year, important lessons have been learned in the course of such collaboration. Jointly with UNDP, UNHCR has agreed on a framework for inter-agency initiatives to promote a smooth transition from humanitarian assistance to sustainable human development. Both the Office's new memorandum of understanding with UNICEF and a revision of the 1994 memorandum with WFP now under discussion place particular emphasis on the need to develop such linkages further. Consultations with the World Bank and the regional development banks have also continued.

Human rights considerations must also have a central place in post-conflict peace-building. UNHCR has cooperated with the human rights mechanisms of the United Nations within the framework of overall United Nations operations, such as those in Bosnia and Herzegovina, Cambodia, El Salvador and Rwanda, to link human rights concerns with the protection of refugees and the monitoring of returnees. Collaboration has increased with the United Nations High Commissioner for Human Rights, especially at the level of field operations. A memorandum was signed in 1995 between the UNHCR branch office in Rwanda and the Human Rights Field Operation in Rwanda in an effort to enhance complementarity of action in the areas of monitoring and institution-building. Ongoing contacts with human rights working groups, rapporteurs, experts and monitors are also an integral part of UNHCR's approach.

Preventing refugee crises

In the past few years, a number of different factors have combined to bring about a fundamental reassessment of traditional approaches to the refugee problem. These include, for example, the strain placed upon the international relief system by the recent spate of internal wars and complex humanitarian emergencies; the mounting concern of host and donor countries about the financial and other costs incurred in providing refugees with indefinite protection and assistance; and a growing awareness that refugee movements can constitute a serious threat to national, regional and even international security, in particular when they involve countries of asylum that have weak economies, fragile ecologies and a delicate balance of ethnic groups. As a result of these developments, a new international consensus has emerged, recognizing that the mandate of UNHCR to seek permanent solutions for the problem of refugees gives the organization a legitimate interest in the prevention of conditions that lead to refugee movements by means of operational activities within countries of origin.

These include important elements of capacity-building and institutional development. At its forty-sixth session, in 1995, the Executive Committee called on UNHCR to strengthen its activities in support of national capacity-building. UNHCR has, where appropriate, provided advice and assistance to Governments in building legal, judicial and administrative capacity.

A dual preoccupation with solutions and prevention has been the impetus behind efforts to develop, together with interested Governments and intergovernmental organizations, a comprehensive approach to the problems of refugees, returnees, displaced persons an other forms of involuntary displacement in the Commonwealth of Independent States and relevant neighbouring States. In collaboration with the Organization for Security and Cooperation in Europe and the International Organization for Migration, UNHCR organized a regional conference in May 1996. All 12 Commonwealth of Independent States countries and other interested States and intergovernmental organizations participated in the preparatory process and the conference itself The conference endorsed a programme of action and a framework for follow-up activities aimed at managing migratory flows and developing institutional capacity to prevent mass displacement. The regional conference has highlighted, among other issues, the importance of dealing with problems of statelessness as part of preventive strategies.

Recognizing the importance of this question in other parts of the world, UNHCR has also played a more active role in regional discussions aimed at resolving certain nationality issues. The Executive Committee in 1995 adopted a conclusion on the prevention and reduction of statelessness and the protection of stateless persons. Stressing that the prevention and reduction of statelessness and the protection of stateless persons are important in the prevention of potential refugee situations, the Committee encouraged UNHCR to continue its activities on behalf of stateless persons and, in particular, actively to promote accessions to the statelessness conventions.

Protection and Assistance to Refugees and Stateless Persons

1. The United Nations has been concerned since its inception with the situation confronting refugees, displaced persons, stateless persons and "returnees", and has adopted a number of measures to protect their human rights and to find appropriate and durable solutions for their problems.

2. At its third session, in 1948, the General Assembly initiated United Nations assistance to Palestine refugees, and in 1949 it established the United Nations Relief and Works Agency for Palestine Refugees in the Near East. Since May 1950 this Agency, which is supported by voluntary contributions, has been providing relief, education, training, health and other services to Arab

refugees from Palestine. In 1967 and 1982, the functions of the Agency were widened to include humanitarian assistance, as far as practicable, on an emergency basis and as a temporary measure, to other displaced persons in serious need of immediate assistance, as a result of the 1967 and subsequent hostilities. In 1986, the Agency mandate was extended until 30 June 1990.

3. At its fourth session, in 1949, the General Assembly established the Office of the United Nations High Commissioner for Refugees. The original three-year mandate of the High Commissioner was extended periodically, and the current term ends on 31 December 1993.

4. In recent years the international community has been particularly concerned about mass exoduses of refugees and displaced persons from areas of armed conflict, and in particular about the growing number of refugees in Africa. With the assistance of governmental experts, the General Assembly has endeavoured to find ways and means of preventing new massive flows of refugees which often have given rise to adverse consequences for the countries of origin as well as for the receiving States.

United Nations Relief and Works Agency for Palestine Refugees in the Near East

5. The Agency is headed by a Commissioner-General, assisted by an Advisory Commission composed of 10 Member States. The Commissioner-General reports annually to the General Assembly on the work of the Agency, and to the Secretary-General on matters to be brought to the attention of the United Nations or its appropriate organs.

6. Although the Agency is doing all it can within the limits of available resources, its financial situation has

deteriorated seriously in recent years. In 1970, the General Assembly established a Working Group on the Financing of the United Nations Relief and Works Agency for Palestine Refugees in the Near East and requested it to study all aspects of the financing of the Agency. The Working Group submitted to the Assembly, at every subsequent session, recommendations to help solve the financial problems. However the continuing critical financial situation of the Agency permits the provision of only minimum services to the Palestine refugees.

7. In resolution 42/69 A of 2 December 1987, the Assembly noted with profound concern that, despite the commendable and successful efforts of the Commissioner-General to collect additional contributions, this increased level of income was still insufficient to cover essential budget requirements and that, at the foreseen levels of giving, deficits will recur each year.

Office of the United Nations High Commissioner for Refugees

8. The United Nations High Commissioner for Refugees serves as the spearhead of the international community's current efforts to solve the problems of refugees, displaced persons, stateless persons and "returnees" in the spirit of the Charter of the United Nations and the provisions of article 14 of the Universal Declaration of Human Rights, which reads as follows:

1. Everyone has the right to seek and to enjoy in other countries asylum from persecution.
2. This right may not be invoked in the case of prosecutions genuinely arising from non-political crimes or from acts contrary to the purposes and principles of the United Nations.

9. The Office of the United Nations High Commissioner for Refugees was established for a three-year term by the General Assembly in resolution 319 (IV) of 3 December 1949. The High Commissioner's work is entirely humanitarian and non-political. In 1954 and again in 1981, this work won for the Office the Nobel Peace prize. The 1 million Swedish kroner awarded with the 1981 prize was used to establish a Trust Fund for Handicapped Refugees.

10. The Office of the United Nations High Commissioner for Refugees replaced the International Refugee Organization (IRO), an agency established by General Assembly resolution 62 (1) of 15 December 1946 to assist victims of the nazi, fascist or falangist régimes and others unable or unwilling to avail themselves of the protection of the Government of their country of nationality. The IRO terminated its activities on 30 June 1950, leaving about 180,000 refugees to be repatriated or resettled.

11. The terms of reference of the Office were first set out in General Assembly resolution 319 (IV) of 3 December 1949 and further elaborated in Assembly resolution 428 (V) of 14 December 1950. According to paragraph 8 of the annex to the latter resolution, which annex constitutes the Statute of the Office, the High Commissioner shall provide for the protection of refugees falling under the competence of his Office by:

(a) Promoting the conclusion and ratification of international conventions for the protection of refugees, supervising their application and proposing amendments thereto;

(b) Promoting through special agreements with Governments the execution of any measures calculated to improve the situation of refugees and to reduce the number requiring protection;

(c) Assisting governmental and private efforts to promote voluntary repatriation or assimilation within new national communities;

(d) Promoting the admission of refugees, not excluding those in the most destitute categories, to the territories of States;

(e) Endeavouring to obtain permission for refugees to transfer their assets and especially those necessary for their resettlement;

(f) Obtaining from Governments information concerning the number and conditions of refugees in their territories and the laws and regulations concerning them;

(g) Keeping in close touch with the Governments and intergovernmental organizations concerned;

(h) Establishing contact in such manner as he may think best with private organizations dealing with refugee questions;

(i) Facilitating the co-ordination of the efforts of private organizations concerned with the welfare of refugees.

Paragraph 9 of the annex stipulates that the High Commissioner shall engage in such additional activities, including repatriation and resettlement, as the General Assembly may determine, within the limits of the resources placed at his disposal.

12. The Office concerns itself with persons who come within its competence under the terms of its Statute. Through subsequent resolutions of the General Assembly, its mandate has been widened to include also displaced persons who are in a refugee-like situation.

13. By resolution 3274 (XXIX) of 10 December 1974, the General Assembly requested the Office of the High

Commissioner "provisionally to undertake the functions foreseen under the Convention on the Reduction of Statelessness [of 28 August 1961] in accordance with its article 11 ... ;" and by resolution 31/36 of 30 November 1976, the Assembly requested the High Commissioner "to continue to perform these functions".

14. In accordance with paragraph 2 of its Statute, "The work of the High Commissioner shall be of an entirely non-political character; it shall be humanitarian and social..

Organisational and procedural arrangements

15. The High Commissioner is elected by the General Assembly on nomination of the Secretary-General. He appoints, for the same term as his own mandate, a Deputy High Commissioner of a nationality other than his own.

16. The Office of the High Commissioner is located in Geneva, Switzerland. In accordance with paragraph 16 of the Statute of his Office, the High Commissioner maintains a number of representatives in areas or countries where there are significant refugee problems.

17. The High Commissioner reports annually to the General Assembly through the Economic and Social Council. By a decision of 27 October 1969, the Economic and Social Council arranged that in future the annual report of the United Nations High Commissioner for Refugees would be retained on the agenda of the Council's summer session on the understanding that the report would be transmitted to the General Assembly without debate, unless the Council were to decide otherwise, at the specific request of one or more of its members or of the High Commissioner, at the time of the adoption of the agenda.

18. Assistance provided by the High Commissioner is normally channelled through Governments or governmental bodies or non-governmental organizations. Assistance programmes are submitted for authorization to the Executive Committee of the High Commissioner's Programme and a report on the implementation of these programmes is also submitted to this body.

19. Pursuant to paragraph 4 of the Statute, an Advisory Committee on Refugees was established by Economic and Social Council resolution 393 (XIII) B of 10 September 195 1. The Committee was reconstituted as the Executive Committee of the United Nations Refugee Fund, which was in turn replaced by the Executive Committee of the Programme of the United Nations High- Commissioner for Refugees, established by Council resolution 672 (XXV) of 30 April 1958. The terms of reference of the Executive Committee were set out in General Assembly resolution 1166 (XII) of 26 November 1957 as follows:

(a) To give directives to the High Commissioner for the liquidation of the United Nations Refugee Fund;

(b) To advise the High Commissioner, at his request, in the exercise of his functions under the Statute of his Office;

(c) To advise the High Commissioner as to whether it is appropriate for international assistance to be provided through his Office in order to help to solve specific refugee problems remaining unsolved after 31 December 1958 or arising after that date;

(d) To authorize the High Commissioner to make appeals for funds to enable him to solve the refugee problems referred to in subparagraph (c) above;

(e) To approve projects for assistance to refugees coming within the scope of subparagraph (c) above;

(f) To give directives to the High Commissioner for the use of the emergency fund to be established under the terms set out in paragraph 7 of resolution 1166 (XII).

20. The Executive Committee meets once a year at Geneva. The Committee consists of 40 representatives of States Members of the United Nations or members of any of the specialized agencies, elected by the Economic and Social Council on the widest geographical basis from those States with a demonstrated interest in, and devotion to, the solution of the refugee problem.

International protection and assistance

21. In accordance with paragraph 1 of the Statute of his Office, the United Nations High Commissioner for Refugees, acting under the authority of the General Assembly, shall assume the function of providing international protection, under the auspices of the United Nations, to refugees who fall within the scope of the present Statute . . . The provisions of paragraph 8 of the Statute, reproduced in paragraph 11 above, determine the means whereby the High Commissioner provides for the protection of refugees falling under the competence of his Office.

22. The protection activity of the High Commissioner has developed in accordance with the provisions of the Statute, particularly within the framework of international legal instruments such as the 1951 United Nations Convention and its 1967 Protocol relating to the Status of Refugees, the Convention on the Reduction of Statelessness and the Convention relating to the Status of Stateless Persons. In his report to the forty-second session of the General Assembly,' the High Commissioner pointed out that there is widespread recognition that persons who have been displaced from their countries as a result of

armed conflicts, foreign aggression, occupation or internal upheavals should also be protected from danger through the granting, as a minimum, of temporary asylum, i.e. until such time as conditions in the country of origin permit their safe return.

23. Paragraph 1 of the Statute provides that the United Nations High Commissioner for Refugees, acting under the authority of the General Assembly, shall assume the function ... of seeking permanent solutions for the problem of refugees by assisting governments and, subject to the approval of the governments concerned, private organizations to facilitate the voluntary repatriation of such refugees, or their assimilation within new national communities.

24. Furthermore, paragraphs 9 and 10 of the Statute of his Office provide that:

> The High Commissioner shall engage in such additional activities, including repatriation and resettlement, as the General Assembly may determine, within the limits of the resources placed at his disposal.
>
> The High Commissioner shall administer any funds, public or private, which he receives for assistance to refugees, and shall distribute them among the private and, as appropriate, public agencies which he deems best qualified to administer such assistance.

25. At the time when the Statute of the Office of the High Commissioner was adopted it was considered that its principal function would be to provide international protection for refugees and that its activities in the field of material assistance would assume less prominence. The Office's functions in regard to material assistance were subsequently, however, extended. In resolution 538 (VI) of 2 February 1952, the General Assembly authorized the

High Commissioner, under paragraph 10 of the Statute of his Office, to appeal for funds to enable emergency aid to be given to the most needy groups of refugees within his mandate.

26. In resolution 832 (IX) of 21 October 1954, the General Assembly authorized the High Commissioner to undertake a programme designed to achieve permanent solutions for refugees and authorized him to make appeals for funds for this purpose. Finally, in resolution 1166 (XII) of 26 November 1957, the General Assembly requested the Economic and Social Council to establish the Executive Committee of the High Commissioner's Programme, the functions of which include approving projects for assistance to refugees and authorizing the High Commissioner to make appeals for funds for the financing of such assistance. The Executive Committee of the Programme of the United Nations High Commissioner for Refugees approves the expenditures of the Office of the High Commissioner.

27. The ever-increasing number of refugee situations throughout the world, and the requests for assistance directed to the High Commissioner by the Governments concerned, have contributed to a considerable development of the activities of the United Nations High Commissioner for Refugees with respect to facilitating voluntary repatriation, resettling refugees in countries of durable asylum and various forms of material assistance to refugees, aimed primarily at durable solutions in the country of asylum.

28. In recent years, the High Commissioner has also provided assistance, in accordance with the relevant resolutions of the General Assembly, to an increasing number of displaced persons. Thus, in 1986, he was obliged to respond to urgent assistance needs of refugees

with whom he was concerned in Somalia, in the Sudan, in Djibouti, and to help voluntary returnees and displaced persons in Ethiopia and Chad.

29. In accordance with the Statute of his Office, the High Commissioner reports annually to the General Assembly through the Economic and Social Council. He is entitled to present his views to the Assembly, the Council, and their subsidiary bodies. The mandate of the Office is extended by the General Assembly for periods of five years. Most recently, in resolution 42/108 of 7 December 1987, the Assembly decided to continue the Office for a further period of five years from 1 January 1989.

30. After examining the 1987 report of the High Commissioner on the activities of his Office, the General Assembly in resolution 42/109 of 7 December 1987 noted with satisfaction that 103 States had ratified or acceded to the 1951 Convention and/or the 1967 Protocol relating to the Status of Refugees, and appealed to all States to consider acceding to these instruments in order to enhance their universal character. It condemned all violations of the rights and safety of refugees and asylum-seekers, in particular those perpetrated by military or armed attack against refugee camps and settlements and other forms of violence; recognized the importance of attaining durable solutions to refugee problems and, in particular, the need to address in this process the causes that force refugees and asylum seekers to flee their countries of origin in the light of the report of the Group of Governmental Experts on International Co-operation to Avert New Flows of Refugees; and urged all States to support the High Commissioner in his efforts to achieve durable solutions to the problem of refugees and displaced persons of concern to his Office, primarily through voluntary repatriation or return, including assistance to returnees, as appropriate or, whenever appropriate, through integration

into countries of asylum or through resettlement in third countries.

31. The Assembly, further, expressed deep appreciation for the valuable material and humanitarian response of receiving countries, in particular those developing countries which, despite limited resources, continue to admit, on a permanent or temporary basis, large numbers of refugees and asylum-seekers; and urged the international community to assist those countries in order to enable them to cope with the additional burden that the care for refugees and asylumseekers represents.

32. As an integral part of the United Nations system, UNHCR participates fully in all arrangements for cooperation established within that system.

33. With regard to international protection, the High Commissioner maintains direct contact with the Centre for Human Rights, the Commission on Human Rights and the, Human Rights Committee and with inter governmental organizations such as the Council of Europe, the League of Arab States, OAU and the Organization of American States (OAS). In addition, close contact is maintained with the International Committee of the Red Cross (ICRC) and other nongovernmental organizations directly concerned with the problems of refugees, displaced persons and stateless persons.

34. With regard to assistance activities, a number of United Nations agencies and programmes have provided help to the High Commissioner, ranging from the implementation of specific sectors of assistance projects to the provision of technical advice and expertise. For example, UNICEF has carried out activities in the fields of health, education and community development; UNDP has assigned United Nations Volunteers in various areas of need; UNFPA has helped in the taking of censuses in refugee camps; and

WFP has provided most of the basic food needs of refugees either from its own resources or by channelling bilateral contributions.

35. Of the specialized agencies, ILO has provided technical expertise in such areas as vocational training and income-generating activities for refugee settlements and for women refugees. UNESCO has helped to ascertain, and provide for, the educational needs of refugees, and WHO has provided health co-ordinators for several countries, as well as health supplies.

Convention relating to the status of refugees

36. In accordance with General Assembly resolution 429 (V) of 14 December 1950, a Conference of Plenipotentiaries met in Geneva in 1951 to consider a draft convention relating to the status of refugees and a draft protocol relating to the status of stateless persons, prepared by an ad hoc Committee on Refugees and Stateless Persons which had been established by the Economic and Social Council. On 28 July 1951 the Conference adopted the Convention relating to the Status of Refugees, revising and consolidating previous international agreements on the status of refugees and extending the scope of, and the protection accorded by, such instruments.

37. The Convention sets out, in article 1, a definition of the term "refugee" for the purposes of the Convention. Articles 2 to 11 contain general provisions and provide for non-discrimination as to race, religion, or country of origin; religious freedom, at least to the extent granted to nationals; safeguarding of rights apart from the Convention; equal treatment with aliens unless the Convention contains more favourable provisions, and exemption from legislative reciprocity after three years' residence; exemption from exceptional measures which might be taken against the person, property or interests

of nationals of a foreign State solely on account of such nationality; recognition of continuity of residence; and sympathetic consideration of the position of refugee seamen.

38. Articles 12 to 16 pertain to the juridical status of the refugee, articles 17 to 19 concern the rights of refugees to engage in gainful employment, articles 20 to 24 concern the welfare of the refugee in regard to such matters as rationing, housing, public education, public relief, labour legislation and social security. Article 25 deals with the provision of administrative assistance to refugees and article 26 with their freedom of movement.

Articles 27 and 28 deal respectively with the issue of identity papers to refugees and of travel documents to enable them to travel outside their country of lawful residence. (The Schedule to the Convention contains detailed provisions regarding the issue of such travel documents, their period of validity, their renewal or extension, etc.) Article 29 deals with the applicability of fiscal charges to refugees and article 30 with the right of refugees to transfer their assets from the territory of a Contracting State to another country where they have been admitted for resettlement.

Articles 31 to 33 contain important provisions which are relevant to the question of asylum. According to these articles, a refugee requesting asylum in the territory of a contracting State may not be subjected to penalties on account of his illegal entry or presence provided he presents himself without delay to the competent authorities; if he has resided in the territory of a contracting State he may not be expelled save on grounds of national security and public order and in any event he may not be expelled or returned in any manner whatsoever to the frontiers of territories where his life or freedom would be threatened on account of his race, religion, nationality, membership of a particular social group or political opinion.

Article 34 of the Convention requires contracting States as far as possible to facilitate the assimilation and naturalization of refugees and in particular to make every effort to expedite naturalization proceedings and to reduce the charges and costs of such proceedings. Article 35 of the Convention requires the contracting States to co-operate with the Office of the United Nations High Commissioner for Refugees in the exercise of its functions and in particular to facilitate its duty of supervising the application of the provisions of the Convention.

Protocol relating to the status of refugees

39. As a result of a dateline contained in the definition of the term "refugee" the Convention relating to the Status of Refugees only applied to persons who had become refugees "as a result of events occurring before 1 January 1951". In order to remove this dateline and to make the Convention applicable in all new refugee situations, a Protocol relating to the Status of Refugees was prepared and submitted to the General Assembly at its twenty-first session. In resolution 2198 (XXI) of 16 December 1966 the Assembly took note of the Protocol and requested the Secretary-General to transmit its text to States with a view to enabling them to accede. The Protocol was opened for signature on 31 January 1967 and upon accession thereto by six States, came into force on 4 October 1967.

Declaration and draft convention on territorial asylum

40. Proposals for the inclusion of a provision on the right of asylum were put forward at various stages in the preparation of the International Covenants on Human Rights, but were rejected because of the difficulty of reaching agreement on the categories of persons who

should be granted asylum. While there was a general understanding that States should be generous in granting asylum it was not found possible to translate this principle into a positive obligation in the Covenants.

41. As no article on asylum had been included in the draft covenants, the Government of France submitted to the Commission on Human Rights, in 1957, a draft declaration on the right of asylum.' The Commission, after considering the comments of Governments, the United Nations High Commissioner for Refugees, and non-governmental organizations concerned, adopted the draft declaration at its sixteenth session, in 1960, and transmitted it to the Economic and Social Council, which in turn forwarded it to the General Assembly.

42. The Third Committee of the General Assembly considered the draft declaration at its fifteenth, sixteenth, and seventeenth sessions, held in 1960, 1961 and 1962. In 1965 the Assembly referred the question to the Sixth (Legal) Committee. In 1966, a Working Group of that Committee prepared a revised draft declaration on the basis of the work which had been done by the Commission on Human Rights and the Third Committee.

43. By resolution 2312 (XXII) of 14 December 1967, the General Assembly adopted the Declaration on Territorial Asylum. The Declaration lays down a series of fundamental principles in regard to territorial asylum. It states in the first place that the granting of asylum "is a peaceful and humanitarian act and that, as such, it cannot be regarded as unfriendly by any other State".

Moreover, where a State finds difficulty in granting or continuing to grant asylum, other States "individually or jointly or through the United Nations shall consider, in a spirit of international solidarity, appropriate measures to lighten the burden on that State". Finally the

Declaration gives expression to the basic humanitarian principles of non-refoulement according to which no person shall be rejected at the frontier, expelled, or returned to a country where he may be subjected to persecution.

44. At its thirtieth session the General Assembly, in resolution 3456 (XXX) of 9 December 1975, requested the Secretary-General, in consultation with the United Nations High Commissioner for Refugees, to convene a conference of plenipotentiaries on territorial asylum from 10 January to 4 February 1977, to consider and adopt a convention on territorial asylum.

45. The United Nations Conference on Territorial Asylum met at Geneva as scheduled but did not succeed in adopting the proposed draft convention. It recommended that the General Assembly consider the question of convening, at an appropriate time, a resumed session of the Conference. As at 31 December 1982 a resumed session had not been convened.

Assistance to student refugees in Southern Africa

46. In resolution 31/126 of 16 December 1976, the General Assembly expressed its concern about the continuing influx of large numbers of South African student refugees to Botswana, Lesotho and Swaziland, which imposed a heavy burden on the limited resources of those countries; and requested the Secretary-General to consult with the three Governments and the liberation movements concerned with a view to organizing and providing appropriate emergency financial and other forms of assistance for the care, subsistence and education of these refugee students.

47. At its thirty-second and thirty-third sessions the General Assembly endorsed the measures taken by the

Secretary-General and the United Nations High Commissioner for Refugees to mobilize assistance to the South African student refugees, and urged the international community to contribute generously to the assistance programme. At its thirty-fourth session, in resolution 34/174 of 17 December 1979, the Assembly decided to enlarge the assistance programme for South African student refugees to include student refugees from Namibia and Zimbabwe, and reiterated its appeals for increased and sustained assistance.

48. At recent sessions the General Assembly continued its annual review of assistance to student refugees in southern Africa. In resolution 42/138 of 7 December 1987 it noted with concern that the discriminatory and repulsive practices that continue to be applied in South Africa and Namibia cause a continued and increased influx of student refugees into Botswana, Lesotho, Swaziland and Zambia; and expressed its appreciation to the Governments of those countries for granting asylum and making educational and other facilities available to the student refugees in spite of the pressure that the continuing influx of those refugees exerts on facilities in their countries.

49. The Assembly requested the High Commissioner, in co-operation with the Secretary-General, to continue to organize and implement an effective programme of educational and other appropriate assistance for student refugees from Namibia and South Africa granted asylum in the countries mentioned above, and appealed for contributions to the assistance programme for such students.

International co-operation to avert new flows of refugees

50. The item, "International co-operation to avert new flows of refugees", was included on the agenda of the General Assembly at the request of the Federal Re public

of Germany. In resolution 35/124 of 11 December 1980, the Assembly, deeply disturbed by the human suffering affecting millions of men, women and children who fled or were forcibly expelled from their homelands and sought refuge in other countries, expressed the view that the United Nations was called upon to consider, in addition to humanitarian and social relief, suitable means to avert new flows of refugees. Strongly condemning all policies and practices of oppressive and racist régimes as well as aggression, alien domination and foreign occupation, which in its view were primarily responsible for the massive flows of refugees throughout the world and which resulted in inhuman suffering, the Assembly invited all Member States to convey to the Secretary-General their comments and suggestions on international co-operation to avert new flows of refugees and to facilitate the return of those refugees who wished to do so. The Secretary-General was requested to report to the Assembly on this question.

51. At its thirty-sixth session, in 1981, the General Assembly examined the Secretary-General's report, and adopted resolution 36/148 of 16 December 1981, in which it reaffirmed the inviolability of the provisions of the Charter of the United Nations and the Universal Declaration of Human Rights land of other existing international instruments, norms and principles relevant to responsibilities of States with regard to averting new massive flows of refugees, as well as to the status and the protection of refugees; and noted that, in addition to creating individual human misery, massive flows of refugees could impose great political, economic and social burdens upon the international community as a whole, with dire effects on developing countries.

The Assembly further emphasized the right of refugees to return to their homes in their homelands and reaffirmed the right of those who did not wish to return to receive adequate compensation.

52. Under resolution 36/148 the General Assembly established a group of governmental experts of 17 members and requested it to undertake as soon as possible a comprehensive review of the problem in all its aspects. The Group of Governmental Experts on International Co-operation to Avert New Flows of Refugees was called upon to take into account the comments and suggestions which had been communicated to the Secretary-General, the views expressed in the Assembly and the Commission on Human Rights, and the study on human rights and mass exoduses which a Special Rapporteur was preparing for submission to the Commission.

53. The final report of the Group of Governmental Experts' was examined by the General Assembly at its forty-first session, in 1986. In the report, the Group analysed the circumstances causing new massive flows of refugees and the appropriate means to improve international co-operation to avert such massive flows.

54. The analysis of causes and factors led to the conclusion that the emergence of massive flows of refugees is a result of a number of complex and often interrelated economic and social problems related to, and influenced by, the overall international situation; it may affect the political and social stability, as well as the economic development, of the receiving States, and also carry adverse consequences for the economies of the countries of origin and entire regions, thus endangering international peace and security. Moreover, in view of its complex nature and magnitude, as well as its potentially destabilizing effects, averting massive flows of refugees is a matter of serious concern to the international community as a whole.

55. In its recommendations, the Group proposed that the General Assembly should call upon Member States, for the purpose of averting new massive flows of refugees, to respect a number of obligations, among them:

(c) In view of their responsibilities under the Charter of the United Nations and consistent with their obligations under the existing international instruments in the field of human rights, States, in the exercise of their sovereignty, should do all within their means to prevent new massive flows of refugees. Accordingly, States should refrain from creating or contributing by their policies to causes and factors which generally lead to massive flows of refugees;

(d) States should promote civil, political, economic, social and cultural rights and accordingly refrain from denying them to, and from discriminating against, groups of their population because of their nationality, ethnicity, race, religion or language, thus directly or indirectly forcing them to leave their country;

(e) States should co-operate with one another in order to prevent future massive flows of refugees. They should promote international co-operation in all its aspects, in particular at the regional and subregional levels, as an appropriate and important means to avert such flows;

(f) States should, wherever new massive flows of refugees occur, respect the existing generally recognized norms and principles of international law governing the rights and obligations of States and refugees directly concerned, including those pertaining to the rights of refugees to be facilitated in returning voluntarily and safely to their homes in their homelands and to receive adequate compensation therefrom, where so established, in cases of those who do not wish to return;

56. The Group further recommended that Member States should be called upon to co-operate with one another and

with the Security Council, the General Assembly, the Economic and Social Council, the Secretariat and other relevant organs of the United Nations in a fuller and more timely manner for the prevention of new massive flows of refugees, and that the main organs of the United Nations, and the Secretary-General, should make fuller use of their respective competences to prevent such massive flows.

57. The General Assembly, in resolution 41/70 of 3 December 1986, endorsed the conclusions and recommendations of the Group of Governmental Experts, called upon Member States to respect the recommendations, and requested the main organs of the United Nations, and the Secretary-General, to make fuller use of their respective competences for the prevention of new massive flows of refugees.

Human rights and mass exoduses

58. In resolution 30 (XXXVI) of 11 March 1980, the Commission on Human Rights noted the continuing great distress of refugees and displaced persons in various regions of the world and the immense burden imposed on the first host countries and territories which received the victims of these sudden and massive movements of population, which were frequently the result of violations of human rights. The Commission requested the Secretary-General, in cases where any large-scale exoduses became a matter of international concern, to consider establishing direct contacts with appropriate Governments, to assess the relationships between the situation and full enjoyment of human rights and to make concrete recommendations for ameliorating such situations.

59. Later that year the General Assembly, in resolution 35/196 of 15 December 1980, also expressed deep concern at the continued incidence of large-scale exoduses and

displacements and the resulting hardships and problems for the persons and States concerned, expressed its determination to facilitate solutions to those problems, and requested the Commission on Human Rights to make recommendations for further action.

60. At its thirty-seventh session, in resolution 29 (XXXVII) of 11 March 198 1, the Commission decided to appoint a special rapporteur to study the question of human rights and mass exoduses, and invited its Chairman to appoint an individual of recognized international standing as special rapporteur. The Council approved that action in decision 1981/145 of 8 May 1981.

61. The Special Rapporteur, Sadruddin Aga Khan, presented his study on human rights and massive exoduses to the Commission at its thirty-eighth session. In resolution 1982/32 of 11 March 1982, the Commission commended him for the study and requested the Secretary-General to transmit it to the General Assembly and to bring it to the attention of the Group of Governmental Experts on International Co-operation to Avert New Flows of Refugees established by Assembly resolution 36/148 of 16 December 1981.

62. At its forty-second session, in 1987, the General Assembly reviewed the Special Rapporteur's Study, together with the report of the Group of Governmental Experts on International Co-operation to Avert New Flows of Refugees and the Secretary-General's Exeport on human rights and mass exoduses. In addition, its attention was drawn to the Secretary-General's decision to establish an office for research and the collection of information responsible, inter alia, for the provision of early warning of developing situations requiring his attention and the monitoring of factors related to possible flows of refugees and displaced persons and comparable emergencies and the preparation of plans for possible responses, as

mentioned in his report on the work of the Organization to the General Assembly.

63. The Assembly, in resolution 42/144 of 7 December 1987 welcomed the steps taken by the Secretary-General and other steps taken within the United Nations to examine and deal with the problem. Conscious of the fact that human rights violations are one of the multiple and complex factors causing mass exoduses of refugees and displaced persons, as indicated in each of the studies and report, the Assembly invited the Commission on Human Rights to keep the question of human rights under review.

International Conferences on Assistance to Refugees in Africa

64. The General Assembly, in resolution 35/42 of 25 November 1980, noted with deep regret the inadequacy of the assistance provided to the growing number of African refugees, and requested the international community to contribute substantially to programmes designed to help them. It requested the Secretary-General, in close co-operation with the Secretary-General of the Organization of African Unity and the United Nations High Commissioner for Refugees, to convene at Geneva on 9 and 10 April 1981, at the ministerial level, an International Conference on Assistance to Refugees in Africa.

65. The report of the Secretary-General on the Conference was considered by the General Assembly at its thirty-sixth session. In resolution 36/124 of 14 December 1981, the Assembly expressed its appreciation and gratitude to all donor countries and to the international community at large for their very positive response to the appeal for assistance to African refugees and for their contribution to such assistance, and urged them to continue to support programmes undertaken on behalf of refugees in Africa.

66. As requested in paragraph 6 of resolution 36/124, the Secretary-General submitted a report to the Economic and Social Council at its second regular session of 1982, providing detailed information on post conference activities, including data on pledges and contributions made at the Conference as known at 3 May 1982. He submitted information on activities after 3 May 1982 to the General Assembly. These reports indicated that one of the results of the Conference had been the receipt of pledges of approximately $573 million.

67. In resolution 37/197 of 18 December 1982 the General Assembly expressed its appreciation to all donor countries, the United Nations High Commissioner for Refugees and the international community for their continued support and assistance to African refugees, and its concern that the assistance available fell short of the urgent needs of refugees and returnees in Africa. It requested the Secretary-General, in close co-operation with the Secretary-General of the Organization of African Unity and the United Nations High Commissioner for Refugees, to convene a second International Conference on Assistance to Refugees in Africa at Geneva in 1984.

68. A second International Conference on Assistance to Refugees in Africa was held at Geneva from 9 to 11 July 1984 to launch collective action by the international community aimed at achieving lasting solutions. The report of the Conference was examined by the General Assembly at its thirty-ninth session, in 1984.

69. The Declaration and Programme of Action adopted by the Conference pointed out the persistent and serious problem of large numbers of refugees on the African continent and the economic and social burden borne by African countries of asylum on account of the presence of those refugees. On the basis of these findings the General Assembly, in resolution 39/139 of 14 December

1984 recognized the universal collective responsibility of sharing the urgent and overwhelming burden of the problem of African refugees through effective mobilization of resources to meet the urgent and long-term needs of the refugees and to strengthen the capacity of countries of asylum to provide adequately for them, as well as to assist the countries of origin in the rehabilitation of voluntary returnees. It thanked all who had contributed to alleviating the plight of the refugees and urged the international community to maintain the momentum created by the Conference and to translate its principles and programmes into action.

70. However in 1987 the Assembly, after reviewing a later report by the Secretary-General on assistance to refugees in Africa noted with deep concern in resolution 42/107 of 7 December 1987 that many of the projects submitted to the Second International Conference on Assistance to Refugees in Africa had yet to be funded and implemented, and called upon all Member States and organizations of the United Nations system to intensify their support for the speedy implementation of the recommendations and pledges made at the Conference.

Group of Governmental Experts on International Co-operation to Avert New Flows of Refugees

71. Taking into account paragraph 4 of General Assembly resolution 40/166 of 16 December 1985, in which the Assembly called upon the Group of Governmental Experts on International Co-operation to Avert New Flows of Refugees which it had established by resolution 36/148 of 16 December 1981 "to work expeditiously on the fulfilment of its mandate", the Group concluded its study in May 1986.17

72. In its conclusions, the Group of Experts stated that its analysis of causes and factors showed that the emergence

of massive flows of refugees is a result of a number of complex and often interrelated political, economic and social problems related to, and influenced by, the overall international situation. It added that massive flows of refugees may affect the political and social stability, as well as the economic development, of receiving States, and may also have adverse consequences for the economies of the countries of origin or even entire regions, thus undermining international peace and security. In its recommendations, the Group expressed the view that States, in the exercise of their sovereignty, should do all within their means to prevent new massive flows of refugees, and should refrain from creating, or contributing to, such massive flows.

73. On the basis of the Group's report, the Assembly in resolution 41/70 of 3 December 1986 urged the main organs of the United Nations to make fuller use of their competences under the Charter of the United Nations to prevent new massive flows of refugees, and requested the Secretary-General to bring the report of the Group of Governmental Experts to the attention of Member States and all relevant organizations, organs and programmes of the United Nations system.

The essential problems of refugees, and the necessary solutions to them, have been the same throughout history and around the world: refugees need to be fed, clothed and sheltered; the want to go back home if they can, and often need help to do so; and they need to find new homes if they cannot return to their old ones. The basic function of UNHCR is to extend international protection to refugees who, by definition, do not enjoy the protection of their former home country. UNHCR seeks to ensure that refugees receive asylum and are granted a favourable legal status in their asylum country. An essential element of this legal status is the safeguard provided by the generally accepted principle of non-refoulement, which prohibits expulsion or forcible return of a person to a country where he may have reason to fear persecution.

UNHCR also seeks to ensure that persons claiming to be refugees are identified as such so as to enable them to take advantage of the standards in international instruments or under international law. The legal status of refugees has been defined more specifically in two international instruments—the 1951 Convention relating to the Status of Refugees and its 1967 Protocol which define the rights and duties of refugees and contain provisions dealing with such matters as protection from refoulement, unlawful expulsions and detentions, and the refugee's employment, public education and assistance, artistic rights and industrial property.

In regard to many of these matters, refugees are to receive the same treatment as nationals of their country of residence. Material assistance is also essential, to enable refugees or displaced persons to achieve permanent solutions to their problems, whether it be through voluntary repatriation, local settlement in the country of first asylum or migration to another country. Measures vary widely according to need.

Integration through rural settlement is in general the best solution for refugees of rural background who cannot hope to repatriate for some time; in Africa, in particular, UNHCR helps refugees to settle on the land through the establishment of new rural communities or through strengthening the infrastructure of areas where the refugees can be absorbed spontaneously into the local population. Assistance in voluntary repatriation may involve a large-scale transportation and settlement operation, or may simply entail the payment of travel expenses for individuals.

UNHCR has for many years helped to organize special resettlement schemes for refugees who could not qualify under normal immigration criteria because of physical or social handicaps. In addition, family reunion is an essential activity. Finally, counselling plays an important role in helping individual refugees find the most appropriate solutions to their problems.

The Second International Conference for Assistance to Refugees in Africa (ICARA II) was held at Geneva in July 1984. It adopted a Declaration and Programme of Action aimed at initiating a long-term strategy to deal with Africa's 4 million refugees and returnees. Going beyond the first International Conference (ICARA 1) (Geneva, 1981), which focused primarily on emergency assistance, ICARA 11 linked humanitarian aid to refugees with the need to help host countries develop their social and economic infrastructures.

One problem facing the U.N. and other efforts to protect refugees has been the narrow interpretation of who constitutes a refugee, as defined by U.N. and other treaties. The Universal Declaration of Human Rights, considered binding on all states, "affirms a full range of civil, political, economic and social rights for all persons, citizens and refugees alike. It also significantly provides the right to seek and enjoy asylum, the right to freedom of movement, and the right to a nationality". Other pacts, such as, the International Covenant on Civil and Political Rights, cover all people within a nation's territory and prohibit expulsion of aliens or limitations on movement. But other pacts that spell out refugee rights define protected refugees more narrowly. The 1950 Statute of the UNHCR and the 1951 Convention Relating to the Status of Refugees prohibit forced return of refugees and state they must be treated almost as well as Citizens.

Refugees must be accorded free movement, ownership of property, legal rights, access to education, work, and other human rights. The instruments define refugees as people with a well-founded fear of persecution based on racial, religious, national, social, or political grounds. This definition covers some-but not all-émigrés fleeing civil strife, war, or poverty related to political persecution or ethnic conflict. It applies to individuals who fear persecution on personal grounds but leaves out the millions who know they will probably die or suffer if they return to countries torn by war or civil conflict. The General Assembly adopted the Declaration on Territorial Asylum in 1967. It seeks to bar states from rejecting asylum seekers at the nation's frontiers and would bar the return of asylum seekers to countries in which they would be persecuted. But like all other Assembly resolutions, it is nonbinding. Efforts to draft a binding convention collapsed in 1977.

Many of the problems facing refugees stem from disagreement over these definitions of who deserves asylum. Politically it has been a good year for tens of thousands of anticommunist, generally educated Warsaw Pact refugees whose flight has vindicated years of Western criticism of Moscow and its satellites. But it has been a terrible year for more simple masses fleeing persecution and war, or merely life-threatening poverty, in the developing world.

Countries continue to show a preference for refugees fleeing the host nation's enemies as well as for migrants with good skills and education. Welcoming countries also tend to favor exiles supported by powerful, domestic groups. How to define a refugee-as opposed to someone merely seeking economic opportunity—continues to be an issue, one that some governments use as a fig leaf to cover their choice of which refugees to admit and which to reject.

A document drafted by the region's first-asylum countries for an International Conference on Indo-Chinese Refugees earlier in 1989 had established a process for screening Indochinese boat people to distinguish political refugees from economic migrants, but the United States and Vietnam rejected the notion of forced repatriation for those denied refugee status. In the summer of 1990, as the refugee/migrant waves continued and Washington and Hanoi stood their ground vis-a-vis forced repatriation, the countries of first asylum threatened to refuse landing rights to all new arrivals. It was to avoid formalizing this lack of consensus, say observers, that both sides requested the UNHCR to postpone indefinitely a conference scheduled for mid-July.

U.S. refugee policies-intended to protect those in political danger reveal similar contradictions. Washington usually accepts those fleeing governments it opposes or refugees who bring skills and education with them. Of 125,000 annual openings for refugees, the lion's share goes to Soviet-bloc and other exiles fleeing communism.

In late 1989, Arab countries mounted a major diplomatic effort to convince the Soviet Union and transit countries not to aid the flow of Soviet Jews to Israel, claiming they would colonize the occupied Arab territories-this despite the fact that only a few hundred so far have chosen to settle in the occupied lands. Most countries have done little to aid tens of thousands of Kurds fleeing intense persecution and chemical bombardment in Iraq for fear of alienating the influential Baghdad regime or Turkey, a member of the North Atlantic Treaty Organization.

Eritrean migrants in Gulf states are often carted out to sea and dumped on islands off the Ethiopian coast, where conditions often lead to death. Both Sudan and Ethiopia use food and aid as weapons against their own and refugee populations in their countries' civil wars. The United Nations itself must negotiate these tricky political issues supporting refugee rights without aggravating major donors or countries sheltering exiles. Critics say it sometimes plays the political game too well. The High Commissioner for Refugees, Jean-Pierre Hocké, resigned on October 26, 1989, amid widespread charges that he undercut the agency's management and had misused hundreds of thousands of dollars for entertainment and travel. But Hocké, a Swiss native, was also accused of catering to the interests of UNHCR's big donors at the expense of the interests of refugees.

The new High Commissioner, Thorvald Stoltenberg, has been a more vocal advocate of greater support for those under his protection. Complaining of budget constraints, he told The New York Times on March 18, "I can't fulfill my mandate-levels of care are falling, I have only half the resources per refugee today that we had in 1980."

The General Assembly, for its part, continues to pass dozens of resolutions each year calling attention to specific refugee issues and the needs of refugee groups around the world. On December 8, 1989, it adopted 11 resolutions on Palestinian refugees who fall under the mandate of the United Nations Relief and Works Agency (UNRWA). The resolutions appealed for more funding for UNRWA, demanded that Israel not resettle any refugees in the Occupied Territories, affirmed the need for scholarships and strengthened educational facilities, and in general sought to further the Palestinians' cause.

While the resolutions may have been worthy, they reflect the fact that only refugees with vocal political supporters-in this case the Arab group-tend to get major political support in the General Assembly. On December 15 the Assembly adopted by consensus a resolution supporting UNHCR. It called for all states to grant asylum in accordance with international law, noted the fact that many of those seeking asylum are held in detention or forced to serve in armed forces, and affirmed other UNHCR programs, including an emphasis on aiding refugees through development.

Another December 15 consensus resolution called for support for South African refugees. Other texts praised the International Conference on Indo-Chinese Refugees and the May 1989 Guatemala City conference on Central American refugees. Still other texts adopted that day by consensus called for aid to refugees and displaced persons in Malawi, Djibouti, the Sudan, Somalia, Chad, Ethiopia, and student refugees in southern Africa. These resolutions help draw attention to pressing refugee needs, but they do not always translate into sufficient resources or political will to solve refugee crises. In the face of this ambivalent world attitude toward refugees, the United Nations has tried several strategies.

On another tack, the United Nations is attempting to develop early warning systems designed to predict when a large group of people may flood a country. This effort would allow agencies to meet exiles' needs quickly while laying the ground for their proper reception. But at base, most refugees' decisions to flee their homelands stem from political and social crises in these homelands; only the ending of these crises will convince most to return home. Sometimes the United Nations tries to nudge refugees to return in the hope that this will help move a nation toward settling its conflicts. This has been the effort with $ million Afghan refugees in Pakistan and Iran.

Operation Salaam has mounted a major effort to prepare refugees for their return home and the rebuilding of their country, hoping this would goad Afghan belligerents toward a settlement of the nation's civil war.

But critics say that few refugees have chosen to return, adding that the United Nations may be overstating its success in this area. Only peace can convince exiles to go home. A settlement of the Nicaraguan civil war-if it sees the return of contra rebels under U.N. auspices, as called for under regional peace treaties-would prove this simple thesis. In the expectation of a successful conclusion to the peace process, the U.N. Secretary-General, the U.N. Development Programme, and UNHCR called an international meeting on Central American refugees and displaced persons, June 27-28-a follow-up to the May 1989 conference in Guatemala City. Their hope was to gather support for 59 projects to resettle, settle, or otherwise benefit Central America's 2 million refugees.

Meanwhile, the situation for most refugees will remain delicate as long as resources are scarce and nations fail to address the gap between their stated humanitarian goals and actual policies.

3
Rights of the Child

There is no way to thoroughly enumerate the various ways in which children around the world are economically exploited and physically mistreated. But the numbers are great—and the suffering widespread. Behind the hideous imagery—of children beaten or sexually abused by parents; ravaged beyond their years by hard living and drug abuse on the streets; maimed by landmines or turned into killers by war; stricken with AIDS—are the all-too-common struggles against disease, hardship, and family or social traditions that compromise children's humanity or subject them to physical and emotional suffering.

While victims of injustice and poverty have always had trouble being heard, none have had more trouble, historically, than children. Whether exploited as child labourers or prostitutes, drafted as young teenagers into armed forces, forced as young girls into a lonely life as domestic workers, deprived of an education to work on the family farm, or denied adequate nutrition and health care, children need help and protection from an adult world that perpetrates most of the abuse.

To highlight the existence of the most egregious violations of international human rights law and encourage Governments to investigate particular cases, the United Nations Commission on Human Rights has appointed a Special Rapporteur on the sale of children, child prostitution and child pornography. The Special Rapporteur, an expert in the field, works to gather and analyse facts for the Commission.

The condition most common to children who suffer, or are deprived of, opportunity is the poverty resulting from economic injustice. "The most perverse form of denial of child rights is poverty, because poverty makes it impossible to satisfy those needs that are basic rights," says Tereza Albenez, Special Advisor to the United Nations Children's Fund (UNICEF) on the Convention on the Rights of the Child.

According to figures compiled by UNICEF—the United Nations Organisation most directly concerned with children's issues—there are now well over a dozen countries in which conditions for children are far below the norms to be expected for their levels of economic development. This includes such gauges as malnutrition levels; under-five mortality rates; percentage of children reaching the fifth grade of primary school; and low literacy rates for women.

In many poor countries, children work to supplement meagre family income or otherwise to help the family business. Although they may not always work under the most desirable conditions, most are not being intentionally exploited by their families. The real issue in such cases is not whether the children work or not, but whether the conditions under which they work are just, and whether they are being denied other basic rights because of their work—such as the right to education, to freedom from abuse, and to proper health care.

Solving a Complex Dilemma

A number of those working on behalf of child rights have come to realise that in many of the poorer countries, if children are to stop working, some form of financial compensation must be found for their families.

One creative response to this kind of complex dilemma has come from Bangladesh. In reaction to United States Congressional legislation mandating a boycott of companies in the garment industry that use child labour, companies in the garment industry in Bangladesh began ousting children from their jobs—as many as 50,000 in a four-month period. The result was that many of the children were worse off than they had been when they were working, having taken other, less desirable jobs or living in the street—but not going to school.

In July 1995, after negotiations with non-governmental organisations (NGOs), as well as UNICEF and the International Labour Organisation (ILO), the Bangladesh Garment Manufacturers and Exporters Association (BGMEA) signed a Memorandum of Understanding stipulating that BGMEA would ask "that no underaged worker will be terminated until the appropriate school programmes for the workers can be put in place."

UNICEF has committed itself to supporting the education of the children, and the ILO has pledged to contribute money and technical assistance to the establishment of a labour inspection system to monitor implementation of the Memorandum of Understanding. Under the agreement, stipends will be provided to child workers attending the school programmes. All parties also agreed to take steps 'to create positive public awareness' with respect to issues of child labour and education.

The direct injustices perpetrated largely by adults—and manifested in the large numbers of children exploited as labourers and prostitutes or maimed by war—require further public exposure and protective laws that are actually enforced. In the last decade, an estimated two million children have been killed in armed conflict, many of them by some of the 100 million landmines thought to be concealed in 62 countries. A total of perhaps four to five million more have been disabled as a result of their experience in war, and more than 12 million have been made homeless.

As for child labour, while experts agree that there are few accurate statistics available, the best estimates from the ILO are that there are nearly 80 million children under 15 working as labourers. It is also estimated that the number of children under 18 involved in prostitution exceeds two million, one million of whom are in Asia and 300,000 in the United States.

"Poverty cannot be accepted as a pretext and justification for the exploitation of children," wrote Vitit Muntarbhorn, until 1995 the Special Rapporteur on the sale of children, child prostitution and child pornography. "It does not explain the huge global demand with, in many instances, customers from rich countries circumventing their national laws to exploit children in other countries. Sex tourism has spread its illicit wings wide, and paedophiles search for their victims in all parts of the globe. The problem is compounded by the criminal networks which benefit from the trade in children, and by collusion and corruption in many national settings."

"It has become increasingly obvious that many children used for labour and sexual exploitation are lured from particular racial or social groups, rather than from the well-endowed groups in power," the Special Rapporteur went on, in a January 1994 report to the United Nations Commission on Human Rights. "In South Asia, it is the children of the 'untouchables' who are most often victimised in child labour situations."

The Special Rapporteur said a field visit to Nepal showed that "it is primarily girls from hill-tribe groups in that country who are tricked and sold into prostitution, both local and transnational. The pattern is repeated in other parts of the world, where the children of minorities, migrant workers and/or indigenous peoples, who are already margi-nalised, are often the main victims of such exploitation."

The Special Rapporteur—Mr. Muntarbhorn was succeeded by Mrs. O. Calcetas-Santos—has often had difficulty obtaining information from governments in response to queries about such matters as the sale and abduction of children; bonded labour; child prostitution; or sale of child organs. But in certain cases the Rapporteur's inquiries have added an international level of accountability in otherwise domestic cases.

Abuses against Street Children

In August 1993, to cite one example, the Special Rapporteur communicated with the Brazilian government concerning allegations of the exploitation and abuse of street children by law-enforcement officials. The officials were alleged to have killed eight street children and injured others in Rio de Janeiro in July 1993. The allegation followed a long list of others noted in the Special Rapporteur's report on Brazil submitted to the Commission on Human Rights in 1992.

The Brazilian government responded by acknowledging the charge. "As pointed out in your communication, this incident is not an isolated case," the government said in its response. "The Brazilian government is well aware that the killings of street children are not a new phenomenon and that certain elements of the policy may be implicated in the actions of 'death' squads." Three policemen and a fourth man were in prison awaiting trial for murder, and the commander of the Fifth Police Corps in Rio de Janeiro, to whom the three policemen were subordinated, was dismissed from his post.

Non-governmental organisations have played an important role in pressuring governments to respect both international law and in many cases similar laws in their own countries, particularly when it is clear that they have been partly or largely responsible for violations of those laws. Human Rights Watch, a non-governmental human rights organisation with offices in Europe and the United States, has investigated numerous allegations. These include trafficking of women and girls from Nepal into India for use as prostitutes; the conditions of bonded labourers in Pakistan, many of whom are children; and the improper detention of juveniles by the criminal-justice system in Jamaica. The Human Rights Watch recently released reports on India and Pakistan in mid-1995 that were highly critical of government complicity.

In the United States, new tools for fighting sexual abuse of children overseas and international child pornography have been incorporated into the Mann Act, a 1910 Act of Congress originally aimed at prohibiting the interstate transportation of women 'for immoral purposes'. The amendments, approved after several years of lobbying by voluntary agencies, make it illegal for American citizens and resident aliens to travel abroad to engage in sexual acts with minors. The measures would bring the law into line with US domestic policy. The law—part of the Violent Crime Control and Law Enforcement Act of 1994, which was signed into law by President Clinton—also pertains to those who conspire to commit such acts, such as sex-tour operators. A 1986 amendment to the Mann Act made it a crime to transport a person under 18 between states or abroad with the intention of having the young person engage in sexual activity.

Halting Unlawful Jailings

In response to an earlier report on conditions in Jamaica, where juvenile offenders were being unlawfully locked up with adults, some of the children were released. Local government agencies and organisations began to explore alternatives to imprisonment for juvenile offenders, and training programmes on the rights of juveniles was begun for guards. "If you get people out of custody or get Governments to change their policy," says Lois Whitman, Director of the Children's Rights Project at Human Rights Watch, "that is progress."

It was not until recently that children have become a constituency in their own right, on whose behalf a number of international organisations, government laws and human rights decrees have been created to advocate more equitable treatment for children under existing laws and for a more equitable share of resources and opportunities.

Prior to the 20th century, children were for the most part regarded as inferior and subordinate to adults, and childhood was a period of life that was often brief and regarded as a stage of passage to adulthood. Now, in the latter half of the century, childhood is regarded as a relatively sacred part of life among many of the more affluent. But it is still a period of great struggle and deprivation for children in most of the rest of the world.

Children have been included, either directly or indirectly, in most of the nearly 80 treaties and decrees on human rights in this century. The first major step on behalf of children taken by the United Nations was UNICEF's creation in December 1946.

Two years later, the Universal Declaration of Human Rights was adopted by the General Assembly. The provisions of that Declaration and its two International Covenants on human rights, adopted in 1966, recognised that child rights need protection. The 1959 Declaration on the Rights of the Child was the first United Nations statement devoted exclusively to the rights of children, but served more as a moral rather than legally binding framework. The special plight of girls was addressed in part by the Convention on the Elimination of All Forms of Discrimination Against Women, adopted in 1979. The Working Group on Contemporary Forms of Slavery annually addresses such issues as child labour and debt bondage.

It took until the 1990s, however, for all of the pieces to come together in the form of the Convention on the Rights of the Child, which was adopted by the General Assembly in 1989. The Convention's 54 articles cover everything from a child's right to be free from sexual and economic exploitation, to the right to his or her own opinion, and to the right to education, health care, and economic opportunity.

By September 1995, 178 countries had ratified the Convention. A dozen more, some of which had been created since the Convention was adopted six years earlier, were considering it. As a result of this growing support, according to Ms Albenez of UNICEF, childhood is coming to be widely seen not as "some kind of probation period before becoming an adult." Instead, she said, "the child emerges as an individual with dignity who has all the rights of a full human being."

The initiative for the Convention came from the Government of Poland, which submitted a Draft Convention to the Commission on Human Rights in 1978, prior to celebration of the 20th anniversary of the Declaration on the Rights of the Child during the International Year of the Child in 1979. That led to a decade of collaboration between a small group of non-governmental organisations, including Radda Barnen of

Sweden, the International Child Catholic Bureau, and Defence for Children International, and United Nations human rights experts. After a lengthy period of careful negotiations, the Convention on the Rights of the Child was adopted in November 1989 by a vote of the General Assembly. By September of the following year, the Convention had obtained the 20 ratifications required for its entry into force as international law. Its importance as a foundation of modern human rights law was later underscored at the 1993 World Conference on Human Rights in Vienna. I. A Landmark for Children and Their Rights. The Convention on the Rights of the Child was adopted by the General Assembly of the United Nations by its resolution 44/25 of 20 November 1989.

This was the end of a process which had begun with the preparations for the 1979 International Year of the Child. That year, discussions started on a draft convention submitted by the Government of Poland. Children had been discussed before by the international community. Declarations on the rights of the child had been adopted by both the League of Nations (1924) and the United Nations (1959). Also, specific provisions concerning children had been incorporated in a number of human rights and humanitarian law treaties. Nevertheless, some States argued that there was a need for a comprehensive statement on children's rights which would be binding under international law.

That view was influenced by reports of grave injustices suffered by children: high infant mortality, deficient health care, limited opportunities for basic education. There were also alarming accounts of children being abused and exploited as prostitutes or in harmful jobs, of children in prison or in other difficult circumstances, and of children as refugees and victims of armed conflict.

The drafting of the Convention took place in a working group set up by the United Nations Commission on Human Rights. Government delegates formed the core of the drafting group, but representatives of United Nations bodies and specialised agencies, including the Office of the United Nations High Commissioner for Refugees (UNHCR), the International Labour Organisation (ILO), the United Nations Children's Fund (UNICEF) and the World Health Organisation (WHO), as well as a number of non-governmental organisations, took part in the deliberations. The original draft submitted by the Polish government was extensively amended and expanded through the long discussions.

The unanimous adoption of the Convention by the General Assembly paved the way for the next stage: ratifications by States and the setting up of a monitoring committee. Within less than a year, by September 1990, 20 States had legally endorsed the Convention, which thereby entered into force.

In the same month, the World Summit for Children was held in New York on the initiative of UNICEF and six States (Canada, Egypt, Mali, Mexico, Pakistan and Sweden). The Summit encouraged all States to ratify the Convention. By the end of 1990, 57 had done so, thereby becoming States parties. In 1993, the World Conference on Human Rights held at Vienna declared that the goal was universal ratification by the end of 1995. By 31 December 1995, no less than 185 countries had indeed ratified the Convention. This number is unprecedented in the field of human rights.

The Convention on the Rights of the Child has the same meaning for people in all parts of the world. While laying down common standards, the Convention takes into account the different cultural, social, economic and political realities of individual States so that each State may seek its own means to implement the rights common to all.

There are four general principles enshrined in the Convention. These are meant to help with the interpretation of the Convention as a whole and thereby guide national programmes of implementation. The four principles are formulated, in particular, in articles 2, 3, 6 and 12.

Non-discrimination (art. 2): States parties must ensure that all children within their jurisdiction enjoy their rights. No child should suffer discrimination. This applies to every child, "irrespective of the child's or his or her parent's or legal guardian's race, colour, sex, language, religion, political or other opinion, national, ethnic or social origin, property, disability, birth or other status."

The essential message is equality of opportunity. Girls should be given the same opportunities as boys. Refugee children, children of foreign origin, children of indigenous or minority groups should have the same rights as all others. Children with disabilities should be given the same opportunity to enjoy an adequate standard of living.

Best interests of the child (art. 3): When the authorities of a State take decisions which affect children, the best interests of children must be a primary consideration. This principle relates to decisions by courts of law, administrative authorities, legislative bodies and both public and private social-welfare institutions. This is, of course, a fundamental message of the Convention, the implementation of which is a major challenge.

The right to life, survival and development (art. 6): The right-to-life article includes formulations about the right to survival and to development, which should be ensured 'to the maximum extent possible'. The term 'development' in this context should be interpreted in a broad sense, adding a qualitative dimension: not only physical health is intended, but also mental, emotional, cognitive, social and cultural development.

The views of the child (art 12): Children should be free to have opinions in all matters affecting them, and those views should be given due weight 'in accordance with the age and maturity of the child'. The underlying idea is that children have the right to be heard and to have their views taken seriously, including in any judicial or administrative proceedings affecting them.

Highlights of the Convention

— Every child has the inherent right to life, and States shall ensure to the maximum child survival and development.

— Every child has the right to a name and nationality from birth.

— Children shall not be separated from their parents, except by competent authorities for their well-being.

— States shall facilitate reunification of families by permitting travel into, or out of, their territories.

— Parents have the primary responsibility for a child's upbringing, but States shall provide them with appropriate assistance and develop child-care institutions.

— States shall protect children from physical or mental harm and neglect, including sexual abuse or exploitation.

— States shall provide parentless children with suitable alternative care. The adoption process shall be carefully regulated and international agreements should be sought to provide safeguards and assure legal validity if and when adoptive parents intend to move a child from his or her country of birth.

- Disabled children shall have the right to special treatment, education and care.
- Children are entitled to the highest attainable standard of health. States shall ensure that health care is provided to all children, placing emphasis on preventive measures, health education and reduction of infant mortality.
- Primary education shall be free and compulsory. Discipline in schools shall respect the child's dignity. Education should prepare the child for life in a spirit of understanding, peace and tolerance.
- Children shall have time to rest and play and equal opportunities for cultural and artistic activities.
- States shall protect children from economic exploitation and from work that may interfere with their education or be harmful to their health or well-being.
- States shall protect children from the illegal use of drugs and involvement in drug production or trafficking.
- All efforts shall be made to eliminate the abduction and trafficking of children.
- Capital punishment or life imprisonment shall not be imposed for crimes committed before the age of 18.
- Children in detention shall be separated from adults; they must not be tortured or suffer cruel or degrading treatment.
- No child under 15 shall take any part in hostilities; children exposed to armed conflict shall receive special protection.
- Children of minority and indigenous populations

shall freely enjoy their own culture, religion and language.

— Children who have suffered mistreatment, neglect or exploitation shall receive appropriate treatment or training for recovery and rehabilitation.
— Children involved in infringements of the penal law shall be treated in a way that promotes their sense of dignity and worth and aims at reintegrating them into society.
— States shall make the rights set out in the Convention widely known to both adults and children.

Constructive Monitoring

A number of international human rights bodies contribute to improving respect for the rights of the child in their particular areas of competence. In addition to the Commission on Human Rights, the Sub-Commission on Prevention of Discrimination and Protection of Minorities and its Working Group on Contemporary Forms of Slavery, which deals with aspects of the exploitation and mistreatment of children, relevant international human rights bodies include the following:

— Human Rights Committee;
— Committee on Economic, Social and Cultural Rights;
— Committee on the Elimination of Racial Discrimination;
— Committee on the Elimination of Discrimination against Women;
— Committee against Torture.

These five committees are commonly referred to as treaty bodies, since they were established to monitor the implementation of particular United Nations human rights treaties by States which have ratified or acceded to the instruments in question. The creation of the Committee on the Rights of the Child, established under article 43 of the Convention, reinforced the activities of these bodies on behalf of children.

Committee on the Rights of the Child

In early 1991, a meeting of representatives of States parties to the Convention on the Rights of the Child was convened for the first election to its monitoring body: the Committee on the Rights of the Child. Some 40 candidates had been nominated for the 10 seats. The experts elected on this first occasion came from Barbados, Brazil, Burkina Faso, Egypt, Peru, the Philippines, Portugal, the former Soviet Union, Sweden and Zimbabwe. Six were women, four men. They represented a variety of professional backgrounds, including human rights and international law, juvenile justice, social work, medicine, journalism and governmental and non-governmental work.

The Committee on the Rights of the Child currently holds three sessions a year, each of four weeks' duration. The last week is always reserved for preparation of the next session. The Committee is serviced by the United Nations Centre for Human Rights in Geneva.

Under article 44 of the Convention, States parties accept the duty to submit regular reports to the Committee on the steps they have taken to put the Convention into effect and on progress in the enjoyment of children's rights in their territories. First implementation reports are to be submitted within two years of ratification of or accession to the Convention and thereafter every five years. The first initial reports were due in September 1992. More than 70 State reports had reached the Committee by December 1995.

At its first session, in October 1991, the Committee adopted guidelines to help States parties writing and structuring their initial reports. Governments are recommended to prepare their reports according to these guidelines, which stress that the report should indicate 'factors and difficulties' encountered by the State in the implementation of the Convention—in other words, that it should be problem-oriented and self-critical. States are also asked to specify 'implementation priorities' and 'specific goals for the future'. Relevant legal texts and statistical data are to be submitted with the report.

In establishing its procedures, the Committee has emphasised the importance of a constructive dialogue with government representatives. In this context, it has also made clear that it seeks close cooperation with relevant United Nations bodies and specialised agencies, as well as with other competent bodies, including non-governmental organisations.

Working Procedure

A working group of the Committee meets prior to each of its sessions for a preliminary examination of reports received from States parties, and to prepare the Committee's discussions with the representatives of reporting States. In addition to State reports, the working group considers information provided by other human rights treaty bodies. The Committee also receives information from mechanisms established by the Commission on Human Rights to investigate human rights problems in specific countries or on thematic issues, for example the Special Rapporteurs on torture, on extrajudicial, summary or arbitrary executions, and on violence against women. A key partner in this context is the Special Rapporteur on the sale of children, child prostitution and child pornography.

General Discussions and Studies

A procedural innovation was introduced by the Committee in January 1993 when it recommended to the General Assembly that it request the Secretary-General to undertake a study on the protection of children in armed conflicts. This request was the result of a full-day 'general discussion' on the subject organised by the Committee in 1992, in which United Nations bodies and non-governmental organisations were invited to participate.

General discussions have since been held on economic exploitation of children, on the rights of the child in the family context, on the rights of the girl child, and on juvenile justice. Such thematic discussions are held about once a year and may lead to requests for studies, but can also serve as a basis for work on interpreting the articles of the Convention.

United Nations bodies and specialised agencies may take part in the deliberations of the working group and provide information. On the basis of written information received from relevant non-governmental organisations, the Committee has also often invited such organisations to take part in the preparatory meetings on State reports.

The end result of the pre-sessional working group's discussion on a State report is a 'list of issues'. This list, which gives a preliminary indication of the issues which the Committee considers to be priorities for discussion, is sent to the government concerned with an invitation to participate in a forthcoming plenary session of the Committee at which its report will be considered. The government is invited to respond to the issues in writing, before the session.

This approach gives governments the opportunity better to prepare themselves for the discussion with the Committee. Other points not included in the list of issues may emerge during the discussion, which is one reason why the Committee prefers to discuss with high level officials, such as ministers or deputy ministers, rather than with representatives who lack the authority to make decisions.

Discussions with States parties are concrete and detailed, and tend to deal with both results and processes. Although all Committee members usually take part in the deliberations, in most cases two members take the lead on each country as 'rapporteurs'.

At the very end of the process, the Committee adopts 'concluding observations', which are a statement on its consideration of a State's report. Concluding observations are meant to be widely publicised in the State party and to serve as the basis for a national debate on how to improve the enforcement of the provisions of the Convention. They therefore constitute an essential document: governments are expected to implement the recommendations contained therein.

Notes are taken at the meetings of the Committee. The United Nations publishes both press releases on the discussions and more detailed summary records of the proceedings. The Committee encourages the publication of the State party's report, the summary records and the concluding observations on each country as a consolidated document. Some governments whose reports have already been discussed have undertaken to do so.

The whole process of discussion of States parties' reports is designed to promote public debate. The Committee's discussions are normally open to the public; only the preparatory discussions of the pre-sessional working group and the drafting of the Committee's concluding observations are conducted in private. Likewise, it is important that the national reporting procedure be open and transparent; the Committee encourages such an approach.

The reporting procedure is constructive and oriented towards international cooperation and exchange of information. The aim is to define problems and discuss what corrective measures should be taken. The Committee can also transmit requests for assistance to the specialised United Nations bodies and agencies, including UNHCR, ILO, UNICEF, WHO, the United Nations Educational, Scientific and Cultural Organisation (UNESCO) and other competent bodies.

Urgent Procedure

There is no procedure outlined in the Convention for individual complaints from children or their representatives. The Committee may, however, request "further information relevant to the implementation of the Convention" (art. 44, para. 4). Such additional information may be requested from Governments if, for instance, there are indications of serious problems.

In drafting its reporting guidelines for States, the Committee on the Rights of the Child placed emphasis on concrete implementation measures which would make a reality of the principles and provisions of the Convention. More specifically, the Committee paid special attention to necessary reforms within the spirit of the Convention and procedures for constant scrutiny of progress.

Under article 4 of the Convention, States parties are required to undertake all appropriate legislative, administrative and other measures to implement the Convention. With regard to economic, social and cultural rights, they must "undertake such measures to the maximum extent of their available resources and, where needed, within the framework of international cooperation."

An early step in the implementation process is for a State party to review its legislation and ensure that laws are consistent with the Convention. For instance, laws are needed for the protection of children against exploitation, in both the formal and informal labour market, and to ensure free and compulsory primary education.

Mechanisms may be introduced at the national and local levels to coordinate policies and monitor the implementation of the Convention, including through an ombudsman's office. The political decision-making process is important. What procedures are there to ensure that children's affairs are taken seriously in all relevant governmental structures, as well as in both the parliament and local assemblies? Are there opportunities for children themselves and their representatives to make themselves heard?

The gathering of reliable and relevant information on the situation of children is another important step to be taken. With precise data, discussions regarding remedies will be better informed and focused. Improvement of the capacity of the national statistical office can therefore be an essential contribution to the implementation of the Convention.

Other means of genuine realisation of the principles and rights enshrined in the Convention are education and training of personnel working with children, such as nursery school and other teachers, child psychologists, paediatricians and other health personnel, the police and other law enforcement personnel, social workers and others. A broader awareness and knowledge of the Convention among people at large can also serve as a basis for implementation. It is an obligation under the Convention (art. 42) for States parties to disseminate such information—to both children and adults-in understandable languages. States' reports on implementation must also be made 'widely available to the public' (art. 44, para. 6).

What is meant by the wording that States should implement economic, social and cultural rights "to the maximum extent of their available resources" (art. 4)? How does the Convention relate to financial constraints?

The Convention recognises that some of the more costly reforms cannot take place overnight. It specifies, for instance, that the rights to health care (art. 24) and education (art. 28) may be achieved 'progressively'. It also makes it clear that there is an international duty to assist other States in their efforts to protect children's rights—although each State party always has its own obligations. Rich or poor, a State must allocate the maximum extent of its available resources for the implementation of the Convention: priority should be given to children.

Donor countries are encouraged to review their development cooperation programmes in the light of the Convention. At the same time, developing countries may identify a need for international cooperation in their reports on their implementation of the Convention.

Advisory Services

The Convention on the Rights of the Child and the Committee on the Rights of the Child attach special importance to international cooperation and assistance as ways of achieving the effective protection of children's rights. Article 45 (b) authorises the Committee to transmit to the relevant agencies and bodies any reports from States parties that contain a request or indicate a need for technical advice or assistance, along with the Committee's observations and suggestions. The Committee often makes recommendations for technical cooperation in its concluding observations addressed to States parties as an outcome of the reporting dialogue.

The United Nations High Commissioner for Human Rights, whose mandate includes the enhancement of international cooperation for the promotion and protection of all human rights, is providing assistance in this regard and encourages governments to respond favourably to the Committee's recommendations.

General guidelines regarding the form and contents of initial reports to be submitted by States parties under article 44, paragraph 1 (a), of the Convention on the Rights of the Child.

1. Article 44, paragraph 1, of the Convention on the Rights of the Child provides that:

   "States parties undertake to submit to the Committee, through the Secretary-General of the United Nations, reports on the measures they have adopted which give effect to the rights recognised herein and on the progress made on the enjoyment of those rights:

   "(a) Within two years of the entry into force of the Convention for the State Party concerned;

   "(b) Thereafter every five years."

2. Article 44 of the Convention further provides, in paragraph 2, that reports submitted to the Committee on the Rights of the Child shall indicate factors and difficulties, if any, affecting the degree of fulfilment of the obligations under the Convention and shall also contain sufficient information to provide the Committee with a comprehensive understanding of the implementation of the Convention in the country concerned.

3. The Committee believes that the process of preparing a report for submission to the Committee offers an important occasion for conducting a comprehensive review of the various measures undertaken to harmonise national law and policy with the Convention and to monitor progress made in the enjoyment of the rights set forth in the Convention. Additionally, the process should be one that encourages and facilitates popular participation and public scrutiny of government policies.

4. The Committee considers that the reporting process entails an ongoing reaffirmation by States parties of their commitment to respect and ensure observance of the rights set forth in the Convention and serves as the essential vehicle for the establishment of a meaningful dialogue between the States parties and the Committee.
5. The general part of States parties' reports, relating to matters that are of interest to monitoring bodies under various international human rights instruments, should be prepared in accordance with the "Consolidated guidelines for the initial part of the reports of States parties", as contained in document HRI/1991/1.

   The present guidelines, which were adopted by the Committee on the Rights of the Child at its 22nd meeting, held on 15 October 1991, should be followed in the preparation of the initial reports of States parties relating to the implementation of the Convention on the Rights of the Child.
6. The Committee intends to formulate guidelines for the preparation of periodic reports that are to be submitted pursuant to article 44, paragraph 1(b), of the Convention in due course.
7. Reports should be accompanied by copies of the principal legislative and other texts as well as detailed statistical information and indicators referred to therein, which will be made available to members of the Committee. It should be noted, however, that for reasons of economy they will not be translated or reproduced for general distribution. It is desirable, therefore, that when a text is not actually quoted in or annexed to the report itself, the report should contain sufficient information to be understood without reference to those texts.

8. The provisions of the Convention have been grouped under different sections, equal importance being attached to all the rights recognised by the Convention.

9. States parties are requested to provide relevant information pursuant to article 4 of the Convention, including information on:

   a) The measures taken to harmonise national law and policy with the provisions of the Convention;

   b) Existing or planned mechanisms at the national or local level for coordinating policies relating to children and for monitoring the implementation of the Convention.

10. In addition, States parties are requested to describe the measures that have been taken or are foreseen, pursuant to article 42 of the Convention, to make the principles and provisions of the Convention widely known, by appropriate and active means, to adults and children alike.

11. States parties are also requested to describe those measures undertaken or foreseen, pursuant to article 44, paragraph 6, of the Convention, to make their reports widely available to the public at large in their own countries.

12. States parties are requested to provide relevant information, pursuant to article one of the Convention, concerning the definition of a child under their laws and regulations. In particular, States parties are requested to provide information on the age of attainment of majority and on the legal minimum ages established for various purposes, including legal or medical counselling without parental consent, end of compulsory education, part-time employment, full-time

employment, hazardous employment, sexual consent, marriage, voluntary enlistment into the armed forces, conscription into the armed forces, voluntarily giving testimony in court, criminal liability, deprivation of liberty, imprisonment and consumption of alcohol or other controlled substances.

13. Relevant information, including the principal legislative, judicial, administrative or other measures in force or foreseen, factors and difficulties encountered and progress achieved in implementing the provisions of the Convention, and implementation priorities and specific goals for the future, should be provided in respect of :
    a) Non-discrimination (art. 2);
    b) Best interests of the child (art. 3);
    c) The right to life, survival and development (art. 6);
    d) Respect for the views of the child (art. 12).
14. In addition, States parties are encouraged to provide relevant information on the application of these principles in the implementation of articles listed elsewhere in these guidelines.
15. States parties are requested to provide relevant information, including the principal legislative, judicial, administrative or other measures in force; factors and difficulties encountered and progress achieved in implementing the relevant provisions of the Convention; and implementation priorities and specific goals for the future, in respect of:
    a) Name and nationality (art. 7);
    b) Preservation of identity (art. 8);
    c) Freedom of expression (art. 13);
    d) Access to appropriate information (art. 17);
    e) Freedom of thought, conscience and religion (art. 14);

f) Freedom of association and of peaceful assembly (art. 15);

g) Protection of privacy (art. 16);

h) The right not to be subjected to torture or other cruel, inhuman or degrading treatment or punishment (art. 37 (a)).

16. States parties are requested to provide relevant information, including the principal legislative, judicial, administrative or other measures in force, particularly how the principles of the "best interests of the child" and "respect for the views of the child" are reflected therein; factors and difficulties encountered and progress achieved in implementing the relevant provisions of the Convention; and implementation priorities and specific goals for the future, in respect of:

a) Parental guidance (art. 5);

b) Parental responsibilities (art. 18, paras. 1 and 2);

c) Separation from parents (art. 9);

d) Family reunification (art. 10);

e) Recovery of maintenance for the child (art. 27, para. 4);

f) Children deprived of a family environment (art. 20);

g) Adoption (art. 21);

h) Illicit transfer and non-return (art. 11);

i) Abuse and neglect (art. 19), including physical and psychological recovery and social reintegration (art. 39);

j) Periodic review of placement (art. 25).

17. In addition, States parties are requested to provide information on the numbers of children per year within the reporting period in each of the following groups, disaggregated by age group, sex, ethnic or

national background and rural or urban environment: homeless children, abused or neglected children taken into protective custody, children placed in foster care, children placed in institutional care, children placed through domestic adoption, children entering the country through intercountry adoption procedures and children leaving the country through inter-country adoption procedures.

18. States parties are encouraged to provide additional relevant statistical information and indicators relating to children covered in this section.

19. States parties are requested to provide relevant information, including the principal legislative, judicial, administrative or other measures in force; the institutional infrastructure for implementing policy in this area, particularly monitoring strategies and mechanisms; and factors and difficulties encountered and progress achieved in implementing the relevant provisions of the Convention, in respect of :

    a) Survival and development (art. 6, para. 2);
    b) Disabled children (art. 23);
    c) Health and health services (art. 24);
    d) Social security and child-care services and facilities (art. 26 and art. 18);
    e) Standard of living (art. 27, paras. 1-3).

20. In addition to information provided under paragraph 9 (b) of these guidelines, States parties are requested to specify the nature and extent of cooperation with local and national organisations of a governmental or non-governmental nature, such as institutions of social workers, concerning the implementation of this area of the Convention. States parties are encouraged to provide additional

relevant statistical information and indicators relating to children covered in this section.

21. Under this section, States parties are requested to provide relevant information, including the principal legislative, judicial, administrative or other measures in force; the institutional infrastructure for imple-menting policy in this area, particularly monitoring strategies and mechanisms; and factors and difficulties encountered and progress achieved in implementing the relevant provisions of the Con-vention, in respect of:

    a) Education, including vocational training and guidance (art. 28);

    b) Aims of education (art. 29);

    c) Leisure, recreation and cultural activities (art. 31).

22. In addition to information provided under paragraph 9 (b) of these guidelines, States parties are requested to specify the nature and extent of cooperation with local and national organisations of a governmental or non-governmental nature, such as institutions of social workers, concerning the implementation of this area of the Convention. States parties are encouraged to provide additional relevant statistical information and indicators relating to children covered in this section.

23. States parties are requested to provide relevant information, including the principal legislative, judicial, administrative or other measures in force; factors and difficulties encountered and progress achieved in implementing the relevant provisions of the Convention; and implementation priorities and specific goals for the future, in respect of:

a) Children in situations of emergency:

    i) Refugee children (art. 22);

ii) Children in armed conflicts (art. 38), including physical and psychological recovery and social reintegration (art. 39);

b) Children in conflict with the law:

i) The administration of juvenile justice (art. 40);

ii) Children deprived of their liberty, including any form of detention, imprisonment or placement in custodial settings (art. 37 (b), (c) and (d);

iii) The sentencing of juveniles, in particular the prohibition of capital punishment and life imprisonment (art. 37 (a));

iv) Physical and psychological recovery and social reintegration (art. 39);

c) Children in situations of exploitation, including physical and psychological recovery and social reintegration (art. 39):

i) Economic exploitation, including child labour (art. 32);

ii) Drug abuse (art. 33);

iii) Sexual exploitation and sexual abuse (art. 34);

iv) Other forms of exploitation (art. 36);

v) Sale, trafficking and abduction (art. 35);

d) Children belonging to a minority or an indigenous group (art. 30).

24. Additionally, States parties are encouraged to provide specific statistical information and indicators relevant to the children covered by paragraph 23.

Human Rights and Development

By the late 1980s, progress in attracting support for the Convention had drawn the attention of UNICEF. While the organisation has always devoted itself to the improvement of social and economic conditions for children, primarily in the fields of health and education, it was not until then that it saw the potential for integrating human rights objectives with more traditional development programmes.

While UNICEF originally included the Convention as one of a number of its programme and advocacy concerns, by late 1994 UNICEF's Executive Director, James P. Grant, announced that the Convention would become the framework for all of UNICEF's programming. In May 1995, UNICEF announced a new procurement policy on child labour, pledging to purchase materials and supplies only from companies that do not exploit child labour. The UNICEF Representative in each country is required to assess the local situation and evaluate the child labour practices of local companies.

Historically there had been a conceptual divide between those who acted as advocates on behalf of human rights and those who pursued the development of economic and social policies and social welfare programmes. Because the Convention on the Rights of the Child covers so much ground, it has provided a conceptual and legislative umbrella for both traditions. The child-protection issues normally associated with human rights are included — among them those of sexual and economic exploitation, of refugee status, and of juvenile justice.

Making Needs a Matter of Rights

Advocacy for many things that had previously been considered as needs and dealt with by government programmes, the success of which often depended upon political considerations—such as food, shelter, and access to education and health care—can now be fortified by their inclusion as one of a larger number of human rights.

"Needs you can't claim," says Ms Albenez of UNICEF. "Rights you can claim. Now you have claims for each of those needs."

Social reformers and human rights lawyers have defended individual children's rights or pursued political or policy objectives deemed advantageous to children for many years. But with the Convention the concern can now be regarded as universal.

The ratification of the Convention by so many countries means that its articles and principles are now being adapted to, and becoming part of, national laws. The World Conference on Human Rights called for universal ratification of the Child Convention by 1995. While the recent intensification of interest and concentration of resources devoted to child rights following adoption of the Convention has not yet yielded particularly dramatic or even measurable results directly affecting the daily lives of most of the world's children, it has spawned efforts at legislative reform in countries around the world—particularly in Latin America and Southeast Asia.

"The Convention is our essential framework," said Mrs. Raadi-Azarakhchi of the Centre for Human Rights who serves as the Secretary of the Committee on the Rights of the Child, a United Nations body. "It's really a catalyst for action at national level. It provides universal standards—but there are ways it can be interpreted that can be suited to various cultural situations."

The Committee on the Rights of the Child was established by the Convention as a means of monitoring and aiding governments in bringing their national laws and practices into conformity with the treaty. By late 1995, the Committee, which consists of 10 international members with backgrounds in law, education and social work, had reviewed some 40 reports on implementation plans since 1993 from countries that had ratified the Convention. Reports are required within two years of ratification, and are used as a means of opening a dialogue between members of the Committee, the government of a ratifying state, and the public in that country.

Non-governmental organisations are invited to contribute information or comment, and in over 20 countries have published alternative reports that either add to or take issue with the government reports. The Committee reviews the reports and releases its recommendations, which the government is subsequently obligated to make public. A follow-up report from each government is required five years later. It has provided one way of measuring just how serious a government is about honouring the Convention with legislative or social policy reform.

According to UNICEF's 1995 Progress of Nations, by the end of February 1995 there were 35 countries that were more than two years late in submitting their reports, and 21 that were more than a year overdue. About one-third of the 174 countries that had ratified the Convention by April 1995 had done so while lodging reservations about certain provisions with the Secretary-General of the United Nations.

In some cases countries have felt the Convention doesn't go far enough. Several countries have stated that it would be better for the Convention to stipulate 18 rather than 15 as the minimum age for participation in armed conflict. Other countries have expressed reservations about matters such as the precise definition of a child and freedom of conscience and religion. Still others have more sweeping and potentially problematic reservations, such as those of several Islamic countries that reserve the right not to apply articles in the Convention that are incompatible with shariah law.

In some cases, government reports have been challenged as insufficient. In the Philippines, the government report was challenged by both the National Coalition of NGOs for Monitoring the Convention on the Rights of the Child and the Committee on the Rights of the Child. The Committee noted "a lack of reliable qualitative and quantitative data, a shortcoming of means for programs of implementation, and a lack of indicators and mechanisms to evaluate the progress and impact of policies adopted." The Committee ultimately encouraged the government to support wider participation of governmental agencies and non-govern-mental organisations in the process of bringing their national laws into line with the provisions of the Convention.

Much of the power of the Convention comes from mutual example and pressure from the public and from donor countries rather than any real enforcement power. Those that fail to take action or do not take it seriously enough can be admonished by governments that have taken steps to abide by the Convention.

But more persuasive pressure may come from those countries that ratify the Convention and, in turn, receive donor funding for various national initiatives, or assistance with the drafting of laws or establishment of child-advocacy bureaus.

"We have seen enough in five years to know that this approach works," writes Hoda Badra, Chairperson of the International Committee on the Rights of the Child in 1995, in UNICEF's Progress of Nations. "When the government of Vietnam, for example, accepted that we were more interested in helping than criticising, they submitted an open and self-critical report. Subsequently, Vietnam acted: laws covering the protection, care and education of children have all been passed."

Others countries have done the same. The government of Tunisia has made an unusual effort. The Council of Ministers adopted a Code for the Protection of the Child on 17 May 1995, and a delegate for child protection has been appointed in each of the 23 governorates to oversee implementation of the Convention at the sub-national level. Since July 1991, education has been mandatory for children from 6 to 16 years old, and legal action can be taken against parents who do not comply.

The Indonesian government has increased budget allocations for health services to mothers and children during a period of austerity, developed manuals for law enforcement training on the Convention, and established a Child Protection Institute.

In Costa Rica, a new Legal Code for Minors is being developed using the Convention as the framework. In response to comments from the Committee on the Rights of the Child on the great number of national and international child adoptions in Costa Rica, the Legislature has started reviewing the Hague Convention on international adoption. In Jamaica, the government has started a legislative review and, despite heavy debt payments, is increasing its expenditures for children.

In Nicaragua, the government report to the Committee has been made public, a basis is being established for a Child and Adolescent legal code, and a public policy for children is being considered. And in 1991, the government of Colombia created the State Information Agency for Child Rights.

In the best spirit of the Convention, the government of Nepal is seeking input from children as part of its preparation for reporting to the Committee. In April 1995, 29 children participated in a four-day workshop on the Convention sponsored by a consortium of NGOs and UNICEF. Included were working children, a street boy, a disabled girl, children from refugee communities and those from both urban English-language schools and

Nepali schools. Ultimately, they took discussion of the Convention back to their communities and met with the Prime Minister.

Even in countries where both the legality and morality of human rights covenants have been abandoned or repeatedly violated, efforts are being made in the name of the Convention. In Sudan, UNICEF and Operation Lifeline Sudan (OLS) partners have solicited support for the Convention from the Sudan Peoples' Liberation Movement (SPLM) and the South Sudan Independence Movement (SSIM), the rebel movements in control of much of southern Sudan. This is happening in an area where there are no national laws, and where military rule prevails. Relations between OLS and political authorities are governed by ground rules which OLS recently rewrote to include a statement of humanitarian principles.

These principles include a statement of support both for the Convention and the Geneva Convention, according to the Report from Sudan. "Both rebel movements have signed the ground rules", the Report said. "This is an important step forward since it is the first time the movements have made such pledges toward child rights and will provide UNICEF/OLS with a much better opportunity to address breaches and violations."

But the realities in much of the world are that despite national laws that conform to a United Nations Convention, enforcement will be the determining factor in whether or not children's rights are protected. Even in countries with sophisticated legal systems the lack of enforcement is a problem.

"In India," according to the Special Rapporteur, "despite laws prohibiting children under 14 from working in hazardous industries, violations are widespread. They include transgressions in industries such as those producing matches, fireworks, glass and bricks, in diamond cutting and lock making, and in stone quarries."

The hope is that the Convention will continue to stimulate the kind of debate that often leads to attitudinal change. Child rights need to be actively respected rather than simply acknowledged, and advocates admit that more than the passage of laws and publicising of the Convention will be required. "It really is a matter of a change of mentality," says Mrs. Raadi-Azarakhchi of the International Committee on the Rights of the Child.

"We believe the Convention is a wonderful instrument," says Ricardo Domenici, secretary-general of the NGO group Defense of Children International and an advocate of the Convention for more than a decade. "But unless there are really socially conscious policies in the country, the Convention won't make that much of a difference. It is still true that things are not very good for children."

"Even if they have never seen a gun, millions of children suffer from wars, as resources that could have been invested in development are diverted into armaments. Indeed, one of the most distressing realities of our time is that most wars have been fought in precisely those countries that could least afford them."

The wounds inflicted by armed conflict on children - physical injury, gender-based violence, psychosocial distress, are affronts to every impulse that inspired the United Nations Convention on the Rights of the Child. Armed conflict affects all aspects of child development—physical, mental and emotional. Such effects accumulate and interact with each other. To be effective, assistance must take account of each. The impact of armed conflict cannot be fully understood without looking at the related effects on women, families and the community support systems that provide protection and a secure environment for development. Children's well-being is best ensured through family and community-based solutions that draw on local culture and an understanding of child development.

The disruption of food supplies, the destruction of crops and agricultural infrastructures, the disintegration of families and communities, the displacement of populations and the destruction of educational and health services and of water and sanitation systems, all take a heavy toll on children. Article 39 of the Convention on the Rights of the Child states that "States Parties shall take all appropriate measures to promote physical and psychological recovery and social reintegration of a child victim of: any form of neglect, exploitation, or abuse; torture or any other form of cruel, inhuman or degrading treatment or punishment; or armed conflicts. Such recovery and reintegration shall take place in an environment which fosters the health, self-respect and dignity of the child." Ensuring that health and nutrition, psychosocial well-being and education are priority components of humanitarian assistance is the best way to ensure children's physical and psychological recovery and social reintegration.

"The sources of conflict and war are pervasive and deep. To reach them will require our utmost effort to enhance respect for human rights and fundamental freedoms, to promote sustainable economic and social development for wider prosperity, to alleviate distress and to curtail the existence and use of massively destructive weapons."

Armed conflict, more than any other force, has transformed the lives of millions of children and women. Children and their families are not just getting caught in the crossfire. Many are being targeted. Nothing is spared, held sacred or protected. It is the singular characteristic of armed conflict in our time that children suffer most.

In the past decade alone, an estimated two million children have been killed in armed conflict. Three times as many have been seriously injured or permanently disabled. Countless others have been forced to witness or even to take part in horrifying acts of violence. These statistics are shocking enough, but more chilling is the conclusion to be drawn from them: more and more of the world is being sucked into a desolate moral vacuum, a space devoid of the most basic human values, a space in which children are slaughtered, raped and maimed, where children are exploited as soldiers, starved and exposed to extreme brutality.

Calling a Halt to Attacks on Children

The lack of control and the sense of dislocation and chaos that characterise contemporary armed conflicts can be attributed to many factors, such as political upheavals and struggles for control over resources in the face of widespread poverty and economic disarray. The callousness of modern warfare may be a natural outcome of the social revolutions that have torn traditional societies apart. But whatever the causes, the time has come to call a halt. The international community must proclaim attacks on children for what they are—intolerable and unacceptable.

As a result of a recommendation of the United Nations Committee on the Rights of the Child, the General Assembly in 1993 requested the Secretary-General to appoint an expert to study the impact of armed conflict on children. After two years of research, field visits and consultations, G. Machel, the Secretary-General's Expert on the subject and a former Minister for Education in Mozambique, submitted a report, titled

Impact of Armed Conflict on Children (document A/51/306 and Add. 1), to the 1996 session of the General Assembly. The report's most fundamental premise is that children simply have no part in warfare. It reveals the full extent of children's involvement in the armed conflicts raging around the world, and sets out the findings and recommendations aimed at governments, entities of the United Nations system, inter-governmental and regional bodies, civil society organisations and individuals. This booklet is aimed at raising awareness among the widest possible audience of the impact of all forms of armed conflict on children. It focuses on some of the report's main recommendations for action. The examples provided in this publication have been drawn from research for the report on Impact of Armed Conflict on Children.

Health and Nutrition

Armed conflict is a major public health hazard that cannot be ignored. Any disease that caused as much large-scale damage to children would long ago have attracted the urgent attention of public health specialists. When armed conflict kills and maims more children than soldiers, the health sector has a special obligation to speak out.

Thousands of children are killed every year as a direct result of fighting—from knife wounds, bullets, bombs and landmines, but many more die from malnutrition and disease caused or increased by armed conflicts. In Mozambique alone, between 1981 and 1988, armed conflict was the cause underlying 454,000 child deaths. Many of today's armed conflicts take place in some of the world's poorest countries, where children are already vulnerable.

Children are the most vulnerable to collective assaults on health and well-being. At the height of the conflict in Somalia, more than half the deaths of children in some places were caused by measles. Diarrhoea is another common and often deadly disease. Cholera is a constant threat as exemplified in refugee camps in Bangladesh, Kenya, Malawi, Nepal, Somalia and Zaire. The World Health Organisation (WHO) estimates that half the world's refugees may be infected with tuberculosis, as crowded conditions in refugee camps provide a breeding ground for infections. Malaria and acute respiratory infections, including pneumonia, also claim many lives.

Disrupted Health Services and Food Supplies

In most wars, health facilities come under attack, in direct violation of international humanitarian law. Those facilities that remain open during a conflict are often looted or forced to close down, and the remainder are sometimes difficult to reach because of curfews. Restrictions on travel also hamper the distribution of drugs and other medical supplies, causing health systems' referral services and logistic support to break down. Many of the health services of a country are diverted to the needs of military casualties. Hospitals are forced to neglect the regular care of patients or to shift them to health centres. A concentration on military needs also means that children injured in a conflict may not get effective treatment or rehabilitation. Children living with disabilities get little, if any, support. For children, a dangerous implication of the breakdown of a country's health facilities during conflicts is the disruption of vaccination programmes.

Claiming children as 'zones of peace' has become an important concept of humanitarian relief programmes. Commitment to this principle by all warring parties has taken various forms. In El Salvador, beginning in 1985, Government and rebel forces agreed to three 'days of tranquillity' during which 250,000 children were immunised against polio, measles, diphtheria and other diseases, a process that was repeated annually for six years until the end of the civil war. In Afghanistan in 1988-1989, health teams were permitted to operate in both government and rebel-held areas, raising vaccination levels in some areas above 80 per cent. In the case of Operation Lifeline Sudan, arrangements were made for 'corridors of peace' so that relief supplies and vaccines could be delivered during relative lulls in the conflict.

One of the most immediate effects of armed conflict is the disruption of food supplies. Farmers, who are often women and older children, become fearful of working on plots of land too far from their homes. They reduce the area under cultivation, and their water sources, systems of irrigation and flood control may also be destroyed. Restrictions on movement limit access to such necessities as seeds and fertilisers and stop farmers from taking their produce to market. Most households in developing countries, including many farm households, rely on market purchases to meet their food needs. Economic disarray heightens unemployment, reducing people's ability to buy food.

Sometimes, damage to food systems is deliberate. For example, in the early 1980s in Ethiopia, the government's scorched earth policies destroyed hundreds of thousands of acres of food-producing land. In many countries, landmines prevent the use of agricultural land. In contravention of international law, warring parties may block relief supplies or divert them for their own use. Feeding centres for children and vulnerable groups are frequently bombed or attacked.

Warfare also takes its toll on livestock. This creates particular problems for young children who rely on milk as part of their basic diet. In the Kongor area of Sudan, the massacre of cattle reduced livestock from around 1.5 million to 50,000.

Adequate nourishment depends on the way food is distributed, the way children are fed, hygiene and the time parents have available to care for children. Malnutrition can affect all children, but it causes the greatest mortality and morbidity among young children, especially those under three years of age. Breastfeeding provides ideal nutrition for infants, reduces the incidence and severity of infectious diseases and contributes to women's health.

During conflicts, mothers may experience hunger, exhaustion and distress that can make them less able to care for their children. Breastfeeding may be endangered by the mother's loss of confidence in her ability to produce milk. The general disruption in routine can separate mothers from their children for long periods. As conflicts proceed, social structures and networks break down. Knowledge about breastfeeding is passed from one generation to the next, and this can be lost when people flee and families are broken up. Yet artificial feeding, risky at all times, is even more dangerous in unsettled circumstances. Unless mothers are severely malnourished, they can breastfeed adequately despite severe stress. In times of armed conflict, it is important to support women's capacity to breastfeed by providing adequate dietary intake for lactating women and ensuring that they are not separated from their children.

The effects of armed conflicts—the fragmenting of family and community, rapid social change, the breakdown of support systems, increased sexual exploitation and rape, malnutrition, and inadequate health services, including poor ante-natal care—make it imperative that reproductive health care be given high priority. Health education, care and counselling are especially important for women and girls who have been raped or who have been forced into prostitution. The potential for the spread of sexually transmitted diseases, including HIV/AIDS, increases dramatically during conflicts. The breakdown of health services, and blood transfusion services lacking the ability to screen for HIV/AIDS, contribute to the increase in transmission.

In war-affected populations, gynaecological and paediatric health services are often unavailable. An obstacle to the full use of health services in emergencies is that they are often dominated by men, whether expatriate or from the host country. As a result, many women and girls, for cultural or religious reasons, underutilise the services despite risks to their health. One way to overcome this obstacle is to increase the numbers of available female health and protection professionals.

Some recommendations for action.

a) Parties to a conflict should be obliged to maintain basic health systems and services and water supplies.

b) Special attention should be paid to primary health care and the care of children with chronic or acute conditions. Adequate rehabilitative care, such as the provision of artificial limbs for injured or permanently disabled children, should be ensured to facilitate the fullest possible social integration.

c) Child-focused health needs assessments involving local professionals, young people and communities should be speedily carried out by organisations working in conflict situations, and should take into account food, health and care factors and the coping strategies likely to be used by the affected population.

d) During conflicts, governments and non-State entities should be encouraged to facilitate 'days of tranquillity' or 'corridors of peace' to ensure continuity of basic child health measures and delivery of humanitarian relief.

e) Parties in conflict should refrain from destroying food crops, water sources and agriculture infrastructures in order to minimise disruption of food supply and production capacities.

f) Emergency relief should give attention to the rehabilitation of agriculture, livestock and fisheries and to employment or income-generating programmes, to enhance local capacities to improve household security on a self-reliant and sustainable basis.

— Health professionals must be advocates of the rights of the child. WHO, in collaboration with professional, humanitarian and human rights organisations, should encourage paediatricians and all other doctors and health workers to disseminate child rights information and to report rights violations encountered in the course of their work.

Historically, those concerned with the situation of children during armed conflict have focused primarily on their physical vulnerability. But the loss, grief and fear a child has experienced must also be taken into account. For increasing numbers of children living in war-torn nations, childhood has become a nightmare. Armed conflict destroys homes, separates families, splinters communities, breaks down trust among people and disrupts health and education services, undermining the very foundation of children's lives. The psychosocial concerns intrinsic to child development must be taken into account. Seeing their parents or other important adults in their lives as vulnerable can severely undermine children's confidence and add to their sense of fear. As bad as these experiences are, many children have witnessed their parents' torture, murder or rape, and have been threatened with death themselves.

In a UNICEF survey of 3,030 children in Rwanda in 1995, nearly 80 per cent had lost immediate family members, and more than one-third of these had actually witnessed the murders.

When children have experienced traumatic or other events in times of war, they may suffer from increased anxiety about being separated from their families, or they may have nightmares or trouble sleeping. They may cease playing and laughing, lose their appetites and withdraw from contact. Younger children may have difficulty concentrating in school. Older children and adolescents may become anxious or depressed, feel hopeless about the future or develop aggressive behaviour.

Experience has shown that with supportive caregivers and secure communities, most children will achieve a sense of healing. Helping war-affected children to build on their own strengths and resilience, in collaboration with trusted caregivers, is an important strategy in the process of healing. Integrating modern knowledge of child development and child rights with local concepts and practices will result in more effective and sustainable ways to meet children's needs. Although many symptoms of distress have universal characteristics, the ways in which people express, embody and give meaning to their distress are largely dependent on social, cultural and political contexts and are based on different belief systems.

All phases of emergency and reconstruction assistance programmes should take psychosocial considerations into account, while avoiding the development of separate mental health programmes. Such programmes should also give priority to preventing further traumatic experiences, such as preventing family separation, undertaking practical measures to prevent gender-based violence, and avoiding the isolation and stigmatisation that can result from institutionalisation.

Exploring a child's experience with violence and the meaning it holds in her or his life is important to the process of healing and recovery. While many forms of external assistance can help to promote psychosocial recovery, such explorations with children should take place in a stable, supportive environment, by caregivers who have solid and continuing relationships with the child. Ethical issues and confidentiality must be carefully considered. When journalists or researchers encourage a child to relate 'horror stories', the interview can open up old wounds and tear down a child's defences. Children who are photographed and identified by name can become vulnerable to additional harassment.

It is important that those who wish to help with the healing process have a deep understanding of and respect for the societies in which they are working. Aside from knowing the basic principles of child development and the way it is understood locally, they should also understand local culture and practices, including the rites and ceremonies related to growing up and becoming an adult, as well as those associated with death, burial and mourning.

An African girl at the age of 10 was made to witness her mother's rape and murder, and was herself forced to serve for two years as a concubine for rebel soldiers. After finally managing to escape, she went for treatment at the provincial hospital. A nurse realised there was something particularly wrong with the girl. In addition to having contracted a sexually transmitted infection, she was very withdrawn and sad. Encouraged by the nurse's soft and caring treatment, the girl told her story. She repeated it later to a social worker and was moved to a foster home, where she developed a close relationship with her foster mother. At the girl's wish, a traditional cleansing ceremony was held to rid her of all the bad things that had befallen her.

Children who have been continually exposed to violence almost always experience a significant change in their beliefs and attitudes, including a fundamental loss of trust in others. This is especially true of children who have been attacked or abused by people previously considered neighbours or friends, as happened in Rwanda and the former Yugoslavia. Rebuilding the ability to trust is a universal challenge in the wake of conflicts, but it is particularly important for those who are a part of children's daily lives.

A number of activities have been identified as supporting healing by fostering in children a sense of purpose, self-esteem and identity. These include establishing daily routines such as going to school, preparing food, washing clothes and working in the fields; providing children with the intellectual and emotional stimulation through structured group activities such as play, sports, drawing, drama and story-telling; and providing the oppor-tunity for expression, attachment and trust that comes from a stable, caring and nurturing relationship with adults.

Through training and raising awareness of central caregivers, including parents, teachers and community health workers, a diversity of programmes can enhance the community's ability to provide for children and vulnerable groups. Rather than focusing on a child's emotional wounds, programmes should aim to support healing processes and re-establish a sense of normalcy.

The family is essential to children's care and protection and is an important social, economic and cultural factor in child development. But often, families are worn down by conflicts, both physically and emotionally, and face increased impoverishment.

The most effective and sustainable approach to recovery is to mobilise the existing social care system.

This could involve mobilising a refugee community to support suitable foster families or extended family systems for the care of unaccompanied children. Another alternative is to provide care through peer-group living arrangements that are strongly integrated into communities. Institutional approaches can contribute to isolation and stigmatisation and have proven ineffective.

Some recommendations for action.

a) All phases of emergency and reconstruction assistance programmes should take psychosocial considerations into account, while avoiding the development of separate mental health programmes. They should also give priority to preventing further traumatic experiences.

b) Rather than focusing on a child's emotional wounds, programmes should aim to support healing processes and re-establish a sense of normalcy.

c) Programmes to support psychosocial well-being should include local culture, perceptions of child development, and an understanding of political and social realities and children's rights. They should mobilise the community care network around children.

d) Governments, donors and relief organisations should prevent the institutionalisation of children. When groups of children considered vulnerable, such as child soldiers, are singled out for special attention, it should be done with the full cooperation of the community so as to ensure their long-term reintegration.

Education has a crucial preventive and rehabilitative part to play in fulfilling the needs and rights of children in conflict and post-conflict situations. Education also serves much broader functions. It gives shape and structure to children's lives and can instil community values, promote justice and respect for human rights and enhance peace, stability and interdependence.

Unfortunately, not even schools are safe from attack during times of armed conflict. In rural areas the school building may be the only substantial permanent structure, making it highly susceptible to shelling, closure or looting. Often, local teachers are prime targets because they are important community members or because they may hold strong political views. The destruction of education networks represents one of the greatest developmental set-backs for countries affected by armed conflict. Lost education and vocational skills take years to replace, making the overall task of postwar recovery even more difficult.

If countries continue to employ four times as many soldiers as teachers, education and social systems will remain fragile and inadequate, and governments will continue to fail children and break the promises made to them through ratification of the Convention on the Rights of the Child.

During armed conflicts, fear and disruption make it difficult to create an atmosphere conducive to learning, and the morale of both teachers and pupils is likely to be low. As conflicts drag on for months or even years, economic and social conditions suffer and educational opportunities become more limited or even cease to exist altogether. Sometimes, even when educational opportunities exist in war-torn areas, parents may be reluctant to send their children to school. They may be afraid that the children will not be safe while they are on their way to and from school, or during classes. Mothers and fathers may need their children to work in the fields, in shops or at home caring for the youngest children.

Educational activity must be established as a priority component of all humanitarian assistance. When children have been forced to leave their homes and are crowded into displaced persons camps, establishing schooling systems as soon as possible reassures everyone by signalling a degree of stability and a return to normal roles and relationships within the family and community. Refugee children can sometimes attend regular schools in host countries, as provided for in international law, though very few get the opportunity to do so. Some host governments refuse to provide—or to allow international agencies to provide—educational activity for refugee children. The efforts of United Nations agencies and other organisations to meet the educational service needs of children affected by conflict require significantly increased support.

Even in situations of armed conflict, it is important to carry on educating children and young people, no matter how difficult the circumstances. Education promotes their psychosocial and physical well-being. Teachers can recognise signs of stress in children as well as impart vital survival information on issues such as personal safety and health or the dangers of landmines. They can also promote tolerance and respect for human rights. Since schools are likely to be targets for military attack, alternative sites for classrooms can be established, as was done in Eritrea in the late 1980s when classes were often held under trees, in caves or in camouflaged huts built from sticks and foliage. Similar arrangements were made during the height of the fighting in many places in the former Yugoslavia, where classes were held in the cellars of people's homes, often by candlelight.

One important innovation in educating children in emergency situations has been the development by the United Nations Educational, Scientific and Cultural Organisation (UNESCO) and UNICEF of a Teacher's

Emergency Pack (TEP), otherwise known as 'school-in-a-box'. The pack contains basic materials: brushes and paints, chalk, paper, pens, pencils and exercise books. It was first used in Somalia in 1992 and further refined in the refugee camps in Djibouti. The packs were widely used for Rwandan refugees at Ngara in Tanzania, where children attended primary schools in tents on a shift basis.

Education can also incorporate flexible systems of 'distance learning': home or group study using pre-packaged teaching materials complemented by broadcast and recorded media. Such systems are especially valuable for girls when parents are reluctant to have them travel far from home. Education can also be strengthened through a variety of community channels. In Sierra Leone, non-traditional teachers, including mothers and adolescents, were trained and deployed. When public sector agencies are absent or severely weakened, community groups and non-governmental organisations (NGOs) can support local educational administrators in their efforts to keep children in schools. For example, a group of Sri Lankan children who had lost one or both parents in the civil war were refused entry to primary school because they had no birth certificates and no money to pay the high fee demanded to issue a new one. An international NGO working in the country brought the situation to the notice of the National Child Rights Coalition, which took it up with the education authorities. The children received their birth certificates and were able to attend school.

All sectors of society must come together to build 'ethical frameworks', integrating traditional values of cooperation through religious and community leaders with international legal standards, such as the United Nations Convention on the Rights of the Child. Some of the groundwork for this can be laid in schools. Both the content and the process of education should promote peace, social justice, respect for human rights and the acceptance of responsibility. Children need to learn the skills of negotiation, problem solving, critical thinking and communication that will enable them to resolve conflicts without resorting to violence. To achieve these goals, a number of countries have already undertaken peace education programmes. In Lebanon, the Education for Peace Programme, jointly undertaken in 1989 by the Lebanese Government, NGOs, youth volunteers and UNICEF, now benefits thousands of children. The Student Palaver Conflict Management Programme in Liberia employs adolescents as resources in peer conflict resolution and mediation activities in schools.

In Sri Lanka, an Education for Conflict Resolution Programme has been integrated into primary and secondary school education. An innovative element is the programme's use of various public media to reach out-of-school children and other sectors of the community. While such initiatives are not always successful, they are indispensable to the eventual rehabilitation of a shattered society.

Some Recommendations for Action are

— All possible efforts should be made to maintain education systems during conflicts. The international community must insist that government or non-State entities involved in conflicts not target educational facilities, and indeed promote active protection of such services.

— Preparation should also be made for sustaining education outside of formal school buildings, using community facilities and strengthening alternative education through a variety of community channels.

— Donors should extend the boundaries of

emergency funding to include support for education. The establishment of educational activity, including the provision of teaching aids and basic education materials, should be accepted as a priority component of humanitarian assistance.

— As soon as camps are established for refugees or internally displaced persons, children and youth should be brought together for educational activities. Incentives for attendance should also be encouraged through, for example, measures to promote safety and security.

— Support for the re-establishment and continuity of education must be a priority strategy for donors and NGOs in conflict and post-conflict situations. Teachers should be trained to understand the ways in which conflict affects children as well as to impart vital survival information on issues such as landmines, health and promoting respect for human rights.

Parenting and Child Health

The care of children has always been important to philosophies, and religions, and from all over the world we have fragments of concern about the rearing of children. Both Aristotle and Plato discussed appropriate rearing of children of various ages. Their concerns in some ways were very similar to those of parents today: How do we balance the necessity for teaching children to control their impulses and behavior with allowing them to explore the world enough to develop their skills? This problem of balance between too much and too little discipline echoes down through the ages, across the face of the globe, and is reflected today in modern theories and research studies, as well as in how-to-do-it books for parents. Most early treatises on parenting were written by men, and they were concerned with the upbringing of boys more often than girls. While there is the occasional sensitive treatment of the necessity for providing love and warmth for the young child, most information on parenting emphasizes the importance of the child's mind, in terms of either what we call intellectual abilities or what we now call moral values. It is also clear that most discussion is about the training of the upper-class child, and we have little information concerning the rearing of the large majority of children. One of the most complete treatises on child-rearing in modern Western culture was that of John Locke. Some Thoughts on Education, which is basically a practical guide to a father about raising a son. As might be expected from the culture of the time (17th century), much of the essay concerns the necessity of establishing early authority over the child. There are warnings about too much love, about the problems of material rewards, and the concern that children might be spoiled by servants. Yet there are surprisingly modern recognitions of individual differences in children, of the superiority of discipline through reasoning rather than corporal punishment, of the importance of parental role models, and the recognition that the best motivator for the child is the esteem of parents. As might be expected, Locke presents a very rational view of child-rearing, remaining above much of the turmoil of actual parenting, perhaps because Locke was a bachelor and himself had no children. Approximately a century later (late 18th century), Mary Wollstonecraft wrote about the care of children. Her works are heavily influenced by John Locke's rational approach but also touch upon early care. There is a concern that mothers nurse their own infants, that young children need a warm, loving environment, and most of all, a concern for daughters. Her Thoughts on the Education of Daughters expressed a concern that girls were not taught to discipline their minds but allowed to grow without intellectual skills or moral discipline. Wollstone-craft's essays were very popular in her day, suggesting some influence and some concern on the part of parents that child-rearing was not simply the intellectual process suggested by Locke. However, most essays concerning the history of parenting and children have ignored the works of Wollstonecraft, and it is only within the last 20 years that copies of her work have become widely available.

It is likely that such families were relatively rare, as upper-middle-class children were cared for by servants and the poor for the most part did not have the time to follow such strict roles. However accurate this characterization was in reality, it has had a profound effect on our thinking about parenting and about the roles of the mother and father within the family. Prior to Freud, most treatises on parenting emphasized the education and moral development of the child. With Freud's emphasis on the satisfaction of drives came a clearer articulation that the quality of early care would influence later development. While Locke and others emphasized the importance of helping the child to become a rational thinking human, and the Romantics emphasized the innocence and purity of the child, Freud placed human pathologies as firmly rooted in the child's early development.

To some extent, the child's development as pictured by Freud is as seemingly unreasonable and irrational as many of his patients' later meanderings. Freud's influence on the modern mind should not be underrated, for we cannot really understand the theoretical and empirical literature on parenting since 1900 without understanding how Freud's views have permeated our thinking. Our emphasis on providing a sensitive caretaking environment during early childhood as well as our articulations of family roles are influenced either directly by or in opposition to Freudian thinking.

Parsons, writing in the middle of this century, articulated family roles and transformed these roles into gender traits. Women were more expressive, nutrient, and emotionally sensitive, and thus should be in charge of management of relationships, children, and the home. Men were more instrumentally competent, and should therefore be in charge of setting the rules, and be employed outside the home. According to Parsons, such roles are necessary for family life and child rearing. A good deal of empirical work on family relations and parenting has been done to refute the necessity or the benefits of such a rigid roles structure. In fact, in one long-term study of successful men and women of the very generation most influenced by these ideas, regrets were expressed in old age by women because they had not used their talents in the world and by men because they had not spent enough time with their families in building relationships. Most studies suggest that both men and women have expressive and instrumental qualities and that they are happier when both are expressed. It is interesting to see feminist criticism bring back this rigid role structure, this time with more emphasis put upon the superior expressive qualities of women and their lack in men, The data for the current wave of such theorizing are as scant as for such theories of the past.

Robert Sears and his colleagues, writing in the middle of this century, attempted to rework Freudian theory within the framework of learning theory. For the first time in one theory, two qualities to parenting, warmth and control, were made explicit. However, Sear's concepts of parenting, influenced by Freud and Parsons, still made the assumption that mothers would provide warmth and emotional support, and fathers discipline and control. In fact, Sears work, like most studies of the time, concentrated mostly upon the mother as informant, so that we had a view of the father filtered through the eyes of the mother. Throughout the 1950s and 1960s, there were tests of this supposedly optimal family role division, most of which found, first, that such families were in actuality few and far between and, second, that when they existed, they did not appear to be as functional as families in which both parents shared expressive and instrumental qualities. Diana Baumrind published an extensive reappraisal of parenting in 1971 in which she concentrated upon the dimension of parental control to characterize three parenting styles. Parental control in Baumrind's work refers to the attempts of the parents to socialize the child into the family and society.

Clearly ail parents do this with more or less success. Baumrind found that children need a balance of control and warmth and are better off when both mothers and fathers can give both. She described three types of parenting in which the types of control varied. The first type of parenting she called authorization, in which the parent attempts to shape and control the child in accordance with a set standard of conduct. Such parents value obedience, believe in punitive measures to curb the child's self-will and do not allow discussion about the correctness of the standard.

Authoritative parents also believe the child should behave in accordance with their rules and standards, but within a context of rational discussion. Such parents encourage communication and share reasons for conduct with the child. The authoritative parents do not see themselves as infalliable and are open to change as circumstances change. Permissive parents do not put as much emphasis on the child conforming to a set of rules: instead, the child is consulted, and self-regulation by the child is emphasized. The parent is seen as a resource but not necessarily as the final word in setting external standards for the child's behavior. Within each of these parenting types, the parent can vary on warmth, and both the type of control and the use of warmth can influence the child's development.

Baumrind argued strongly that authoritative parenting appeared to be a more effective style in that it produced a situation that gave the child a structure, but which was open to change. Much of the parenting work of the 1970s were attempts to validate Baumrind's categories and her suggestion that authoritative parenting would be the most effective style of parenting. There has been a great deal of support for this within the well-functioning, middle-class families favoured by Baumrind for her research; however, recent work has suggested that in situations of high risk, such as an urban ghetto, boys in particular may benefit from authoritarian parenting. However, one problem with using Baumrind's typologies is that many parents do not fit the definitions, and within each type the variations are often greater than the differences between groups.

More recently, Eleanor Maccoby has used Sear's initial formulation of warmth and control and Baumrind's emphasis on style of control to attempt a reformulation of parenting which takes into account all these different components of parenting. Maccboy and her colleagues have used the social learning approach to reformulate parenting into two major divisions: demandingness and responsiveness. Parents can vary in their demandingness (that is, the number and types of demands they make upon the child) and in their responsiveness to the child's bids for attention. This framework has allowed Maccboy and other researchers to move beyond the types of families studied by Baumrind, into families of divorce, of differing ethnic groups, etc. In addition, families are no longer forced into categories that may not be a good fit to their individual styles. In her recent writings, Baumrind uses the categories of demandingness and responsiveness to define parental characteristics. Interestingly enough, that while we get consistency from the one informant, very often the information contradicts other measures of both parenting procedures and child behaviors. Consequently, researchers have looked for other ways to study parenting. One technique that has evolved has been to train an impartial observer to code parenting behaviors.

The most common type of behavioral observation has been the social interchanges within the family in their home environment. This procedure forces an examination of the dual role of each subject as a reactor and as an initiator. Researchers who use these techniques believe that the day-to-day interactions between the parent and child underline the way parents learn, maintain, and deploy different child management skills. Patterson, a pioneer in the use of behavioral observations since the early 1960s, has shown that control processes studied through behavioral observation show that parents who use harsh punishment and noncontingent punishment have children who respond with similar techniques, and that such families become locked into coercive cycles, which are very hard for family members to end without escalation. A rigorous test of this reciprocity requires two kinds of investigation. First, it should follow that, for a dyad assessed over a series of days, coercion scores would covert. Second, it should be possible to demonstrate experimentally that an increase in coercive techniques by one member produces an increase in coercive reactions by the other. Such coercive cycles are found in families where both parents report a great deal of stress and poor marital adjustment. Observation has also been used to confirm that, within authoritative families, parents encourage reciprocal communication and do more listening, questioning, and reframing than an authoritarian families. However, observation techniques in naturalistic settings are very expensive and by their very nature are under-standardised, so that family researchers are making increasing use of family interactions in more standardized settings in a laboratory.

One of the currently more popular ways to study the outcome of parenting techniques with young children is the Strange Situation. This laboratory technique infers parenting procedures from a short standardized encounter. Developed by Mary Ainsworth in the late 1960s, this procedure examines the child's reactions to separation from the parent, usually the mother, in a strange environment. Children are brought into a laboratory for a 21-minute session in which mother and child first are together in a room with toys, then a stranger enters, the mother leaves the child with the stranger, the mother returns and the stranger leaves, the child and mother are alone together, then the mother leaves the child alone in the room, the stranger enters again, and finally the mother returns. Each episode takes 3 minutes. Individual differences in the way the child reunites with the mother are considered to be reflections upon the mother's sensitivity to the child's needs and demands.

Rogoff has used another type of laboratory study to understand parental instructional techniques. The parent and child are put together in a room and confronted with a task that requires the parent to help the child. The parent's behaviors are coded, and inferences are drawn concerning parenting skills in terms of helping the child in other situations.

Laboratory methods have many benefits. They place all individuals in the same situation and produce information that can be coded by someone other than the parent. They allow the researcher to manipulate variables so that they can observe the effects of changing certain aspects of information presented to the parent or child. However, like other methods of study, there are limitations. The behavior samples we get in the laboratory are influenced by many variables over which we have no control. Too often such studies manipulate trivial variables and leave more interesting variables unstudied simply because they are too difficult to control.

Recently there have been attempts to examine parenting via the report of children. These have been conducted in two ways: either is interviewed about what his or her parents do in certain situations using a structured set of questions or the child is allowed to describe his or her family situation in an unstructured way. Child reports have all the same strengths and weakness of parent reports. In addition, it is more difficult to gain information from children, as they may be more easily influenced by the interviewer than adults, and young children often simply do not have the cognitive capacity to understand some questions.

There are no completely adequate ways to study parenting, but by using a combination of methods, one can begin to understand the different aspects of parenting. Below are reports of three differing concepts of parenting, all of which have developed through the use of multiple methods to study parents.

Gerald Patterson has suggested four variables as crucial in effective parentage. He calls these variables together family management. First, some parents apply consistent and effective controls on problem behavior; other parents frequently threaten, scold, and matter but seldom back up their threats with effective action. The variable measuring this family management skill is called discipline. Second, some parents carefully track the whereabouts of their children, while others do not note any but the most obvious changes in their children's behavior. The variable constructed to measure this skill is called monitoring. Third, some parents can negotiate, can solve problems, and can cope with crises arising inside and outside the family; others cannot. The variable that assesses these skills is termed problem solving. A fourth variable is positive reinforcement where the parent reinforces the child for those behaviors he wishes to maintain. By employing certain techniques in their own lives, parents inevitably foster these same techniques in their children, well or ill. Children learn to relate to others in part by watching adults relate, to help themselves by watching parents fend for themselves, and to work or learn by watching others do so. Patterson's theory focuses more upon the control or demand aspects of parenting, but has the advantage of very clearly defining what processes are behind the general concept of control.

In the early part of the 20th century, Vygotsky attempted to create a psychology of child development that included the social origins and influences on human cognitive functioning. For Vygotsky, the social world of the child channels development. He emphasized that development occurs in situations where the child's problem solving is guided by an adult who structures and models ways to solve a problem, a process he called scaffolding. Adults can arrange the environment so that children can reach a level beyond their present capabilities when working on their own. This is called the zone of proximal development, defined as the distance between the child's capabilities when working on a project independently and the child's capability when an adult or more capable peer has arranged the environment. The child's individual mental functioning develops through experience in the zone of proximal development. The structure provided serves as a scaffold for learning, providing contact between old and new knowledge. Thus, to understand development, we must attend to formal and informal instruction provided by the parents in the course of the child's daily activities.

Considerable work has been done in this area, first by Sigel and his colleagues, who examined the effect of what they label distancing techniques on the child's competence. Distancing techniques within this model are cognitive strategies parents use to help a child understand a problem. They can range from concrete (such as asking a child to label) to abstract (such as synthesizing new structures for the child). More recently, Rogoff and her colleagues have applied Vygotsky's for children's problem solving. Again, the techniques studied have been cognitive strategies to increase the child's understanding of the problem and to help the child move to a new level of thinking. The work on scaffolding has focused upon the responsiveness aspect of parenting. The role of the parent as teacher is recognized, and the dimensions that go into this aspect of parenting have been more carefully defined, so that we have a better idea of the process behind this dimension of parenting.

The third component of parenting that has received a great deal of attention in the research literature recently has been that of emotional support, but as noted in the historical review, this component of parenting does not have a long history. The Freudian point of view emphasized the importance of satisfaction of children's drives, but the discussion was mostly in terms satisfaction of physical needs rather than satisfaction of emotional needs. In the 1960s, this began to change. First, Harry Harlow published his much cited work with infant monkeys and their surrogate mothers. Harlow paired a warm, soft surrogate mother who did not feed the infant monkey with a wire surrogate who fed the infant. If the Freudian view were correct, the infant should identify with the surrogate who fed him or her, but instead the infants went to the warm, soft cloth mother when they were distressed. At approximately the same time, John bowlby began to publish his theory on the importance of attachment during the first year of life. Bowlby made the point that social responsiveness was necessary for development and that, without a care giver that provided warmth and security, the child could not develop normally. Bowlby's second important point was that the child developed an internal working model of relationships from the early caregiving relationships. He called this whole process attachment.

Recent literature in the field of the child and family has emphasized the importance of the attachment relationship. Mary Ainsworth developed the Strange Situation to test individual differences in patterning of infant's attachment behaviors. This procedure allows one to classify the child in terms of security and in terms of reaction patterns toward the mother.

Work within the area has related the child's attachment relationship to material sensitivity, warmth, and intrusiveness. However, the most clear-cut findings with attachment are at the extremes of caregiving. Parents who are abusive or neglecting have children who show extreme avoidance or resistance in the Strange Situation. The classification system also has been used to predict the way that children will behave in new situations as they grow older. Again, the clearest findings are in terms of extreme behavior, but a growing literature suggests that children do approach new relationships in a manner similar to their attachment relationship.

While the traditional view of the family is one of the mother providing warmth and caretaking and the father providing discipline and support for the family, these characterizations of family life do not appear to describe parenting today. While mothers do spend more time with their children than fathers, and this is as true of mother who work outside the home as those who spend their days at home with the children, the roles of present day mothers and fathers appear to have evolved somewhat differently. Mothers do most of the routine caretaking, but the father's role is not the abstract disciplinarian that we see represented in many texts. Instead the father appears to have taken over many of the qualities of playmate. Michael Lamb found in one study that when fathers spent time with toddler-aged children, it was play time; whenever the child needed some type of care, then the child was given back to the mother.

Jeanne Block suggested that fathers will be more important to the sex-role development of children than mothers and that they will interact with boys and girls in very different ways whereas mothers will behave similarly to boys and girls. Boys will be sought out by the father and will be encouraged to take on an instrumental, independent style of behavior. Whereas both mothers and fathers are expected to encourage traditional sex typing, the father will make a greater distinction between sons and daughters. Recent articles from several researchers have found minimal support for the uniqueness of the father's role. While fathers in some studies played physically with boys more frequently than with girls and were more consistent in their encouragement of sex-typed toys, there was actually little support for a differential effect on other sex-role variables. Differences, when they were found, were likely to occur with respect to reported attitudes about the differences between boys and girls rather than in differences in behavior toward boys and girls.

We do know, however, that mothers spend far more time with their children, do most of the caretaking, and if the family breaks up, are far more likely to raise the children as single parents. There is some movement within the middle class for more involvement of the father within the family; however, even in families choosing a equalitarian type of child-rearing in which both parents are employed outside the home, mothers continue to do most of the caretaking. Consequently, when one looks at parenting variables which predict future performance of the child in either the social or cognitive realm, mother variables in most studies tend to be stronger predictors than father variables. Father absence does predict problems for the child, but such studies tend to be highly confounded with economic well-being and social stress, so it is difficult to know whether it is father absence or other variables predicting negative outcome.

One thing that should be noted about the literature is that fathers are extremely understudied. Much of our information concerning the role of fathers comes from mothers. What we know directly from fathers is very biased toward well-educated fathers and concerns interactions in infancy and early childhood. The role of the father in the child's life after school entry and on into adolescence and adulthood remains a mystery.

Parents report different levels of pleasure in their child at different ages. In one study in Fagot's laboratory, both mothers and fathers of 12 month olds appeared to be more comfortable with their roles than did parents of 18 month olds. Parenting an 18-month-old child, who is now quite mobile and starting to assert independence, calls for new skills, and it was clear that many of these parents were findings this transition a challenge. For instance, toddlers spend almost half of their time in communication attempts, and while a communication attempt may be considered a positive behavior, it also calls for an immediate response and can be extremely difficult for a busy parent. The tasks of parenting will change as the child grows. Parents use instruction and direction at much greater rates with 18 month olds than with 12 month olds. One consequence is that purely positive interaction decreases. Eighteen-month-old children require more management skills than 12 month olds, and this change is reflected both in the children's behavior and in the change of style of interaction seen in home observations. We need more studies which carefully define the parent's role as the child grows to understand the interaction between the age of the child and the parent's attitudes and behaviors toward the child.

Whether parents provide differential socialization for boys and girls is a question that has been debated for a number of years. In he early 1970s, Maccoby and Jacklin reviewed the literature and declared that there were few differences in the socialization of boys and girls. Blocks questioned this finding. Specifically, she concluded that few of the studies dealt with fathers, who might be expected to provide stronger sex-role socialization than mothers, and that the studies were biased toward younger children. In the early 1980s, block suggested several areas in which parental treatment might make a difference. Several subsequent attempts to examine parental differences in the treatment of boys and girls still have not yielded conclusive results.

Another of Block's contentions was that pre-school-aged children were overrepresented in the literature, and she hypothesized that sex-role socialization should increase with age. However, recent reviews have suggested that preschool boys and girls are treatment more differently than are middle-school children. There are very few studies concerning socialization of adolescent boys and girls, and many think that parents treat children of this age very differently.

Fagot's laboratory examined behavioral differences in mothers' and fathers' reactions toward boys and girls at three different ages: 12 months, 18 months, and 5 years of age. Home observations were chosen as the best method to look at socialization differences for several reasons. Home observations allow both the children and the parents to react more naturally than do more tightly controlled laboratory studies. There were some differences in mothers' and fathers' styles of interaction; for instance, mothers gave more instructions and directions than did fathers, while fathers spent more time in positive play interaction. There were also differences in parents' reactions to 12- and 18-month-old boys and girls; most differences were quite expected, with the exception that boys received more negative comments for attempts to communicate than did girls. There were no differences in the ways that parents reacted to boys and girls at age 5. Fagot argued that differences in parenting for boys and girls would occur at critical transitions in the child's life when it was important to the parent that the child behave in sex-stereotyped ways. For example, we see more differences at 18 months when the child is establishing a gender identity, and we should expect to see larger differences in adolescence when sex-role behaviors become very important.

There is an old joke among parents that the first child should be considered a practice try and only later children should count in evaluating their skills as parents. Certainly, the effects of birth order exist. However, the first child in many ways appears advantaged, particularly in terms of achievement in school and in later career choices. Why might this be? The first child in general receives more parent attention during the early years, including attention to the child's language development. Parents, particularly mothers, talk to their first-born children more. However, the literature on birth order is sometimes difficult to follow, as the findings are not always the same. At this time, researchers think more in terms of the spacing of children and the adult-child ratio. Families in which children are more closely spaced seem to have more difficulties, perhaps because of the financial and physical stress on the parents. When children are spaced 4 or more years apart, the effects of birth order tend to disappear.

Clearly, the culture in which child is raised has great implications for the child's well-being. Some cultures believe that children should be carefully nurtured and, because they do not yet understand the world, must be protected from harsh consequences. Other cultures seem to believe that children are born evil tendencies and must be sharply are born with evil tendencies and must be sharply curbed if they are not to grow up morally depraved. Some cultures cherish both boys and girls, while in others boys are of great value while girls are costly, and hence more likely to suffer infanticide. In some cultures, children are reared by many members of the community, while in others only the mothers participate in a child's upbringing. Humans seem to have an almost unlimited capacity to develop expectations and values about what is truly tight. Some wish their children to be very communally oriented, and the children are trained never to be outstanding. Other, such as the United States, put a great emphasis on individual achievement, and the child is taught to try to stand out. Cultures are very effective at molding the types of individuals that are most acceptable to the culture. The medium by which this is done is the parenting process.

There is great concern today about the failure of the family and hence the failure of parenting. Certainly if one examines the rise in reported child abuse rate, there is cause for concern. It remains unclear whether such reports reflect a rise in child abuse or an increased awareness of child abuse.

As recently as the 1950s, family violence was not widely recognized as a problem in American society. Since that time, the body of literature on child abuse and other forms of domestic violence has grown to be both extensive and diverse. A great deal of effort has been focused on understanding the causes and correlates of family violence. A rather diffuse field has developed, consisting of a number of indirectly related theories that focus on different aspects of family violence. Much of the literature of child abuse today suggests that many types of trauma in childhood lead to far-reaching problems, and often reactions to childhood trauma are considered in the same category as trauma suffered in wars and natural disasters. These reactions have come to be classified as post-traumatic stress syndrome

Why do parents abuse their children? There are many theories, most of which can be grouped in one of three categories. Psychological theories propose that the violence arises from within certain individuals with deviant personalities and various forms of psychology. Social-international theories point to interpersonal, most often within-family processes such as reciprocal reinforcement of aversive behaviors as the origin of violence. Sociocultural theories suggest the etiology of violence may be found within general societal factors such as poverty, stress, and crowded living conditions, or within the values of a particular cultural subgroup. Each of these theories has contributed in important ways to our understanding of domestic violence. However, the solution to child abuse is quite different depending upon the theory. If the problem is psychological, then it might make sense to focus upon diagnosis of an abusing personality and work with that individual. However, if abuse originates in the social interaction of the family, then intervention with the family is called for. If child abuse is a result of societal pressures, then the solution would be best handled at the societal rather than the individual level. Many who work with abused children have adopted the social-interactional approach, not because they feel that societal conditions have no part in the cycle, but because they can do something about interactions within the family. They also find that most child abusers do not have recognizable forms of pathology. In effect, the tendency within the field has been to adopt educational approaches to failures of parenting.

The mother-child relationship has been a primary focus of both clinical and developmental investigations, and hence most of the parenting programs focus upon the mother-child relationship. Mothers may provide different social learning experiences for a child depending on the mother's style of interaction and the child's gender. Angry mothers typically have young children who display anxious and resistant behaviors, and this is particularly true for boys. Depressed mothers have been shown to spend less time taking care of their children, to use more physical punishment, and to be less affectionate. Comparisons of children's responses showed that daughters were more likely to display behaviors similar to mothers' depressive behaviors, especially during adolescence.

Studying the family has been given a prominent role in trying to understand both the antecedents of problem behaviors and healthy adjustment out-comes. Effective parents for both boys and girls have been characterized as nurturant, positive, and loving, as being sensitive to their children's individuality, and as having developed reasonable expectations and effective behavior management skills. How do we translate the research findings into effective treatment programs? At this point, there are several programs around the country that are developing prevention programs. Here the idea is that parents who are having difficulty or feel they may have difficulty are exposed to parenting programs. The components of such program usually include information on family management, on increasing the warmth and emotional support of the parent, and on teaching the parent to help the child learn new skills.

Biological parents are given a great deal of control over their children's lives. Perhaps this is due to very root of the term parenting, meaning to give birth. There are some recent changes of this control; for instance, a boy in Florida was allowed to divorce his biological parents whom he claimed had neglected and abused him. However, the quality of parenting is rarely considered in placement of children in disputes, and the child continues to be at the mercy of his birth. As the process of parenting becomes better understood, perhaps in the future judgements of suitability will be made in terms of quality rather than biology.

At the turn of the 20th century, a number of influential investigators of human development wrote about the significance of peer relationships for children; however, it was not until the 1920s, when the first child welfare research stations blossomed throughout North America, that the empirical study of children's peer relationships and social skills gained a large and influential following. In these new research laboratories, investigators developed novel methodologies to examine develop-mental and individual differences in children's sociability, assertiveness and aggression, altruism, group dynamics, peer acceptance, and group composition. Although the exigencies of the second World War drove the study of children's social relationships to a virtual standstill, the topic regained new "breath" with the rediscovery of Jean Piaget's theory of cognitive and social cognitive development, on the one hand, and with the preschool and day-care movements of the 1960s and 1970s on the other. Concerning the latter, children in North America are now entering organized peer group settings at earlier ages than ever before. Dual-income and single-parent families require that nonmaternal infant and early child care be made available. For the most part, such care is provided in out-of-the-home peer group venues. Furthermore, given the growing significance of education for life success, today's children remain with peers in age-segregated schools for more years than their cohorts of previous generations. Form this applied perspective, it would be shortsighted to ignore the significance of children's peer group experiences and relationships for normal development and adjustment.

Theoretically, the significance of children's peer relationships is well described in the writings of Jean Piaget. In one of his first books, Piaget suggested that children's relationships with peers could be distinguished clearly, in form and function, from their relationships with adults. The latter relationships could be construed as being complementary, asymmetrical, and falling along a vertical plane of dominance and power assertion. Children normally accept adults' rules, not necessarily because they understand them, but rather because obedience is required. Alternatively, adults are far less likely to follow the dictates of children.

On the other hand, children' peer relationships were portrayed as being balanced, egalitarian, and as falling along a more-or-less horizontal plane of power assertion and dominance. As such, it was within the peer context that Piaget believed children could experience opportunities to examine conflicting ideas and explanations, to negotiate and discuss multiple perspectives, and to decide to compromise with or to reject the notion held by peers. These peer interactive experiences were posited to result in positive and adaptive developmental outcomes for children. For example, positive outcomes included, among others things, the ability to understand others' thoughts, emotions, and intentions.

Armed with these new social understandings, children were believed able to think about the consequences of their social behaviors, not only for themselves, but also for others. The abilities to take into account the perspectives of others and to identify the potential consequences of one's social actions have long been posited to result in the production of socially competent behavior. The relative lack of such skills, conversely, has been thought to predict incompetent social behavior. These Piagetian derived notions have influenced a good deal of contemporary research concerning children's peer relationships. One of the principal off-shoots of this research has been the examination of relations among social cognition (or how children think about their social worlds or about social issues), social behaviour, and the quality of children's peer relationships.

Several other authors have provided a rich perspective on the significance of peer relationships for normal development. For example, Harry Stack Sullivan wrote that the concepts of mutual respect, equality, and reciprocity developed from the "special relationships" that children developed with their chums. During the late elementary school years, children were thought to be able to recognize and value each other's personal qualities; as a consequence, peers gained power as personality shaping agents. Peers were thought to help each other understand the constructs of cooperation, competition, and social roles such as deference and dominance. Sullivan suggested further that during preadolescence, children gained a more complex understanding of social relationships as the concepts of equality, mutuality, and reciprocity became central to their own close friendships. Once acquired between friends, these concepts were thought to be extended to other relationships.

Like Piaget, George Herbert Mead emphasized the importance of the development of perspective-taking through peer interaction. Mead suggested that the ability to reflect on the self developed gradually over the early years of life, primarily as a function of peer play and social interaction experiences. Participation in rule-governed games and activities with peers was believed to lead children to understand and coordinate the perspectives of others with relation to the self. Thus, perspective-taking experiences led to the conceptualization of the "generalized other" or the organized perspective of the social group, which in turn led to the emergence of an organized sense of self. Learning and social learning theories have guided current research on children's peer relationships. It was suggested originally, and subsequently established empirically, that children learn about their social worlds, and how to behave within these contexts, through direct peer tutelage and indirect observation of peers "in action." From this perspective, peers are viewed as behavior control and behavior change agents for each other. Children punish or ignore nonnormative social behavior and reward or reinforce positively those behaviors viewed as culturally appropriate and competent.

Finally, ethological theorists have suggested that there is a relation between biology and the ability to initiate, maintain, or disassemble particular relationships. A basic focus of contemporary human ethological research has been the provision of detailed descriptions of the organization and structure of social behaviors and groups. For example, prosocial, playful, and aggressive displays have been examined within the contexts of parent-child attachment, and peer dominance and affiliative relationships. Those who have studied children's social behaviors from an ethological perspective have focused their attention on the organizational structure and functions of childrens of children's peer groups.

Generally, peer groups are characterized by participants who feel a strong desire to belong to a social unit, generate shared norms or rules of conduct beyond those maintained by society at large, and develop a hierarchical social structure of roles and relationships that govern their interaction with one another. The peer group serves several unique and significant functions for the growing child. For one, participation in peer groups teaches children how to engage in cooperative activities aimed at collective rather than individual goals. Such activities allow children to transcend the traditional egocentric or self-focused perspective traditionally attributed to young children. For another, participation in peer groups provides children with a venue in which control of hostile and aggressive impulses is socialized; when hostility is demonstrated, it is directed at members of other definable groups. Finally, through group membership, children gain first-hand experience with social structure, and are afforded the opportunity to practice skills associated with leadership and "following." For example, there are times when members of the group must step forward and offer suggestions and solutions for the group to abide by. Furthermore, group participants must learn to accept and abide by the will of the collective even if they are not in full agreement with a group decision. Given the significance of the peer group, it seems worthwhile asking how it is that groups are formed and how they look once formed.

From classic social psychological research with children, the means by which groups are formed are well-known. When unfamiliar children are brought together, those children who display competencies in areas designated as important tend to acquire high status among peers. Oft-times the group has several leaders, each of whom takes on a particular role defined by his or her own areas of expertise. These leaders tend to set the norms for the group.

Once norms are established, members of peer groups develop a sense of belonging and a group identity. These affective components of group structure often result in competition (and in some subcultures, conflict) with other identifiable groups. Competition increases group solidarity and cohesion and adherence to norms. Thus, confirmity to group norms is often intense and those who ignore the dictates of the peer group risk being rejected. Interestingly, there appears to be a developmental course of conformity to peer group norms. During early childhood, cognitive egocentrism, or the inability to understand the perspectives of others, often poses a problem concerning conformity to group norms; for example, preschoolers often follow their own sets of norms and they may shift rules in the middle of any given interaction in order to benefit themselves. With age and growth in social-cognitive understanding from middle childhood through early adolescence, conformity to norms increases. Conformity to norms is greatest when the sources of influence are older or more competent than the child.

Norms bind peer groups, and leaders play critical roles in determining norms for the group. but what determines group leadership? The most commonly investigated organizing principle in determining group structure is dominance. Dominance refers to an asymmetrical balance of power between two individuals in a social group. Dominance hierarchies represent a "pecking order" of individuals within a given group. Such hierarchies can be seen in groups of children as young as 3 years of age; they allow the prediction of who will prevail under various conditions of conflict or disagreement between any two group members.

Dominance hierarchies become increasingly stable during middle childhood and adolescence. These group structures serve the function of reducing aggression between group members: thus, even in pre-school groups, overt acts of aggression diminish once a status hierarchy is established. When hostility does occur between group members, it is usually very restricted, often taking the form of playfully delivered verbal insults. As well, dominance hierarchies serve the adaptive function of helping to divide up tasks of labor and group resources. It is also often the case that "rank has its privileges"; lower status members typically assume most of the work and high status members benefit maximally from limited resources.

Although dominance represents a significant organizing function in children's peer groups, its role diminishes with age. Thus, by adolescence, group structures are less dependent on physical size and prowess, and more dependent upon characteristics that support a group's present normative activities. These characteristics include athletic ability, intelligence, and engagement in friendly or sociable behaviors. As such, since groups may vary in their normative orientations, social power among group members will be distributed differently in different social situations. There is also evidence that children's peer groups can be characterized along other dimensions, such as affiliation and attention.

Thus, children's group structures are very complex and become increasingly so with the increasing age of its members.

It is clear that peer groups offer children a unique context within which they learn about themselves and others. Peer group membership affords children the opportunity to learn about common goals, normative behaviors, and the complexity of maintaining relationships. It is important to note, however, that within the child's peer group, "special relationships" may develop. These more intense dyadic friendships serve their own distinct functions. Thus, we turn now to the literature on the significance of friendship.

Friendship is defined by the presence of a close, mutual, and dyadic bilateral relationship that is built upon the principles of equality, mutuality, cooperation, and intimacy. During childhood, the constituent factors associated with friendship formation and maintenance change with age; in fact, the very meaning of friendship undergoes developmental change. In the following sections we discuss the functions of friendships, children's changing understandings of friendship, children's interactive behaviors in friend and non-friend peer groups, and the friendship formation process.

Developmental theories have proposed that friendships in childhood serve a multitude of functions. For example, friendships in childhood serve a multitude of functions. For example, friendships in childhood serve to provide mutual validation of interests, expectations, and concerns; enhance one's feelings of personal worth; provide affection and opportunities for intimate self-disclosure; foster the growth of interpersonal understanding and establish a foundation upon which later interpersonal relationships are built (e.g., romantic, marital, and parental relationships. Friendships are also thought to provide guidance and instrumental aid; offer significant sources of reliable alliance; provide companionship and excitement; enhance social perspective-taking skills; and offer a forum for the transmission of social norms and knowledge. Perhaps most important of all, friendships in childhood offer children an extra-familial base of security from which they may explore the effects of their behaviors on themselves, their peers, and their environments.

Recently, it has been proposed that friendships serve different functions for children at different points in development. In early childhood, friendship maximizes excitement and amusement levels in play, and helps to regulate emotions in the face of arousal (e.g., during conflict). In middle childhood, friendships assist children to learn those social skills necessary for successful self-presentation and impression management. These skills become crucial in middle childhood when anxiety about peer relationships develops. Finally, in adolescence, friendships serve to assist children in their quest for self-identity, and to help them integrate logic and emotions.

It is one thing for theorists to posit the functions of friendship; it is quite something else to know how children think about the phenomenon. In the typical study, children are asked questions such as "What is a best friend?" or "what do you expect from a best friend?" It has been found that children's ideas about friendship progress through three broad stages. In the initial "reward-cost" stage (7-8 years), children characterize friends as companions who live nearby, have nice toys, and are willing to share them. In the "normative stage" (10-11 years), shared values and rules become important, and friends are expected to be cooperative, agreeable, and loyal. In the "emphathetic stage" (11-13 years), friends are viewed as sharing similar interests, and as understanding, intimate confidants.

In summary, it is generally assumed that children's understanding friendship becomes increasingly sophisticated and complex with age. Children's conceptions about friendship reflect their own transitions from the concrete world of the "here and now" to the more abstract world of the way things could or ought to be. What children may require and desire in a friendship develops as a function of their growing understanding of the world.

Why is it that children are drawn into close relationships with each other? A facile first response is that observable characteristics such as racial/ethnic background, age, and sex are important magnets serving to pull children together. However, it is also the case that unfamiliar children who become friends are more likely to communicate clearly, self-disclose more often, engage in more positive interpersonal exchanges, and resolve conflicts more effectively than children who do not eventually become friends. Thus, childhood friendships form partners are able to establish some sense of commonality and community.

Once formed, early childhood friendships are maintained because the partners direct positive affect to one another and share similarities in play preferences and cognitive sophistication. With increasing age, similarities in attitudes and aspirations aid in friendship maintenance.

Friends interact with each other differently than non-friends. Positive social exchanges and mutuality occur more often among than non-friends at all ages. Children as young as 3½ years direct more social overtures, engage in more social and cooperative interaction, and play in more complex ways with their friends than with non-friends. Developmentally, it has been shown that altruistic or prosocial behaviors between friends increase with age until adolescence. Interestingly, conflicts are not uncommon between friends. Friends not only engage in more positive interactions, but they also quarrel and engage in active (assaults and threats) and reactive (refusals and resistance) hostility more often than non-friends. Most likely, this seemingly contradictory finding can be attributed to the fact that friends spend much more time actually interacting with each other than do non-friends. Moreover, friends resolve their conflicts differently than non-friends. Friends, as compared with non-friends, have less intense conflicts; also, their conflicts are resolved more quickly. Friends are more likely to have equitable resolutions following conflict. Finally, following conflict resolution, friends are more likely than neutral associates to stay in physical proximity and continue to interact.

Childrens show a strong preference to play and be with same-sex peers; this tendency becomes stronger as children move from the preschool years through to middle childhood. The preference for same-sex playmates may emanate from children's increased awareness of culture's prescribed roles for males and females, and for the motivation to be included in the peer group.

The structural organisation of friendships differs for boys and girls. For example, boys tend to have "extensive" (large) friendships networks, whereas girls' friendships are embedded in smaller, more "intensive" groups. Also, girl's dyadic relationships are more "exclusive" than those of boys. Boys are less likely to self-disclosure and to share secrets with their friends than are girls. Finally, boys tend to be more competitive with their friends than girls. The experience of being liked and accepted by the peer group is known popularity. This construct reflects the view of the group vis-a-vis any given individual. Presumably, children who are not accepted by their peers experience some difficulty in their interactions with their peers. In the following sections, we examine the findings concerning the possible determinants of peer acceptance, and the outcomes that persistent difficulties with peers may entail.

Why is it that some children gain popularity amongst their peers while others are actively disliked? Most of the research extant concerning this question is purely descriptive; that is, investigators have provided a reasonable description of popular and rejected children. They have not, for the most part, focused directly on the causes of acceptance and rejection. Nevertheless, a review of the correlational database is revealing in that it provides reasonable hints about the determinants of peer reputations.

A wide range of variables, behavioral and non behavioral, social and non-social, have been associated with acceptance and rejection. Although variables such as physical attractiveness, typicality of the child's first name, and minority group status have been found to be related to peer acceptance, it is clear that the strongest correlates of popularity are children's social behaviors. In general, it has been found that popular children are more socially competent than their rejected counterparts. That is, they are better able than rejected children to achieve their personal goals in social interaction in socially acceptable ways. They are generally more friendly, cooperative, and altruistic than their rejected counterparts. There is no one set of characteristics that is associated with peer rejection. Some rejected children are unable either to take into account others' perspectives or to plan the solution of interpersonal dilemmas by taking into account the consequences of their actions for themselves and their social "targets." As a result, these children deal with their interpersonal problems by striking out against their social worlds; that is, they are aggressive. Needless to say, in studies concerned with the causes of rejection, the relatively frequent display of aggressive behavior is a well-worn route to isolation by the peer group.

Other rejected children do not have difficulty thinking about the perspectives of others or about the most optimal solutions to interpersonal dilemmas. Rather, they appear to be anxious and wary of others, and as a result, they avoid interacting with their peers. By the mid-years of childhood, such passively withdrawn children gain negative reputations amongst their peers.

Interestingly, the relation between social competence and popularity appears to hold universally across cultures. The same may be said for the relations between aggression and peer rejection. However, in some cultures (e.g., Asia) wary or careful behavior in the peer group is encouraged by peers and parents; consequently, in these cultures, what is generally referred to in Western cultures as "passive-withdrawal" is associated with peer acceptance and not with rejection.

The distinction between aggressive-rejected and withdrawn-rejected children is important because it appears that these two groups carry with them different types of psychological problems-problems that appear to be associated with different "outcomes" or consequences for them during adolescence. For example, aggressive-rejected children do not think poorly of their social relationships; nor do they express feelings of loneliness or social anxiety. This may be explained by the findings that rejected-aggressive children do not report difficulties with the self-system. Although this group is generally disliked by classmates, rejected-aggressive children do tend to affiliate with others like them. Thus, the social support available to them albeit from a deviant subgroup, may buffer them from developing negative self-perceptions and loneliness. On the other hand, withdrawn or socially anxious children who are rejected do think poorly of their own social prowess and of their social relationships; they are also more likely than aggressive-rejected children to acknowledge feeling lonely or depressed.

4

Religion and Human Rights

In the years since World War II religious liberty has been proclaimed as a human right in several United Nations documents, and all the major Christian churches have affirmed their commitment to the same ideal. It was not always so. A leading scholar in this field observed recently that "for several thousand years the history of religion was marked by religious intolerance and persecution." After mentioning specifically the persecutions of one another by Christians of various persuasions, he added: "Clearly religion and freedom have not been natural allies." This is the situation we have to bear in mind when we reflect on the historical background to the modem idea of religious rights. Of course, all the great religious cultures of the world have given expression to ideals of justice and right order in human affairs, but they have not normally expressed those ideals in terms of subjective natural rights. Even in the West, a doctrine of religious rights emerged only painfully and belatedly, out of a tradition that had earlier found it much easier to acknowledge other kinds of rights. Nowadays it has become commonplace to maintain, as Pope John Paul II recently asserted, that religious rights are the "cornerstone" of all other rights. But, viewed in historical perspective, religious rights came last; these rights were the most difficult to conceive of, let alone put into practice. The Roman Catholic Church was the last of the great Christian denominations to embrace wholeheartedly the principle of religious freedom. This at least had the advantage that its leaders could form a mature and well-considered version of the doctrine. Hence the *Declaration* on Religious Liberty of Vatican Council II, promulgated in 1965, provides an appropriate starting point for our discussion:

> This Vatican Council declares that the human person has a right to religious freedom. This freedom means that all men are to be immune from coercion on the part of individuals or of social groups and of any human power... the right to religious freedom has its foundation in the very dignity of the human person as this dignity is known through the revealed word of God and by reason itself.

This passage of the Declaration referred, in all-embracing fashion, not only to coercion by the state but by "any human power." It defined religious freedom specifically as a "right" and a right inherent in the human person, a natural or human right therefore. This natural right, discernible by human reason, was also said to be rooted in divine revelation and so intrinsic to the Christian faith. The Declaration contained only a bland and innocuous hint that these affirmations represented a radical reversal of a policy of religious repression that the Catholic church (and the mainstream Protestant churches too) had maintained for centuries. The hint came in an observation that the demands of human dignity "have come to be more fully known to human reason through centuries of experience." How true these words are can be gathered from a decree of another general council, promulgated in 1215, just 750 years before the Declaration of Vatican Council II.

The most obvious way in which the leaders of the medieval church contributed (unintentionally of course) to the emergence of modern religious liberty was by their insistence on the freedom of the church from control by temporal rulers. In the Middle Ages there was never just one hierarchy of government exercising absolute authority, but always two—church and state as we say nowadays—often contending with one another, each limiting the other's power. This duality of government was a rather unusual development in human history. In societies larger than a tribal unit or a city-state the most common form of rulership has been some form of theocratic absolutism. The Pharaohs of Egypt, the Incas of Peru, the emperors of Japan were all revered as divine figures. The order of society was seen as a part of the divine order of the cosmos; the ruler provided a necessary link between heaven and earth. Typically, in such societies, religious liberty was neither conceived of nor desired.

Christianity was different from the beginning. It grew up in an alien culture, the sophisticated classical civilization of Greece and Rome. To become a Christian or to persist in the religion was a matter of free personal choice, often involving considerable self-sacrifice. For early Christians, the emperor was not a divine ruler but a persecutor of the true faith. The tension between Roman state and Christian church was expressed classically in the words of Jesus himself: "Render to Caesar the things that are Caesar's and to God the things that are God's" (Mark 12:17). In all ages Christians have remembered, too, the words of Peter: "We ought to obey God rather than man" (Acts 5:29). After the conversion of Constantine and the establishment of a Christian empire there was indeed a possibility for a time that the church might become merely a sort of department of religious affairs in an imperial theocratic church-state. But, as the imperial power crumbled in the West, the independent role of the church was vigorously reasserted by Pope Gelasius: Two there are, august emperor, by which this world is chiefly ruled, the sacred authority of the priesthood and the royal power... in the order of religion, in matters concerning the reception and right administration of the heavenly sacraments, you ought to submit yourself rather than rule.

There were two authorities in the world; whole areas of religious thought and practice were excluded from the control of the temporal ruler. The text of Gelasius was assimilated into the medieval corpus of canon law and endlessly quoted and discussed in later disputes. The whole issue of empire and papacy arose again when Charlemagne sought to establish a new theocratic empire, and his claims were reiterated by his successors of the Ottoman and Salian dynasties of Germany. Claiming to be vicars of God on earth, the kings assumed the right to control their churches; they regularly appointed bishops in the lands they ruled and invested them with the ring and staff that were the symbols of spiritual office. When, from time to time, a German emperor invaded Italy and occupied Rome, he chose and appointed popes, just as he appointed other bishops.

The church seemed to be drifting into another form of theocratic monism. But a dramatic change came in the pontificate of Gregory VII. Gregory condemned the whole existing order of society as radically contrary to divine justice. He declared himself willing to fight to the death for the "freedom of the church," a phrase he used like a kind of battle-cry. To implement his policy, he forbade the prevailing practice of lay investiture (the appointment of bishops by kings) and so inaugurated a struggle that historians used to call the Investiture Contest but that is now often referred to simply as the

Papal Revolution. Henry IV, king of Germany and later emperor, denounced Gregory as a pseudo-pope and a heretic; Gregory responded by deposing Henry from his kingship. The fight that ensued between pope and emperor was both a war of propaganda and a real civil war in Germany and Italy. At one point Henry had to humiliate himself before the pope at Canossa and humbly beg his forgiveness; but later his armies occupied Rome and drove Gregory into exile. In the end neither side could prevail and, after both of the original protagonists had died, a compromise peace was patched up in the Concordat of Worms.

The struggle between popes and kings was reenacted over and over again in the following centuries. After denouncing the theocratic pretensions of kings, the popes were often tempted to assert a theocratic role for themselves. Sometimes they put forward extreme claims to a kind of overlordship of Christian society in both spiritual and temporal affairs. The point is, however, that such claims were always resisted and never generally accepted by medieval kings or their peoples. The theocratic claims of the papacy reached a high-water mark in Boniface VIII's Bull, *Unam sanctan,* with its uncompromising declaration: "It is altogether necessary for every human creature to be subject to the Roman pontiff." But Boniface was defeated and humiliated in the struggle with the king of France that had been the occasion of his pronouncement.

Because neither side could make good its more extreme claims, a dualism of church and state persisted in medieval society and eventually was rationalized and justified in many works of political theory. The French theologian, John of Paris, for instance, writing in 1302 wrote a treatise on Royal and Papal Power which presented a carefully balanced dualism, assigning to each power its proper function. "The priest is greater than the prince in spiritual affairs," John wrote, "and, on the other hand, the prince is greater in temporal fairs."

The persistent dualism in medieval society that we have descried was far removed from a modern "wall of separation." In the Middle Ages, the powers of church and state constantly overlapped and interacted and impinged on one another; but the church remained commute to a radical limitation of state power in the sphere of religion. By the ci of the Middle Ages, the Catholic kings had again acquired a large measure of control over church appointments; but, in the Reformation era, the revived theory of royal divine right was challenged by new forms protest that led to new ways of asserting religious rights.

Freedom of the church from control by the state is one important of modern religious liberty. But it is only a part. 'The libertas ecclesiac that medieval popes demanded was not freedom of religion for each individual person but the freedom of the church as an institution to direct own affairs. It left open the possibility, all too fully realized from the twelfth century onward, that the church might organize the persecution of its own dissident members. And, when the interests of church a state happened to coincide, as they often did in dealing with heresy, there was room for a savage suppression of religious dissent. But, even during the centuries of persecution, there were some aspects of medieval thought and practice that could have been conducive to an alternative tradition of religious toleration.

For one thing, medieval canonists and moral theologians often held the overriding value of the individual conscience as a guide to rig conduct. When Paul wrote: "Everything that is not from faith is sin", the Ordinary Gloss to the Bible (the standard medieval commentary on the text) explained that the words "not from faith" meant "all that is contrary to conscience." In the twelfth century, Peter Abelard expanded the argument. He taught that to act against one's conscience was always sinful, even if the conscience erred in discerning what right. A century after Abelard, Thomas Aquinas addressed this same question. It might seem that we are not obliged to follow an erring conscience, he wrote, because we are not obliged to obey the command of a lower authority when it conflicts with that of a higher one; but conscience might favour our acting contrary to the law of God, who was the supreme authority. In reply, Thomas quoted the Ordinary Gloss to Romans 14:23 and explained that we are only obliged to follow the command of the higher authority when we know that it conflicts with our present judgment. An erring conscience could be formed in good faith if one were ignorant of the higher law. A person was always obliged to do what his conscience discerned as good, even though the conscience might be mistaken.

The same, doctrine was taught by the canonists. It was expressed in two judgments of Pope Innocent III that were incorporated into the corpus of medieval canon law. The Ordinary Gloss to the Decretals, a work studied in law schools throughout Europe, explained their implication, "One ought to endure excommunication rather than sin... no one ought to act against his own conscience and he should follow his conscience rather than the judgment of the church when he is certain... one ought to suffer any evil rather than sin against conscience. "

We are not dealing here with a right to religious liberty but with a duty to obey, one's conscience. Still, an emphasis on the primacy of the individual conscience was an important element in later theories of religious rights The medieval position was that a person was right to follow his conscience but that he might suffer at the hands of the authorities if his conscience led him to illicit behaviour. Similarly, in the modern world, individuals may be led by a sincere conscience to violate the law-as in some forms of civil rights or anti-war protest-but the law will hold them responsible for their actions. There is one further point: medieval moralists did not hold that people should act on mere subjective whims. Everyone was required to use the utmost diligence and every resource of knowledge and understanding to form a correct conscience. Failure to do this was sinful. In practice, it was assumed that most cases where an erring conscience led to illicit behaviour involved culpable ignorance or culpable negligence.

In one sphere, the emphasis on individual conscience did lead to a degree of religious toleration. Medieval doctrine always taught that non-Christians could not be forcibly converted to Christianity. God's grace was a free gift, and it had to be freely accepted. In practice the only substantial populations of non-Christian people scattered throughout the Western church were Jewish communities, and the principle of toleration was explicitly applied to them. The attitude of the medieval church toward the Jews, as toward heretics, was shaped by the teaching of Augustine, though in this case it had a more benign effect. Augustine held that, although the Jewish people had erred at the time of Christ, still it was God's will that they should always survive. They existed to give permanent independent witness to the divine law revealed in the *Old Testament*. They could also attest to the words of the prophets which Christians understood as foretelling the coming of Christ. And accordingly, to fulfil this role, some of the Jewish people would exist until the end of time. The acceptance of this theology shaped the official attitude of the medieval church toward the Jews. They were indeed discriminated against-made to wear a distinctive dress, excluded from positions of authority in government-but they were allowed to have their own synagogues and to practice their own religion. The attitude of the papacy was one of toleration, grudging toleration no doubt, but still a recognition that Jews had a right to exist in a Christian society, 'the policy was defined by Gregory 1 in a letter that became a part of the permanent canon law of the church. 16 "Just as the Jews ought not to be allowed more than the law concedes," he wrote, "so too they ought not to suffer harm in those things that the law does concede to them." From the beginning of the twelfth century onward it became customary for the Jewish community of Rome to obtain a restatement of Jewish rights from each new pope at the beginning of his reign. In the real-life world of the Middle Ages, needless to say, savage outrages against Jewish communities occurred all too often; but they were due to outbursts of mob violence or actions of secular rulers. They were contrary to the law and teaching of the church.

Natural Rights

There was one further area in which medieval thinkers began to develop a doctrine that would be important for later theories of religious liberty-the idea that all persons possess natural rights. No consensus exists among modern scholars about the origin of this doctrine or how it is related to the tradition of Christian thought. Jacques Maritain simply assumed that the idea of human rights was always implicit in the Judeo-Christian teaching on the dignity and value of each human person. At the opposite extreme, Leo Strauss focused on the supposedly atheistic philosophy of Thomas Hobbes, whom he regarded as the founder of modern rights theories, and concluded that the idea of natural rights was alien to the whole preceding classical and Christian tradition. Disciples of Strauss will still maintain that "the very idea of natural rights is incompatible with Christian doctrine." But this view seems untenable if only because there certainly were Christian natural rights theorists before Hobbes—Suarez and Grotius for instance.

According to the most recent work, the origin of the later natural rights theories is to be found in the Christian jurisprudence of the late twelfth century, especially in the works of the canonists of that era. The twelfth century was an age of renewal in many spheres of life and thought. New networks of commerce grew up. There was new art, new architecture a new literature of courtly romance. Religious thought placed a new emphasis on the individual human person-on individual intention in assessing guilt, on individual consent in marriage, on individual scrutiny of conscience. And in the secular sphere, at every level of society we find an intense concern for individual rights and liberties. Above all, the twelfth century was an age of legal renaissance marked by the recovery of the whole corpus of classical Roman law, and by the first adequate codification of the accumulated canon law of the church in Gratian's Concord of Discordant Canons, completed circa 1140. In the following decades a succession of great jurists, inspired by the old texts, found ways to express all the new impulses of their own age in juridical language. For us the crucial development was that the new personalism in religious life, and the everyday concern with rights in secular society, infected the language of the canonists when they came to discuss the concept of ius naturale, natural right. Earlier the phrase his naturale had been understood in an objective sense to mean natural law or "what is naturally right." But the canonists who wrote around 1200, reading the old texts in the context of their more humanist, more individualist culture, added another definition. In their writings, his naturale was now sometimes defined in a subjective sense as a faculty, power, force, ability inhering in individual persons. From this initial subjective definition, the canonists went on to develop a considerable array of natural rights.

By around 1300 a sophisticated legal language had grown up in which a doctrine of natural rights could be expressed. The next step was the assimilation of the juristic idea of rights into works of political philosophy. William of Ockharn was indeed important here. He drew on the earlier canonistic tradition but went beyond it, One of his major contributions was to reshape the scriptural idea of evangelical liberty into a doctrine of natural rights. When Paul wrote about Christian freedom he meant freedom from the law of the Old Testament or freedom from sin, but Ockharn used Paul's texts to argue for freedom from any tyrannical government, especially within the church. Not even the pope, he wrote, could injure "the rights and liberties conceded to the faithful by God and nature." Ockharn also developed a concept of "suppositional" or contingent natural rights, related to basic human needs, but applied in different ways in different circumstances. The idea could perhaps have some relevance for modern problems concerning the applicability of general norms in a world of cultural diversity.

Ockharn's ideas were developed further by Jean Gerson, an eminent theologian who wrote around 1400. Gerson gave a very influential definition of ius as "a power or faculty belonging to each one in accordance with the dictate off right reason" and argued that, even in man's fallen state, humans retained many such rights. Also, Gerson took up and developed further the idea that Christ's law was a law of liberty. In the existing church this was no longer the case, Gerson complained. On the contrary, Christians were oppressed by an intolerable burden of laws and regulations and obligations imposed by human authority, that is by the church hierarchy.

Such enactment were like snares and nets to trap the soul, he wrote. By fusing Paul's doctrine of Christian liberty with his own idea of natural rights, Gerson went on to argue that the essential obligation of a Christian was to accept freely the divinely revealed law of scripture and the natural law that his reason and conscience could discern. In the last resort one could exercise an inherent natural right of self-defence that no human law could take away against any oppressive authority, even an oppressive pope. Gerson's words sometimes have an almost modern sound, and his ideas were indeed very important in the growth of later natural rights theories. They were transmitted to the early modern world mainly by the Spanish scholastics of the sixteenth century, especially in the course of their debates about the rights of American Indians. Bartolomee de las Casas in particular tried to defend the Indians against subjugation and forced conversion by appealing to a doctrine of natural rights based on medieval legal and theological sources.

Given all these aspects of medieval thought-an insistence on the primacy of the individual conscience, a rejection of forced conversion, a nascent theory of natural rights-one might reasonably hope that at least some medieval thinkers would have moved on from these premises to assert a full-fledged doctrine of religious liberty. Nothing of the sort happened.

Every medieval writer who discussed this question saw heresy as a sin and a crime that was properly judged by the church and properly punished by the secular power. Even Gerson had no conception of religious freedom as we understand it; indeed, he participated in the trial and burning of John Hus.

Gerson could defend the rights of Christians within the church, but it never occurred to him to assert that heretics had rights against the church. Before we can understand how real religious rights emerged in the early modern world, we need to consider why they were so persistently denied in the preceding centuries.

In his classic little book, The Whig Interpretation of History, Herbert Butterfield warned historians against "present- mindedness." We should not impose our own ideas on the past, he urged, but rather seek to understand each historical era "in its own terms." The sort of question we ought to ask, Butterfield suggested, is not: How did we get our religious liberty? But rather: Why were people in former ages so given to persecution?

In the late Roman empire, laws against heresy, sometimes imposing the death penalty on offenders, were enacted by imperial authority, But in the centuries after the fall of the empire there was little organized persecution, though heretics or people suspected of heresy were sometimes lynched by fanatic mobs. When cases came before church courts, the usual penalty was excommunication. A more systematic repression began from the twelfth century onward, even as new doctrines of natural rights were growing into existence.

This was partly because of the spread of new heresies and partly because of the growing institutionalization of the church. As the church became more aware of itself as an ordered society with its own system of law and organs of government, it became less tolerant of those who rejected its authority. In 1199, Pope Innocent III declared, in the decretal *Vergentis,* that heresy was equivalent to treason. Heretics were traitors to God, he wrote, just as others guilty of treason were traitors to the emperor. The most threatening heresy of the time was that of the Cathars or Albigensians who had come to dominate substantial areas of southern France. In 1208 Innocent counterattacked by unleashing the Albigensian Crusade, an invasion of southern France by Catholic 'forces from the north which perpetrated savage massacres in cities that were strongholds of the heretics and effectively destroyed the Cathar civilization in Provence. Heretics try to tear the seamless robe of our God. They are violent wolves.... They are sons of depravity.... Therefore we draw the sword of vengeance against them.... Committed to the judgment of the flames, they should be burned alive in the sight of the people.

Other rulers enacted similar legislation, and burning at the stake be came the common punishment for heresy. About this same time, Pope Gregory IX first began to commission groups of inquisitors, usually Dominican and Franciscan friars, to seek out and punish heretics. By the mid-thirteenth century, such inquisitors were at work in all parts of the church. In some areas of political thought, medieval ideas were not so different from our own. Medieval people had quite well-developed concepts of representation and consent and government under law. But, when we turn to the idea of individual religious rights, their whole mindset was so alien to ours that it takes a considerable effort of historical imagination to enter into their world of thought. Perhaps we can find a starting point in a remark of the great legal historian, Frederic Maitland: "In the Middle Ages the church was a state." The church, he pointed out, had its own institutions of government, its own bureaucracy, its own laws and law courts. In the Middle Ages, secular political power was fragmented. The old Roman empire had passed away, and the attempt to found a medieval Christian empire had failed-partly indeed because of the struggle between popes and emperors that we have considered. National monarchies in France and England were only just beginning to grow into existence. The only bond of unity that held Western Christian society together was the bond of a common religion. Nowadays the focus of our loyalty is the state; we look to the state to protect our security and our liberty; to be a "stateless person" in the twentieth century is a most unhappy fate. The other side of the coin is that we do not tolerate people who are perceived of as traitors to the state. We charge them with treason; we punishment on them, sometimes capital punishment in extreme cases. A plea of personal sincerity, that the traitor has acted from good motives, in accordance with his own conscience, is not a sufficient defence. Medieval people regarded heretics in much the same way, held them guilty of treason to the church, and they treated them as traitors. When a common religion defined the whole way of life of a Society to reject it was to cut oneself off from the community, to become a sort of outlaw-and a dangerous outlaw from a medieval point of view.

When Thomas Aquinas first discussed the issue of heresy he be by presenting a series of apparently cogent arguments in favour of toleration. In the first place, there was the parable of the wheat and the tares from Matthew 13. In this story the good grain and the weeds were allowed to grow together until the time of harvest lest, in destroying weeds, some of the wheat was destroyed too. In commenting on his, Aquinas quoted John Chrysostom, an early church father, who had explicitly interpreted the text as meaning that heretics were not to be killed because, if this were permitted, some of the innocent would probably suffer along with the guilty. Again, Aquinas noted, canon law taught that Jews were not to be forcibly converted. Moreover, faith required the free assent of the will; and God himself had said, through the prop Ezekiel: "I do not will the death of a sinner." Against all this, Aquinas quoted one text of Scripture, the one Augustine had already us "Compel them to enter." And Aquinas understood it in the same sense as Augustine. The texts in favour of toleration applied to Jews and infidel was true that they could not be converted by force. But those who had ready accepted the faith could be compelled to return to it if they fell in heresy. To explain this, Aquinas used the analogy of a vow or promise man could not be compelled to take a vow, but if he chose to do so was obliged to fulfil it. In a later discussion, Aquinas compared heretics to counterfeiters of false money. It was a more serious offence to corrupt the faith than to corrupt the currency, he argued. Hence, just as counterfeiters were executed, so too heretics could be Put to death. Sometimes the health of the whole body required that a diseased limb be cut away.

John Noonan, discussing these texts from the standpoint of a law rather than a theologian, has pointed out that they are based on a series of legal fictions and unpersuasive analogies. It was a fiction that persons baptized in infancy had freely vowed to accept the faith; the comparison between counterfeiters and heretics confused the material realm of property with the spiritual realm of truth; and the use of the phrase *compelle intrare* transferred the words from the context of a parable about kingdom of God to a context of law and earthly jurisdiction. However cogent such objections may appear to us, one has to add that the arguments of Aquinas seemed entirely convincing to the medieval audience he was addressing.

Medieval people were so convinced of the truth of their religion that they could never see dissent from the accepted faith as arising simply from intellectual error, from a mistake in judgment. They thought that heresy must somehow stem from malice, from a perverted will that deliberately chose evil rather than good, Satan rather than God. Aquinas wrote: "Unfaithfulness is an act of the intellect, but moved by the will." This was the root cause of the medieval hatred of heresy. The heretics were seen, not only as traitors to the church but as traitors to God. To medieval people it seemed that they had rejected God's truth and God's love out of pride and self-love, the love of their own self-contrived errors. They had set themselves on a path that could lead only to eternal dam nation and, unless they were restrained, they would lure countless others to the same terrible fate. Elementary justice and charity, it seemed, required that they be rooted out. The Inquisition that pursued this task with increasingly harsh and cruel measures, including the use of torture to extort confessions, was accepted as a necessary safeguard of Christian society.

Thinking about the Inquisition may remind us of two aphorisms that Lord Acton quoted. The first is the well-known saying of Mme de Stael: "To understand all is to forgive all." The other, less indulgent, is from the Duke de Broglie: "We should beware of too much explaining lest we end up with too much forgiving." Neither aphorism is altogether satisfying for a historian. Our task is surely to understand and explain as fully as possible; but we do not have to condone everything that we have tried to understand, and, when everything possible has been said in mitigation, the medieval theory and practice of religious persecution will seem abhorrent to most modern people. Over a period of centuries, thousands of persons were hunted down, tortured, and killed for a crime that, to us, might seem a mere eccentricity of personal belief.

A critical observer, looking back over the history of the West for the past thousand years and at the policies pursued in many parts of the world during the present century, might suppose that persecution is a normal pattern of human conduct. He might think that Butterfield had got his question upside down after all. Perhaps the real question a historian has to answer is not: Why were they so given to persecution? But rather: Why are we so committed to an ideal of religious liberty" This the final topic that we have to consider.

Religious Rights

In the context of medieval life, religious persecution seemed both right and necessary. No one could see that "freedom of the church" could mean freedom of conscience for each individual Christian or that the duty to obey one's conscience might imply a right to act in accordance with it, or that a natural right to liberty was radically incomplete if did not include a right to freedom of religion. The Reformation of the sixteenth century created a new historical context in which all these matter were reevaluated in the light of new understandings of Christian teaching shaped by new historical experiences in the centuries after Martin Luther's first protests.

The changes that came about were not due to any intangible "spirit of Protestantism" or to the specific teachings of the first great reformers. Thomas Carlyle observed that new historical events do riot spring from one single cause but from a whole web of causation, from "all other events, prior or contemporaneous. "39 Then, he noted, the new event combines with all the other ones to give birth to further change. This is the sort of situation we have to deal with in considering religious liberty Between 1500 and 1700, a new web of causation was created. Europe experienced a series of savagely destructive wars of religion that ended in stalemates and a splintering of religious unity into innumerable competing sects. Eventually, this led on to a growth of national states that could command the loyalty of subjects who professed a variety of religious beliefs. But before that final outcome was achieved, religious groups who rejected an established faith found themselves persecuted in many countries-Huguenots in France,

Roman Catholics and Puritan separatists in England, Lutherans in the Catholic principalities of Germany, and every kind of dissenter from Catholic orthodoxy in Spain.

In each country, the groups that were being persecuted sought toleration for their own beliefs; but these demands were not at first based on any devotion to religious liberty as such. The right and duty of the ruler to punish religious error was taken for granted; it was just that each group was convinced that it alone held fast to the truth. At the other end of the religious spectrum, the Jesuit Robert Parsons protested against an oath of allegiance demanded of Catholics with an eloquent plea against coercion: "For he that should force a Jew or a Turke to sweare, that there were a blessed Trinity... against their conscience should synne grievously. But Parsons was defending a church that persecuted religious dissidents wherever it had the power to do so. Each religious group believed that it should be tolerated because it was right and, usually, that its adversaries should be persecuted because they were wrong. Oliver Cromwell said, in a moment of exasperation: "Everyone desires to have liberty, but none will give it." Looking back rather disdainfully on the whole situation, J.N. Figgis wrote of the competing sects: " It was... the inability of any single one to destroy the others, which finally secured liberty."

There is truth in this, but it is not quite the whole truth. From the middle of the sixteenth century onward a few voices were raised in defence of a genuine religious freedom. Among Protestant groups, the Anabaptists and Baptists always condemned coercion in matters of religion. And the execution of Servetus for heresy in Calvin's Geneva evoked a response from Sebastian Castellio, On Heretics, Whether they Should be Persecuted that provided the first full-scale argument for freedom of conscience. A century later, a volatile and complex situation that arose during the English Civil War made England for a time the principal forcing ground for the ideal of religious freedom.

Their position was summed up in a statement of Thomas Edward, is against the nature of reformation, a reformation and a diametrically opposite; the commands of God given in his word for reformation do not admit of toleration. "But the armies that had one Parliament's victories were filled with members of dissenting sects—Congregationalists, Baptists, Unitarians, Fifth Monarchy Men, Muggletonians, and many others. They all demanded and, under Cromwell, enjoyed for a time a measure of toleration. Moreover, in the literature that grew up, some spokesmen went further and began to argue for a real religious liberty for all, not just toleration for one group. The Presbyterian Richard Baxter, when serving as a chaplain to one of Cromwell's regiments, noted disapprovingly that, among the soliers "their most frequent and vehement disputes were for science as they called it; that... every man might not hold but preach and do in matters of religion what he pleased." Perhaps the most impassioned plea came from Roger Williams, who had known persecution both in old England and New England. In The 131 Persecution, Williams wrote:

It is the will and command of God that (since the coming of his Sonne the Lord Jesus) a permission of the most Paganish, Jewish, or Antichristian consciences and worships be gran all men in all Nations and Countries. It was not unusual for seventeenth-century Protestant to urge toleration for "Jews and Turks." This was just a way of reaffirming the old medieval doctrine against forced conversion. But William was exceptional in his willingness to tolerate even Roman Catholics even Catholics had consciences "more or less," and that their consciences were to be respected.

In the early modern world, the practice of persecution by three main lines of argument which we might characterize as based on skepticism, or on expediency, or on an appeal to the underlying principles of the Christian faith itself. The arguments were no value. The first two could lead on only to a plea for some li of toleration; only the third could provide a basis for a principled commitment to an ideal of religious freedom.

The skeptical approach was rooted in Renaissance humanism. The humanists began by dismissing all the finespun arguments of scholastic philosophy as dreary nonsense; then some of them carried over the same attitude in considering the arcane theological disputes that divided the Christian churches of their own day. This was the underlying attitude of Castellio. The skepticism of the humanists was not (at least not at first) a skepticism about the fundamental truths of Christian faith. Castellio wrote: "No one doubts that there is a God, whether He is good and just, whether He should be loved and worshipped... " On the other hand, the things that Christians did not agree about-doctrines concerning predestination, free will, baptism, the eucharist, the Trinity-were matters of controversy precisely because they were not clearly revealed in scripture. The truth about such things could not be known with certainty, Castellio thought. So it was futile and cruel for Christians to persecute one another over these matters. This line of argument was continued by the Italian, Acontius, and then, in mid-seventeenth-century England, by writers like William Walwyn and Francis Osborne.

The Huguenot exile, Pierre Bayle, presented a more radically skeptical attack on religious persecution. His work provides a link between the questioning of the Christian humanists and the more thoroughgoing skepticism of the Enlightenment, when a defence of toleration was often associated with indifference or hostility to all religious teaching. We should not underestimate our debt to the Enlightenment. No doubt, the skeptical mockery of a Voltaire was needed to expose the lingering cruelties and superstitions of established religion. But perhaps in the end skepticism is -not enough. Humans are religious animals, and if their old faiths are worn away by too much doubt they are likely to invent new and more savage substitutes, The Enlightenment did not lead on to a new era of peace and harmony; it led to a reign of terror in revolutionary France and a new round of religious persecution.

The second line of argument in favour of toleration was simple expediency. This attitude was typified in Henry IV of France who changed his religion from Protestant to Catholic in order to gain the French crown but then, as a Catholic king, issued the Edict of Nantes that granted substantial liberties to Protestants. Henry's contemporary, Queen Elizabeth of England, also pursued a religious policy guided mainly by reason of state. Reasons of economic policy were cited too. The Spanish regent in the Netherlands, Don Juan of Austria, wrote in 1577: "The Prince of Orange has always insisted... that freedom of conscience is essential to commercial prosperity." The greatest theoretical exponent of the argument from expediency was the political philosopher jean Bodin. He acknowledged that religious uniformity was desirable, and he doubt that the state could lawfully suppress religious dissent; but he argued that, when a new religion had become so entrenched that not be suppressed without a danger of civil strife, the most re~ policy was to tolerate it. A king's duty to maintain the public took precedence over his obligation to uphold religious truth. A problem with the argument from expediency is that, in many circumstances, toleration is not the most obviously expedient course of action.

The third argument for toleration was ultimately the most important one. Over and over again the idea was asserted-though not indeed generally accepted, for these are still dissident voices-that the practice of persecution was radically contrary to the teaching of Jesus himself. This argument was included in the works of many different thinkers. C wrote of persecution that "Satan could not devise anything more repugnant to the nature and will of Christ." Pierre Bayle argued ;In a fashion. He framed his case for toleration as a commentary on the text, "Compell them to enter," the text that Augustine and Aquinas had used to justify persecution; but Bayle argued in a different spirit that to understand the words of Christ in this way was "contrary to the essential spirit of the Gospel itself."

The awareness that religious liberty needed to be ground Christian principles as well as on pragmatic considerations of expediency was well expressed in an English pamphlet of 1614. The author wrote: "A man would think we had been schooled and whipt long enough to it by our calamities." That is to say, recent practical experience had shown the ill-effects of persecution. But the author added at once that "liberty of conscience is no new doctrine." Rather, he declared, it was "as old certainly as the blessed word of God." The new exigencies of the time led discerning Christians to understand more deeply the implications of their old faith. The more learned authors quoted the early patristic texts in favour of religious freedom. Often the parable of the wheat and tares was cited as an argument for toleration. A Baptist pamphlet of 1661 declared that liberty of conscience was "a part of the Christian religion." In the Netherlands, Dirck Coornhert, arguing against the skeptical views of Justus Lipsius, defended religious freedom as a part of the authentic teachings of Christ, and insisted that the truth of those teachings could be known with certainty. Among the English writers, John Milton took up St. Paul's texts about Christian liberty, the texts that Ockham and Gerson had appealed to earlier, and derived from them an argument that the use of force in matters of faith was contrary to "the very weightiest and inmost reasons of Christian religion."

In this new climate of opinion, when persecution was increasingly condemned as contrary to the teachings of Jesus, all the old medieval strands of argument about the freedom of the church from secular control, the overriding authority of conscience, and the existence of natural rights were taken up again and woven into new patterns. These arguments, could all have been conducive to a doctrine of religious liberty, but in the context of medieval life they never led on to that result. In the post-medieval world, in a new historical context, the arguments were carried further to conclusions that perhaps had always been implicit in them but that had never been explicitly affirmed.

The old claim that the church ought not to be controlled by secular rulers was now taken to mean that the civil magistrate had no right to interfere with any person's choice of religion. Protestant dissenters often pointed out that the magistrate was no more infallible than the pope or the bishops. It followed that, as William Walwyn observed, "he who is in an error may be the constrainer of him who is in the truth. Another argument against government coercion of religion pointed out that progress in the understanding of divine revelation could be achieved only through free and reasoned discourse. When Milton wrote of "the reforming of the Reformation itself" in a coming new age., he was arguing specifically for freedom of the press. Medieval theologians had sometimes envisaged a gradual progress in the understanding of scripture through the course of the centuries. The new insight was that such progress required freedom of thought and expression.

The view that any meaningful freedom of the church required that the civil magistrates refrain from interfering in matters of religion was widespread among members of the separatist groups in England. During the army debates held at Whitehall in 1648, one of them declared: "No man or Magistrate on the earth hath power to meddle in these cases." A Leveller pamphlet written in the following year set out the same doctrine that the First Amendment would eventually proclaim for Americans:

> [W]e do not impower or entrust our said representatives to... compell by penalties or otherwise any person to any thing in or about matters of faith, Religion or Gods worship or to restrain any person from the profession of his faith, or exercise of his Religion according to his conscience...

Another strand of medieval argumentation that underwent radical development in the early modern era concerned the authority of the individual conscience. In the middle of the seventeenth century, the prevailing view was still that religious disagreements sprang "from malice, rooted in sin.. But by then alternative opinions were also being expressed. The Latitudinarian Anglican, Chillingworth, declared in 1638: "An honest man, a true lover of God, and of his truth... may embrace errour for truth". In the subsequent years of civil war it became increasingly difficult for men of good will and good sense to believe that their neighbours, sometimes men they had fought with side by side in a common cause, were really inspired by active malice to do the work of the devil because, of a disagreement about some obscure point of theology. Yet this belief in the malice of the dissenter had been the essential basis of the medieval abhorrence of heresy. When differences of religious opinion could be, seen as effects of intellectual error rather than of perverted will, the way was open to reconsider the proper attitude to a mistaken conscience. William Walwyn took up the text "Whatever is not of faith is sin," the same text that medieval authors had used to defend the primacy of conscience, but arrived at a conclusion that no medieval theologian had -reached: "Every man ought to have Liberty of Conscience of what Opinion so ever." Walwyn argued that a person's conscience could be directed only by his own individual reason. A person could not be compelled to believe as true something that reason and conscience told him was false. If, under compulsion, he acted against his conscience, fie sinned; but, and this was the new twist to the argument, the one who compelled him was a party to the sin and was acting like a tyrant. This became a common argument among those who defended freedom of conscience. Even an extreme royalist like Michael Hudson argued that a magistrate who compelled a man to act against his conscience forced him to commit the sin of hypocrisy, and that the magistrate himself was guilty of "sacrilegious intrusion upon those sacred prerogatives which God hath preserved unto himself." The Anglican divine Jeremy Taylor argued at length that a person who followed an erring conscience did not sin in doing so and, again, concluded with a plea for religious freedom: "If God will not be angry at men for being invincibly deceived, why should men be angry one at another?" Sometimes the forcing of a person's conscience was compared to physical rape; in the pungent language of Roger Williams it was "spiritual and sole rape."

The final outcome of all the new argument about conscience was fusion of the new ideal of religious liberty with the older doctrine of natural rights. Freedom of conscience came to be seen as one of the natural rights of man, guaranteed by natural law and discernable by the "light of reason" or "light of nature." The parliamentary leader, Hen Vane, for instance, asserted that freedom of religion could be claimed "upon the grounds of natural right." Roger Williams has also been called an extreme exponent of natural rights because of his all-embracing argument for freedom of conscience, but this seems to be a misunderstanding of his position. Williams ever used the language of natural rights. William Penn, however, did so, and with "classic clarity," according to Searle Bates. Penn wrote: "I ever understood an impartial liberty of conscience to be the natural right of all men... I argued that the people did not and could not give up this natural right any government formed by the original contract that first established a political society. Hence, subsequently, government could have no law power to invade this right of the individual. As one might expect, in constitution of Pennsylvania in due course echoed the words of founder and proclaimed "a natural and unalienable right" to freedom of worship. As a Quaker, Penn stood outside the mainstream of the religious thought of his age, but his eminently respectable contemporary Bishop Burnet, expressed a similar view: "I have long looked on liberty of conscience as one of the rights of human nature, antecedent to society, which no man could give up.... "Going back to the roots of Christian tradition Burnet also undertook a translation of Lactantius and, in preface to it, again argued for toleration. John Locke, too, in his influential Letter Concerning Toleration, wrote that "liberty of conscience is every man's natural right." Outside England, Pierre Bayle defended the rights of conscience and Spinoza drew on his own idiosyncratic doctrine of natural rights in asserting an inalienable right to freedom of religion.

By the end of the seventeenth century, reasonably adequate theories of religious rights had been formulated. Implementing them took much longer. Persecution became more sporadic in the eighteenth century, but it was not until the liberal revolutions of the nineteenth century that freedom of religion became widely established in the constitutions of Western states and not until the twentieth century that the major Christian churches proclaimed religious rights as an essential feature of the Christian faith itself.

Any thoughtful person who surveys the human rights scene around the globe today cannot help but notice how central is the religious dimension. Scholars in the Western world and, no doubt, many of their colleagues elsewhere, have good reason to rub their eyes in wonder over this central position of religious concerns. At least since the eighteenth-century Enlightenment in Europe and the Americas, through the course of the modern experience, the situation was different. It became almost a matter of reflex for observers from the academic, literary, and diplomatic worlds to expect religion to diminish in significance, if not disappear altogether from many public spheres.

A visit to the mental attic of historical impressions that most of us carry around would reinforce a single impression. It was consistently assumed that as Enlightenment reason and science spread, something else must decline. That something included the sense of the sacred and the transcendent and the institutions of "superstition and priestcraft." Religion, in most of its forms, would lose significance and power. If religion had ever represented interests involving the case for human rights, or if it had ever motivated people to seek such rights and the case for most religions having done so was frail no longer would this be the circumstance. Philosophy, anthropology, and politics would provide the new language for rights.

Furthermore, it was assumed in most academic circles that whatever of religion survived would be of a genial, tolerant, philosophically-enlightened sort. This meant that faith would not be a motor for dissent against establishment, a bond between people, who suffered deprivation of rights, or an element in the assurance of rights.

All those dreams of the Enlightenment, not easy to isolate in doctimentation because of their protean reach but pervasive in the West in any case, have been replaced by realistic scenes of a very different character. The monstrous totalitarian systems of the twentieth century, be they Fascist, Nazi, Communist, Maoist, or whatever, set out to suppress rights, beginning with those of religious people. Yet the systems and structures of Fascism, Nazism, Communism, and in many ideological respects Maoisrn, have imploded and are shattered. Their progenitors have been exposed and repudiated, their strategies have been seen to have failed, and their repressions to have been finally found ineffective.

What has outlasted these inventions have been the voices of religions. Often these appeared in the form of small and despised sects, whose adherents kept insisting on their own rights through all the years of oppression until at last they prevailed. Also outlasting the anti-spiritual ideologies have seen some religious voices that present rationales for assuring rights not only of adherents of a single group in question but also, beyond it, of other-believers, nonbelievers, and victims of repression in general.

Such a surprising change in ethos and turn in world affairs demands and deserves examination, an examination that thematically unifies the chapters in this collection. The logic of their three-part sequence is clear and manifest.

First, a set of scholars has laid a ground work by

engaging in historical and theological inquiries that will help provide a different accounting of rights than that which was part of reflexive thought and scholarly instinct for so long. None of the authors in this section writes in an uncritical or triumphalist tone about the past contribution of religious thought and action to the talk about rights or to the acts of helping assure human rights. These scholars are all aware of the sorry record of religion when it was legally established, as was characteristically the case. They know that religious leaders were often those who repressed rights, and that believers were often apathetic about making the case for these, and were frequently submissive to oppressive authorities.

On the other hand, these scholars help disinter long obscured facts and understandings. They demonstrate that many religious expressions have, been supportive of human rights. Quite naturally, many of these were expressly religious rights. One expects this to be the case, as much as one expects lawyers to examine legal rights, journalists and academics to defend the liberty of the press and academic freedom, or philosophers to explore freedom to propagate in public what they had been thinking. Yet to those who study these cases it becomes clear that just as religions freedom is in many ways the first freedom, so religious rights are the primary rights, and that they imply and produce corollaries from far beyond religious realms. Protect religious beliefs, exercises, and organizations, they observe with some consistency, and you are likely to be ex tending other rights further.

A second group of essayists looks at the "rights structure" of religions communities and traditions. If it is rather difficult to relocate ideas that generate religious support for religious and other rights, as the first group of scholars has done, it is very simple to examine the record, especially the record of "unfinished business." However well-intended the religious may be, and however bold their talk of concern for rights, their leaders have often been quite selective in choices of their ways to put their language of defense to work. Ancient texts, long traditions, and perduring interests of the powerful to retain power has led and often leads leadership to fail to provide this "rights structure" in ways that will assure rights to the whole community. Historically three groups have apparently suffered most, or at least their sufferings are most vivid in the consciousness of our contemporaries. These include women, who have often been overlooked or even trampled on in many traditions marked by male religious authority. Second are children, who may be victims of parental and other adult deprivations or rights, Then come dissenters and dissidents, who trouble religious and other authorities. A study of the records in all three cases may be a contribution to the enlargement of human rights concern on the part of the religious.

A third group of scholars deals with inconsistency, anomaly, or shortsightedness on the part of religious leadership. Urgent as these leaders may be in their expressions of the religious rights of their own group, and insistent as they can be about the validity of these and the hearing that they deserve, they are not always consistent. They want their own rights, but they are not always on the front lines in conflicts whose outcome is to be the assurance of rights for others. Even more problematic is the record of people who hold power in religions and often go out of their way to re strict the rights of many in their own believing communities and traditions. One must ask whether there is something distinctive about religion that leads to such contradictory behavior or shortsightedness. Is failure to assure rights on this front typical of behavior in other spheres of life as well, or is it especially obvious when religious agents speak in favor of rights but often act like their secular counterparts in simply trying to hold power and limit the rights of others?

An introductory thesis might serve readers well as they follow the logic of the sequence of essays here. I shall argue that among all the other ways to explore the situation of rights, one has been neglected but, if re covered, it should contribute to understanding and action. This is what we might call a religious approach to discussion of religious human rights. However we may define "religion" or "religious"—issues of definition cannot be fully addressed on these pages—one can argue a case for such an approach at the outset and, sustain the argument to the end. This argument centers on the notion that there are religious dimensions to struggles over religious human rights, and that religious studies In their many forms can illumine the inquiry.

Such a proposal and understanding does not require every religious phenomenon to be the subject of reductionism, as currently is often the case. When reductionism is privileged, religious issues simply and quickly get translated to psychological, anthropological, sociological, or economic and political factors. The quest for religious human rights in Such cases is reduced to "nothing but." This reduction would lead to a situation in which when one hears the voice of the religious there is a temptation to say, "this concern for religious rights is nothing but a power move by dissenters who want to be victorious insiders." Or "this talk about rights by the religious amounts to nothing but their psychological impulses to find identity." Or "they want a better economic deal for their class, and make their way by invoking religious claims."

Religious approaches would find scholars and

diplomats suspending disbelief in the presence of homo religious. They would take seriously the claims of individuals and groups to be grounded in "ultimate concern," and see their individual and group identity issuing from response to myths and symbols, rites and ceremonies, metaphysical claims and behavioral correlates of that concern.

When religions oppress the religious

A different version of the thesis instead leads one to contend that a religious problem needs a religious address. For examples of where this subject comes up, here is a catalog:

> A Catholic theologian complains that the freedom that is claimed to be a possession or quality of Catholicism is not extended to someone like that theologian herself when and insofar as she calls into question any aspect of churchly authority. Her freedoms to engage in such inquiry are denied, and she is ostracized if not actually driven from employment by any institution connected with the church.

A religions organization does not respect the rights of its employees to bargain collectively and form unions, even while its leaders are occupied with advocacy for such unionizing and bargaining rights in other spheres of employment. Where, one asks, is the consistency?

A teacher in a church-related college is threatened with loss of tenure, shunned, and virtually or actually driven out because academic rights are always secondary to religious claims as these are being guarded and professed by the momentarily-in-power leaders of that religion who support and represent the authority but never freedom in such a college.

The child of Christian Scientists, Jehovah's Witnesses, or one or an other of the small "healing sects" is deprived of the rights to life and health, thanks to the parental obedience to churchly teaching that is disrespectful of such rights—and the child needlessly dies. A woman in a strict Jewish or Muslim group is victimized by her husband, by male authority, or the executors of rites and ceremonies of passage. She has nowhere to escape and no way to find an advocate who will help her enjoy rights of protest against such ceremonies and deprivations. Where are her rights?

A couple in Israel refuses to recognize the religious authority of the Orthodox rabbis who are established in power in an otherwise secular state, and has to leave Israel for the marriage to be performed. A novelist who writes experimentally and takes imaginative risks to the point that his or her work is perceived as heresy or blasphemy is the victim of a *fatwa*, becomes a marked person, and has to hide in exile in order to enjoy the primal human right of "life," of getting to stay alive when religious authority would do the killing.

A Pakistani woman is raped by her employer. When her father would prosecute her case, she learns with him that while the rapist, if found guilty, might suffer some penalty, that she would be put to death for adultery according to the legal prescriptions of her religion in her culture—and she has nowhere else to go to enjoy the right to stay alive. Here, as elsewhere, it is the religion itself that produces the need for defenders of religious freedom.

Members of religious groups in numbers of nations are virtually, bound by authority so that they cannot challenge their own communities' prohibitions against birth control at United Nations conferences on the subject.

Native Americans get reservated, and few non-Indians pay attention to their needs, including their need to defend rights to practice tribal rites of a sacred character and to do this apart from the superimposition of the will of their conquerors and reservators.

In all these frequent and typical kinds of cases, religious rights are issue within traditions where many claim that a language and a polity exist to help assure rights.

A special challenge presents itself in all such cases when religions problems suggest religious addresses, if not always solutions. An array of these present themselves at once.

For beginnings, one asks: What business does one religion or set of religious leaders have intruding on the religious practices of another group? When is such intrusion appropriate and when is it not? What rights do religionists have to protect themselves from efforts to convert them, especially when this is done by the use of instruments of power or deception? What rights do people have to impose their views on those who practice rites that are offensive to others? A vivid example is female circumcision. Many cultural relativists who fight for the right of other religions simply to be themselves find that there are boundaries beyond which such defense will not go. Thus they find religiously legitimated practices like female circumcision offensive and, on grounds alien to the practitioners of such a rite, want it stopped. Closer to home: it must be asked: Were the rights of religious groups unprotected and misunderstood when the United States government moved against the Branch Davidians in Waco, Texas?

Such questions do not permit easy answers. They do show that understandings of what religion is or what religions are about are important for addressing issues of law or even of preference and taste. An old saying has it that "it takes a thief to catch a thief." It may take a religious scholar or jurist of religious sensibilities to throw special light on the is sue of what is at stake in the sensibilities of other religionists. Such a per son may not produce satisfying or sufficient addresses to the problem of rights, but he or she may throw welcome light on the subjects when they are at issue.

A second, counterpart question introduces a cautionary note: Might it not be that a religious inquiry or understanding could actually complicate rights talk? Maybe the secularist, tone deaf to or opposed to the claims of any and all religion, can be a safeguard. Not without reason did the partisans of Enlightenment toleration argue that there was a special calling for those who sought universal patterns of reasoning to defend rights across cultural and sectarian boundaries. So the question is in place: Might not religious impulses only make matters worse when rights are being suppressed?

Third, one is prompted to ask, what is it about religion that leads partisans to adduce it with such passion and self-assurance on all sides in discussions of rights, including religious rights? Certainly some answers to that question would include the fact that most religions regard them selves as rooted in the transcendent, the supra-mundane, the extraordinary realms of existence. Since that is the case, when they speak up, in gambling terms, they "raise the stakes" over talk about rights in the mundane and ordinary spheres. Thus, a person or community claims an experience of the sacred, one that induces awe. Consequently, a communal or social expression takes form, in order to help fortify those who experience a hierophany and to help inspire them to share knowledge of it. Such an experience is always empowering; it authorizes action toward various outcomes, some of them murderous against those who are not moved by the originating vision, or who oppose its propagation.

These experiences of the sacred, these responses to revelation or enlightenment, do not always match each other across the boundaries in other religions. Thus in interfaith dialogue on human rights, one might hear the monotheist make a case. Only when the one God does the revealing and when this God speaks, insisting that the human is made in the divine image and has consequent rights, can there be a realization of rights. Well and good for fellow monotheists who worship the same God. But their witness is quickly countered by the Buddhist who believes that it is precisely the presence of *theos*, of God, that limits rights. The question from the dialogue partner then comes: What must the Jew or Muslim or Christian "give up" to advance dialogue about rights and rights them selves? For a beginning sample, says the Buddhist, dogma and monotheism must go. Clearly, when sincere but opposing voices like these are heard, a new realism is manifest in discussions. The interests "thicken" and grow more complex.

Fourth, the introduction of specifically religious voices into religious and other rights talk makes the speakers and what they say both less compre-hensible to outsiders and more vivid and satisfying to insiders in the particular traditions and communities. People of various faith communities live in and develop what phenomenologist Alfred Schutz calls different "universes of discourse." These might include universes related to race, ethnicity, tribe, gender, class, culture, aesthetics, or national experience. Religious experience connected with any of these raises everything to a new plane of complication or to a new depth of understanding. In either case, faith and practices associated with it cannot be ignored.

One further must deal with the disparity of understandings within each religious community, or with the conflict resulting from the disparities. Thus family quarrels within religions often lead to suppression of rights. Islamic fundamentalist groups, by insisting on literal application of Shari'a, religious law, often embarrass, inconvenience, and thwart more moderate Muslim leaders and citizens, for example, in the matter of the rights of women. The winners and losers in the Southern Baptist Convention or Missouri Synod Lutheran fights make appeals to the same primal texts and long elaborative traditions. But their interpretations vary, and the winners find the losers *de trop* and expel them from responsible positions or respectability within the denomination. Both Pope John Paul II and dissenting theologians appeal to biblical texts, but the Pope holds the power to take away license to teach priests if he disagrees with the theologians, whose resort to arguments for academic freedom and the accuracy of their interpretations of the Catholic tradition go unheeded and are ineffectual in the power situation.

A sixth creative complication when one introduces religious concerns to rights talk comes when a mediator seeks some sort of common ground. This is done se, that there can be meaningful conversation across the boundaries of these separate universes of discourse or family conflicts. The cultural absolutist has it easy: my religion is the only right one, the only one that assures and deserves rights; others are all wrong. They have no rights, or at least can make no compelling case for expressing and defending them.

The cultural relativist seems to have an equal advantage, though probably at the expense of any satisfactory outcome when there is conflict. Such a relativist says that anthropologists can always find some where, in some tribe or communion, a religiously-certified practice that violates any conception of common grounding, natural law, or whatever. This is the case with human rights as with everything else.

In this context, a basic dispute surfaces in every kind of cross-cultural conclave. This has to do with whether rights belong to the individual or to the community. In many inquiries, the pro-community voices often speak up in terms that are disturbing to advocates of individual rights. Thus one hears: "Human rights are a product of modern, post-Enlightenment, liberal, secular humanism. This is a religiously alienating humanism because it elevates the individual to the point that the group is forgotten"—yet it is precisely the group that makes the strongest religious claims. Conversation across the boundaries of debate over "rights of individuals over groups" versus "rights of groups" is always more difficult. This is especially the case when either side is or both sides are eager to ground their positions and claims in religious revelation or tradition.

Given complications like these and the many more that one can easily imagine, there is good reason to ask a basic question about the thesis that a religious problem needs a religious address. If religion is so complicating, so difficult, why deal with it? Why not be content with casual recourse or willful reversion to non or antireligious arguments derived from Enlightenment era understandings of secular reasoning? If religion brings as much heat as light, why not extinguish it, or at least bracket it in polite discourse? At least, the practice of using such language in 1945 and 1948 helped the United Nations come to sufficient consensus or sufficient assertion of persuasive power that there could even be a UN Charter. Such an approach made it possible for the nations to speak of "faith in fundamental human rights" and to produce a Universal Declaration of Human Rights. On its grounds, the UN could produce contentions like these: "Everyone has the right to education," and education should pro mote "understanding, tolerance and friendship among all nations, racial or religious groups. . . . "

It is often asked, on credible grounds, whether in today's religiously expressive world such lines could be written and forwarded with any hope of approval. Would Islamic, Jewish, Christian, Sikh, Hindu, and other fundamentalists and their spiritual kin be able to argue their cases on such grounds of shared "faith" and "understanding?" Hardly. Then, the question reoccurs: Why introduce language that reflects an awareness that there are millions of such voices today, voices of people who would not accept the Declaration language? Why not leave well enough from 1945 and 1948 alone? Why not hope that no one who notices the shifts in presuppositions within the international community, since then not acquire power to upset the UN? Again, why bring up religion?

The realist has answers ready: The world community deals with religion because it is there and will not go away. If some forms of faith and institutions have dwindled, cooled, or even disappeared in the northern spiritual ice belt, there are temperate and tropical zones of spirituality where religion prospers. There it is the main motivator in the discussion of rights or their limits. The scholar or the adjudicator deals with religion because its professor claims that its impulses have derived from the vertical dimensions of experience. They issue from God or the heavens before respondents connect them with the horizontal elements. On that secondary plane, humans interact with each other both within and beyond the boundaries of religious communities. Because of their transcendent and absolute source, these are seen as nonnegotiable.

Some assets of religion in the field of human rights

To write as we have here is to deal one-sidedly with religion, and it is reassuring to note that many authors in this book and its sequel have much to say compensatorily, on the assets, not the liabilities, of religions advocacies. It is easy to portray the complications and neglect to mention the solaces and aids that religion can and does bring. Thus it is tempting for one to be passive in the face of the manifest differences among and the intractable oppositions of many religions to each other and of some or all citizens against the nonreligious. Yet in practice, the boundaries between faith communities or those who differ within them are not always so impermeable as here suggested. Potential alliances of elements from differing communities are not always simply so out of range and reach as militants and dogmatists often suggest. Especially in free and thus pluralist republics, there are boundary-crossings of many sorts on diverse occasions. One might here speak of a crisscrossing of interests, goals, affiances.

To illustrate from North America: When colonial America was turning into the national United States, the issue of religious rights was prime. Political and philosophical leaders like George Washington and Patrick Henry, inspired by the God of Reason and Nature in the courts of the American Enlightenment, squared off against other Enlightenment advocates like Thomas Jefferson and lames Madison. They debated whether any trace of religious establishment should survive and asked whether there would be ample religious human rights if it did. Both sets of founders used arguments grounded in witness to the God of Reason or Reason itself.

On the other hand and at the same time, the Protestant religious community was also divided among advocates of vestigial religions establishment and the voice of protest. Thus a dissenter like Elder John Leland, who believed in all the orthodox Protestant stories of salvation effected through Jesus, made profound practical as well as emotional common cause with Thomas jefferson, who emphatically did not share that basis of belief. Both Enlightened and dissenting Christian advocates were strengthened in their pro-human rights stance by their religions outlook. Both used the depth of their own commitments to what they believed as an instrument for comprehending why the other found so much to be at stake and fought so vigorously for these rights.

If a religious problem needs a religious address and if religion does not seem to be disappearing globally or nationally, it is understandable that citizens and believers among them, would want to peer into the future in order to prepare themselves for debate, action, and further coin prehension. Here as elsewhere, no single profile presents itself under the simple category "religion," but a new range of problems comes into view to demand attention.

Thus, the observer reckons with the fact that historically the issue of human rights in religion has not been perceived as being clearly anticipated or enjoined in ancient sacred texts. The writers of these texts, in response to revelation or transcendent experience, had what to them were wider, deeper, and longer interests. For example, they would have de scribed themselves as having been busy saving souls and not setting up government or argument. When supporting such interests they may of ten have obscured or neglected human rights or even worked against realizing them, to the glory of the God of authority.

Second, religious cultures evolve, just as the ancient texts are rarely rich in the use of explicit rights language, so they do not freeze traditions, even those that claim to be frozen in literalist interpretations. They all belong to history, and they experience inevitable cultural change. An ex ample that courses along in the background as a figurative stream in this essay has been the regionalist but not irreligious Enlightenment as experienced and expressed in the European and American contexts and followed agents of both, their cultural offspring. On the soil of Christendom at a particular moment there developed what Crane Brinton called a new religion, an invention called the Enlightenment, with a big "E." Its advocates spoke of human rights in new terms. Most religious groups, whether they immediately supported the new talk or were dragged screaming into the sphere that it defined and illuminated, soon found it congenial and began to make claims that promoting such rights was their impulse all along. Hannah Arendt, among many others, noted how almost all the religions liked to claim that they were present at the creation of such rights-frameworks. She politely suggested, in effect, that such religious spokespersons might at least send a card of thanks to modernity, to the Enlightenment, for having led them to the delayed—fifteen century late!—discovery of the latent prohuman rights, proreligious rights, ele. ments in their treasury.

In on Revolution, Arendt deals almost ironically with this subject:

> A few words need still be said about the not infrequent claims that all modern revolutions are essentially Christian in origin, and this even when their professed faith is atheism.... Secularization, the separation of religion from politics and the rise of a secular realm with a dignity of its own, is certainly a crucial factor in the phenomenon of [democratic] revolution.... The fact is that no revolution was ever made in the name of Christianity that no revolution was ever made in the name of Christianity prior to the modern age, so that the best one can say in favor of this theory is that it needed modernity to liberate the revolutionary germs of the Christian faith, which obviously is begging the question.

Thus some have discovered what Glen Tinder has spoken of as a stress on "the exalted individual" within a faith like Christianity because there exist a prime belief in human creation "in the image of God" and the sharing of a human nature with Jesus Christ, who is God "incarnate" in human form. Certainly, that exalted individual, who was often obscured when the human was described only in "total depravity" terms, possessed rights that Christian faith had to assure, it was subsequently and effectively argued in many circles. The exalted individual might indeed belong to the believing community, but his or her individual rights in the West were regarded as being prior to the collective or communal rights that were more appropriately understood as prime with religious tribal communities.

Religious revelation, community, and expression, as these "thickened" discourse about rights, could not solve arguments about them. Religion, it has been argued in the twentieth century as it was by people like James Madison and Baptist elder and rights advocate John Leland in the eighteenth century, can help assure the rights of others. This assurance, say some advocates, need not result because of the obscuring or muting of religious concerns. It is not necessary to reduce them to only highly noncommittal, low-conviction, "tolerant" forms of faith in order to make them ready to be brought to bear on the issue. Indeed, properly understood and cultivated, it might well yet turn out to be the case that it is now often the religions of deep commitment and high conviction that are of greatest aid. In that case, it is not the corrupted heir of eighteenth-century Enlightenment philosophy that best promotes tolerance by arguing that all beliefs have the same claims and quality all others.

In our deliberations on the reciprocal relationships of religion and human rights, one key issue is the question of whether there are any common ethical standards, especially in an emerging global society where multiple religions, the sources and sustainers of morality in most cultures, encounter both each other and a variety of doubts about the place of religion in the common life. On the one hand, the concept of human rights stands in "fie modern world as a set of universalistic ethical norms that state ideals for all human societies. They identify first principles and goals by which the community of nations may legitimate (or delegitimate) various legal systems or cultural practices (including religious ones, where religions are viewed as part of a culture), and limit the use of state power against persons and groups.

On the other hand, the very idea of universalistic norms is viewed by some as nothing more than the imposition of some particular set of religio-cultural values on the other peoples of the world. That is due to the fact that in most of human history and in much of the world still today, ethical norms are rooted in religious orientations that seldom embrace human rights except insofar as they advance the particular religion. The idea of ethical principles standing beyond religions, cultures, and societies, and able to evaluate and alter them, is to many a strange and hostile notion. Such an understanding of ethics requires that we tie thought and faith together in a philosophical theology, which is able to defend itself in public discourse, critically evaluate the relative adequacy of various religions on key questions, and provide the deep guidance system for complex societies and cultures.

What an irony we face. Modern articulations of human rights were born out of the attempt to constrain the great barbarisms of the twentieth century. In this context, ancient insights, which had been obscured or suppressed, were retrieved and made the basis for what is today called human rights. For the most part, the surge of interest in human rights that occurred after

World War II turned to the formulations of human rights and democracy that grew out of the Enlightenment. However, it was only sometimes noted that these developments were themselves rooted in previously established theological assumptions that derive from antiquity—which the Enlightenment had claimed to overcome. While the great thinkers of the Enlightenment were familiar with the ancient sources, their heirs were not. Hence, the interpretations of human rights that have come to triumph in the West are both derived from and opposed to their deeper religious roots. They nearly always ignore the greatest contribution of faith to human rights: namely, that some religious positions in alliance with selected philosophical traditions developed a transcendental view of the world and began to conceive of it as a whole, and thus to recognize that there is a perspective which is beyond the time and space, culture and society, religion and morality which we inhabit when we imagine the unity. If we grasp something of this perspective, or are grasped by it, we think and experience theologically, and see the nature of justice more clearly, for we see it sub species aeternitatis.

If the world is a unity, and we can conceive of if as a whole-this, of course, means that we transcend it in some degree and do not simply live within it, trapped by its horizons-then we begin to suspect that it is governed by a unified moral law, even though the customs and habits of many people in the world and their ways of modelling the whole differ. Further, these customs, habits, and models can be altered according to a more ultimate and reliable pattern. The most pertinent developments of modernity, in this view, have to do with the recovery, radicalization, propagation, and relative institutionalization of an ethical vision of this sort. The late twentieth century has been the period in which these principles have become spread throughout the world. Human rights provisions are now built into the constitutions of more peoples than any previous civilization could have imagined, and are among the decisive criteria as to whether a religion, a culture, a regime, or a society should be honoured or altered, isolated or revolutionized.

However, this has also been the century in which we have faced dramatic challenges to these ideas. These challenges have taken and continue to take many forms—most notably the quests for the solidarity of a particular community against such universal and transcendental claims. Indeed, the greatest struggles of the twentieth century are of this order one against the pagan anti-modernism of Hitlerian-Fascist National Socialism, another against the secularist hyper-modernism of Marxist Leninist Proletarian Socialism. Each manifested itself in massive political military movements that became the chief threats to human rights and to modernity in this century. Both have, in substantive measure, been defeated, although, like ail great terrors, they writhe in their bonds and threaten to reappear from their graves in new forms.

For instance, a direct challenge to human rights from these defeated forces appeared in new conspiracy of anti-modernists and hyper-modernists who, while having apparently abandoned the Nazism of Hitler's politics and Communism of Stalinist economics, now join the internal entrepreneurs of Asia's "liberalizing" economic policies and the business interests of the West who want access to Asia's cheap labour and vast markets to echo the defeated arguments. In 1993, China led a coalition of nations, including Indonesia, Vietnam, Burma, Syria, and Iran that posed concepts of national sovereignty and state-supported development against democracy and human rights, as stated in the "Bangkok Declaration," which became 'the basis for their postures in the U.N. conference on human rights in Vienna.

The triumph of these developments in the long run is unlikely, unless the fundamental conception of human rights itself begins to collapse. The maledictive of political or economic gain may be decisive in many matters of indeterminate policy, but the deeper theological and ethical influences shape determinate matters of polity, and over time polity guides, leavens, and sets boundaries for policy. The more profound threat to the idea of human rights as a determinate of polity, thus, is an attack from both it detractors and, unwittingly, from many of its defenders.

A number of contemporary philosophers, social theorists, and religious thinkers of note have begun to doubt that there are such things a human rights, or have attempted to defend them in such terms as to make them impossible to sustain. In perhaps the most famous absolutist denial of the validity of human rights, one of the premier philosophers of our day, Alasdair Maclntyre, wrote that the concept has no meaning at, all:

> [T]he truth is plain: there are no such rights, and belief in them is one with belief in witches and unicorns.... The best reason for asserting so bluntly that there are no such rights is [the same]... reason for asserting that there are no witches.... [E]very attempt to give good reasons for believing that there are such rights has failed.... Natural or human rights... are fictions.

Although MacIntyre has been discerningly criticized, he is not alone. Leo Strauss, the widely regarded political philosopher who taught at Chicago for many years, has convinced a generation of young minds to become "neo-conservative" on the grounds that the classical ethical notion of natural rights (*physis*) and the proper exercise of virtue especially of "prudence" (*phronesis*) are subverted by this modern ideology of "rights.

On the other side of the ideological spectrum, a major attempt to defend human rights from a "liberal" point of view has been advanced by Rhoda E. Howard and Jack Donnelly. They use sociological and anthropological theory to argue that human rights involve the affirmation of the autonomy and equality of every individual, in contrast to all the tribalisms, feudalisms, socialisms, communisms, and Communitarianisms, old and new, that view the individual as a part of a whole. They argue that the idea of rights "is rooted in structural changes that began to emerge in late medieval and early modern Europe, gained particular force in the eighteenth and nineteenth centuries, and today are increasingly the norm throughout the world. The creation of the private individual separate from society is closely linked to the rise of a new, more complex division of labour, the resulting changes in class structure... and [thus] a new vision of the individual's relationship to God, society and the state.

Leaving aside historical questions as to whether Abraham, Moses, Sara, Ruth, Jeremiah, Amos, Jesus, and Paul, or for that matter, Cleopatra, Socrates, Plato, Aristotle, Confucius, or the Buddha were in any serious sense individuals, we do not view human rights as an imaginative literary or political fiction on the order of unicorns. Instead, we view ethical norms such as human rights as the cultural by-products of socio-evolutionary processes. Thus, human rights (and the persons and groups to which they apply) are seen to be an historical artifact, pertinent only insofar as social conditions stand at a particular stage of development, and subject to disappearance if those conditions do not obtain or eventually pass away. These philosophical and sociological views would be a great comfort to those in closed societies who use torture as a policy of governance or allow slave labour, for they can claim that they are at a particular stage of development. And neither are these scholars alone. Literally hundreds of social commentators and clergy share this understanding of morality, even if they read the "signs of the times" of societal evolution differently.

What is missing in these philosophical and sociological views is an account of why such matters as human rights, which cannot be derived from the empirical analysis of the world, prudentially or socio-historically, are plausible or why people should be committed to them, since it is empirically obvious that human rights are violated often and not everyone believes in them. Two things are required for a full analysis: (1) a social hermeneutical theory of how such things come into consciousness- a matter that shall take us into questions of religion and social theory; and (2-1) a way of evaluating which kinds of normative, but non-empirical, matters like human rights might be valid-a matter that requires theology.

This is not to suggest that we can abandon all philosophy and social theory. Some forms of them can be extremely useful when they are stabilized or undergirded by a theological perspective-a perspective that they can help analyse, but which they can neither generate nor surpass. An historically and cross-culturally comparative view of these questions suggests that ideas of human dignity, human rights, and the great liberties of speech and association derive from certain kinds of religious views, indeed, a distinct set of religious views developed in dialogue with key strands of philosophy and particular theories of social life that are different from, and in fact contended against, positions analogous to the ones we have just noted. In fact, it is quite likely that human rights are based on nothing less than decisive theological convictions, distinct from but incorporating and utilizing some of the best insights of philosophy and social theory.

The challenges to human rights today, thus, are more subtle than the threats of Nazism and of Communism, for what we face is not likely to be overcome so quickly as these rose and fell-in a mere century or so The three great challenges for human rights in the next century are these (1) the decay of philosophy, and the consequent suspicion of any onto-theological account of how things are; (2) the attempt to establish normative principles for civil society on the basis of social description alone—the sadly unfulfilled promise of the social sciences; and (3) the power of resurgent, ancient religions, particularly Islam and Hinduism, which have a normative metaphysical-moral vision and which have shown their capacity to organize complex and vast civilizations over long periods of time. In their present forms, it is doubtful that any one of these three car sustain the idea of human rights in the long run--although it may turn out that Islam and Hinduism, or at least key strands of them, like key strands of Christianity critically refined by theology, will come closer than philosophy and sociology insofar as these try to remain detached from religion and theology. To be sure, all of these are potential companions of the kind of ethic that could sustain human rights, if and when they develop a "public theology" in the sense that they seek to discern, under God, the moral and spiritual architecture whereby just and humane civilizations can be constructed. But it is also the case that if any one of them should become the dominant view without substantial reform, human rights are likely to be subordinated or lost.

As this volume and its sequel testify, the place of

religion in human rights discussions is an area of considerable debate, John Witte has rightly argued that the study of this interaction has been underway for a long time, and that the echoes of the older debates continue to shape us in many ways. But a new interest has erupted since World War II, and however much it presumes the older discussions, it rarely explicitly refers to them. Instead, the discussion has focused domestically on the removal of discrimination based on sex, race, and culture,... the enhancement of freedoms of speech, press, and association.... [and] the safeguarding of criminal and cultural rights." Similarly, the international debate has centered on the "democratic/socialist" polarity, with each. It tempting to show that it can best provide for "the eradication of sexual, cultural, and ethnic discrimination" and economic injustice. And, throughout this recent period, the place of religion in human rights has been relatively muted, except that religion became one item on the list of sociocultural factors to be protected, and the hegemony of any one religion became something to be feared.

The remarkable resurgence of the question of religion in relation to human rights over the past few years, however, has many causes. Perhaps the most profound cause is that societies and souls cannot flourish without a deep substratum of awareness about the moral basis of life, a substratum that generally does not occur without a religious orientation. This is not to say that all religious orientations are good or equal or supportive of human rights, 'They are not; some religions are quite destructive of all that human rights stands for, and the very intensity and potency of religion makes the destructiveness all the more vicious. It therefore makes a good deal of difference what sort of religion is at hand. But the key point here is that such intensity and potency has at times been supportive and even generative of human rights, and that the commitment to a moral substratum which can guide the common life seems to appear most strongly in those societies informed by certain kinds of religious influence, and to be least vigorous in those societies shaped by other religious traditions or by anti-religion. We have a situation, thus, in which the freedom and vitality of religion at one level appears to depend on human rights, but in which the intensity and viability of human rights in society at another level seems to depend on the extent of certain kinds of religious influence. In the vast literature on religion and human rights, this second aspect is the least discussed and often the most superficially treated.

Although there is considerable evidence that human rights are deeply and fundamentally dependent on religion and specifically on certain kinds of theological issues, it is equally clear that not all are convinced of this rather substantive point. Indeed, it is probable that for human rights to be recognized and sustained in the common life, two things are necessary: a theological understanding of normative reality, and a set of concrete institutional channels to actualize these normative visions in society and make them accessible in a civilization.

The main contentions of this chapter are (1) that the very idea of human rights is rooted in a theological ethic; and (2) that this ethic needs to be defended from contemporary challenges-philosophical, sociological, and religious-in order that, as an ethical norm, human rights may more fully be actualized in societies, and so that philosophy, social theory, and religion supportive of human rights may flourish among all peoples. The challenges to human rights are based upon doubts about the nature of theology as well as the confusion between confessionalism and theology. Religion is often treated as a strictly personal, cultural, or historical experience, and theology is understood to be its formal, dogmatic articulation. Thus, to root human rights in religion or theology is seen as a form of personal, cultural, or historical imperialism. Further, since we have come to wider awareness of the variety of religions in the world, it is hard for some to imagine that not all the religions contribute equally to moral matters. Although the world religions have been around for centuries, they did not seem to many to be present as living options or necessarily related to human rights.

Yet historically, the evidence is rather clear, as Brian Tierney has, already suggested. The deep roots of human rights ideals are rooted nowhere else than in the biblical tradition, for it is here that we find the decisive unveiling of a perspective in which moral first principles demanding the respect for the neighbour are made known to humanity by a reality that is universal and absolute. This reality, which the Western traditions call "God," is neither a figment of human imagination, a projection of our personal needs or tribal consciousness, nor a product of human creativity. Nor is this God morally neutral. This is an ethical God, the source and norm of a kind of justice and righteousness and contends against what we often find as we look around the world. Richard Deats puts it this way:

> The universal implications of this faith in the righteous God, creator of the earth and all living things... [permeated] the life of Israel, expanding their faith to widened horizons of inclusiveness and compassion. "Am I my brother's keeper?" and "Who is my neighbour?" are questions that never ceased to stir the conscience of the people of God.... [T]he universality of this faith.... is to be a "light for all the peoples."

This heritage was applied to all the peoples of the world in the prophetic traditions, when the prophets protested the exploitation of the poor and weak, and demanded that the various nations, especially those who claimed to be most loyal to this God, must submit to a moral law not of their own making. Some things simply ought not be done by one human to another, even if they are approved or commanded by an impious political authority.

In this context, Christianity arose and radicalized the prophetic point of view, carried it into the Graeco-Roman world, and linked it to philosophical and jurisprudential theories that, on quite other grounds, also had begun to articulate a -notion of a universal normative moral order. This interaction of faith and philosophy created theology and ethics as basic modes of discourse to guide thought and action on the most universalistic bases Possible."

These developments remained a minority tradition for centuries, and were often suppressed by pagan tendencies, power interests, and forms of myth and magic that could not be said to be universalistic, moral, faithful, or philosophically sound. But periodically this tradition was retrieved and made central, to attempts to reform life, and to establish it on a more universalistic, more humane, and more godly foundation. This we can see in the revolutionary trans-formations of law and society so central to the history of the West, in the theological theories of "conciliarism" that anticipated and approximated constitutional democracy and especially in parts of the Reformation that influenced the modern formation of human rights.

However, it was periodically the case that precisely this tradition was distorted by both the ideological use of religion at the hands of political power to legitimate its interests, and the betrayal of the rational and ethical character of theology by religious leaders who made Christianity into a series of arbitrary dogmas to be accepted on blind faith, without intellectual justification, moral rigor, or a sense of what it meant to be "a for all peoples." When the wars of religion of early modern Europe combined these perversions, the heritage was discredited in the eyes of All sorts of post-Christian views of human moral a *priori*, self-evident truths and natural rights were developed to attempt to guide and strain political authority without religion, and to develop a cosmopolitan ethic that would allow the various obscurantist religions to hold their own dogmas-albeit only as private preferences. Theology, in-a public sense, was destroyed in favour of apolitical or pietistic fideism, on one side, and an ontologically free-floating rationality, on the other. The destruction was called Enlightenment. However, the Enlightenment col not carry the full load of what it attempted, and its rational fruits became instruments of oppression, even as it struggled to establish and maintain a sense of universal moral order. Its godless foundations could not bear the weight of all that the Enlightenment philosophers confidently placed upon them. The Enlightenment's initial success depended upon the deeper, but hidden, foundations which had been laid by theology, Apart from them, philosophy began to deconstruct—into romanticism, historicism, existentialism, and now postmodernism.

Our argument is not only that we need to get and keep our history straight, although that would be a very good idea. Our argument is a Is that it is quite possible for an idea that is generated out of one context to be found valid in another, and to become contextualized in forms of thought and life in ways that enhance possibilities within those adopted forms of thought and life that were only latently central to the new host This, of course, produces "revisionist" history in the secondary tradition as happened to Greek philosophy and Roman law when they were wedded to biblical insights to form a theology which surpassed these original sources. Our argument is, in brief, that today human rights can best be seen as a part of the process of the recognition of the validity of decisive ethical concepts that, while offered and made actual by a particular tradition, are recognizably valid for all people and are essentially true for the world. Human rights are a modern way of speaking about cross-cultural ethical concepts that actualize certain valid theological presuppositions and in turn legitimates constraints on what humans or states can do to each other, where theology is understood to be the critically examined and systematically stated interpretation of what humanity is sinful creatures not driven entirely by nature and nurture, that know we live under a God who establishes moral laws and ends and contexts of life we cannot attain alone.

Theology, in this view, is not merely the rationalized form of a social or cultural view legitimated by a privileged religion. It is also a necessary partner of philosophy and the social sciences, and a critic of religions, in clarifying, and establishing universal and valid ethical norms for an emerging global civilization. Theology tells us whether this or that religion, our own or someone else's, is valid or whether it ought to be challenged on the grounds of its truth or its justice. This hypothesis then bears within it an ironic implication: it suggests the likelihood of religious, philosophical, and social conflict, for not all religions are equally capable of developing or sustaining a theology that can generate a universalistic ethic of jurisprudential importance. Indeed, in its strongest form, this argument suggests that it is doubtful whether human rights can be sustained without a theology that has certain definable characteristics, which we will attempt to indicate.

Yet, as the threats of the anti-modernists on the right and the hyper-modernists on the left fade, increasingly frequent attacks are made upon the theological genealogy of human rights and the very possibility of anything being universal especially anything with normative content. A new surge of pragmatic anti-Enlightenment and anti-theological philosophy has attempted to deconstruct all aspects of culture, including language, with the reductive techniques of the social sciences, and to view the great world religions as evidence against the possibility of developing and sustaining a universalistic theological ethic. These deconstructive arguments suggest that both theology and modernity are to be faulted for trying to supply a basis for human rights, for they rest on strictly untenable universalistic claims.

In what follows, first consider aspects of these deconstructive philosophical arguments, and then we use a preliminary discussion of postmodern social theory as a segue into a consideration of Islam and Hinduism as interlocutors in the rights dialogue. We argue (1) that the postmodern case against universalistic theological principles is inconsistent and not convincing; (2) that certain postmodern social theories already realize this; and (3) that aspects of classical Hinduism and Islam can be enlisted as allies in the struggle for the global recognition of human rights, even if aspects of them, along with aspects of historical Christianity, also are judged to contain features which could potentially subvert human rights.

Postmodern philosophy and human rights

Philosophers since the Enlightenment have frequently argued that only human reasoning carried out as philosophy adequately grounds human rights, for religions are usually enemies of rights, unless they relegated to optional personal preference. Theology, in this view, is less passe for it is but the rationalization of fideist belief. The serious work of establishing ethical and political values is accomplished by philosophy. This view, it is widely acknowledged, is in considerable difficulty today, and it is doubted whether human reasoning carried out philosophy can justify anything, let alone human rights. Reason no longer speaks with the booming confidence of Archimedes, nor even in the conversational and receptive tones of Hermes. Both the "clear and distinct" arguments of epistemology and subtler shades of hermeneutics are thought to be maniacal ravings of the pompous predicament of Enlightenment reason. Modern philosophy here thought to be a kind of pretentious insanity, as was religion and theology.

Two thinkers represent this "postmodern" turn of mind with special clarity: Jean-Francois Lyotard and Richard Rorty. They believe that theoretical defence or justification of human rights is neither possible nor desirable. Yet they have both recently given lectures in the Oxford Amnesty Lecture Series, the funds of which are used to support Amnesi International and human rights. The ambiguity in Lyotard's and Rorty arguments is this: they are opposed to all universalistic theory-religious theological, or epistemological-that attempts to establish first principles. And yet they want a world where the "dignity" of each self, and each unique locale, story, biography, and group identity is honoured.

The substantiality of this view is not at all clear, for human rights are by definition both universalistic, practical, and highly theoretical. Rorty has argued that it is possible to "de-universalize" and "de-theorize" both democracy and human rights, and yet to maintain them as a good way to live. As ways of life, democracy and human rights are prior to philosophy. Enlightenment philosophy's most profound self-deception, he argues, was to believe that its theory of rights was foundational and Prioi to the form of democratic life. Rorty argues, to the contrary, that Enlightenment justifications were always justifications of this way of life; and this way of life can be "justified," or made sense of, in a number of ways. But, better yet, it needs no justification. In lieu of a theoretical defence of rights and democracy, one has to say merely that these forms of life work well; they have helped us to stop killing one another. That pragmatic justification, if one can call it that, involves certain understandings about what is desirable, but these understandings should be recognized as strictly contingent products of our historical experience.

Rorty is surely correct that the Enlightenment justifications were not prior to democracy and human rights, for in fact it was key theological and ecclesial traditions that established them for at least parts of the human community, long before the Enlightenment. Furthermore, it can easily be argued that democracy and human rights were based upon universalistic theories of right and wrong that were, in fact, resisted by particular local traditions, stories, biographies, and group identities that would have lost the arbitrary power they held over people if rights and democracy were acknowledged. Also, Rorty's theory presupposes a touching vision of a naturally harmonious state of affairs for all life that is not touched by the sin of grand theory. This wonderful polytheistic paradise, with no trees of knowledge since it is "beyond good and evil," is as universalistic and religious a theory as any he rejects, although it is not theological and thus has no grounding beyond arbitrary preference. Finally, he cannot provide a reason why we would stop killing one another, especially if it is to the great advantage of some that the killing continue.

Lyotard also believes, echoing aspects of Heidegger and Neitzsche, that the fundamental error in Western philosophy is that grand narratives storm through history by swallowing up and silencing alternatives and otherness. Grand narratives reign by "terror," even though they are guided by a profound humanism. This humanism is supported by the grand narratives of Marxism and liberalism, which measure all things by their ability to produce results for humanity. Marxism promises a catastrophic liberation of humanity; liberalism promises humanity's gradual unfolding and flowering. Yet both liberalism and Marxism agree that human beings stand at the center of history, and that history told' rightly tells the story of the ineluctable emancipation of humans from tyranny and need.

Lyotard believes, however, that the ideas of real subjects, gene humanity, or the meaning of life or history are pretenses that cannot survive contemporary experience. With Rorty, Lyotard argues that humans are much more "put together" than such an anthropocentric theory, history would indicate. Modern views constitute themselves by denying the constructed character of the self, and thus they invent a mythology of a completely new, unfettered beginning: that it is in this way possible to "set the clock back to zero,"' to return to or take one' clues for living from a "state of nature." Postmodernity believes such confident new beginnings merely deny the past and are thus doomed to repeat it. Lyotard's postmodern way forward is much more like psychoaualysis: one can see the pros and cons of one's parents and past but cannot imagine a personal story without them. History is, or rather histories are like that, too. People are so "put together" that even their new starts a in *medias res;* they are much more ambiguous, gritty, and semi-form than modernity's Self. Universalistic narratives, public philosophy, theology conceal and overwrite this "put togetherness

The idea that some universally conferred dignity stands behind the Enlightenment doctrine of human rights is, in this interpretation, the product of a false consciousness. The recurrence of grand narratives, or bold declarations like claims c natural rights, are a sign that cultural psychotherapy has gone badly awry-that the therapeutic process has mistaken the content of it-conversation for an authoritative and normative remembering of "history. Spinning grand narratives, like theoretical defences of universal human rights, entail a "primal repression" all such attempts are tied to a philosophy of consciousness, which is doomed to repeat the horrors of the past. In Western history, the chief example is the Jews:

What is most real about the Jews is that Europe, in any case, does not know what to do with them: Christians demand their conversion; monarchs expel them; republics assimilate them; Nazis exterminate them.

The grand narratives of the Enlightenment, with their promise of equality, did nothing in Lyotard's view to protect the Jews from extermination. Their most benevolent face was to require the abandonment of all of the distinctive features of judaism. Lyotard wants human rights to be much less than a theoretically comprehensive articulation of the rights and duties of humanity, and so to provide much more of a shield for simply being human. At the core, human rights are about the right to talk with others, and to tell one's own stories. One's stories ensure that one is always "other," not reduced to some alien scheme:

> [T]he strangeness of the other seems to escape any totalization.... It is precisely when we think we have reduced the abject or the sacred to transparent meanings that it becomes most opaque. The discontent from which contemporary societies are suffering, the postmodern affliction, is the foreclosure of the Other. It is the reverse of the triumphant identification with the Other which effects modern republics at their birth.

Lyotard is surely correct that the Enlightenment conception of the Self, as autonomous, complete, whole, and unique, is unconvincing. But his view of the socially and narratologically constituted person is equally unconvincing, and it is doubtful that his view can provide the shield from "terror" that he wants, Lyotard recognizes one of the emphases of the biblical and theological tradition, namely, that humans are creatures made from the dust, to which they return after a brief life. The biblical and theological tradition, however, also affirms that humans are created in the image of God. The self does not have an automatic dignity; it has a conferred dignity. The weak, the fragile, the foolish, the faulty also are to be treated with dignity. The biblical view is paradoxical; these creatures from the dust, made in the image of God, may not be violated-in prophetic voice, their heads may not be crushed-at least not without incurring God's wrath. Lyotard cannot provide a convincing reason why we may not manipulate one another's stories and crush each other's heads, even though he desires that we do not.

Just as Rorty falls into an unwitting romantic and presumptively harmonious polytheism, Lyotard falls into a soulless vacuity of chatter. Rorty needs God; Lyotard needs the image of God. Their arguments are insufficient, even though they have helped us see more clearly the insufficiency of key philosophical arguments of the Enlightenment. Nonetheless, if it comes to it, the world would probably be wise to choose the Enlightenment views over their efforts, for in the notions of a universal moral law and a self with inherent dignity, there is a closer approximation to what these two philosophers want to protect than in what they themselves proffer as alternatives.

Several other lines of argument could be marshalled against this vision of Rorty and Lyotard. First, plurality does not take care of itself, in a structural and historical form, plurality without a larger sense of unity is tribalism. Various forms of ethnic exclusiveness and pluralism constitute themselves in terms of "the other" by constant hostility, and it is romantic and historically blind to argue otherwise, Second the so-called totalistic impulses of the Enlightenment can be criticized, along the lines laid out by Rorty and Lyotard, without denying the importance of inclusivistic narratives. In fact, the lack or denial of comprehensive narratives is historically the source of violence. The problem is that the Enlightenment was not inclusive enough. Its narrative was petty, not grand, for it lacked depth. The Enlightenment conception has only selves, not souls; it has humanism, but neither God nor creation. Rorty and Lyotard are right, then, that the Enlightenment does not deliver on its promise to secure some kinds of particularity and plurality, and thus these are subject to deconstruction, because they have no ground for being honoured. Yet that has as much to do with the Enlightenment's denial of the theological foundations of its own presumptions as anything else. The doctrine of the trinity, for example, enables the articulation of ultimate reality, marked by a non-reductive inclusivity, with principles and freedom, otherness and identity. Third, it is possible to see vestiges of the "Enlightenment" all through Rorty's and Lyotard's writings, especially when they are read from a Christian theological point of view. The premature dismissal of theology as a voice in public discussion represents the Enlightenment in its most dubious philosophical aspect, and they accept the dismissal at face value. Fourth, it is not at all clear how one can have a non-theoretical practice or form of life, without falling prey to self-referential inconsistencies. It is a noble impulse that should be nurtured, one that has people pause and ask, "Is this practice just, and therefore theoretically justifiable?" Human rights apply to more than one form of practice, because they are highly theoretical, Yet, beyond these issues, there is reason for a deeper critique of Rorty and Lyotard from the perspective we are advancing here.

For all their insights, Rorty and Lyotard undermine the chief source of human rights and obscure the character of the contemporary ethos in which human rights will be advanced or retarded. In short, theology is an indirect, and often a direct, target of their critiques, as it is for enlightened liberals. Moreover, their focus upon the smaller fragments of life leads them to ignore a manifest feature of the ethos of our time, namely that the world's increasingly unified economic, political, ideational, and legal global ethos can support a nonviolent plurality. Rorty and Lyotard spool together these features of bad theology and a misunderstood ethos because they believe that the Enlightenment best spoke for its own presuppositions and correctly analysed the nature and character of religion. But, since they have challenged the Enlightenment on a dozen points, it is not clear why they remain dependent on it for this one. Rorty and Lyotard simply assume that theology is inherently heteronomous and that an irreducible plurality is better than the stifling singularity which theology ostensibly desires. The social hermeneutic of Rorty and Lyotard blinds them to the emerging global ethos, or to view it as some demonic Leviathan, and no more.

The fate of human rights as a sustainable cluster of doctrines is likely to require the apologetical refutation of these sorts of claims. For, on the one hand, if theology cannot enter into first-order dialogue about the nature of humanity, without being destructive or heteronomous, it is hard to see how religious human rights can mean anything. On the other hand, if they show that classical and enlightenment philosophy and all of theology is inherently dehumanizing, it is also hard to see where substantive accounts of "humanity" will come from, since nearly all of the current human rights proclamations depended, directly or indirectly upon the normative anthropotogical assumptions of biblically influenced philosophical theology.

Rorty's denial of "metanarratives" turns out to be a particular metanarrative that systematically denies the reality of the world. In fact, both Rorty and Lyotard presume a metaphysical and epistemological ethically normless polytheism at the level of experience. Their social hermeneutic has decided a priori that it will see nothing other than fragments which are threatened by comprehensive unities. That means that, the bases for rights which might be used to stave off intrusions on inviduality are undermined. To be sure, in the emerging global ethos, there is an intensive plurality that which cannot be denied and that which often be celebrated, but there is also a quite real unity, There is one system with multiple climates, one global economy with highly differentiated markets, one emerging cosmopolitan global civilization with many cultures and subcultures, and one need to communicate with many languages. Human rights as a normative concept adds that there is one humanity with a rich variety of individual lives, traditions, community and religions that ought not be violated. This is a theological hermeneutic that includes unity and difference. Rorty and Lyotard undermine the dialectic by focusing upon difference; this is quite directly related to their denial of theology as a form of public discourse, since theology join unity to difference and articulates the real differences found in and under ultimate unity.

The course travelled by these postmodern philosophers is odd. Rorty and Lyotard tacitly accept several key presumptions of the Enlightenment, turn them on the greatest achievements of modern humanistic thought, and thus destroy the foundations of the very values that they want to affirm. Further, they finally have to rest their case on a socio-historical reading of how things work in the common life and on a priori convictions about what is valuable. Yet they can defend neither, some thing they disavow at the outset, in any event.

Rorty and Lyotard, however, are not the only contemporary philosophers to address human rights. Terry Nardin and David Maple of the Thikon Institute, for example, are editing a major volume on The Constitution of International Society, in which both classical (conservative) and Enlightenment (liberal) theories of law, in dialogue with certain theological positions, are being tetrieved and revised to guide the common life in ways that support and sustain human rights. Similarly, certain self consciously "conservative" and "liberal" moral philosophers, and some self-consciously liberal, and conservative "Christian philosophers," are making very similar arguments against both the reductionism of the Enlightenment and the moral emptiness of many postmodern alternatives.

The Enlightenment thinkers would surely have found it odd that some of the most serious arguments against human rights come not from religion or theology but from philosophy. That may not be enough, were we able to discuss these matters with the Enlightenment thinkers, to turn them to a reconsideration of religion and theology. For a number of social theorists in our day, however, it has been enough, even if the turn these theorists make to religion is not always fully adequate. The work of Jdrgen Habermas, for example, represents an attempt to go beyond the narrowness of both Enlightenment philosophy and sociology by commingling their insights in a program of critical theory. He joins Rorty and Lyotard by rejecting a philosophy of consciousness, monological justifications of the social contract, and the foundationalism of Enlightenment philosophy; he also joins them by turning to language and communication theory. Yet here is precisely where Habermas turns away from Rorty and Lyotard, for he attempts to extract a normative justification for rights Out of the very nature of communication.

Scholars in the sociological tradition of Weber, Emile Durkheim a Talcott Parsons, such as Robert Bellah, are also increasingly, though cautiously, engaging in dialogue with religion. This move is not without controversy. Some writers in this tradition challenge the use of the sod sciences as a companion to religion and theology." Others, such a Peter Berger, question whether sociology alone can provide any guidance, about human rights as normative claims. To the contrary, other sociologists argue that social sciences are the only disciplines that can provide normative guidance to post-religious civil society. It is not clear whether contemporary sociology, any more than contemporary philosophy, can offer normative guidance about human rights, though both discipline point to the necessity of dealing with religions as decisive factors in human rights discourse.

It may be that the more urgent approach to human rights is to raise, the question of the world religions directly. To do so, however, we need a method that both focuses directly on religious realities and joins the study of religion to philosophy and social theory. Such a method is found in theological ethics, or what some traditions call social theology, philosophical theology or natural theology. Theological ethics, along with certain forms of philosophy of religion and jurisprudence which are alert to theological issues,"' goes to the deepest normative perspective in which human rights can be talked about without sacrificing concrete socio-historical institutions.

Surely, human rights would be on a more secure footing if we could place them on a foundation that has both a sustainable normativity and a concrete, institutional footing. The theological ethical considerations of the world religions bring these concerns together, because all of the axial religions express metaphysical-moral visions that entail normativity, and their civilizational expansiveness verifies their sustainability. The major religions also interactive the chief and indispensable social structures—familial, political, economic, and cultural. Indeed, in many classic societies, religion is identified with one or more of these social structures, so that it is not strange to speak of a tribal, clan, or caste religion, an imperial, political or civic religion, a religion focused around the hunt, the harvest, or the expected "cargo, or a religion of a cultural-linguistic grouping. In some societies, however, where religion is focused upon a culture-transcending, ethical reality, it becomes distinguished from these so that it is not to be identified with any one of them. There, quite often, we find the formation of voluntary associations-centers of bonding and meaning that are intentionally not tied to any of these, even if these associations continue to influence any or all of them. When this begins to happen, we find also the emergence of other independent institutions of society-law, science, medicine, and business-which also segregate particular activities into distinctive institutions and shape the fabric of the whole society.

Historically, it has been in certain kinds of traditions—those which on ecclesiological grounds, have spawned voluntary associations, an thereby institutional pluralism—nearly always populated by minorities at the outset, that we find the most promising institutional focus for the creedal recognition, affirmation, and nurture of human rights." Such associations are primarily called into existence by proselyting, ethical religions, where these transcend family, governments, special economic of cultural interests and try to influence them to approximate justice.

Voluntary associations are also created in secular forms, once the space is established and rationalized by religious groups, and these associations can transmit the ethical ideas in routine institutions, quite often in forms which are not recognized as religious. Anthony Giddens' thesis may be promising here with some modification, for he argues that globalization is the "radicalization of modernity," the realization of its consequences.- Giddens' "discontinuist" account, however, does not sufficiently engage the question of the religious and theological antecedents of modernity. It is likely that the global radicalization of modernity is the most recent actuation of the deep fount of modernity, that is, of what Max Weber saw in his treatment of "the city," and more fully in his study of the spirit of capitalism-the "secular" rationalizations of life prompted by religious transformations. But Giddens' thesis holds that we are now experiencing the consequences of that ethic in ways that Weber did not and could not envision. Newly emerging global patterns, reflected in international law, media, and markets, but largely evoked and facilitated by new forms of the multinational corporation, concretely shape the world in which we live and in which human rights are recognized or violated. We should investigate what drives these new patterns, because they harbour the ability to create inclusive institutions and to nurture normative ideas about what is true and just, at least latently.

This raises the question: do global institutions, since they are universal in scope, bear within them an ethic which can be allied to that of human rights?- If so, with theological ethical guidance, they may support human rights more securely than either philosophy or sociology alone, that is, of either an uninstitutional normativity or an institutional anomie. Answering that question requires a consideration of the chief fount of voluntary associations, the world religions. It requires a theological ethical consideration of them, a consideration that seeks to articulate which religious claims are true, and how one could know their truth. In sum, important as philosophy and sociology are, both finally depend upon religion-the investigation of which finally requires theological analysis, if a universalistic ethic such as human rights is to be sustained by religion.

For our purposes, only some religions are interesting—those that have demonstrated a capacity to shape large scale civilizations. Only these religions can reach toward human rights in the relevant respects; only these make claims to universality. The world's major civilizational religions are, to use postmodernism's contemptuous phrase, totalizing theories. God's covenant with Israel commissions it to be a prophet to the nations. The Christian gospel is to be taken into all the world. The Qur'an is the Arabic words of Allah. The sounds of the Sanskrit words preexist the cosmos itself. These traditions know something about what Christians also say, "In the beginning was the word." Indeed, in what Karl Jaspers called the religious, of the axial age (*Achsenzeit*), several traditions discovered that the cosmos could be comprehended as a single whole thousands of years before such an idea could begin to make empirical sense, as it does now in what social theorists call globalization, internationalization, or the world system.

Three distinct elements are present in the ethics of each of these religions; these need to be sorted if we are to find out where and how we are similar, and where and how we are different in regard to human rights.

First, the world religions are allies in identifying a fundamental need to transform reality as we now find it, and together they form a cluster of formal deontological claims that categorically address all humans and all human societies. Every religion has something like universal moral laws that condemn murder, rape, lying, stealing, dishonouring religion and proper authority, and commanding truth-telling, promise-keeping, and upright living. In broad terms, members of the religions can agree with each other, and often with philosophies that also seek to know the "right order" of things, and can cooperate on these bases about many matters concerning human rights.

Second, however, all the great religious traditions have a way of interpreting and guiding the social context of life. There is considerable tension on this point, although it does not perhaps involve ultimate differences. This second area of ethics has to do with the ways in which commonly held first principles and final aims become embedded in the necessary contexts of life. Frequently, they become attached to a socially and historically conditioned ideal, which determines what the most fitting context of life ought to be, and what kinds of concrete social arrangements best allow the right order of things to be actuated.

If we look briefly at Islam and Hinduism, we can see important elements of this dimension of religious ethics that bear upon human rights. As we already noted, every society has to have a way of dealing with familial, political, economic', and cultural matters; if the societies are complex, they must also have independent institutions for law, science, medicine, and business. Religious institutions and loyalties have been, and presumably always wilt be, closely allied with these, but how that connection is made from- the standpoint of the religion will be decisive for the actual functioning of the first principles of right and wrong, including the ways in which human rights operate.

Islam was led by Mohammed, of blessed memory, who was not only professionally given to commerce, but also a political-military leader who, by being the mediator of the Qur'an and the first judge in legal cases, established a direct and immediate connection between the faith and political and legal rule. It would, indeed, be very strange if religious organizations in that tradition did not draw a close connection between political, military, and legal principles, especially as they dealt with property, trade, and agreements among the heads of households, clans, tribes, and nations. Over the centuries, that has been quite characteristic, from the rise of the Caliphate, to the Iranian Revolution, to the new militancy nearly every Islamic country is now facing. Religion encouraged political and military expansion and thereby the establishment of the Shari'a and of trade. When political and military expansion went well, religion flourished, marked by wider establishment of the sacred law and commercial success. When any one these declined, the others fell into frustration or disrepair.

To be sure, there have been grand moments in the history of Islam, when issues of cultural and philosophical genius, medicine, science, commercial fairness, and generosity to the poor have surpassed most other civilizations, and these "arenas of life" remain highly regarded by many devotees of the tradition. And, of course, Islam, has quite distinctive teachings about family life, presumably born out of the political, military, and legal history of the faith, and quite supportive of an ethic which nourished their common life. In general it might be said that the of Islam basically supports the "nation of Islam," and that both bring political power, law, and religion into intimate proximity.

In contrast, Hinduism is organized by a priestly caste that is viewed as superior to the military-political-legal custodians of public order, and they, in turn, are superior to those given to commerce and production. The fact that priestly domination triumphed over political and military rule in India is of basic significance; the priests have first-order contact with the first principles of morality, in a way that no other vocational group does. A casted hierarchy, determined by birth, sets the extended familial patterns at the core of religious association in a way that has no real analogy in Islam or Christianity. Thus, dynastic institutions, guided by a marriage-conscious and highly educated literate dynasty tends to dominate life in those areas where Hinduism is predominant.

Both traditions have elements of transcendence, of the dignity of the human soul, and of the necessity of legal protections for life. But neither has developed a general theory of human rights. However, these deeply embedded social orders are not beyond change, any more than the imperial and feudal structures of medieval Christianity were. Further, once the concept of human rights is presented to these traditions, and once the possibilities of a pluralistic and open civil society becomes accessible to them, and people within these faiths begin to adopt patterns of organization that are neither totally given to political-legal militancy or to familiar-dynastic hierarchy, elements in their own traditions can be found that support the notion of human rights. Human rights can be used to catalyse growth in the latent depths of these traditions which are already have profound universalistic dimensions.

In brief, religious traditions can alter and reform themselves in the light of new ideas and circumstances. Gandhi is the great symbol of what that kind of transformation might look like in Hinduism, and present debates in Islam suggest that some changes in a comparable direction are available to Islam. Great traditions change only uneasily, and some traditions get lost or simply become minority themes in other grand traditions-as the history of Hinduism poignantly suggests, but as is also evident in the heterodox sects of Islam. Even more important is how the religions react to cosmopolitan, inter-cultural, and inter-religious contact-a crisis that is currently confronting Islam, Hinduism, and Christianity. To be sure, the direction of change is not fully predictable, and it is ambiguous whether these will bring about recognition of human rights. Under the impact of the emerging formation of a global civilization, various principles and trends that are revealed to, or discovered in, one tradition refuse to remain within a single societal, cultural, political, economic, or familial framework. They influence and are selectively and voluntarily adopted by other traditions, including other religious traditions.

Third, the world religions offer constructive, forward-looking visions or teleologies, that is, guidance about how to discern good from evil consequences of our actions by considering them in reference to ultimate aims. This third, teleological dimension of ethical discourse is rather decisive in this process of selective adoption. As the traditions now stand, they have deeply formed, rich contexts, and these make the deontological and teleological conceptions concretely available to people. While all the religions deconstruct the world with the absolute spectre of religious criticism and the call to transformation, they all also reconstruct it through imagination, doctrine, practice, and ritual so as to redeem or sanctify the world realities. They acknowledge the moral and spiritual legitimacy of the basic institutions of life, although the kind and character of the religion', and specifically its affinities to particular kinds of institutions, will shape the context in quite distinctive ways.

All the world religions also know that without a vision the people perish. Here, however,, no hasty synthesis is possible: the Kingdom of God is neither Nirvana nor the Paradise of the Qur'an, and liberation in Latin America means something quite different than the *moksa* and *bhakti*. Thus human rights find possible support in the metaphysical moral visions of the world religions, though these are indigenized in various contexts, sometimes in ways that suppress the deontological insights. But what shall be made of the world (and what shall become of the soul) is not so clear. It may well be the case, as many human rights advocates argue, that a high degree of agreement and clarity exists about the possible cooperation of religious believers on some matters bearing on human rights. Most also agree 'hat contexts should be treated with care, although some appeals to context become contextualist ideologies of identity and pluralism that effectively resist every call to transform society toward greater justice. On the question of teleology, however, there is neither agreement nor clarity. Often the role played by teleology ill human rights is ignored, and when it is treated, it usually compromises the deontological character of rights. Undoubtedly this is partly the case because of the conflict between communitarians and universalists." We have been Pressed from both sides to adopt either/or positions. However, one also wonders whether some of the failure to treat the issue is not a way of avoiding the difficulty it entails.

We are delighted that we can invoke the dharma, the *dhamma*, the Mosaic law, the Qur'an, the Holy Spirit, and, in times past, the proletariat against the injustices we perceive in the world. However, that is not enough; for we must also speak about what we and the various constituencies of the world's religions are for. And that moves us into an area where many are not comfortable—an area where one must not only be against the injustices of the world, but also ready to claim that some teleologies see farther arid more than others, an area in which apologetics is a chief form of dialogue.

5

Prisoners and Human Rights

Agonies of prisoners in Indian jails undergoing life-imprisonment remain largely unknown. All of them are not dreaded professional criminals who habitually commit heinous crimes. Many of them had committed serious crimes like murder in a fit of sudden impulse or under very grave and unsettling circumstances. Indeed, each case of life convict is different and the causes and motivation of criminal conduct by him are also different. An ad-hoc and uniform approach towards all is incorrect and also not desirable from the viewpoint of their subsequent rehabilitation in society. None will disagree that dangerous and notorious criminals should be out off streets and kept in jails for long periods of time since they pose a threat to peace-loving citizens. However, not many dreaded criminals are languishing in jails and suffering long-term imprisonment. For the average, run of long-term prisoners, long sentences do not have any constructive impact nor do they serve any therapeutic purpose. Suspension, remission and commutation of sentences of the prisoners suffering various terms of imprisonment are governed by the provisions of the Criminal Procedure code. Section 433-A of the Criminal Procedure Code prescribes that "if a person is convicted of an offence for which death is one of the punishments provided by law, or whereas the sentence of death imposed on a person has been commuted under section 433 of Criminal Procedure, Code into one of imprisonment for life, such person shall not be released unless he had served atleast fourteen years of imprisonment". This section of the Criminal Procedure Code, in the opinion of the Justice A.N. Mulla committee on Jail Reforms had the effect a sacrificing the Values of rehabilitation and reformation on the lifers altogether".

In selected cases, the power of the Governor to grant pardon or remit or commute sentences can be invoked under Article 161 of the Constitution so that the prisoners can be released even before completing 14 years of imprisonment. However, it has been noticed that the exercise of this power by the Governor for premature release of the prisoners has not always been based on objective criteria. The Supreme Court, in the well-known case of Maruram Vs. Union Government of India in 1981 has laid down that Section 433(a) of the Criminal Procedure Code does not affect the power conferred by Article 161 on the governor to grant remission of sentences. The Governor, on the advice of Council of Ministers, can thus prematurely release prisoners sentenced to life imprisonment.

Further, different states have different rules regarding release of the life convicts. The National Human Rights Commission gets petitions from life convicts over 70 years of age who are languishing in prisons for more than 30 years. A life convict in a Central Jail in Lucknow told me that he remained incarcerated for nearly 30 years. In a letter to all Chief Ministers, the Chairman of National Human Rights Commission has requested them to undertake a review of the system of release of prisoners and avoid any inconsistency in the application of the law.

At present, in most jails there is no well-laid programme of training for lifers and preparing them for suitable rehabilitation after their release. Indeed, a life convicts receives very little individual attention. Quite often he gets huddled together With the short-term and medium termers, casuals and adolescent offenders. There is no special provision for a comprehensive study of a life convict. He is allotted work on the same basis as other medium or long-term prisoners. His individual needs and problems get submerged in the routine of prison administration. As years roll by, he gets steeped in the typical subculture of the prison and develops allegiance to criminal groups. His value system gets seriously undermined.

The all India Jail Manual Committee in its report recommended that on admission a comprehensive social and psychological study of the life convict should be undertaken. The treatment programme should consist of diversified education work, vocational training, training in responsible community living etc. Such a programme should be balanced and take note of the needs of each inmate. While allotting work or planning training programmes, the possibility of imparting multiple skills according to the abilities of each life convict should be kept in mind. The acquisition of multiple skills will improve his prospects of employment after he steps out of prison.

Indeed, pre-release preparations and planning for aftercare and follow-up need special attention in the case of the life convicts. The prison administration and aftercare services must work in tandem. In these respects, there is need for a positive outlook. Rule 58 of the United Nations Standard Minimum Rules for the treatment of Prisoners prescribes that the period of "imprisonment should be used to ensure as far as possible that on his return to society, the offender is not only willing, but also able to lead a law-abiding and self-supporting life".

An enormous amount of criminal research in various parts of the world has shown that very often prisoners return with an increased commitment to criminal lifestyles. Hence prison regimes must focus on prisoners' return to society and encourage al. and opportunities that would facilitate a law-abiding life after release. Many life convicts also complain of harassment by the police when they are released on furlough or proceed on annual leave. Senior police officers must curb firmly such vexatious acts by their subordinate staff.

There are advisory committees in each district comprising the District Judge, District Magistrate and Superintendent of Police to review the cases of premature release of the life convicts along with cases of convicts sentenced to medium terms of imprisonment. Unfortunately, working of most these Advisory Committee in considering cases of premature releases of the long-term convicts is very unsatisfactory. Their method of review of sentences is often found to be haphazard and cursory. Scores of cases, as pointed out in the reports of the Mulla Committee, are disposed of hurriedly within a couple of hours without properly studying relevant fact and background of each case.

Advisory committees should hold separate meetings for reviewing cases of the life convicts only. This will facilitate proper and careful reviewing. Order of the government on the recommendations of the Advisory Committee should also be issued expeditiously. At present the life convicts have very little faith in the efficacy of the Advisory Committees because of the lackadaisical manner of their functioning.

As things stand now, life convicts in different Indian prisons feel bitter and discontented. Urgent action by state Government is called for to deal with their various problems and grievances. They feel very strongly about the inclusion of section 433 A in the Criminal Procedure Code. This has dashed their hopes of early release from prisons by getting benefits of remission. They will thus have to go through imprisonments of 14 years. This makes them sullen and bitter and destroy chances of any meaningful endeavour on their part for self-improvement.

The Indian socio-legal system is based on nonviolence, mutual respect and human dignity of the individual. If a person commits any crime, it does not mean that by committing a crime, he ceases to be a human being and that he can be deprived of those aspects of life which constitute human dignity. Even the prisoners have human rights because the prison torture is not the "'last drug in the Justice Pharmacopoeia" but "a confession of failure to do justice to living man". For a prisoner all fundamental rights are an enforceable reality, though restricted by the fact of imprisonment. Article 21 of the Constitution guarantees the right of 'personal liberty" and thereby prohibits any inhuman, cruel or degrading treatment to any person whether he is a national or foreigner. Any violation of this right attracts the provisions of article 14 of the Constitution which enshrines right to equality and equal protection of laws. In addition to this, the question of cruelty to prisoners is also dealt with specifically by the Prison Act. If any excesses are committed on a prisoner, the prison administration is responsible for that. Any excesses committed on a prisoner by the police authorities not only attract the attention of the legislature but also of the judiciary. The Indian judiciary, particularly the Supreme Court in the recent past has been very vigilant against encroachments upon the human rights of the prisoners.

It is the inhuman treatment meted out to the prisoners in the prison that the Supreme Court, which is last in the Indian pyramid of justice, is compelled to delineate the broad boundaries of judicial jurisdiction, vis-a-vis, prison justice. The province of prison justice, the conceptualization of freedom behind bars and the role of judicial power as constitutional sentinel in a prison setting, are of the gravest moment in a world of escalating torture by the minions of state, and in India, where this virgin area of jurisprudence is becoming painfully relevant.

The judicial pen also recognized other rights of the prisoners, viz., protection against torture in the prison, right not to be put in solitary confinement and saving from handcuffing and bar fetters save in the cases provided by this protective organ of the State itself. The prisoners' right to bail and right to meet friends, relatives and lawyer are also considered by the Apex Court. Being conscious to human dignity, the court also granted the right to medical examination. Judicial conscience recognized the human rights of the prisoners because of its reformistic approach and belief that convicts are also human beings and that the purpose of imprisonment is to reform them rather than to make them hardened criminals.

Rights of the prisoners and judiciary

In *Charles Sobraj v. Supdt, Central Jail, Tihar, New Delhi,* the Apex Court observed:

> Imprisonment does not spell farewell to fundamental rights although, by a realistic reappraisal, courts will refuse to recognize the full panoply or Part III enjoyed by a free citizen... Art. 21, read with Art.19 (1) (d) and (5), is capable of wider application than the imperial mischief which gave it birth and must draw its meaning from the evolving standards of

> decency and dignity that mark the progress of a mature society.

In *Sunil Batra v. Delhi Admn.*, the Supreme Court stated

> (I)n out constitutional order it is axiomatic that the laws do not swallow up the fundamental rights of the legally unfree and as sentinels on the *qui vive*, courts will guard freedom behind bars, tempered, of course by environmental realism but intolerant of torture by executive echelons. The policy of the law is beyond purchase by authoritarians glibly invoking 'dangerness' of inmates and peace in prisons.

The court further held:

> Part III of the Constitution does not part company with the prisoner at the gates, and judicial oversight protects the prisoner's shrunken fundamental rights, if flouted, frowned upon or frozen by the prison authority.

Thus, it is evident that the Supreme Court has taken the view that every fundamental right of the prisoner cannot be infringed. The procedure for restriction should have been found in article 21, its reasonableness should be tested under article 19(5) and if the "anathema" by virtue authority" is used arbitrarily, it would be an of article 14.

The dynamism of the Summit Court beautifully expressed the admission of this court that "right jurisprudence" was important only if it was followed by remedial jurisprudence. The court was satisfied that 'protection of the prisoner within his rights is part of the office of Art. 32". After Sunil Batra (11), "the dynamic role of judicial remedies" painted the writ of habeas corpus as "a versatile vitality" and "operational utility" in order to make "the healing presence of the law live up to its reputation as bastion of liberty even within the secrecy of the hidden cell. The Court observed:

> When prison trauma prevails, prison justice must investigate and hence we broaden our 'habeas' jurisdiction. Jurisprudence cannot slumber when the very campuses of punitive justice witness torture

In *Sunil Batra (II)*, the writ petition originated through a letter by a prisoner, Batra, to a judge of the Supreme Court in which it was complained that the head warder caused assault on another prisoner, Prem Chand. This letter was admitted as writ petition forsaking the formal procedure because the freedom of a prisoner was at stake. So this case changed the picture of habeas corpus. Previously, it used to be available to help the release of the person. But now it can be evoked even to save the prisoner from prison torture. And moreover, no formal procedure is needed now.

The Summit Court has favoured the application of fair procedure in prisons and held that," whether inside prison or outside, a person shall not be deprived of his guaranteed freedoms save by methods, "right, just and fair'. "Solitary Confinement", according to Black's Law Dictionary, in a general sense, means the separate confinement of a prisoner, with only occasional access of any other person, and that too only at the discretion of the jail authorities and in stricter sence, it means the complete isolation of a prisoner from all human society and his confinement in a cell so arranged that he has no direct intercourse with or sight of any human being or no employment or instruction.

The Apex Court in *Sunil Batra* (I) held that solitary confinement could be imposed only in exceptional cases where the convict was of such a dangerous character that he must be segregated from other prisoners.

The dehumanizing effect of solitary confinement was picturised by the court as follows:

> To see a fellow being is a solace to the soul. Communication with one's own kind is a balm to the aching spirit. Denial of both with complete segregation superimposed is the journey to insanity.

In *Sunil Batra* (I), it was contended that Batra was put in "statutory confinement" and not "solitary confinement" and the court rightly responded to this contention:

> If solitary confinement is a revolt against society's human essence, there is no reason to permit the same punishment to be smuggled into the prison system by naming it differently. Law is not a formal label, nor logomachy but a working technique of justice.

Justice Desai while delivering separate judgement remarked:

> Solitary confinement has a degrading and dehumanising effect on prisoners. Constant and unrelieved isolation of a prisoner is so unnatural that it may breed insanity. Social isolation represents the most destrutive abnormal environment. Results of long solitary confinement are disastrous to the physical and mental health of those subjected to it.

In *Kishore Singh* again the court held keeping of petitioners in separate solitary rooms for long periods from eight months to eleven months as barbarous on the basis of what this court had decided in Sunil Batra. The Court also held that "solitary confinement" could be imposed in "rarest of rare cases" and with strict adherence to the procedural safeguardes contained in the decisions of this court relating to the punishment of prisoners. The court warned that the violation of article 21 as interpreted by this court in its recent decisions, if repeated, would be visited with serious consequences, because :

> Human dignity is a dear value of our Constitution not to be bartered away for, mere apprehensions entertained by jail officials.

Keeping in view the human rights and recognizing human dignity, the Apex Court forbade putting any prisoner in bar fetters. The picture of the prisoners subjected to fetters was pointed in the real colours of life by this court:

> (A) large number of prisoners a few hundred at times minors and under trials too are shackled day and night for days and months on and by bar fetters too shocking to contemplate with cultural equanimity. And this, prima facie shows up the class character of jail injustice for an incisive Sociologist.

In *Sunil Batra* (I), the Additional Solicitor General feared dangerousness of the prisoner in case he escaped. Therefore, he favoured bar fettters, in order to prevent such escape. The activist court responded to this fear in the following words:

> Chaining all prisoners, amputing many, caging some, can all be fobbed off, if every undertrial or convict were painted as a potentially dangerous maniac. Assuming a few likely to escape, would you shoot a hundred prisoners or whip everyone every day or fetter all suspects to prevent one jumping jail? These wild apprehensions have no value in our human order, if Articles 14, 19 and 21 are the prime actors in the constitutional play.

The court rightly emphasised that continuously keeping a prisoner in fetters day and night reduced the prisoner from a human being to, an animal and that the treatment was so cruel and unusual that the use of bar fetters was anathema to the spirit of the Constitution.

In *Sunil Batra* (II) also, the court expressed its concern over putt jug fetters in the following words:

> (T)o fetter prisoners in irons is an inhumanity unjustified save where safe custody is otherwise impossible. The routine resort to handcuffs and irons bespeaks a barbarity hostile to our goal of human dignity and social justice.

The human rights conscious Supreme Court took the matter of bar fetters to a logical extent in *Prem Shankar Shukla v. Delhi Administration.* In this case, in spite of the decision in Batra (I), the petitioner, who was an undertrail, was handcuffed. In the present case the dilemma of human rights jurisprudence could be seen in the questions raised by Justice Krishna Iyer: "Can the custodian fetter the person of the prisoner, while in transit, with irons, may be handcuffs or chains or bar fetters? When does such traumatic treatment break into the inviolabel zone of guaranteed rights? When does disciplinary measure end and draconic torture begin ? What are the constitutional parameters, viable guidelines and practical strategies which will permit the peaceful coexistence of custodial conditions and basic dignity?',

Justice Krishna Iyer emphasised that handcuffs should not be used in routine and they were to be used only when the person was "desperate", "rowdy" or the one who was involved in non-bailable offence. Justice Krishna Iyer righthly observed:

> Handcuffing in prima facie inhuman and, therefore, unreasonable, is over-harsh and at the first flush, arbitrary. Absent fair procedure and objective monitoring, to inflict 'irons' is to resort to zoological strategies repugnant to Article 21.

It was also observed that it being "sadistic, capricious, despotic and demoralising " was violative of article 14 and that the minimal freedom of movement which even a detainee was entitled to under article 19 could not be cut down with cruelty through the handcuffs.

In this case, Justice Iyer did not agree with the argument that handcuffing was insurance against escape because he felt that there were other measures whereby an escort could keep safe custody of a detenu without the indignity and cruelty implicit in handcuffs or other iron contraptions. According to him, this method could be resorted to only when there was no other practical way of forbidding escape, the prisoner being so dangerous and desperate and the circumstances so hostile to safe-keeping.

In *Kishore Singh,* the Supreme Court held that bar fetters should be imposed only in "rarest of rare cases" and that is also for "convincing security reasons" and must comply with the principles of natural justice.

In gross violation of the decision of the Summit Court in *Sunil Batra* (I) the case of undertrial prisoners, who were kept in leg irons again gave a shock of the court in *Kadra Pehadiya.* The court ordered to immediately remove leg irons from the feet of the four petitioners and also directed that no convicted or undertrial prisoners would be kept in leg irons except in accordance with the ratio of the *Sunil Batra.*

Despite the eye-opening judgments of the Supreme Court against handcuffing, the question of alleged handcuffing of an advocate practising in Delhi was raised before the court in *Aeltemesh Rein v. Union of India.* It was urged before the court that the Union Government and the Delhi Administration had not issued necessary instructions to the police authorities with regard to the circumstances in which an accused, arrested in a criminal case, could be handcuffed or fettered in accordance with the judgement of this court in *Prem Shankar Shukla.* In this case, the Attorney General of India very fairly conceded that it was for the Union of India to issue necessary instructions in this behalf to all the State governments and the government of Union Territories. The Supreme Court has directed the Union of India to frame rules or guidelines regarding the circumstances in which handcuffing of the accused, should be resorted to in conformity with the judgement of this court in *Prem Shankar Shukla and* to circulate them amongst all the State governments and the governments of Union Territories.

In *Harbans Singh v. State of U.P.*, the Supreme Court once again reiterated that undertrial prisoners should not be kept in fetters in jail as it is inhuman to keep them in fetters while they are awaiting trial.

In spite of such clear rulings of the Apex Court against handcuffing, the high headedness of the police authorities came to the light in *Delhi Judicial Service Asson. Tis Hazari. Court v. State of Gujarat.* This case relates to a horrendus incident which took place in 1989 in the town of Nadiad in Gujarat State. This case exhibited the berserk behaviour or police undermining the dignity and independence of judiciary. The Inspectors of Police of Nadiad Police Station arrested, assaulted and handcuffed the Chief Judicial Magistrate of Nadiad town and tied him with a thick roap like an animal and made a public exhibition of it by sending him in the same condition to the hospital for medical examination on an alleged charge of having consumed liquor in breach of the prohibition law enforced in the State of Gujarat.

The Supreme Court found that the object was to work vengeance and humiliate Chief Judicial Magistrate who had been policing the police by his judicial orders. The court took a serious note of the whole incident and held that this extraordinary and unusual behaviour of police was not proper. It amounts to interference with administration of justice, lowering of its judicial authority and hence amounts to criminal contempt. The Supreme

Court laid down detailed guidelines which should be followed in case of arrest and detention of a judicial officer. The guilty police inspector was given the simple imprisonment for a period of six months and also directed to pay a fine of Rs. 2,000/- The Court also sent other guilty police officials to jail and imposed fine and further directed the State government to take disciplinary action against them.

Sunil Gupta V. State of M. P is yet another instance where the police ignored the Supreme Court ruling against handcuffing and handcuffed the social workers sitting on peaceful dharma for espousing public cause and who voluntarily submitted themselves for arrest.

In *State of Maharashtra v, Ravi Kant S. Patil.,* an undertrial prisoner was handcuffed and taken through streets in a procession by police during investigation. The Court held that it is violative of article 21 of the Constitution and Rs. 10,000/ compensation was directed to be paid to the undertrial prisoner by the State. The Court also held that since the police officer was acting in his official capacity so he cannot be made personally liable to pay compensation. However, the court left it open to the authorities to hold an enquiry, if considered necessary, against the police officer and then decide whether any further action is to be taken against him or not.

It is submitted that wherever any police official acts contrary to the clear directions against handcuffing as laid down by the Supreme Court and thus violates the basic human right to "human dignity", he should be made personally liable to pay the compensation. Recently, the Supreme Court has also favoured this view in *Khedat Mazdoor Chetna Sangath v. State of M.P.*

In this case human rights violation by handcuffing of tribals and commission of inhuman atrocities on them by police officials and local administration was alleged by the petitioner tribal organisation. The allegations were not proved by sufficient evidence but the court, observing that the police had not recorded the happening faithfully and misrepresented locking up of six persons, held that handcuffing is illegal and to uphold human values and to protect the rights guaranteed under, the Constitution it was further directed that CBI should investigate and register cases and prosecute, the officers howsoever high or low. 'The Court relied upon *Prem Shankar* and *Sunil Gupta.*

It is submitted that this ruling of the Supreme Court is in consonance with the spirit of the Indian Constitution.

The human rights saviour Supreme Court has protected the prisoners from all type of torture. The Court has rightly observed in *Sunil Batra* (I):

> The humane thread of jail jurisprudence that runs right through is that no prison authority enjoys amnesty for unconstitutionality, and forced farewell to fundamental rights is an institutional outrage in our system where stone walls and iron bars shall bow before the rule of law.

In *Kishore Singh v. State of Rajasthan,* the Supreme Court brought home the deep concern for human rights by observing against police cruelty in the following words:

> Nothing is more cowardly and unconscionable than a person in police custody being beaten up and nothing inflicts a deeper wound on our constitutional culture than a State official running berserk regardless of human rights.

The basic question is who will police the police? The Government should pay serious attention to any possibility of police cruelity. The Supreme Court has made it clear beyond doubt that any form of torture of cruel, inhuman or degrading treatment is offensive to human dignity and constitutes an inroad into the right to life and therefore, prohibitive of article 21 of the Constitution. This approach of the Supreme Court is in consonance with article 5 of the Universal Declaration of Human Rights, article 7 of the International Covenant on Civil and Political Rights and Declaration on the Protection of all Persons from being Subjected to Torture and other Cruel, inhuman or Degrading Treatment or Punishment.

The horizon of human rights is expanding. Prisoner's rights have been recognized not only, to protect them from physical discomfort or torture in the prison but also to save them from mental torture. Therefore, the Supreme Court in Sunil Batra (H) recognized the right of the prisoners to be visited by their friends and relatives. The court favoured their visits but subject to "search and discipline and other security criteria". It was observed:

Visits to prisoners by family and friends are a solace in insulation, and only a dehumanized system can derive vicarious delight in depriving prison inmates of this humane amenity.

In *Francis Coralie Mullin,* the Summit Court again stressed upon the need of permitting the prisoners to meet their friends and relatives. The Court held that the prisoner or detenu could not move about freely by going outside the jail and could not socialise with persons outside jail. It was rightly stated:

> (P)ersonal liberty would include the right to socialise with members of the family and friends subject, of course, to any valid prison regulations and under Arts. 14 and 21 such prison regulations must be reasonable and non-arbitrary.

In this case, the court went a step ahead from *Sunil Batra* (II) when it recognized the prisoner's right to consult legal adviser also. The court held that this right could be included in the right to live with human dignity and it was part of "personal liberty". A prison regulation might regulate the right to have interview with a legal adviser in a manner which was reasonable, just and fair but it could not prescribe an arbitrary or unreasonable procedure for regulating such an interview and if it was so done, it would be violative 4 Articles 14 and, 21.

In *Prabha Dutt v. Union of India,* the Supreme Court went to the extent of allowing the prisoners who were death sentencees, to give interview to the press.

In *Joginder Kumar v. State of Up.,* the Supreme Court noticed that in a large number of cases human rights violation takes place because of indiscriminate arrests. The arrestee has right to have his friend, relative or some other known person informed about his arrest. The police officer must make an entry in his diary about the person who was so informed. It was further directed that the Magistrate must be satisfied about compliance with these requirements in all cases of arrest. In view of the human rights, proper balancing of individual rights and liberties with society's rights and individual's obligation and responsibilities towards the society is needed.

Right to bail

Bail means the procedure by which judge or magistrate sets at liberty one who has been arrested and imprisoned in connection with a legal matter, criminal or civil, upon receipt of security to ensure the released prisoner's latter appearance in court for further proceedings in the matter.

In *Babu Singh v. State of U.P.,* the Apex Court, recognizing right to bail as a part of "personal liberty" under article 21, held:

> Personal liberty, deprived when bail is refused, is too precious a value of our constitutional system recognized under Art. 21 that the crucial power to negate it is a great trust exercisable not casually, but judicially with lively concern for the cost to the individual and the community. To glamorise impressionistic orders as discretionary may, on occasions make a litigative gamble decisive of a fundamental right. After all, personal liberty of an accused or convict is fundamental, suffering lawful eclipse only in terms of 'procedure established by law'. The last four words of Art. 21 are the life of that right.

The court found that a man on bail had a better chance to prepare or present his case than one remanded in custody. This was demand of public justice. And if public justice was to be promoted, mechanical detention should be demoted. The judiciary must take sympathetic attitude towards poor, therefore, the court did not favour taking of heavy bail from poor. In *Moti Ram, v. State of M.P.*, this factor turned the focus of the court on the "aspect of liberty bearing on bail jurisprudence". The court felt that when heavy sums were demanded by way of bail from the weaker segments of the society, and the court was powerless to dispense with surety, the grant of bail would become "stultified" and "impossibly inconvenient. The court, finding this problem as one of human rights, especially "freedom vis-a-vis the lowly", observed that the best guarantee of presence in court was "the reach of the law and not the money tag."

In *Hussainara Khatoon v. State of Bihar,* while dealing with undertrial prisoners, Justice Bhagwati held that the courts must abandon the antiquated concept that pretrial release would be ordered only against bail with sureties. This concept was outdated and it had done more harm than good. Therefore, the court held that if the court was satisfied on a consideration of the relevant factors that the accused had his ties in the community and there was no substantial risk of nonappearance, the accused might, as far as possible, be released on his personal bond.

In another case of *Hussainara Khatoon*, the court again held that when an undertrial prisoner was produced before a Magistrate and he had been in detention for 90 days or 60 days, as the case may be, the Magistrate must, before making an order of further remand to judicial custody, point out to the undertrial prisoner that he was entitled to be released on bail. It was also held that the State Government must also provide at its own cost a lawyer to the undertrial prisoner with a view to enable him to apply for bail.

The right to bail also flows from directive principles enshrined in Part IV of the Constitution having regard to the fact that more than half of the total population of India lives below the poverty line. The prolonged trial of the earning member of a family is bound to result in the negation of the principle embodied in articles 21, 38, 39 and 39-A of the Constitution. It is a travesty of justice that many poor accused, "little Indians are forced into long cellular servitude for little offences" because the bail procedure is beyond their meagre means and the trials do not commense, and even if they do, they never conclude.

Section 438 of the Criminal Procedure Code contains the provision for "anticipatory bail" in certain cases. The Supreme Court in *Kartar Singh v. State of Punjab*, has upheld section 20(7) of Terrorist and Disruptive Activities (prevention) Act, 1987, which exclude the benefit of section 438 of the Criminal Procedure Code. The Court has held that it is not violative of article 21 of the Constitution.

In *Hitendra Vishnu Thakur v. State of Maharashtra*, the Supreme Court has held that the investigation must be completed with the specified period under law and where the same is not completed within the prescribed period, the accused would acquire a right to seek to be released on bail and if he is prepared to and does furnish bail, the Magistrate shall release him on bail, The court has further pointed out that an application for grant of bail has to be decided on its own merit for the default of the prosecuting agency to complete the investigation within the prescribed period and the Court will not be influenced by the merit or the gravity of the case.

From the perusal of the above cases it is evident that the approach of the judiciary is human rights oriented and it has rightly recognised the prisoner's right to bail.

Right to reasonable wages in prison

Whenever during the imprisonment, the prisoners are made to work in the prison, they must be paid wages at the reasonable rate. The wage rate should not be trival or below minimum wages. In *Mohammad Giasuddin v. State of A.P.*, the Court directed the State to take into account this factor, while finalising the rules for payment of wages to prisoners, as well as to give retrospective effect to wage policy.

In the matter of P.R.E. of Wages of Prisoners, the Court has held that labour taken from prisoners, which was not properly remunerated was "forced labour" and hence violative of article 23 of the Constitution.

In *P. Bhaskara Vijay Kumar v, State*, the Court held that imposition of rigorous imprisonment with hard labour does not amount ot extracting forced labour and hence not contrary to article 23 of the Constitution. However, the prisoners would be entitled to be paid adequate wages for their labour otherwise it will violate article 21 of the Constitution.

Again in *Gurdev Singh v. State of H.P.*, the Court held that the prisoner is entitled to get reasonable wage not below the minimum wages prescribed by Minimum Wages Act, otherwise it will violate article 23 of the Constitution. Thus, the Court have taken the consistent view to uphold the human rights of prisoners inside the prisons as well.

Right to speedy trial is a fundamental rights, of a prisoner implicit in article 21 of the Constitution. 'It ensures "just, fair an reasonable" procedure. The fact that a speedy, trial, is also in public interest or that it serves the societal interest also, does not make it any—the less the right of the accused. It is in the interest of all concerned that the guilt or innocence of the accused is determined as quickly as possible in the circumstances.

The shocking and dismaying picture of administration of justice was depicted by *Hussainara Khatoon* in which the writ petition filed before the Supreme Court disclosed that a large number of men and women, including children, were behind prisons for years awaiting trial in courts of law. They had languished in jail for a period for which they, would, have been detained had they been tried for the offences committed by them. The highest judiciary was shocked that while it was climbing the steps of activism, such anguishing state of affairs still existed. It observed :

> It is a crying shame on the judicial system which permits incarceration of men and women for such long periods of time without trial. We are shouting from house tops about the protection and enforcement of human rights... But, are we not denying human rights to these nameless persons who are languishing in jails for years for offences which perhaps they might ultimately be found not to have committed.

The humane court was feeling shame that it was "a travesty of justice" that these "little Indians" had no more remained human beings but were reduced to merely "ticket-numbers". Therefore,

> What faith can these lost souls have in the judicial system which denies them a bare trial for so many years and keeps them behind bars....

The human rights protector Supreme Court gave a timely warning:

> The time has come when the legal and judicial system has to be revamped and restructured so that such injustices do not occur and disfigure the fair and otherwise luminous face of our nascent democracy.

In *Hussainara Khatoon (III) v. State of Bihar,* the court found that continued detention of the undertrial prisoners could not be justified as they, had already been in jail for a period longer than what they would have been sentenced to suffer, if convicted, It was observed:

> This discloses a shocking state of affairs and betray complete lack of concern for human values. It exposes the callousness of our legal and judicial system which can remain unmoved by such enormous misery and suffering resulting from totally unjustified deprivation of personal liberty.

Therefore, the court directed to release the undertrials as continuance of their detention was violative of their fundamental rights under article 21.

As this court had included "speedy trial" as a fundamental right under article 21, so this court held that it was the obligation of the state to devise such a procedure as would ensure speedy trial to the accused and refused to permit the state to deny this constitutional right of speedy trial to the accused on the ground that the state had no adequate financial resources to incur necessary expenditure needed for improving "the administrative and judicial apparatus" in order to ensure speedy trial.

In *Hussainara Khatoon (V) v. State of Bihar,* the court held that the undertrial prisoners, who were accused of multiple offences and who had already been in jail for the maximum term for which they could be sentenced on conviction, even if the sentences awarded to them were consecutive and not concurrent, should be released because the continuance of detention would be clearly violative not only of human dignity but also of their fundamental right under article 21 of the Constitution.

The judicial decisions in Hussainara cases proved to be a Magna Carta to the 1,20,000 undertrial prisoners languishing in jails for years without trial.

In *Mantoo Majumdar v. State of Bihar,* the court again found that the two petitioners had spent six years in jail without trial. The court was shocked to see the indifferent attitude of the state when it was found unwilling even to furnish the basic facts about the imprisonment of the petitioners, the offences for which they were kept in judicial custody, for how long and at what stage were the proceedings and the like. The court felt that it was "an unconscionable aspect of the State's unconcern for human rights.

The activist court, which was on the path of enlivening human rights, wondered at such state of affairs:

> 'If he salt hath lost its savour, wherewith shall it be salted'. If the law officers charged with the obligation to protect the liberty of persons are mindless of constitutional mandates and the Code's dictates, how can freedom survive for the ordinary citizen.

In *Sunil Batra* (II), there was no direct question of release of undertrials but the Supreme Court expressed its opinion that the undertrials, who are presumably innocent until convicted, should not be sent to jail because by being sent to jail, they were, by contamination, made criminals and it was "a custodial perversity" which violated the test of reasonableness in article 19 and of fairness in article 21.

While the Supreme Court was already giving reminders regarding the unfolding of a new dimension of article 21, that is, recognizing rights of the undertrials, at Bhagalpur, a number of suspected criminals were allegedly blinded while they were in prison.

In this case, the court brought into light certain irregularities. In a few cases, the accused persons were not produced before the nearest magistrate within 24 hours of their arrest as required by article 22. In some cases, the accused persons were not produced before the judicial magistrates subsequent to their first production and they continued to be in jail without any remand orders being passed by the judicial magistrate.

According to the court, the provision inhibiting detention without remand was a very healthy provision which enabled the magistrates to keep check over the police investigation and that it was necessary that the magistrates should try to enforce this requirement carefully. The court also expressed its unhappiness at the lack of concern by the judicial magistrate in not enquiring from the blinded prisoners when they were first produced before them and thereafter from time to time for the purpose of remand as to how they had received injuries in the eyes. This gave rise to two inferences; either the prisoners were not physically produced before the magistrates or the magistrates machanically signed the remand orders. The court also regretted that no inspection of the central jail, Bhagalpur, was carried out by the district and sessions judge at any time during the year 1980.

The *Bhagalpur Blinding* case depicted a very sad picture of undertrials. The judiciary again came for the protection of human rights. But the question remains how far judiciary can be successful in preventing such torture to meet "lynch justice" in future.

In *Kadra Pehadiya v. State of Bihar,* four boys were languishing in jail as undertrial prisoners for more than 10 years. Human rights had no significance or meaning for them. The court rightly remarked:

> We fail to understand why our justice system has become dehumanised that lawyers and judges do not feel a sense of revolt at caging people in jail for years without trial.

However where the delay in trial is due to the fault of the accused, then he is not entitled to the benefit of delayed trial.

In *Sant Bir v. State of Bihar,* the court declared the detention of a prisoner as criminal lunatic illegal. He had become perfectly sane and fit for discharge and yet had been kept in detention for a period over 16 years without any justification. The court directed that he should be released from jail forthwith. The Supreme Court observed:

> It is shocking to our conscience that a perfectly sane person should have been incarcerated within the walls of a prison for almost 16 years without any justification in law whatsoever.

One may ask, speedy means how speedy? How long a delay is too long ? These questions were raised in *A.R. Antulay v. R.S. Naik.* The Constitution Bench delivered illuminating and exhaustive judgement which has traversed the entire ground. In regard to speedy trial the Supreme Court has laid down following propositions which will go a long way to protect the human rights of the prisoners:

1. Fair, just and reasonable procedure implicit in article 21 of the Constitution creates a right in the accused to be tried speedily.
2. Right to speedy trial encompasses all the stages, namely the stage of investigation, inquiry, trial, appeal, revision and retrial. There is no reason to take restricted view,
3. The concerns underlying, the right to speedy trial from the point of view of the accused are
   - (i) the period of remand and pre-conviction detention should be as short as possible,
   - (ii) the worry, anxiety expense and disturbance to his vocation and peace, resulting from unduly prolonged investigation, inquiry or trial should be minimal.
   - (iii) undue delay may well result in impairing of the ability of the accused to defend himself, whether on account of death, disappearance or non-availability of witnesses or otherwise.
4. It is usually the accused who is interested in delaying the proceedings because "delay is a known defence tactic". Of course, there may be cases where the prosecution, for whatever reasons, also delays the proceedings. Therefore, in every case, where the right to speedy trial is alleged to have been infringed, the first question to be put and answered is who is responsible for the delay? Proceedings taken by either party in good faith, to vindicate be their rights and interest, as perceived by them, cannot treated as delaying tactice nor can the time taken in pursuing such proceedings be

counted towards delay. Frivolous proceedings taken merely for delaying the day of reckoning cannot be treated as proceedings taken in good faith. The mere fact that an application/petition is admitted and an order of stay granted by superior court is by itself no proof that the proceeding is not frivolous.

5. While determining whether undue delay has occurred one must have regard to all the attended circumstances, including nature of offence, number of accused and witnesses, the work load of the court concerned and prevailing local conditions.

6. Each and every delay does not necessarily prejudice the accused. However, inordinate long delay may be taken as presumptive proof of prejudice.

7. The "demand" rule cannot be recognised or given effect to. Hence, an accused's plea of denial of speedy trial cannot be defeated by saying that the accused did at no time demand a speedy trial.

8. Court after weighing or balancing several relevant factors determine in each case, whether the right to speedy trial has been denied in a given case.

9. Ordinarily speaking, where the Court comes to the conclusion that right to speedy trial of an accused has been infringed, the charges or conviction, as the case may be, shall be quashed. But this is not only course open., The nature of the offence and other circumstances in a given case may be such that quashing of proceeding may not be in the interest of justice. In such a case, it is open to the court to make such other appropriate order, including the order to conclude the trial within a fixed time where the trial is not concluded or

reducing the sentence where the trial has concluded, as may be deemed just and equitable in the circumstance of the case.

10. It is neither advisable nor practicable to fix any time limit for trial of offences. In every case of complaint of denial of right to speedy trial, it is primarily for the prosecution to justify and explain the delay. Non-fixing of outer limit does not infringe the right to speedy trial.
11. An objection based on denial of right to speedy trial and for relief on that account should first be addressed to the High Court which should dispose of such proceedings on priority basis.

In *Santosh De v. Archna Guha* prosecution was pending for 14 years and not a single witness had been examined. The delay was entirely on account of default by prosecution. The prosecution failed to explain the delay. The court held that the right of the accused to speedy trial has been infringed and the proceedings were quashed on this ground.

We hope that the clarion call given by the highest judiciary will awaken the executive and subordinate judiciary from their deep slumber and they will join hands to make this right to speedy trial a living reality for the "little Indians".

The talk of human rights would become meaningless unless a person is provided with legal aid to enable him to have access to justice in case of violation of his human rights. This is formidable challenge in a country of India's size and heterogeneity where more than half of the population lives in far flung villages steeped in poverty, destitution and illiteracy. Legal aid is no longer a matter of charity or benevolence but is one of the constitutional right and the legal machinery itself is expected to deal specifically with it. The basic philosophy of legal aid envisages that the machinery of administration of justice should be easily accessible and should not be out of the reach of those who have to resort to it for the enforcement of their legal rights. In fact, legal aid offers a challenging opportunity to a society to redress grievances of the poor and thereby lay foundation of "Rule of Law". The rule of equality before the law and equal protection of law under article 14 of the Constitution would only remain constitutional shibboleth if a person cannot secure legal protection because he is poor. To begin with article 22(1) of the Constitution provided a right to every arrested person to consult legal practitioner of his choice. In 1976, a new article 39-A dealing with "equal justice and free legal aid" was added in the Constitution of India.

In India, judiciary has played an important role in developing the concept of legal aid and expanding its scope so as to enable the people to have access to courts in case of any violation of their human rights.

Maneka Gandhi v. Union of India, made the "procedure established by law" in article 21 of the Constitution as "just, fair and reasonable". This had impact in the subsequent cases in the area of legal aid as well.

In *M.H. Hoskot v. State of Maharashtra,* the Supreme Court held that the right to legal aid is one of the ingredients of fair procedure. The benefit of article 39-A is available in those cases where public justice suffers.

The Court, taking article 39-A as an interpretative tool of article 21, observed that the power to assign counsel to the indigent person "for doing complete justice" was implicit in the court by virtue of article 142 read with articles 21 and 39-A It was observed:

> Of course, the court may judge the situation and consider from all angles whether it is necessary for the ends of justice to make available legal aid in the particular case.

In *Hussainara Khatoon v. State of Bihar,* the court explained the true scope of article 39-A in the following words:

> This article also emphasises that free legal service is an unalienable element of 'reasonable, fair and just procedure for, without it a person suffering from economic or other disabilities would be deprived of an opportunity for securing justice... it must be held implicit in the guarantee of Article 21 (of the Constitution).

In *Khatri v. State of Bihar* again the court held that the right to free legal services was clearly an essential ingredient of reasonable, fair and just procedure for a person accused of an offence and it was implicit in the guarantee of article 21.

The court emphasised that the state was bound to provide free legal services to an indigent accused person and could not plead financial and administrative inability. The state might have its financial constraints and its priorities in expenditure but the state could not escape this liability.

The court made it obligatory for the Magistrate or the Sessions judge, before whom the accused appeared, to inform the accused that if he was unable to engage the services of a lawyer on account of poverty or indigence, he was entitled to obtain free legal services at the cost of the state. This duty was assigned to the Magistrates due to lack of legal awareness among the people. And this cause led the court to vote for making promotion of legal literacy as one of the principal items of the legal aid movement.

In *Damo v. State,* the Rajasthan High Court held that court has judicial discretion in giving priority and to hear cases even out of turn which would depend on the facts and circumstances of each individual case and this discretion does not in any way violate the right to equality under article 14 of the Constitution.

In *Sheela Barse v. State of Maharashtra,* the Supreme Court once again reiterated that legal assistance to poor or indigent accused is a constitutional imperative mandate not only by article 39-A but also by articles 14 and 21 of the constitution. The Court stated:

> It is a necessary sine quo non of justice and where it is not provided, injustice is likely to result and undeniably every act of injustice corrodes the foundations of democracy and rule of law...

In this case, the court gave a clarion call to the lawyers to rise for the help of those sections of humanity who were poor, illiterate and ignorant and who did not know what to do and where to go when they were involved in the accusation of crime or arrest or imprisonment. They could not impress upon them in better words than used by it.

Lawyers must realise that law is not a pleasant retreat where we are concerned merely with mechanical interpretation of rules made by the legislature but it is a teeming open ended avenue through which most of the traffic of human existence passes. There are many casualties of this traffic and it is the function of the legal profession to help these casualties in a spirit of dedication and service.

In *Suk Das v. U.T. of Arunachal Pradesh,* the Court followed the previous judgement and held that free legal aid at the State expense was a fundamental right of the person accused of an offence. And this right was not conditional upon the accused applying for free legal assistance. The Court made it obligatory on the Magistrate or Session Judge to inform the accused that he was entitled to free legal service at the cost of the State. 'Me court observed:

> It would... make a mockery of legal aid if it were to be left to a ignorant and illiterate accused to ask for free: legal service. Legal aid would become merely a paper promise and it would fail of its purpose.

Another aspect of "fair, just and reasonable" procedure is that while granting free legal aid, professional competence of the lawyer must be considered. If the lawyer provided by the state to the accused is not of equal competence as that of public prosecutor, there is no question of procedure being "fair, just and reasonable" because the accused does not have the equal opportunity of defending himself.

In *R.M. Wasawa v. State of Gujarat,* the Supreme Court observed:

> Indigence should never be a ground for denying fair trial or equal justice. Therefore, particular attention for should be paid to appoint competent advocates, equal to handling the complex cases, not patronising gestures to raw entrants to the Bar.

In *Ranjan Dwivedi v. Union of India,* the Summit Court again considered the question of professional competence of the lawyer provided by the state to the accused. The Court made it incumbent upon the state to provide the accused with a counsel of equal standing "as a matter of processual fair play."

The Supreme Court has also emphasised the role of people, voluntary organisations and social action groups in making legal aid meaningful, effective and purpose oriented. In order to fulfil the objectives of free legal aid, the Parliament has also passed "Legal Services Authorities Act, 1987". The basic aim of this Act is to provide free and competent legal services to the weaker sections ensuring that opportunities for securing justice are not denied to any citizen by reason of economic disability.

Throughout the world two extreme approaches regarding the capital punishment have been advocated. One, for retaining the death sentence for certain offences and the other for abolition of it. The first approach is based on deterrent theory of punishment whereas the Abolitionists have argued in favour of abolition of death sentence because they consider this punishment as cruel and inhuman. Article 6(2) of the International Covenant on Civil and Political Rights says that the countries which have not abolished death sentence, it may be imposed for the most serious crimes in accordance with the law in force at that time after the final judgement of the competent court. Article 6(4) of the Covenant further says that anyone sentenced to death shall have the right to seek pardon or commutation of the sentence. Amnesty, pardon or commutation of the sentence of death may be granted in all cases. On 15th December, 1989, the General Assembly, vide resolution 44/128, adopted and proclaimed the Second Optional Protocol to the International Covenant on Civil and Political Rights, aiming at the abolition of the death penalty. The provisions of the Second Protocol apply as additional provision to the Covenant on Civil and Political Rights. State Parties to the Second Protocol believe that abolition of death penalty contributes to enhancement of human dignity and progressive development of human rights. They are also convinced that all measures to abolish the death penalty should be considered as progress in the enjoyment of the right to life.

In India, the Indian Penal Code, provides for death Penalty for seven types of offences. Even these offences, it is to be noted that death sentence need not necessarily be meted out, for, generally other punishments are also provided for the same offence depending upon the circumstances of each case. Further even when a court has awarded death penalty, the President of India under article 72 of the Constitution has been empowered to grant pardons, commute, suspend or remit death penalty in appropriate cases.

In addition to this there are several procedural safeguards. For example, if a Session Court passed a sentence of death, the proceedings shall be submitted to the High Court for confirmation without which the sentence cannot be executed. Appeal lies from the High Court to the Supreme Court in cases where the High Court has, on appeal reversed an order of acquittal of an accused person and convicted him and sentenced him to death. The Criminal Procedure Code, 1973 further provides that the execution of sentence of death is to be postponed in case an appeal is pending before the Supreme Court. Moreover, when the conviction is for an offence punishable with death, the judgement should state "special reasons" for such sentence. The Criminal Procedure Code, 1973 also requires the High Court to postpone the execution of death sentence on pregnant women and may if it thinks fit, commute the sentence to imprisonment. The Indian Penal Code contains provisions to govern the situations of mass killing and murders. India has also signed and ratified the Covenant on the Prevention and Punishment of the Crime of Genocide. Indian Constitution also prohibits the making of ex-post facto laws and this applies equally to the question of death penalty.

Thus India has no doubt retained the death sentence in certain cases, but from the above statutory provisions And constitutional protections, it is evident that the basic human right to "life" is well protected in India. In spite of these protections the judiciary in India has shown its activist approach and tested various cases of death sentence on the touchstone of articles 14, 19 and 21 of the Constitution, which constitute the golden triangle for the protection of human rights in India.

In *Jagmohan Singh v. State of U.P.*, the Supreme Court held that death sentence is constitutionally permissible and not violative of articles 14, 19, and 21 of the Constitution.

In *Rajindra Prasad v. State of U.P.*, the constitutionality of death penalty was tested again on the touchstone of articles 14, 19 and 21 of the Constitution. In this case the court followed the humanist approach. The Court insisted that before putting out "the very flame of life" the judge must decide whether it is reasonably necessary. The court emphasised on "special reasons" under section 354 (3) of the Code of Criminal Procedure, 1973 which should be given by the judge before imposing death sentence. The Court observed:

> (I)t has now become necessary to have a second look at the life versus death question, not for summarising heither to decided cases and distilling the common factors but for applying the Constitution to cut the Gordian Knot.

The Court was also of the view that unusually cruel punishment should not be imposed because wherever there is unusual cruelity, it spells arbitrariness and "what is arbitrary is *per se* unequal" and ultimately violative of article 14 of the Constitution. The Court felt that the Indian Penal Code and the Code of Criminal Procedure must be read in the "humane light of Parts III & TV, further illuminated by the Preamble to the Constitution.

In *Dalbir Singh v. State of Punjab,* there was again a proposal towards abolition of death penalty. The Apex Court held that the imposition of death penalty violates dignity of the individual which is the sublime value of the Constitution, so it must be abolished. In this case the majority reduced the death sentence to one of life imprisonment despite the appellants guilty of four murders by stating that counting of casualities is not the main criterion for sentencing them to death.

In *Bachan Singh v. State of Punjab,* the Constitution Bench held that death sentence was not violation of article 21 but it should be awarded in "rarest of rare case", which is demanded by a real and abiding concern for the dignity of human life postulating resistance to taking life through law's instrumentality. The court is required to take into consideration all "aggravating circumstances" as well as "mitigating circumstance". There is no strict formula to define "rarest of rare cases". The court has to determine it in the facts and circumstances of each case.

In the case of *Kuljeet Singh alias Ranga v. Union of India,* where two young children Sanjay Chopra and Gita Chopra were murdered and in *Kehar Singh v. State (Delhi Admn.)* relating to the assassination of former Prime Minister of India, death sentence was awarded on the touchstone of the aforesaid criterion.

In Kehar Singh the Supreme Court has also considered the scope of article 72 of the Constitution and laid down following guidelines.

First, that it is open to the President in the exercise of the power vested in him by article 72 to scrutinise the evidence on record of the criminal case and come to a different conclusion from that recorded by the court in regard to the guilt of, and sentence imposed on the accused. In doing so the President does not amend or modify or supersede the judicial record which remains intact and undisturbed. The President is entitled to go into the merits of the case notwithstanding that it has been judicially concluded with !he consideration given to it by the court. Secondly, that order of the President cannot be subjected to judicial review on its merits except within the strict limitations defined in *Maru Ram v. Union of India.*

Thirdly, that there is no right in the condemned person to insist on an oral hearing before the President. The proceedings before the President are of an executive character, and when the petitioner files his petition, it is for him to submit with it all the requisite information necessary for the disposal of the case.

Mandatory death sentence unconstitutional

In *Mithu v. State of Punjab,* the Supreme Court declared section 303 of the Indian Penal Code, as unconstitutional being violative of articles 14 and 21 of the Constitution. The court remarked that a savage sentence was anathema to the civilised jurisprudence of article 21 of the Constitution. The Court gave following reasons for declaring it unconstitutional.

Firstly, it did not give the accused an opportunity to show cause why that sentence should not be imposed. Secondly, it did not require the court to state the reasons why death penalty was imposed. Thirdly, death sentence was mandatory in all the cases under section 303. Thus, the Court has protected the society from the clutches of cruel punishment.

Delay in execution of death sentence

The Supreme Court in *Ediga Anamma v. State of A.P.,* observed:

> (T)he brooding horror of hanging which has been haunting the prisoner in her condemned cell for over two years... has ameliorative impact (and was a factor of human significance in the sentencing context).

This view of the Supreme Court was followed in subsequent cases as well. The dehumanising effect of prolonged delay in execution after the sentence of death was explained by the Court in *T.V. Vatheswaran. v. State of T.N.,* in the following words:

> (T)he dehumanising factor of prolonged delay in the execution of a sentence of death has the constitutional implication of depriving a person of his life in an unjust, unfair and unreasonable way as to offend the constitutional guarantee that no person shall be deprived of his life or personal liberty except according to procedure established by law. The appropriate relief in such a case is to vacate the sentence of death.

The Court further observed:

> (T)hat delay exceeding two years in the execution of a sentence of death should be considered sufficient to entitle the person under sentence of death to invoke article 21 and demand the quashing of the sentence of death.

In *Sher Singh v. State of Punjab,* the Supreme Court refused to fix any time limit of delay for quashing the sentence of death and observed:

> Prolonged delay in the execution of the death sentence is unquestionably an important consideration for determining whether the sentence should be allowed to be executed. But no... hard and fast rule can be laid down... that "delay exceeding two years in the execution of a sentence of death should be considered sufficient to entitle the person under sentence of death to invoke Article 21 and demand the quashing of the sentence of death.

Finally, the question about delay has been decided by the Constitution Bench of the Supreme Court in *Triveniben v. State of Gujarat,* where it was held that while the Court has the power to commute sentence of death to life imprisonment in case of prolonged delay in execution, no fixed period of delay could be held to make the sentence of death inexecutable and entitle the accused to the lesser sentence of life imprisonment. The court also held that undue long delay in execution of sentence of death would entitle the condemned person to approach this court under article 32 but this court will only examine the nature of delay caused and circumstances which ensued after the sentence was finally confirmed by the judicial process and would have no jurisdiction to reopen the conclusions reached by the court while finally maintaining the sentence of death. However, this court may consider the question of inordinate delay in the light of all circumstances of the case to decide whether the execution of sentence should be carried out or should be converted into imprisonment for life.

Triveniben has been relied upon by the Supreme Court in subsequent cases as well. Thus, the human rights conscious court braught a mutation change in Criminal Law jurisprudence and made basic human right to "life" a living reality for the convicts at the execution stage.

Hanging by neck

The Supreme Court has also examined the question whether hanging by neck to execute death sentence can be said to be violative of article 21 of the Constitution on the ground that it is a cruel method of taking life.

Section 354(5) of the Code of Criminal Procedure, 1973 says that any person sentenced to death, the sentence shall direct that he shall be hanged by the neck till he is dead. In *Deena v. Union of India* while testing the method prescribed under section 354(5) of the Code of Criminal Procedure for executing the death sentence under article 21 of the Constitution, the court observed:

If it is lawful to impose the sentence of death in appropriate cases, it would be lawful to execute that sentence in an appropriate manner. Article 21, undoubtedly has as much relevance on the passing of a sentence, as on the manner of executing it... Substantively, the sentence has to meet the constitutional prescription contained, especially, in Articles 14 and 21. Procedurally, the method by which the sentence is required by law to be executed has to meet the mandate of Article 21. The mandate of Article 21 is not that the death sentence shall not be executed but that it shall not be executed in a cruel, barbarous or degrading manner.

The court held that the method prescribed by section 354(5) of the Code of Criminal Procedure for executing the death sentence did not violate the provision contained in Article 21 of the Constitution. It found that neither electrocution, nor lethal gas, nor shooting, nor even the lethal injection had any distinct or demonstrable advantage over the system of hanging. Therefore, it could not be concluded with certainty that the method of hanging should be replaced by any of these method.

This view of the Supreme Court has been endorsed again in *Shashi Nayar v. Union of India.* Thus, in view of the court, hanging by neck does not involve torture, brutality, barbarity and humilation.

However, in *Attorney General of India v. Lachma Deo,* the Supreme Court while paying great respect to the human dignity of the convicts held that the execution of death sentence by "public hanging" would be a barbaric practice and hence unconstitutional being violative of article 21 of the Constitution. The Court further observed that a barbaric crime does not have to be visited with a barbaric penalty, such as public hanging," which was also regarded as disgrace and shame on any civilised society, which no society should tolerate.

The right to die

Article 21 of the Constitution takes care of not only protection against arbitrary deprivation of life but also takes care of positive life to enable an individual to live a life with human dignity, Therefore, a very interesting as well as an important question which requires consideration is that whether right to live will include also a right not to live or not to be forced to live or in other words, does it include a right to die or to terminate one's life.

This senstive question was initially dealt with by Delhi, Bombay and Andhra Pradesh High Courts. The Delhi High Court in State v. Sanjay Kumar Bhatia, held that continuation of section 309 of the Indian Penal Code, which makes attempt to commit suicide punishable, is an anarchronism unworthy of a human society like ours. The present need is for humane, civilised and socially oriented outlook penology. Therefore, section 309 of the Indian Penal Code has no justification to remain on the statute book.

Andhra Pradesh High Court in *Maruti Shripati Dubal v. State of Maharashtra,* held that section 309 of the Indian Penal Code is violative of articles 14 and 21 of the Constitution and, therefore, struck it down. The High Court reached at this conclusion because freedom of speech guaranteed by article 19 includes freedom not to speak and to remain silent. Similarly other positive freedoms also include the negative aspect as well. Therefore, what applies to article 19 would also apply to article 21 of the Constitution. The Court mentioned various circumstances, including "extremely cruel or unbearable condition of life making it painful to live", in which suicide is committed or attempted. The High Court also considered section 309 as arbitrary because this section treats all attempts to commit suicide by the same measure without referring to the circumstances in which attempts were made.

A contrary view was, however, taken in *Chena Jagdeeshwar v. State of A.P.*, by the Andhra Pradesh High Court which held that it is difficult to hold that right to life impliedly guaranteed by the Constitution includes the right to die. It was stated that every case under section 309 of the Indian Penal Code may not lead to a punishment, because this section by no means mandates that a court should punish attempted suicide; it only lays down the upper limit of such punishment."

Finally, this question has been considered by the Supreme Court in P.Rathinam v. Union of India. The Supreme Court has also held that section 309 of the Indian Penal Code is violative of article 21 of the Constitution and hence unconstitutional. It was held that right to live, of which article 21 speaks can be said to bring in its trail right not to live a forced life. The court further pointed out that though the negative aspect may not be inferable on the analogy of the rights conferred by the different clauses of article 19 of the Constitution, one may refuse to live, if his life be not :According to the person concerned worth living or if the richness and fullness of life were not to demand living further. In any case, a person cannot be forced to enjoy right to life to his detriment, disadvantage or disliking.

The Court repelled the apprehension that if the negative aspect of right to life, Le., to destroy it can be read into article 21, the 'State' can easily embark upon a policy to encourage genocide on the plea that proper management of resources are vital and necessary for the upkeep of life with vigour and dignity in the wake of geometrical progression of population growth. In the opinion of the Court there is "gulf of difference between taking of one's life and allowing the State to go in for genocide". The Court further pointed out that law cannot be cruel, which it would be if persons attempting suicide are treated as criminals and are prosecuted to get them punished, whereas what they need is psychiatric treatment, because suicide basically is a "call for help".

A law which is cruel violates article 21 of the Constitution. However, the Court held that section 309 of the Indian Penal Code cannot be held violative of article 14 of the Constitution. After considering the position in this regard in the leading countries the Court concluded that the view taken by it would advance not only the cause of humanisation, which is the need of the day, but of globlisation also, as by effacing section 309, it would be attuning this part of our Criminal Law to the global wavelength.

It is submitted that the activist approach of the Supreme Court in de-criminalising attempt to commit suicide appears to be timely and thus is welcomed. However, it is difficult to digest the "right to die as fundamental right". On the one hand we all are concentrating in protecting and promoting the human rights of the people of which right to life is "heart and soul". On the other hand, to recognise right to die as fundamental right or a part of basic human right, i.e.., right to life would be self defeating. This process may reverse the whole trend of judicial activism as well.

Police atrocities and exemplary compensation

Judicial activism has not only protected the human rights of the people, but it also led to the granting of examplary compensation to the victims of police atrocities, which resulted in human rights violation. The traditional view supported the theory that "arrest and detention" is a "sovereign function" of the State. Thus, no liability of the state was considered if there was illegal arrest and detention. But the judicial grammar of interpretation of article 21 has undergone a mutation particularly since Maneka Gandhi. One of the impacts of this new interpretation is that in some cases the court has considered the question of giving monetary compensation to one who might have, suffered unduly, detailed illegally or was badly harmed.

Khatri v. State of Bihar, popularly known as Bhagalpur Blinding case, was the first case where the question of granting monetary compensation was considered by the Supreme Court. In this case, it was alleged that police had blinded certain prisoners and the state was liable to pay monetary compensation to them. Thus, an important question of constitutional importance was involved, viz., if a person is deprived of his right to life or personal liberty in violation of article 21 by the state, can the court grant monetary relief to such person? Bhagwati, J. speaking for the court observed:

> Why should the court not be prepared to forge new tools and devise new remedies for the purpose of vindicating the most precious of the precious Fundamental Rights to life and personal liberty.

As regards the liability of the state to pay compensation for infringing article 21, the court answered in the affirmative saying that if it were not so, article 21 would be reduced to a nullity, "a mere rope of sand. But since the matter as to the responsibility of the police officers was Still under investigation, the court did not decide the issue. Belatedly though, justice has finally caught up with the perpetrators of the blinding in Bhagalpur. The three police officers who were involved in the shocking incident of blinding of the undertrials, were finally convicted for taking the law into their own hands.

The Supreme Court brought about revolutionary breakthrough in the "Human Rights Jurisprudence" in

Rudul Sah v. State of Bihar when it granted monetary compensation of rupees thirty-five thousands to the petitioner against the lawless act of the Bihar government which kept him in illegal detention for over fourteen years after acquittal.

An important question to be determined by the Court was whether it could grant some compensation or exemplary costs against the State under article 32 of the Constitution for illegal detention in the jail. The Supreme Court observed:

> (T)he refusal of this court to pass an order of compensation in favour of the petitioner will be doing mere lip-service to his fundamental right to liberty which the State Government has so grossly violated.

It was pointed out that article 21 would be denuded of its significant content if the power of the court was limited to passing of orders of release form illegal detention. The Supreme Court further observed:

> One of the telling ways in which the violation of that right can reasonable be prevented and due compliance with the mandate of Article 21 seemed, is to mulct its violators in the payment of monetary compensation. Administrative sclerosis leading to flagrant infringements of fundamental rights cannot be corrected by any other method open to the judiciary to adopt. The right to compensation is some palliative for the unlawful acts of instrumentalities which act in the name of public interest and which present for their protection of power of the state as a shield... Therefore, the State must repair the damage done by its officers to the petitioner's rights. It may have recourse against those officers.

Thus, the Supreme Court for the first time openly declared that compensation ought to be paid for the violation of basic human right, i.e., right to life and liberty under article 21 of the Constitution.

In *Sebastian M Hongray v. Union of India,* the Supreme Court in habeas corpus proceedings required the Government of India to produce two persons before it. These persons had been taken into, custody by the military jawans in the military camp. The government failed to Produce, them in the court and also expressed incorrect a, ad untenable. In fact, the, truth was that these two persons had met an natural death. The, Court, in the circumstances, keeping in view the torture, the agony and mental oppression undergone by the wives of the persons directed to be produced, instead of imposing fine on the government for civil contempt of the court, required that "as a measure of exemplary costs as is permissible in such cases", the government must pay rupees one lakh to each one of the aforesaid two women.

In yet another important case of *Bhim Singh v. State of J&K,* the Supreme Court noted that the police officer acted in the most high-handed way and it awarded rupees fifty thousand as monetary compensation by way of exemplary costs to the petitioner so as to compensate him "suitable and adequately. In this case, the petitioner, a member of Legislative Assembly of Jammu and Kashmir, was arrested by the police malafide and was not produced before the magistrate within the requisite period. The petitioner alleged that his fundamental rights under articles 21 and 22(l) were violated. The Supreme Court observed:

> When a person comes to us with the complaint that he was arrested and imprisoned with mischievous or malacious intent and that his constitutional and legal rights were invaded, the mischief or malice and the invasion may not be washed away or wished away by his being set free. In appropriate cases we

> have the jurisdiction to compensate the victim by awarding suitable monetary compen-sation. We consider this an appropriate case.

In all the cases from Rudul Sah to Bhim Singh, in which the Supreme Court awarded the monetary compensation, no basis for quantification of the amount of exemplary costs was laid down by the court. And perhaps this was the reason that the amount of monetary compensation varied in all the above mentioned cases. In order words, the discretion to award monetary compensation for the gross violation of article 21 was left to the individual judge who decided, the case, which in our opinion is not a good law or good precedent

The Supreme Court in *Peoples' Union for Democratic Rights v. State of Bihar,* laid down the working principle for the, payment of compensation to the victims of ruthless and unwarranted police firing. In the present case, about twenty-one persons including children died and many more were injured due to the unwarranted firing of the Police. The Supreme Court observed:

> Ordinarily in the case of death, compensation of rupees twenty thousand is paid... We may not be taken to suggest that in the case of death the liability of the wrongdoer is absolved when compensation of rupees twenty thousand is paid. But as a working principle and for convenience and with a view to rehabilitate the dependants of the deceased such compensation is being paid.

The Supreme Court further pointed out that without prejudice to any just claim for compensation that may be advanced by the relations of the victims who had died or by the injured persons themselves, for every case of the death, compensation of rupees twenty thousand and for every injured person compensation of rupees five thousand shall be paid.

From the above observations of the Supreme Court, it is evident that though it has evolved a working principle of awarding compensation to the victims of the police atrocities but it is not a good working principle. Where the life of the person was lost, his dependants were to be paid only the meagre sum of rupees twenty thousand. The Supreme Court, while evolving the working principles of granting compensation, has also failed to differentiate between the major and minor injury to the limb or body of the person concerned. It appears that the Supreme Court evolved the working principle of awarding compensation with the primary object of rehabilitating the victims or their dependants. However, it might happen that the person might not die but with the police atrocities he might lose his eyes, limb and might become unable to earn his livelihood. Can we say that the suggested amount of rupees five thousand to such a person would be, sufficient to "rehabilitate" him. The obvious answer would be no. Therefore, it is suggested that if life and liberty is to have some meaning for the millions of Indians, then for rehabilitating these persons, who are often victims of police atrocities, some larger amount should be paid as compensation and not merely rupees five thousand or so.

In *Rajasthan Kisan Sangathan v. State,* it was held that it is a now wellsettled that a person even during lawful detention is entitled to be treated with dignity befitting any human being and the more fact that he has been detained lawfully does not mean that he can be subjected to illtreatment, much less any torturous beating. The right to be treated even during lawful detention in a manner commensurate with human dignity is a well recognised right under article 21 of the Constitution, and if it is found that the police has maltreated any person in police custody which is not commensurate with human dignity, he is at least, entitled to monetary compensation for the torturous act by the police.

In *R. Ramkonda Reddy v, State,* it was held that where a citizen has been deprived of his life or liberty, otherwise than in accordance with the procedure prescribed by law, it is no answer to say that the said deprivation was brought about while the officials of the state were acting in discharge of the "sovereign function" of the state. Suit for compensation against the state, when an undertrial prisoner in jail lost his life due to failure or neglect of its officers to perform their duties, will, therefore, be maintainable. The Court pointed out that indeed, this is the only mode in which right to life guaranteed by article 21 can be enforced.

In *SAHELI, a Women's Resources Centre v. Commr. of Police, Delhi,* the Supreme Court once again considered the question of granting compensation in case of police atrocities. In this case, a 9 year old child died due to assault and beating by the Police Officer. The Supreme Court held that the state is liable to pay compensation in case of police atrocities and accordingly it directed the State government to pay Rs. 75,000 as compensation to mother of victim.

In State of Maharashtra v. Ravikant S. Patil, under trial prisoner was handcuffed and taken through the streets in a procession by police during investigation. The Court held that article 21 was violated. However, the Court further held that police officer responsible for the act, acted only as an official and cannot be made personally liable. The Court directed that compensation of Rs. 10,000 be paid by the state and authorities may, if consider necessary, hold an enquiry against the police officer and then decide whether any further action is to be taken against him or not.

It is submitted that when the complainant is entitled to compensation for violation of human rights or for physical or mental harassment, then an award of exemplary costs/damages can serve as useful purpose in vindicating the strength of law and promoting and protecting human rights. However, when the court directs payment of damages/compensation against the State, the ultimate sufferer is the common man. It is the tax payers money which is paid for the wrong of public official. Therefore, it is suggested that the state should pay the complainant from the public fund but recover the same from those who are responsible for such unpardonable behaviour.

Nilabati Behera v. State of Orissa, is yet another case of custodial death where the deceased was taken in police custody and next day his body was found on railway track with multiple injuries. The Supreme Court once again reiterated that in case of violation of fundamental rights by State's instrumentalities or its servants, Court can direct the State to pay compensation to victim or his heir by, way of 'monetary amends' and redressal. The principle of sovereign immunity" shall be inapplicable in such cases, Having regard to the age and income of the deceased, the State was directed in this case to pay Rs. 1,50,0001 as compensation to the deceased's mother. The Court further held that other liabilities of the respondents or any other person for custodial death remain unaffected. In other words, compensation in civil law or criminal law can still be claimed in addition to this. The Court clarified that "public law proceedings" are different from "private law proceedings" and the award of compensation in proceedings for the enforcement of fundamental right under articles 32 and 226 of the Constitution is a remedy available in public law. It was rightly observed:

> The Court is not helpless and the wide powers given to the Supreme Court by Article 32, which itself is a fundamental right, imposes a constitutional obligation on the Court to forge such new tools,

> which may be necessary for doing complete justice and enforcing the fundamental rights guaranteed in the constitution which enable the award of monetary compensation; in appropriate cases...

To support the above observations, the court rightly referred to article 9(5) of the International Covenant on Civil and Political Rights, 1966 and held that the said provision indicates that an enforceable right to compensation is not alien to the concept of a guaranteed right.

Dr. A.S. Anand, J., while delivering a separate but concurring judgement in this case pointed out in sonorous terms that convicts, prisoners and undertrials also have the right under article 21 of the Constitution and the State has strict duty to ensure that a person in custody of police is not deprived of his right except in accordance with law.

In *Charanjit Kaur v. Union of India,* where an Army Officer died while in service in mysterious circumstance. On facts, authorities were found guilty of criminal omissions and commissions resulting in great mental agony and physical and financial hardship to the widow and children of the deceased. The Court granted rupees six lakhs as compensation and special family pension and children allowance.

Whenever any case of human rights violation has been brought before the Court, it has always taken a serious note of it and directed to make either judicial enquiry into the allegations or directed the Central Bureau of Investigation (CBI) to conduct an enquiry independently so as to fix the responsibility for violation of human rights.

In *Khedat Mazdoor Chetna Sangath v. State of M.P.,* where the tribals alleged the human rights violation and commission of inhuman atrocities on them by the police, the Supreme Court not only directed the Central Bureau of Investigation (CBI) to investigate the whole matter but also register case and prosecute officers, however, high or low in the hierarchy of administration for these lapses. Further to ensure an independent trial, the Court directed that the trial of such cases should take place outside the district concerned. These directions were given to uphold human values and to protect the rights guaranteed by the Constitution.

Arvinder Singh Bagga v. State of U.P., is yet another case of police atrocities where police officers subjected a married women to her physical, mental and psychological torture calculated to create fright to make her submit to the demands of the police and abandon her legal marriage. Her husband and family members were also tortured. The court took serious note of the human rights violation and directed the State to launch prosecution against the police officials concerned and directed to pay compensation of Rs. 10,000/ to the victim women and her husband and Rs. 50001 to each of the other victim. The Court further pointed out that upon such payment it will be open to the state to recover personally the amount of compensation from the police officers concerned. It could have been better if the Supreme Court had not left it open on the State government to recover the amount of compensation from the guilty officials but directed to recover from them.

It is submitted that this new concept of "personal liability" of the police official concerned for violating the human rights is a welcoming feature of Indian judiciary on the path of protecting human rights of people. This will definitely have some deterrent affect on the police officials. However, in this case the amount paid to the victims was too less.

In *Dhananjay Sharma v. State of Haryana*, the Supreme

Court has once again reiterated that the state "must be held responsible for the unlawful acts of its officers and it must repair the damage done to the citizens by its officers for violating their indefeasible fundamental right of personal liberty without any authority of law." However, in the present case the detenues were disentitled from receiving any compensation, as monetory amends for the wrong done by the state officials because detenues had misrepresented and exaggerated the facts by filing false affidavits in the Court.

No doubt, the police plays vital role in safeguarding our life liberty and freedoms. But the police must act properly showing fall respect to the human rights of the people. They must also remember that they are also under the law and not above the law. They can also be held liable for any violation of human rights. In fact, what the society needs is, well-led, well-trained and well-disciplined force of police which help in protecting and promoting the human rights. The judicial activism has brought the human rights close to the people and the latest trend of the judiciary is in consonance with article 9(5) of the International Covenant of Civil and Political Rights.

Treatment of Prisoners

Preliminary Observations

1. The following rules are not intended to describe in detail a model system of penal institutions. They seek only, on the basis of the general consensus of contemporary thought and the essential elements of the most adequate systems of today, to set out what is generally accepted as being good principle and practice in the treatment of prisoners and the management of institutions.

2. In view of the great variety of legal, social, economic and geographical conditions of the world, it is evident that not all of the rules are capable of application in all places and at all times. They should, however, serve to stimulate a constant endeavour to overcome practical difficulties in the way of their application, in the knowledge that they represent, as a whole, the minimum conditions which are accepted as suitable by the United Nations.

3. On the other hand, the rules cover a field in which thought is constantly developing. They are not intended to preclude experiment and practices, provided these are in harmony with the principles and seek to further the purposes which derive from the text of the rules as a whole. It will always be justifiable for the central prison administration to authorize departures from the rules in this spirit.

4. (1) Part I of the rules covers the general management of institutions and is applicable to all categories of prisoners, criminal or civil, untried or, convicted, including prisoners subject to "security measures" or corrective measures ordered by the judge.

(2) Part II contains rules applicable only to the special categories dealt with in each section. Nevertheless, the rules under section A, applicable to prisoners under sentence, shall be equally applicable to categories of prisoners dealt with in sections B, C and D, provided they do not conflict with the rules governing those categories and are for their benefit.

5. (1) The rules do not seek to regulate the management of institutions set aside for young persons such as Borstal institutions or correctional schools, but in general part I would be equally applicable in such institutions.

(2) The categories of young prisoners should include at least all young persons who come within the jurisdiction of juvenile courts. As a rule, such young persons should not be sentenced to imprisonment.

Part I: Rules of General Applications

Basic principle

6. (1) The following rules shall be applied impartially. There shall be no discrimination on grounds of race, colour, sex, language, religion, political or other opinion, national or social origin, property, birth or other status.

(2) On the other hand, it is necessary to respect the religious beliefs and moral precepts of the group to which a prisoner belongs.

Register

7. (1) In every place where persons are imprisoned there shall be kept a bound registration book with numbered pages in which shall be entered in respect of each prisoner received.

(a) Information concerning his identity;

(b) The reasons for his commitment and the authority therefor;

(c) The day and hour of his admission and release.

(2) No person shall be received in an institution without a valid commitment order of which the details shall have been previously entered in the register.

Separation of categories

8. The different categories of prisoners shall be kept in separate institutions or parts of institutions taking account of their sex, age, criminal record, the legal reason for their detention and the necessities of their treatment.

Thus,

(a) Men and women shall so far as possible be detained in separate institutions; in an institution which received both men and women the whole of the premises allocated to women shall be entirely separate;

(b) Untried prisoners shall be kept separate from convicted prisoners;

(c) Persons imprisoned for debt and other civil prisoners shall be kept separate from persons imprisoned by reason of a criminal offence;

(d) Young prisoners shall be kept separate from adults.

Accommodation

9. (1) Where sleeping accommodation is in individual cells or rooms each prisoner shall occupy by night a cell or room by himself. If for special reasons, such as temporary overcrowding, it becomes necessary for the central prison administration to make an exception to this rule, it is not desirable to have two prisoners in a cell or room.

(2) Where dormitories are used, they shall be occupied by prisoners carefully selected as being suitable to associate with one another in those conditions. There shall be regular supervisions by night, in keeping with the nature of the institution.

10. All accommodation provided for the use of prisoners and in particular all sleeping accommodation shall meet all requirements of health, due regard being paid to climatic conditions and particularly to cubic content of air, minimum floor space, lighting, heating and ventilation.

11. In all places where prisoners are required to live or work,

(a) The windows shall be large enough to enable the prisoners to read or work by natural light, and shall be so constructed that they can allow the entrance of fresh air whether or not there is artificiel ventilation;

(b) Artifical light shall be provided sufficient for the prisoners to read or work without injury to eyesight.

12. The sanitary installations shall be adequate to enable every prisoner to comply with the needs of nature when necessary and in a clean and decent manner.

13. Adequate bathing and shower installation shall be provided so that every prisoner may be enabled and required to have a bath or shower, at a temperature suitable to the climate, as frequently as necessary for general hygiene according to season and geographical region, but at least once a week in a temperate climate.

14. All parts of an institution regularly used by prisoners shall be properly maintained and kept scrupulously clean at all times.

Personal hygiene

15. Prisoners shall be required to keep their persons clean, an to this end they shall be provided with water and with such toilet articles as are necessary for health and cleanliness.

16. In order that prisoners may maintain a good appearance compatible with their self-respect, facilities shall be provided for the proper care of the hair and beard and men shall be enabled to shave regularly.

Clothing and bedding

17. (1) Every prisoner who is not allowed to wear his own clothing shall be provided with an outfit of clothing suitable for the climate and adequate to keep

him in good health. Such clothing shall in no manner be degrading or humiliating.

(2) All clothing shall be clean and kept in proper condition. Underclothing shall be changed and washed as often as necessary for the maintenance of hygiene.

(3) In exceptional circumstances, whenever a prisoner is removed outside the institution for an authorized purpose, he shall be allowed to wear his own clothing or other inconspicuous clothing.

18. If prisoners are allowed to wear their own clothing, arrangements shall be made on their admission to the institution to ensure that it shall be clean and fit for use.

19. Every prisoner shall in accordance with local or national standards, be provided with a separate bed, and with separate and sufficient bedding which shall be clean when issued, kept in good order and changed often enough to ensure its cleanliness.

Food

20. (1) Every prisoner shall be provided by the administration at the usual hours with food of nutritional value adequate for health and strength, of wholesome quality and well prepared and served.

(2) Drinking water shall be available to every prisoner whenever he needs it.

Exercise and sport

21. (1) Every prisoner who is not employed in outdoor work shall have at least one hour of suitable exercise in the open air daily if the weather permits.

(2) Young prisoners, and others of suitable age and physique, shall receive physical and recreational training during the period of exercise. To this end space, installations and equipment should be provided.

Medical services

22. (1) At every institution there shall be available the services of at least one qualified medical officer who should have some knowledge of psychiatry. The medical services should be organized in close relationship to the general health administration of the community or nation. They shall include a psychiatric service for the diagnosis and, in proper cases, the treatment of states of mental abnormality.

(2) Sick prisoners who require specialist treatment shall be transferred to specialized institutions or to civil hospitals. Where hospital facilities are provided in an institution, their equipment, furnishings and pharmaceutical supplies shall be proper for the medical care and treatment of sick prisoners, and there shall be a staff of suitable trained officers.

(3) The services of a qualified dental officer shall be available to every prisoner.

23. (1) In women's institutions there shall be special accommodation for all necessary pre-natal and post-natal care and treatment. Arrangements shall be made wherever practicable for children to be born in a hospital outside the institution. A child is born in prison, this fact shall not be mentioned in the birth certificate.

(2) Where nursing infants are allowed to remain in the institution with their mothers, provision shall be made for a nursery staffed by qualified person, where the infants shall be placed when they are not in the care of their mothers.

24. The medical officer shall see and examine every prisoner as soon as possible after his admission and thereafter as necessary, with a view particularly to the discovery of physical or mental illness and the taking of all necessary measures; the segregation of prisoners

suspected of infectious or contagious conditions; the noting of physical or mental defects which might hamper rehabilitation, and the determination of the physical capacity of every prisoner for work.

25. (1) The medical officer shall have the care of the physical and mental health of the prisoners and should daily see all sick prisoners, all who complain of illness, and any prisoner to whom his attention is specially directed.

(2) The medical officer shall report to the director whenever he considers that a prisoner's physical or mental health has been or will be injuriously affected by continued imprisonment or by any condition of imprisonment.

26. (1) The medical officer shall regularly inspect and advise the director upon:

(a) The quantity, quality, preparation and service of food;

(b) The hygiene and cleanliness of the institution and the prisoners;

(c) The sanitation, heating, lighting and ventilation of the institution;

(d) The suitability and cleanliness of the prisoners' clothing and bedding;

(e) the observance of the rules concerning physical education and sports, in caes where there is no technical personnel in charge of these activities.

(2) The director shall take into consideration the reports and advice that the medical officer submits according to rules 25C2) and 26 and, in case he concurs with the recommendations made, shall take immediate steps to give effect to those recommendations; if they are not within his competence or if he does not concur with

them, he shall immediately submit his own report and the advice of the medical officer to higher authority.

Discipline and punishment

27. Discipline and order shall be maintained with firmness, but with no more restriction than is necessary for safe custody and well-ordered community life.

28. (1) No prisoner shall be employed, in the service of the institution, in any disciplinary capacity.

(2) This rule shall not, however, impede the proper functioning of systems based on self-government, under which specified social, educational or sports activities or responsibilities are entrusted, under supervision, to prisoners who are formed into groups for the purpose of treatment.

29. The following shall always be determined by the law or by the regulation of the competent administrative authority:

(a) Conduct constituting a disciplinary offence;

(b) The types and duration of punishment which may be inflicted;

(c) The authority competent to impose such punishment.

30. (1) No prisoner shall be punished except in accordance with the terms of such law or regulation, and never twice for the same offence.

(2) No prisoner shall be punished unless he has been informed of the offence alleged against him and given a proper opportunity of presenting his defence. The competent authority shall conduct a thorough examination of the case.

(3) Where necessary and practicable the prisoner shall be allowed to make his defence through an interpreter.

31. Corporal punishment, punishment by placing in a dark cell, and all cruel, inhuman or degrading punishments shall be completely prohibited as punishments for disciplinary offences.

32. (1) Punishment by close confinement or reduction of diet shall never be inflicted unless the medical officer has examined the prisoner and certified in writing that he is fit to sustain it.

(2) the same shall apply to any other punishment that may be prejudicial to the physical or mental health of a prisoner. In no case may such punishment be contrary to or depart from the principle stated in rule 31.

(3) The medical officer shall visit daily prisoners undergoing such punishments and shall advise the director if he considers the termination or alteration of the punishment necessary on grounds of physical or mental health.

Instruments of restraint

33. Instruments of restraint, such as handcuffs, chains, irons an straitjackets, shall never be applied as a punishments. Furthermore, chains or irons shall not be used as restraints. Other instruments of restraint shall not be used except in the following circumstances:

(a) As a precaution against escape during a transfer, provided that they shall be removed when the prisoner appears before a judicial or administrative authority;

(b) On medical grounds by direction of the medical officer;

(c) By order of the director, if other methods of control fail, in order to prevent a prisoner from injuring himself or others or from damaging property; in such instances the director shall at once consult the medical officer and report to the higher administrative authority.

34. The patterns and manner of use of instruments of restraint shall be decided by the central prison administration. Such instruments must not be applied for any longer time than is strictly necessary.

Information to and complaints by prisoners

35. (1) Every prisoner on admission shall be provided with written information about the regulations governing the treatment of prisoners of his category, the disciplinary requirements of the institution, the authorized methods of seeking information and making complaints, and all such other matters as are necessary to enable him to understand both his rights and his obligations and to adapt himself to the life of the institution.

(2) If a prisoner is illiterate, the aforesaid information shall be conveyed to him orally.

36. (1) Every prisoner shall have the opportunity each week day of making requests or complaints to the director of the institution or the officer authorized to represent him.

(2) It shall be possible to make requests or complaints to the inspector of prisons during his inspection. The prisoner shall have the opportunity to talk to the inspector or to any other inspecting officer without the director or other members of the staff being present.

(3) Every prisoner shall be allowed to make a request or complaint, without censorship as to substance but in proper form, of the central prison administration, the judicial authority or other proper authorities through approved channels.

(4) Unless it is evidently frivolous or groundless, every request or complaint shall be promptly dealt with and replied to without undue delay.

Contact with the outside world

37. Prisoners shall be allowed under necessary supervision to communicate with their family and reputable friends at regular intervals, both by correspondence and by receiving visits.

38. (1) Prisoners who are foreign nationals shall be allowed reasonable facilities to communicate with the diplomatic and consular representatives of the State to which they belong.

(2) Prisoners who are nationals of States without diplomatic or consular representation in the country and refugees or stateless persons shall be allowed similar facilities to communicate with the diplomatic representative of the State which takes charge of their interests or any national or international authority whose task it is to protect such persons.

39. Prisoners shall be kept informed regularly of the more important items of news by the reading of newspapers, periodicals or special institutional publications, by hearing wireless transmissions, by lectures or by any similar means as authorized or controlled by the administration.

Books

40. Every institution shall have a library for the use of all categories of prisoners, adequately stocked with both recreational and instructional books, and prisoners shall be encouraged to make full use of it.

Religion

41. (1) If the institution contains a sufficient number

of prisoners of the same religion, a qualified representative of that religion shall be appointed or approved. If the number of prisoners justifies it and conditions permit, the arrangement should be on a full-time basis.

(2) A qualified representative appointed or approved under paragraph (1) shall be allowed to hold regular services and to pay pastoral visits in private to prisoners of his religion at proper times.

(3) Access to a qualified representative of any religion shall not be refused to any prisoner. On the other hand, if any prisoner should object to a visit to any religious representative, his attitude shall be fully respected.

42. So far as practicable, every prisoner shall be allowed to satisfy the needs of his religious life by attending the services provided in the institution and having in his possession the books of religious observance and instruction of his denomination.

Retention of prisoners' property

43. (1) All money, valuables, clothing and other effects belonging to a prisoner which under the regulations of the institution he is not allowed to retain shall on his admission to the institution be placed in safe custody. An inventory thereof shall be signed by the prisoner. Steps shall be taken to keep them in good condition.

(2) On the release of the prisoner all such articles and money shall be returned to him except in so far as he has been authorized to spend money or send any such property out of the institution, or it has been found necessary on hygienic grounds to destroy any article of clothing. The prisoner shall sign a receipt for the articles and money returned to him.

(3) Any money or effects received for a prisoner from outside shall be treated in the same way.

(4) If a prisoner brings in any drugs or medicine, the medical officer shall decide what use shall be made of them.

Notification of death, illness, transfer, etc.

44. (1) Upon the death or serious illness of, or serious injury to a prisoner, or his removal to an institution for the treatment of mental affections, the director shall at once inform the spouse, if the prisoner is married, or the nearest relative and shall in any event inform any other person previously designated by the prisoner.

(2) A prisoner shall be informed at once of the death or serious illness of any near relative. In case of the critical illness of a near relative, the prisoner should be authorized, whenever circumstances allow, to go to his bedside either under escort or alone.

(3) Every prisoner shall have the right to inform at once his family of his imprisonment or his transfer to another institution.

Removal of prisoners

45. (1) When the prisoners are being removed to or from an institution, they shall be exposed to public view as little as possible, and proper safeguards shall be adopted to protect them from insult, curiosity and publicity in any form.

(2) The transport of prisoners in conveyances with inadequate ventilation or light, or in any way which would subject them to unnecessary physical hardship, shall be prohibited.

(3) The transport of prisoners shall be carried out at

the expense of the administration and equal conditions shall obtain for all of them.

Institutional personnel

46. (1) The prison administration, shall provide for the careful selection of every grade of the personnel, since it is on their integrity, humanity, professional capacity and personal suitability for the work that the proper administration of the institution depends.

(2) The prison administration shall constantly seek to awaken and maintain in the minds both of the personnel and of the public the conviction that this work is a social service of great importance, and to this end all appropriate means of informing the public should be used.

(3) To secure the foregoing ends, personnel shall be appointed on a full-time basis as professional prison officers and have civil service status with security of tenure subject only to good conduct, efficiency and physical fitness. Salaries shall be adequate to attract and retain suitable men and women; employment benefits and conditions of services shall be favourable in view of the exacting nature of the work.

47. (1) The personnel shall possess an adequate standard of education and intelligence.

(2) Before entering on duty, the personnel shall be given a course of training in their general and specific duties and be required to pass theoretical and practical tests.

(3) After entering on duty and during their career, the personnel shall maintain and improve their knowledge and professional capacity by attending courses of in-service training to be organized at suitable intervals.

48. All members of the personnel shall at all times so conduct themselves and perform their duties as to influence the prisoners for good by their example and to command their respect.

49. (1) So far as possible, the personnel shall include a sufficient number of specialist such as psychiatrists, psychologists, social workers, teachers and trade instructors.

(2) The services of social workers, teachers and trade instructors shall be secured on a permanent basis, without thereby excluding part-time or voluntary workers.

50. (1) The director of an institution should be adequately qualified for his task by character, administrative ability, suitable training and experience.

(2) He shall devote his entire time to his official duties and shall not be appointed on a part-time basis.

(3) He shall reside on the premises of the institution or in its immediate vicinity.

(4) When two or more institutions are under the authority of one director, he shall visit each of them at frequent intervals. A responsible resident official shall be in charge of each of these institutions.

51. (1) The director, his deputy, and the majority of the other personnel of the institution shall be able to speak the language of the greatest number of prisoners, or a language understood by the greatest number of them.

(2) Whenever necessary, the services of an interpreter shall be used.

52. (1) In institutions which are large enough to require the services of one or more full-time medical

officers, at least one of them shall reside on the premises of the institution or in its immediate vicinity.

(2) In other institutions the medical officer shall visit daily and shall reside near enough to be able to attend without delay in cases of urgency.

53. (1) In an institution for both men and women, the part of the institution set aside for women shall be under the authority of a responsible woman officer who shall have the custody of the keys of all that part of the institution.

(2) No male member of the staff shall enter the part of the institution set aside for women unless accompanied by a woman officer.

(3) Women prisoners shall be attended and supervised only by women officers. This does not, however, preclude male members of the staff, particularly doctors and teachers, from carrying out their professional duties in institutions or parts of institutions set aside for women.

54. (1) Officers of the institutions shall not, in their relations with the prisoners, use force except in self-defence or in cases of attempted escape, or active or passive physical resistance to an order based on law or regulations. Officers who have recourse to force must use no more than is strictly necessary and must report the incident immediately to the director of the institution.

(2) Prison officers shall be given special physical training to enable them to restrain aggressive prisoners.

(3) Except in special circumstances, staff performing duties which bring them into direct contact with prisoners should not be armed. Furthermore, staff should in no circumstances be provided with arms unless they have been trained in their use.

Inspection

55. There shall be a regular inspection of penal institution and services by qualified and experienced inspectors appointed by a competent authority. Their task shall be in particular to ensure that these institutions are administered in accordance with existing laws and regulations and with a view to bringing about the objectives of penal and correctional services.

Part II: Rules Applicable to Special Categories

A. Prisoners Under Sentence

Guiding principles

56. The guiding principles hereafter are intended to show the spirit in which penal institutions should be administered and the purpose at which they should aim, in accordance with the declaration made under Preliminary Observation 1 of the present text.

57. Imprisonment and other measures which result in cutting off an offender from the outside world are afflictive by the very fact of taking from the person the right of self-determination by depriving him of his liberty. Therefore the prison system shall not, except as incidental to justifiable segregation or the maintenance of discipline, aggravate the suffering inherent in such a situation.

58. The purpose and justification of a sentence of imprisonment or a similar measure deprivative of liberty is ultimately to protect society against crime. This end can only be achieved if the period of imprisonment is used to ensure, so far as possible, that upon his return to society the offender is not only willing but able to lead a law-abiding and self-supporting life.

59. To this end, the institution should utilize all the remedial, educational, moral, spiritual and other forces

and forms of assistance which are appropriate and available, and should seek to apply them according to the individual treatment needs of the prisoners.

60. (1) The regime of the institution should seek to minimize any differences between prison life and life at liberty which tend to lessen the responsibility of the prisoners or the respect due to their dignity as human beings.

(2) Before the completion of the sentence, it is desirable that the necessary steps be taken to ensure for the prisoner a gradual return to life in society. This aim may be achieved, depending on the case, by a pre-release regime organized in the same institution or in another appropriate institution, or by release on trial under some kind of supervision which must not be entrusted to the police but should be combined with effective social aid.

61. The treatment of prisoners should emphasize not their exclusion from the community, but their continuing part in it. Community agencies should, therefore, be enlisted wherever possible to assist the staff of the institution in the task of social rehabilitation of the prisoners. There should be in connection with every institution social workers charged with the duty of maintaining and improving all desirable relations of a prisoner with his family and with valuable social agencies. Steps should be taken to safeguard, to the maximum extent compatible with the law and the sentence, the rights relating to civil interests, social security rights and other social benefits of prisoners.

62. The medical services of the institution shall seek to detect and shall treat any physical or mental illnesses or defects which may hamper a prisoner's rehabilitation. All necessary medical, surgical and psychiatric services shall be provided to that end.

63. (1) The fulfilment of these principles requires individualization of treatment and for this purpose a flexible system of classifying prisoners in groups; it is therefore desirable that such groups should be distributed in separate institutions suitable for the treatment of each group.

(2) These institutions need not provide the same degree of security for every group. It is desirable to provide varying degrees of security according to the needs of different groups. Open institutions, by the very fact that they provide no physical security against escape but rely on the self-discipline of the inmates, provide the conditions most favourable to rehabilitation for carefully selected prisoners.

(3) It is desirable that the number of prisoners in closed institutions should not be so large that the individualization of treatment is hindered. In some countries it is considered that the population of such institutions should not exceed five hundred. In open institutions the population should be as small as possible.

(4) On the other hand, it is undesirable to maintain prisons which are so small that proper facilities cannot be provided.

64. The duty of society does not end with a prisoner's release. There should, therefore, be governmental or private agencies capable of lending the released prisoner efficient after—care directed towards the lessening of prejudice against him and towards his social rehabilitation.

Treatment

65. The treatment of persons sentenced to imprisonment or a similar measure shall have as its purpose, so far as the length of the sentence permits, to

establish in them the will to lead law-abiding and self-supporting lives after their release and to fit them to do so. The treatment shall be such as will encourage their self-respect and develop their sense of responsibility.

66. (1) To these ends, all appropriate means shall be used, including religious care in the countries where this is possible, education, vocational guidance and training, social casework, employment counselling physical development and strengthening of moral character, in accordance with the individual needs of each prisoner, taking account of his social and criminal history, his physical and mental capacities and aptitudes, his personal temperament, the length of his sentence and his prospects after release.

(2) For every prisoner with a sentence of suitable length, the director shall receive, as soon as possible after his admission, full reports on all the matters referred to in the foregoing paragraph. Such reports shall always include a report by a medical officer, wherever possible qualified in psychiatry, on the physical and mental condition of the prisoner.

(3) The reports and other relevant documents shall be placed in an individual file. This file shall be kept up to date and classified in such a way that it can be consulted by the responsible personnel whenever the need arises.

Classification and individualization

67. The purpose of classification shall be:

(a) To separate from others those prisoners who by reason of their criminal records or bad characters, are likely to exercise a bad influence;

(b) To divide the prisoners into classes in order to

facilitate their treatment with a view of their social rehabilitation.

68. So far as possible separate institutions or separate sections of an institution shall be used for the treatment of the different classes of prisoners.

69. As soon as possible after admission and after a study of the personality of each prisoner with a sentence of suitable length, a programme of treatment shall be prepared for him in the light of the knowledge obtained about his individual needs, his capacities and dispositions.

Privileges

70. Systems of privileges appropriate for the different classes of prisoners and the different methods of treatment shall be established at every institution, in order to encourage good conduct, develop a sense of responsibility and secure the interest and co-operation of the prisoners in their treatment.

Work

71. (1) Prison labour must not be of an afflictive nature.

(2) All prisoners under sentence shall be required to work, subject to their physical and mental fitness as determined by the medical officer.

(3) Sufficient work of a useful nature shall be provided to keep prisoners actively employed for a normal working day.

(4) So far as possible the work provided shall be such as will maintain or increase the prisoner's ability to earn an honest living after release.

(5) Vocational training in useful trades shall be provided for prisoners able to profit thereby and especially for young prisoners.

(6) Within the limits compatible with proper vocational selection and with the requirements of institutional administration and discipline, the prisoners shall be able to choose the type of work they wish to perform.

72. (1) The organization and methods of work in the institutions shall resemble as closely as possible those of similar work outside institution, so as to prepare prisoners for the conditions of normal occupational life.

(2) The interests of the prisoners and of their vocational training, however must not be subordinated to the purpose of making a financial profit from an industry in the institution.

73. (1) Preferably institutional industries and farms should be operated directly by the administration and not by private contractors.

(2) Where prisoners are employed in work not controlled by the administration, they shall always be under the supervision of the institution's personnel. Unless the work is for other departments of the government the full normal wages for such work shall be paid to the administration by the persons to whom the labour is supplied, account being taken to the output of the prisoners.

74. (1) The precautions laid down to protect the safety and health of free workmen shall be equally observed in institutions.

(2) Provision shall be made to indemnify prisoners against industrial injury, including occupational disease, on terms not less favourable than those extended by law to free workmen.

75. (1) The maximum daily and weekly working hours of the prisoners shall be fixed by law or by

administrative regulation, taking into account local rules or custom in regard to the employment of free workmen.

(2) The hours so fixed shall leave one last day a week and sufficient time for education and other activities required as part of the treatment and rehabilitation of the prisoners.

76. (1) There shall be a system of equitable remuneration of the work of prisoners.

(2) Under the system prisoners shall be allowed to spend at least a part of their earnings on approved articles for their own use and to send a part of their earnings to their family.

(3) The system should also provide that a part of the earnings should be set aside by the administration so as to constitute a savings fund to be handed over to the prisoner on his release.

Education and recreation

77. (1) Provision shall be made for the further education of all prisoners capable of profiting thereby, including religious instruction in the countries where this is possible. The education of illiterates and young prisoners shall be compulsory and special attention shall be paid to it by the administration.

(2) So far as practicable, the education of prisoners shall be integrated with the educational system of the country so that after their release they may continue their education without difficulty.

78. Recreational and cultural activities shall be provided in all institutions for the benefit of the mental and physical health of prisoners.

Social relations and after-care

79. Special attention shall be paid to the

maintenance and improvement of such relations between a prisoner and his family as are desirable in the best interest of both.

80. From the beginning of a prisoner's sentence consideration shall be given to his future after release and he shall be encouraged and assisted to maintain or establish such relations with persons or agencies outside the institution as may promote the best interest of his family and his own social rehabilitation.

81. (1) Services and agencies, governmental or otherwise, which assist released prisoners to re-establish themselves in society shall ensure, so far as is possible and necessary, that released prisoners by provided with appropriate documents and identification papers, have suitable homes and work to go to, are suitably and adequately clothed having regard to the climate and season, and have sufficient means to reach their destination and maintain themselves in the period immediately following their release.

(2) The approved representatives of such agencies shall have all necessary access to the institution and to prisoners and shall be taken into consultation as to the future of a prisoner from the beginning of his sentence.

(3) It is desirable that the activities of such agencies shall be centralized or co-ordinated as far as possible in order to secure the best use of their efforts.

B. Insane and Mentally Abnormal Prisoners

82. (1) Persons who are found to be insane shall not be detained in prisons and arrangements shall be made to remove them to mental institutions as soon as possible.

(2) Prisoners who suffer from other mental diseases or abnormalities shall be observed and treated in specialized institutions under medical management.

(3) During their stay in a prison, such prisoners shall be placed under the special supervision of a medical officer.

(4) The medical or psychiatric service of the penal institutions shall provide for the psychiatric treatment of all other prisoners who are in need of such treatment.

83. It is desirable that steps should be taken, by arrangement with the appropriate agencies, to ensure if necessary the continuation of psychiatric treatment after release and the provision of social-psychiatric after-care.

C. Prisoners under arrest or awaiting trial

84. (1) persons arrested or imprisoned by reason of a criminal charge against them, who are detained either in police custody or in prison custody jail but have not yet been tried and sentenced, will be referred to as "untried prisoners" hereinafter in these rules.

(2) Unconvicted prisoners are presumed to be innocent and shall be treated as such.

(3) Without prejudice to legal rules for the protection of individual liberty or prescribing the procedure to be observed in respect of untried prisoners, these prisoners shall benefit by a special regime which is described in the following rules in its essential requirements only.

85. (1) Untried prisoners shall be kept separate from convicted prisoners.

(2) Young untried prisoners shall be kept separate from adults and shall in principle be detained in separate institutions.

86. Untried prisoners shall sleep singly in separate rooms, with the reservation of different local custom in respect of the climate.

87. Within the limits compatible with the good order of the institution, untried prisoners may, if they so desire, have their food procured at their own expense from the outside, either through the administration or through their family or friends. Otherwise, the administration shall provide their food.

88. (1) An untried prisoner shall be allowed to wear his own clothing if it is clean and suitable.

(2) If he wears prison dress, it shall be different from that supplied to convicted prisoners.

89. An untried prisoner shall always be offered opportunity to work, but shall not be required to work. If he chooses to work, he shall be paid for it.

90. An untried prisoner shall be allowed to procure at his own expense or at the expense of a third party such books, newspapers, writing materials and other means of occupation as are compatible with the interests of the administration of justice and the security and good order of the institution.

91. An untried prisoner shall be allowed to be visited and treated by his own doctor or dentist if there is reasonable ground for his application and he is able to pay any expenses incurred.

92. An untried prisoner shall be allowed to inform immediately his family of his detention and shall be given all reasonable facilities for communicating with his family and friends, and for receiving visits from them, subject only to restrictions and supervision as are necessary in the interests of the administration of justice and of the security and good order of the institution.

93. For the purposes of his defence, an untried prisoner shall be allowed to apply for from legal aid where such aid is available, and to receive visits free his

legal adviser with a view to his defence and to prepare and hand to him confidential instructions. For these purposes, he shall if he so desires be supplied with writing material. Interviews between the prisoner and his legal adviser may be within sight but not within the hearing of a police or institution official.

D. Civil Prisoners

94. In countries where the law permits imprisonment for debt, or by order of a court under any other non-criminal process, persons so imprisoned shall not be subjected to any greater restriction or severity than is necessary to ensure safe custody and good order. Their treatment shall be not less favourable than that of untried prisoners, with that reservation, however, that they may possibly be required to work.

E. Persons arrested or detained without charge

95. Without prejudice to the provisions of article 9 of the International Government on Civil and Political Rights, persons arrested or imprisoned without charge shall be accorded the same protection as that accorded under part I and part II, section C. Relevant provisions of part II, section A, shall likewise be applicable where their application may be conducive to the benefit of this special group of persons in custody, provided that no measures shall be been taken implying that re-education or rehabilitation is in any way appropriate to persons not convicted of any criminal offence.

6
Human Rights of Victims of Crime

Representatives of 129 U.N. member states helped to prepare for the Eighth Congress in the course of five interregional and regional meetings in 1988 and 1989. Draft recommendations and resolutions from these conferences were taken up by the Committee on Crime Prevention and Control (CCPC), a 27-member standing body of experts answering to the Economic and Social Council (ECOSOC), which examined and shaped the drafts for submission to the congress.

The Crime Prevention and Criminal Justice Branch of the Centre for Social Development and Humanitarian Affairs at the U.N. Office in Vienna acted as congress secretariat throughout the preparation period. The 44th General Assembly, playing its role as town crier to the world, directed the attention of the international community to the August 27-September 7 event in Havana. The Third (Social, Humanitarian, and Cultural) Committee's two draft resolutions drew from the Secretary-General's report "Crime Prevention and Criminal justice", which noted the danger of all forms of transnational criminality, "thriving at unprecedented levels and in ways previously unheard of," emphasized the necessity of worldwide participation in preparations for the congress, and expressed concern over severe resource constraints that threatened to jeopardize its success. These two resolutions-one on "International cooperation in combating organized crime" and the other a catch-all, which, among other things, invited governments to provide information on the progress made in implementing the Milan Plan of Action [44/72]-passed the Assembly by consensus. The latter also requested the Secretary-General to submit to the 45th Assembly his views and recommendations on implementing the conclusions of the Eighth Congress.

The CCPC's proposal to combat international terrorism, contained in an annex, observes that existing international norms "might" not be sufficient to control all forms of terrorist violence and suggests attacking the problem on several new fronts, ranging from extradition to the creation of an international criminal court. The committee's draft model treaty against the illicit import and export of "movable cultural property" would require states to "confiscate and return such property taken without authorization" and to "introduce measures to prevent the acquisition by museums and similar institutions of such property," imposing sanctions on those responsible. Other agenda items for the crime congress are the CCPCs proposed rules for the protection of juveniles deprived of their liberty, affirming that detention should be the punishment of last resort and for the minimum period necessary.

A related draft offering guidelines on the prevention of juvenile delinquency pays particular attention to children at social risk. The CCPC's draft U.N. "standard minimum rules for noncustodial measures of imprisonment" (dubbed the Tokyo rules) calls for appropriate actions to rationalize criminal justice policies from the standpoint of human rights. A draft offering basic principles for the use of force and, firearms by law enforcement officials is yet another CCPC entry on the lengthy agenda of the crime congress [ibid.].

The overarching theme of the Havana congress is International Cooperation in Crime Prevention and Criminal justice for the Twenty-first Century. Delegates will be offered a workshop on alternatives to imprisonment and another workshop on computerizing the criminal justice system. Beyond the considerable problem of finances, the congress faces a boycott by the United States, which, as expressed by a U.S. Mission spokesman, considers it highly inappropriate to hold the meeting in a country that "flouts" international norms in the area of crime prevention and criminal justice.

Crime scenario in area characterised as 'Urban' is to be viewed differently from the rest of the arm, namely rural. Urbanisation influenced by the increased population, unchecked migration, high industrial activities give rise to rapid development and unorganised settlements. Lack of opportunities, uneven distribution of incomes, diverse socio-religio-cultural disparities make urban areas a breeding ground for criminal activities. Organised groups, Gangsters, professional criminals, new entrants, youths, juveniles etc. find crime a thriving vocation in their quest for an easy and good living in urban environment.

Crime and development are intrinsically linked. The phenomenon of urban crimes is an important feature in metropolitan cities but the pattern varies from city to city. The urban area is generally recognised as breeding ground for the criminals and prone for higher incidence level of crimes compared to rural areas. Criminals brought up in such an environment are known to indulge in crimes as a way of life. The unchecked and unplanned growth of cities as well as large floating population are major contributing factors for urban crimes. Criminal propensity is also known to be higher in urban industrial areas. Migration of Poor, illiterate people-having roots in a simple environment consequent to migration suffer emotional instability in the urban setting. The problem of unemployment is yet another "compounding factor. They are easily lured into theft, robbery, smuggling or even terrorists activities.

India is predominantly a rural country as only 25.7 per cent of its population lives in urban areas (as per 1991 census) while majority, of the population (74.39%) lives in rural areas. Of the estimated total Urban population (2,354.1 lakhs), nearly one-third (825.5 lakhs) constituting 35.06 per cent live in 23 metropolitan cities (one million plus population). The proportion of metropolitan cities population to the national population is 9.01 per cent

There is no demarcation between rural and urban areas as far as the crime statistics are concerned since these were not collected on this basis, but as the crimes in urban areas are peculiar and have shown a consistent rise parallel to the population increase, during the previous few decades, it has generated interest to make a study of such crime phenomenon. For the purpose of crime analysis in Urban areas, the Present effort has been one to analyse the various crimes reported in the 23 mega cities and bring forth the main pattern of crime scene, type of offenders, result of enforcement etc. The analysis would cover the crime patterns and emerging trends.

Of the total 37,464 murder cases reported in the country in 1995, the 23 Urban mega cities together recorded 2,591 such cases comprising 6.9 per cent of the national share against the previous year's figure of 7.1 per cent thus recording a decrease in the reporting. Incidence wise Delhi reported the highest (413) followed by Bombay

(357), Bangalore (212) and a significant fall was observed under Murder cases in Vishakhapatnam (41.7%), Kochi (32%), Kanpur (31.3%) and Coimbatore (30.4%) whereas Vadodara and Ahmedabad reported more such incidence in 1995 over 1994. The total reported cases of Attempt to Commit Murder in the 23 Urban mega cities during 1995 were 2,936 as against 2,765 cases in 1994. The percentage share of these urban cities in 1995 in the national share has slightly increased to 9.9 per cent from 9.2 per cent in 1994 for this form of crime. Two cities viz., Hyderabad (from 31 to 77) and Vadodara (from. 13 to 23) reported significant increases while such cases declined in Madurai City (from 80 to 49).

Interestingly, some urban centres such as Bangalore, Bhopal, Calcutta, Delhi, Indore, Lucknow, Madras, Madurai, Patna, Varanasi and Vishakapatnam reported more cases of attempt to Murder than the cases reported under Murder. This indicates that the life in Urban cities is more prone to insecurity and threats, for various reasons. The magnitude of Kidnapping and Abduction of Women and Girls increased in the cities of Ahmedabad, Bangalore, Calcutta, Indore, Jaijpur, Ludhiana, Madurai, Nagpur, Patna and Surat in this year compared to 1994.

The urban cities reported higher percentage of rape victims in the age-group below 10 years (16.4) and 10 16 years (28.3) than the All-India average (5.4% and 24.1% respectively). Victims in the age-group of 16 30 years (48%) is well below the national average (56.3%) in urban areas. This clearly indicates that girls below 16 years of age are the vulnerable group predominantly in urban areas. Magnitude-wise, Delhi accounted the highest victims of Paedophilia (68) followed by Bombay (30). In the age-group of 10-16 years Bombay (86), Delhi (53) Hyderabad (27), Bhopal (26), Nagpur (16), Pune (15) Calcutta (14), Bangalore (13) and Kanpur (10). Rape victims in the age-group of 16-30 years were more In Delhi (163), Bombay (83) and Pune (42).

The number of Dacoities that have been reported in the Urban Agglomeration when analysed show that 5.8 per cent of the total, recorded Dacoities in the country were reported in these cities against the share of 5.2, per cent in the previous year, clearly, indicating a rising trend in Dacoity cases in Urban areas. Patna city recorded the highest-crime rate among the mega cities in India in this year (6.2). The cities which registered the highest incidence of Dacoity are Bombay (131) followed by Patna (74) and Surat (40). Cases of Preparation and Assembly for Dacoity reported in the mega cities shared 14.9 per cent of cases registered at the national level. This is 1.8 per cent less than the figure accounted in 1994 (16.7%). Ludhiana city registered a higher crime rate for this type of crime in this year (0.9) as against the national average of 0.1. Bombay (51), Calcutta (31), Delhi (18) and Ludhiana (12) fans reported higher incidence under this category.

Cities of Bombay (9), Jaipur (3) and Delhi (2) reported such incidence during this year (1995). During 1994, the reported number of TADA cases in the above cities were 15, Nil (0) and 15 respectively. Lucknow city, which registered one such incidence in 1994 did not record any such incidence in this year. A total of 51 persons were detained under this Act in the Bombay City, whereas at Jaipur and Delhi, Police detained 7 and 2 persons respectively in custody under the TADA Act in 1995. The table presented below provides detailed information regarding incidence (1) crime rate (R) and persons arrested (A) under TADA Act during 1992 1995 from the Cities where such reported crimes are high.

The offences related to Gambling Act that were reported in 1995 in the 23 mega cities accounted for 13.4 per cent of the total such offences reported In the country,

Overall, the offences reported under this Prohibitory Act have shown a declining trend during the last 4 years. From a share of 17.1 per cent in 1992 to the All-India, the share of these cities had fallen to 13.2 per cent in 1993, risen to 13.6 per cent in 1994 and declined to 13.4 in. 1995. Cities such as Bombay (2,826), Vishakhapatnam (2,628), Delhi (2,486), Madras (2,452), Ahmedabad (1,654) and Nagpur (1,263) continued to report high incidence which were registered under this Act. Crime rate-wise. Vishakhapatnam recorded the highest crime rate (196.9) followed by Nagpur (68.3), Ahmedabad (44.6), Bhopal (44.2) and Madras (40.9).

Enforcement of Prohibition is an important regulatory duty of Police in mega, cities. Surat city accounted for the highest incidence under Prohibition Act. 14,361 Males and 15,286 females were taken into custody for 27,362 incidence in this city during the year 1995. An effective enforcement of this Act was also reported, from the following cities: Ahmedabad (9,972), Madras (7,204), Vadodara (6,703), Pune (5,129), and Bombay (5,031). Crime rate-wise, Surat City recorded the highest rate under Prohibition Act (1,447.7) in this year.

Enforcement and registration of offences under the Excise Act was the highest in the city of Delhi (5,303) followed by Calcutta (1,557). Number of persons, both male's and females were arrested during such 'enforcement where In Delhi (5,283) and Calcutta (1,569) accounted for higher number of persons who were taken into custody. Crime rate-wise, Delhi registered the highest crime rate (53.3) during the year 1995 among the mega cities.

Offences in Immoral Trafficking and their prevention is an Urban specific crimes demanding equal attention of the Law Enforcement Agencies of the Cities for their Prohibition. This offence which contributed 24.8 per cent of the All-India share (reported from 23 cities) seems to get disproportionate treatment in enforcement by the city police authorities. The police in the cities of Bombay (530), Bangalore (511), Madras (338), Coimbatore (329), Madurai (179) and Delhi (123) have effectively enforced this act whereas their counterparts in other mega cities have reported least such incidence which clearly calls for intensification of enforcement of this preventive law.

Information in respect of enforcement of Dowry Prohibition Act reveals that the cities such as Bangalore (178), Patna (40), Madras (26) and Hyderabad (19) registered higher number of cases under this Act. Crime rate-wise Bangalore City (3.7), Patna (3.4) recorded higher rate in 1995 among the cities for such offences under Dowry Prohibition Act. In Bangalore city Police took 378 persons in custody (including 124 females) for various offences under this Act. In the cities of Patna and Madras, 61 persons (including 10 females) and 60 persons (including 23 females) respectively were arrested under this Act.

Protection of civil rights act

Instances of violation of 'Civil Rights' was low in Urban areas. The Cities of Jaipur (74), Bangalore (61), Lucknow
areas. The Cities of Jaipur (74), Bangalore (61), Lucknow
(19), Nagpur (13) and Madurai (10) reported the bulk of such cases. Jaipur city recorded the highest crime rate 4.1 followed by Bangalore (1.3) for these offences among the 23 mega cities.

Child marriage restraint act

Of the 33 cases registered under the Child Marriage Restraint Act in the country, during 1995, 4 cases (2 at Surat and 1 each at Ahmedabad and Nagpur) were reported in the urban areas which indicates that this form of crime is more privalent in the rural areas than Urban. In rural areas, the people are innocent, superstitious and are unaware of the consequences of Child Marriage.

Indecent representation of women (Prohibition) act

The offences relating to Indecent Representation of Women, in the 23 mega cities accounted for nearly half (49.3%) of the total such offences, reported in the country, during 1995. The above proportion is a testimony to the urban nature of this crime. Cities of Bombay (106), Surat (79) and Vadodara (51) reported higher incidence, under this Act. The police apprehended 132 persons (including 6 females) in Bombay, 107 in Surat and 51 in Vadodara.

Offences under the copyright act

The notion, that this form of crime is predominantly an urban one, is supported by its percentage contribution (47.9%) from the 23 mega cities towards total such offences reported in the country, during 1995. The higher incidence of violation of this Act were reported from the cities of Bombay (107), Delhi (51), Calcutta (35), Pune (25), Bangalore (22), Hyderabad (21), Indore (15), Ahmedabad (12), Ludhiana and Surat (11 each). The crime rate at Indore (1-2) was not only the highest but was 12 times, the national average (0.1). As far as the arrests made in the above offences are concerned, 188 persons were arrested in 11 cases at Surat, 126 persons in 107 cases at Bombay, 56 persons including a female in 25 cases at Pune, 54 persons in 51 cases at Delhi and so on.

SC/ST (Prevention of atrocities) act

The offences relating to atrocities on SCs/STs (weaker sections of the society) in 23 metropolitan cities accounted for barely 3.8 per cent of the total such offences, reported in the country, during 1995, which strengthens the view that this crime is predominantly a rural one. Cities such as Kanpur (252), Lucknow (157), Indore (75), Bangalore (61) and Varanasi (49) reported high incidence under this Act. The crime rate in Kanpur (11.3), Lucknow (7.5) and Indore (6.0) was observed to be higher than the national average of 1.9. The highest arrests were made at Kanpur (479), (including 10 females) followed by Lucknow (270).

Offences tinder the forest act

The 23 mega cities contributed just 3.9 percent to total offences reported under the Forest Act in the country during 1995. Amongst the cities, Bangalore reported the highest incidence (144), the highest crime rate (3,0) And the highest number of arrests (405). The percentage share of some prominent Special Laws offences in the Metropolitan Cities towards incidence at the national level Is depicted through the following bar graph.

Rule of law is perceived as the foundation for a democratic system of Government in any civilized and developed society. The Constitution of India, a system of laws and precepts established by the sovereign power of the state for its own guidance and governance has been the source from where the laws of the land stem out. Constitution, thus, is the law of all laws. The constitution alone confers the power for enacting laws on the Parliament and State legislatures comprising of duly elected members in a democratic set up.

Essentially, therefore, laws become rates of actions established by the authority -of the state and contravention of which is punishable as provided for by treating them as offences. Origin of our structured legal system in the country dates back to 1860. For maintenance of law, public order and peace, three major and governing law were enacted:

(a) The Indian Penal Code (I.P.C.), 1860.

(b) The Indian Evidence Act, 1872.

(c) The Code of Criminal Procedure (Cr.P.C.), 1898. (Amended 1973).

The *Indian Penal Code* is the general penal code for the country. It identifies such acts that constitute offences and make them punishable under this Act. It provides punishments for offences Committed within India, punishment for offences committed beyond, but which by law may be tried within India and also extends applicability of the Act to extra-territorial offences. Over the years the scope of the Act has been enlarged by few amendments and by insertion of specific provisions as extensions.

The *Indian Evidence Act* is a major law relating to evidence and applies to all judicial proceedings in any, court or court martial. This Act has undergone few amendments to enlarge the scope of acceptance of evidence and presumptions as admissible. The *Criminal Procedure Code* is the major procedural law relating to conduct of investigations, trial and appeal. This procedural law underwent a major amendments in year 1973.

All the major laws are integral in dealing with an offence, its investigation, its trial and judgement. As such they are to be read together. In conformity with the objectives of the Constitution which is the law of all laws, provisions incorporated in all these acts are to conform to the various Articles enshrined in the Constitution as otherwise they are likely to be struck down as ultra vires to the Constitution.

The legal system in the country is now more than a century old. After attaining independence and to realise the constitutional obligations under the various Articles with particular reference to 'Directive Principles', several new laws have been enacted. As such, apart from Indian

Penal Code, several Special Laws and Local Laws have been enacted from time to time to meet the growing crime prevention needs. They are broadly categorised as

(i) *Special Law* (Section 41 of IPC) which is applicable to a particular subject, and

(ii) *Local Law* (Section 42 of IPC) which is Applicable to a particular part of India.

The word 'Offence' (Sec. 40 IPC) denotes any act or omission, made punishable, by any law, for the time being in force. Mens rea or intention is a prerequisite to constitute an offence under this definition. However, it also includes deaths or injuries caused through culpable rashness or culpable negligence as defined under the specified sections of Indian Penal Code. While the term 'offence' may be specific, the term 'crime' is generic largely signifying offences which are serious in nature. The law is dynamic in nature in that the society considers enacting the law for an act which has been committed which in the collective view of society is deemed as offence. In this regard, the law generally tends to be one step behind crime itself.

All cognizable crimes reported in the country in which a police officer may arrest a person without a warrant, are dealt by the police. In such crimes, the police has a direct responsibility to take immediate action on receipt of a complaint or of credible information, visit the scene of the crime, investigate the facts, apprehend the offender and arraign him in a court of jurisdiction. Cognizable crimes are broadly categorised as those failing either under the 'Indian Penal Code (IPC)' or under the 'Special and Local Laws (SLL)'. The incidence level of crime in the country, during the decade 1985 to 1995. As many as 59,93,17-) (Fifty nine lakh ninety three thousand one hundred and seventy two) cognizable crimes were reported in the country during 1995. These comprised of nearly 17 lakh cases under the IPC and nearly 43 lakh cases under the SLL. The ratio of IPC to SLL crimes, which persisted at 1:2 till 1992, has shown a steady increase thereafter, i.e., from 1:2.3 in 1993 to 1:2.4 in 1994 and finally to 1:2.5 during 1995.

Non-Cognizable crimes are generally left to be pursued in courts by the affected parties themselves. Police cannot interfere in non-cognizable crimes except with, magisterial permission to be specifically obtained, if found necessary, in any specific situation. The schedule of the Cr-P.C. lists out all the offences of the IPC and further specifies in each case whether the offence is cognizable or non-cognizable. In out of the three lists delineating subjects for governance viz; State list, Central list and Concurrent list in the 'Constitution of India', 'Police' as a subject falls under the 'State list' making law enforcement the primary responsibility of the States. The total reported crimes (59,93,172) crimes, both IPC and SLL cases, are those, dealt by 25 States and 7 UTs, in the year 1995.

There, yet, are few Central Law Enforcing Agencies characterised as 'Special Investigation Agencies' who also register cognizable crimes, investigate and place results to 'Normal' or 'Special' Courts, for trial. They, include 'the Central Bureau of Investigation', 'the Directorate of Enforcement', 'the Central Board of Direct Taxes', 'the Directorate of Revenue Intelligence', 'the Directorate of Preventive Operations, 'the Narcotics control Bureau', 'the Directorate General of foreign Trade', 'the Directorate of Income Tax' at the Centre and 'the Directorates of Vigilance', 'the Directorates of Enforcement, 'the forest Cells' etc. at each State of the Country.

Law Enforcement requirements and roles are growing in the country as the sophistication levels of traditional crimes are rapidly assuming proportions calling for new enactments and specialised investigation agencies to deal with them. It would be deemed as in order to take into account their roles, the number of criminal cases dealt with by them under the nationally enforceable laws, be they Central Police or State Police in presenting a holistic picture.

For general information and reference new legislations enacted in the country during 1995 are listed below in chronological order:

1. The Cable Television Networks (Regulation) Act, 1995.
2. The National Environment Tribunal Act, 1995.
3. The persons with Disabilities (Equal Opportunities, Protection of Rights and Full Participation) Act, 199.5.

As a pioneering and maiden venture a compilation of all the criminal laws in the country commenced from the previous year. The list of criminal laws duly classified as Special Laws and Local Laws is presented as Appendices. Though it is comprehensive, omission, if any noticed, are expected to be included in the forthcoming issue and maintained on a sustained basis.

The population of the country in the decade (1985-95) increased by (22) per cent, with a compound growth rate of 2 per cent per annum. While a higher percentage growth rate from the decades 1951-61 to 1961-71 was seen establishing an increasing trend, the same in the subsequent decades remained more or less steady with the marginal decrease from 1981-91. Differing trends were noticed in the population growth rate in respect of males versus females. This has resulted in a steady fall in the male-female sex ratio. From a figure of 946 females per thousand males in 1951, presently (1991 census), the same has decreased (2.0%) to 927 females per thousand males. The state-wise position in this regard also shows a widely fluctuating trend.

The density of population per square kilometre has also been steadily increasing. The percentage increase from one decade to the succeeding one indicates a steady increasing trend. Density of population recorded during 1991 census was 267, an increase of 23.6 per cent during the decade (1981-91). Analysis of rural population vis-a-vis Urban population indicates that against an increase of 23.9 per cent in total population of the country, during the decade 1981-91, the increase in urban population was much higher at 36.4 per cent.Data relating to age-wise profile of the population is not readily available. The growth in the population, at a high rate in the decides 1961-71, 1971-81 and 1981-91 is indicative of a trend of large proportion of population being in the younger age-groups.

The total cognizable crimes in the country had been steadily rising as if to keep pace with the population, though at varying rates, over the past 40 years. As many as 59,93,172 cognizable crimes were reported in the country during 1995. The incidence of total cognizable crimes in 1995 increased by 33.7 per cent over 1985 with a compound growth rate of 2.4 per cent per annum.

Population is one of the factors influencing crime incidence. There is a positive correlation between the growth in incidence and the population of the country. The rate of crime defined as the incidence of crime- per lakh of population is universally taken as a more realistic indicator as it balances the effect of growth in population. The rate of total cognizable crimes in, the country during 1995 was 654.3, an increase of 9.6, per cent over 1985 with a compound growth rate of 0.3 per cent annum. The rate of total cognizable crimes recorded an increase of 6.8 per cent over the previous year. The rate in respect of IPC crimes increased by 3.7 per cent while the increase in SLL crime rate was much higher at 10-8 per cent in this year.

The 'Indian Penal Code' defines in precise terms various acts and omission constituting an offence against the State, public tranquillity, religion, human body, property and so on. These are covered under 511 Sections of law which are traditionally and broadly classified into 3 main groups viz., Violent Crimes, Property crimes and Economic crimes. In an effort to clear the murkiness prevailing over the inflated group (comprising more than half) of 'Other cognizable IPC crimes' to a certain extent, it was to bring out a couple of distinct crimes like 'Arson' and 'Hurt (Grievous /simple)' and it was decided to collect detailed information in respect of these crimes, from 1995 onwards.

A consolidated information on 'Crime Against Women' is received on monthly basis, this Bureau also decided to collect detailed information under some important crime-heads like 'Dowry Death', 'Molestation', 'Sexual harassment' and 'Cruelty by Husband' or his relatives. In the absence of classification of 'Hurt' cases (into, Grievous or Simple) it was decided to include only 'Arson' in the group of violent crimes. The states of Bihar, Gujarat and Meghalaya, the UT of Daman and Diu and the Patna city, however, did not furnish data under the above mentioned new crime-heads.

Trends-states IPC crimes

The State, UT and city-wise incidence of total cognizable IPC crimes during 1990 to 1995 and the percentage variations during 1995 over the Q.A. of 1990-94 and over 1994. Madhya Pradesh reported the highest incidence with 1,97,445 cases, accounting for 11.6 per cent of the total IPC crimes reported during the year in the country. The other states which reported more than 1 lakh cases apiece and contributed significantly to the crime at national level during 1995 were Uttar Pradesh (1,77,992 cases, 10.5%), Rajasthan (1,48,26.6 cases, 8.7%), Tamil Nadu (1,26,761 cases, 7.5%), Gujarat (1,23,514 cases, 7.3%), Karnataka (1,20,334 cases, 7.1%), Bihar (1,15,598 cases, 6.8%) and Andhra Pradesh (1,05,016 cases, 6.2%). These 9 states together accounted for more than threefourth (77.2%) of the total cognizable IPC crimes reported in the country during the year.

The State and UT-wise incidence of total cognizable. IPC crimes registered during 1995 along with the percentage contribution of each State & UT, estimated midyear population, crime rate and the rank of criminality. The crime rate was the highest (307.5) in Rajasthan, followed by Mizoram (303.3), Kerala (282.3) and Goa (279-1) which, therefore, ranked as the 1st, 2nd, 3rd and 4th respectively in the, rank of criminality among States. Uttar Pradesh though the third highest contributing state, as far as the crime incidence- is concerned, Tanked quite low (21st amongst the 25 States) mainly because of its high population. 12 States, viz., Arunachal Pradesh, Goa, Gujarat, Haryana, Himachal Pradesh, Karnataka, Kerala, Madhya Pradesh, Maharashtra, Mizoram, Rajasthan -and Tamil Nadu can be grouped under the 'More Crime Prone' States as these recorded higher crime rate than the national average.

In order to assess the crime situation and its trends, prevailing in the centrally administered regions of the country, the 7 union territories were separately earmarked for survey. It is observed that out of 59,93,172 total (IPC + SLL) cognizable crimes reported in the country during 1995, 71,517 cases constituting only 1.2 per cent were reported in the 7 union territories. These incidence recorded an increase of 9 per cent over the previous year.

The crime rate for the total cognizable crimes (IPC + SLL) in the Union Territories was 538, against 656 in States and 654.3 at the national level, thereby showing an increase of 5.3 per cent over the previous years rate of 511.

IPC Crimes

All the Union Territories except Delhi, recorded less than 2,500 IPC crimes during the year 1995, four of these occupied the higher slots, as far as the crime rate is concerned. Delhi which reported 47.686 'such 'crimes during the year, recorded the highest crime rate (434.7) in the country, The next in order were Pondicherry (273.0), Dadra and Nagar Haveli (272.5) and Chandigarh (260.5).

The State and UT-wise Incidence of various IPC crimes along with the crime rate for 1995, while the comparative crime statistics relating to incidence during 1994 and 1995 under various crime-heads and the percentage variations in 1995 over 1994.

The incidence (37,464) of Murder in 1995, increased by 44.3 per cent over the decade 198595, decreased by 2 per cent over the quinquennial average of 1990-94 and by 2.9 per cent over the previous year. The highest incidence (8,774) of Murder, constituting (23.4) per cent of the total cases, were reported from Uttar Pradesh. Bihar also reported significant number (5050) of Murder cases. The other States which reported more than 2,000 cases apiece were Madhya Pradesh (3,416), Maharashtra (2,900) and Andhra Pradesh (2,472). Together, the above 5 states accounted for (60.4) per cent of the total Murder cases reported in the country during 1995. The crime rate varied from a minimum of 1.6 in Kerala to a maximum of 12.7 in Manipur, the national average being 4.1.

The incidence (29,571) of Attempt to commit Murder in this year, registered a decrease of 1.5 per cent over the previous year. As in the Case Of Murder, Uttar Pradesh registered the highest (8,523) incidence of Attempt to Murder, followed by Bihar and Madhya Pradesh with 4,597 and 3,289 cases respectively. Another notable feature was that cases of Attempt to commit Murder outnumbered the Murder cases in the States of 'Orissa',

Rajasthan', 'Chandigarh' and 'Delhi'. The crime rate varied from a minimum of 0.3 in Goa to a maximum of 7.1 in Jammu & Kashmir against the national average of 3.2.

The incidence (3,830) of C.H. not amounting to Murder in this year, recorded a decline of 4.1 per cent during the decade 1985-95 and-8.7 per cent over the Q.A. of 1990-94. and 2.9 per cent over the previous year., As in the cases of Murder and its attempt, Uttar Pradesh recorded a -sizable number of cases (1,383) of C.H. hot amounting, to Murder; accounting for 36.1 per cent of such cases reported at the national level. The crime rate was the highest (1.2) in Chandigarh, followed by 0.9 in Uttar Pradesh and 0.8 in West Bengal against the national average of 0.4.

The frequency of Rape case- have almost doubled during the decade 1985-95 (7,289 in 1985 to 13,754 in 1995) recording an increase of 88.7 per cent over 1985, 19.4 per cent over the Q.A. of 1990-94 and 4.1 per cent over the previous year (1994). Madhya Pradesh, as in the previous few years, recorded the highest (3,119) incidents, which accounted for 22.7 per cent of the total cases reported in the country. Uttar Pradesh also reported a significant number (1,808) of such cases, accounting for 13.1 per cent. 'The other states which reported more than 1,000 cases during the year were Maharashtra (1,362), Bihar (1,312) and Rajasthan (1,036). However, barring - Madhya Pradesh (4.3), Maharashtra (1.6) and Rajasthan (2.1), the crime rate in the above states was either less than or equal to the national average of 1.5. The crime rate varied from the lowest 0.2 in Pondicherry to the highest 5.2 in Mizoram.

During 1995, incidence (20,426) of 'Kidnapping and Abduction' recorded an increase of 27.3 per cent over the decade (1985-95), 2.2 per cent over the Q.A. of 1990-94 while these decreased by 2.7 per cent over the previous year. However, incidence of 'Kidnapping and Abduction of Women and 'Girls' recorded a decline of 0.8 per cent over the Q.A. of 1990-94 and 0.1 per cent over the previous year. The highest incidence (3,842) were reported in Uttar Pradesh accounting for 18.8 per cent of the total cases reported in the country followed by 2,822 cases in Rajasthan and 2,070 cases in Bihar. The other states and UTs which reported more than 1,000 cases during the year were Assam (1,293), Delhi (1,252), Maharashtra (1,163), Madhya Pradesh (1,142), Gujarat (1,120) and Andhra Pradesh (1,064). The crime rate varied largely from 0.5 in Kerala to 11.4 in Delhi against the national average of 2.2. Orissa, A & N Islands and D and N Haveli had the uniquie distinction of not having any case of 'Kidnapping and Abduction of Others'.

The incidence of Dacoity (8,335) showed a steady decline with 25.9 per cent over the decade 1985-95, 19.6 per cent over the Q.A. of 1990-94 and 10.1 per cent over the previous year (1994). Bihar continued to report the highest incidence (2,566) accounting for 30.8 per cent of the total cases reported during the year in the country. Uttar Pradesh with 1,327 cases was the next in order accounting for 15.9 per cent of the total cases. The crime rate varied extensively from 0. 1 in Punjab, Chandigarh and Pondicherry to 6.0 in Tripura against the meagre national average of 0.9.

The incidence (961) of Preparation and Assembly for Dacoity registered a considerable decline of 20.2 per cent over the Q.A. of 1990-94 and a slight Increase of 1.6 per cent over the previous year. West Bengal recorded the largest number (250) of such cases, closely followed by Bihar with 203 cases. Together, these two States accounted for 47.1 per cent of the total cases reported during the year in the country. The crime, rate 0.3 was the highest in Mizoram and West Bengal 'against" the national average of 0.1.

The incidence (22,443) of Robbery showed a declining trend, with 0.3 per cent over the decade 1985-95, 11.4 per cent over the Q.A. of 1990-94 and 6.2 per cent over the previous year. The highest incidence (5,348) were reported from Uttar Pradesh followed by 3,130 and 2,678 from Maharashtra and Bihar respectively. These three states together accounted for 49.7 per cent of ' the" to' 6,1 Robbery cases reported in the country during the year. Nagaland, which had a meagre contribution of 0.5 per cent towards total Robbery cases, recorded the highest crime rate of 7.3 against the national average of 2.5.

The incidence (1,16,507) of Burglary recorded steady decline with 10.6 per cent during the decade 1985-95, 8.3 per cent over the Q.A. of 1990-94 and 4.1 per cent over the previous year (1994). The highest number of burglary cases (18,073) were reported from Madhya Pradesh followed by 16,304 cases in Maharashtra and 13,383 cases in Uttar Pradesh. Together, these three states Accounted to 41 per cent of the total cases reported in the country during the year 1995. The highest increase (52.8%) during the year was noticed in Mizoram while the highest decline (30.1%) was recorded in Pondicherry. The crime rate, was the highest at 48.4 in Goa and the least at 1.1 in the State of West Bengal against the national average of 12.7.

As in the case of other property crime (Burglary), the incidence (2,94,306) of Theft also recorded a decline, with 11 per cent during the decade 1985-95, 13 per cent over the Q.A. of 1990-94 and 3 per cent over the previous year (1994). Maharashtra reported the highest number (49,323) of Theft cases, followed by Uttar Pradesh (36,209) and Madhya Pradesh (30,607). In all, 11 States and UTs recorded more than 10,000 theft cases each, during the year. The highest percentage increase (75.8) during the year was recorded at the UT of Daman & Diu while the highest decline (42%) was noticed at Pondicherry. The crime rate fluctuated largely between 6.4 at Punjab to 157.4 at Delhi against the national average of 32.1.

The incidence (96,520) of Riots registered during the year recorded a decline of 3.2 per cent over the decade 1985-95 and 3.7 per cent over the Q.A. of 1990-94. However, these incidents showed an increase of 2.5 per cent over the previous year (1994), The highest incidence (20,386) were reported in Rajasthan, followed by 12,368 in Bihar. States which recorded between 5,000 to 10,000 Riots cases during the year were Karnataka (9,595), Uttar Pradesh (7,918), Tamil Nadu (7,423), Kerala (6,747), Maharashtra (6,183) and West Bengal (6, 111). These 8 states together accounted for 79.5 per cent of the total Riots cases, reported in the country, during the year. The highest increase (90.9%) in the incidence of Riots was observed in Arunachal Pradesh.

The incidence (15,503) of Criminal Breach of Trust continued to show a declining trend with 15.8 per cent decrease over the decade 1985-95, 9.4 per cent decrease over the Q.A. of 1990-94 and 6.2 per cent over the previous year (1994), Uttar Pradesh recorded the highest incidence (3,142) of this form of crime, followed by Gujarat (2,541), Maharashtra (1,928) and Bihar, (1,440). Together, these four states accounted for 58.4 per cent of the total cases of Criminal Breach of Trust registered during the year, in the country. The crime rate was highest at 6.4 in Chandigarh while it was the least at 0.5 in Tripura and Pondicherry against the national average of 1.7.

The incidence (30,678) of cheating showed a steep rise of 46 per cent over the decade 1985-95, and 7,6 per cent increase over the Q.A. of 1990-94. However, these cases showed a decline of 1.7 per cent over the previous year (1994). The highest incidence (4,972) of Cheating were reported in Rajasthan, followed by Maharashtra (3,282), Uttar Pradesh (3,167) and Gujarat 0,114). These four states accounted for 47.4 per cent of the total cheating cases reported during the year in the country. The crime rate was the highest (14.8) in Delhi while it was lowest at 0.8 in Tripura against, the national average 3.3.

During 1995, a total of 12,028 cases of Arson were registered in the country. Uttar Pradesh recorded the highest incidence (1,643), accounting for 13.7 per cent of the total cases at the national level. Other states which registered more than 1,000 Arson cases were Andhra Pradesh (1,450), Tamil Nadu (1,327), Madhya Pradesh (1,324), Maharashtra (1,314) and Rajasthan (1,117). The crime rate in the turbulent state of Jammu and Kashmir was the highest at 9.1 which was 7 times the national average of 1.3.

IPC crimes, which are though cognizable but do not fall under any of the 20 specified categories are clubbed under 'Other IPC Crimes'. Since this group covers a major part of the total cognizable crimes, it will be appropriate only to discuss its salient features. As many as 7,22,583 such crimes accounting for 42.6 per cent of the total cognizable crimes were registered in the country during the year 1995. Madhya Pradesh with 85,949 such cases accounted for 11.2 of the total cases, reported at the national level.

The District-wise and City-wise incidence of IPC crimes during 1995 are shown. Only those cities which had a population of 5 lakh or more in 1995, have been considered for the purpose of survey. The crime situation in the 23 Metropolitan cities (Cities/Urban Agglomerations which had a population of 10 lakh or more as per the 1991 census) has been separately discussed and analysed.

Out of 584 Police Districts (including Railway Police Districts) in India as many as 100 districts registered more than 5,000 cognizable IPC. crimes during 1995. Out of the above 100 districts as many as 9 districts, viz., Ahmedabad Commissionerate in Gujarat, Bangalore Commissionerate in Karnataka, Ernakulam and Thiruvananthapuram in Kerala, Indore and Jabalpur in Madhya Pradesh, Bombay Commissionerate, in Maharashtra, Jaipur in Rajasthan and Calcutta Commissionerate in West Bengal registered more than 10,000 cognizable IPC crimes. Out of the above 9 districts, while the Bangalore. Commissionerate registered nearly 30,000 (28,899) cases, Bombay registered more than 40,000 (40,512) cases and had the unique distinction of registering the highest number of IPC cakes during the year, amongst all the districts in India. Besides 23 Metropolitan Cities (Cities/Urban Agglomerations) Gwalior and Jabalpur Cities in Madhya Pradesh and Thane City in Maharashtra also registered more than 5,000 IPC cases during the year.

The number of Police Districts in the, country increased from 573 in 1994 to 584 in this year. The number of Districts, attaining the five figure mark in registering IPC cognizable crimes, remained Static at 9 while those in the range of 5,000 10,000 Increased from 77 to 91. Thus majority (nearly 83%,) of the districts have been observed to record less than 5,000 IPC cases per year.

Crimes under the special and local laws (SLL)

The crime head-wise incidence and rate of cognizable crimes under the Special and Local Laws (SLL) during 1985 and 1990 to 1995 are presented in Table. The quinquennial average of incidence and rate for the period 199094 as also the percentage variations during 1995 over

1985, Q.A. and over the previous year (1994). In an effort to explore the 'Other SLL Crimes' constituents, detailed data collection under the following Laws has commenced, from this year (1995).

(1) Child Marriage Restraint Act

(2) Indecent Representation of Women (P) Act

(3) Copyright Act

(4) Sati Prevention Act

(5) Scheduled Castes & Scheduled Tribes (Prevention of Atrocities) Act

(6) Forest Act

The States of Bihar, Gujarat & Meghalaya, the UT of Daman and Diu and the Patna City, however, did not furnish the data under the above crime-heads. During 1995, a total of 42,97,476 cogrizable crimes were reported in the country under various Special Laws enacted by the Union Government and Local Laws by the respective State Governments. These incidents showed a steady increase, with 38.8 per cent over the decade 1985-95, 20,2 per cent over the Q.A. of 1990-94 and 13 per cent over the previous year (1994).

Since most of the Special and Local Laws are preventive In nature, a rise in the registration of these cases In the country could also be viewed as due to the greater preventive role played by the Police and therefore may not be construed as an indicator of deterioration in crime situation. The crime head-wise percentage distribution of various cognizable crimes under the SLL during the last 5 years (1991 to 1995). It is observed that only about one fourth (24.8 %) of the total SLL crimes, accounted for the 21 specified crime-heads while the remaining 75.2 per cent were clubbed as 'Other SLL crimes. The 'Prohibition Act', though prevalent in only a few States, was a major contributor with 15 per cent share towards total SLL crimes. Next in order were the 'Gambling Act' (3.2%) which again appears in different forms in various States, the 'Excise Act' (2.7%) and the 'Arms Act' (1.5%). Each of the remaining 17 specified crimes contributed less than 1 per cent and together accounted for just 2.4 per cent of, the total SLL crimes.

Trends-states

The crime head-wise incidence and rate of cognizable SLL crimes in different States, UTs and metropolitan cities. It does not appear to be justifiable to classify A' State as 'Crime prone' on the basis of highest number of total (IPC + SLL) cognizable crimes registered therein during a year as most of the SLL offences are preventive in nature. Registering of more of SLL cases reflects police's efficacy of enforcement rather than a deteriorating law and order situation. So, it will be appropriate to discuss the position of various Special Laws rather than the Local Laws in various States and UTs.

Arms act

The incidence (64,331) under the Arms Act showed a steady increase with 3.8 per cent each over the decade 1985-95 and over the quinquennial average of 199094 and 6.7 per cent over the previous year. The highest incidence (39,512) constituting 61.4 per cent of the total cases were reported from Uttar Pradesh. The crime rate varied from a minimum of 03 in Karnataka, Tamil Nadu and Pondicherry to a maximum of 32 5 in Delhi against national average of 7.0.

N.D.P.S. act

The incidence (20,194) under the N.D.P.S. Act in 1995 which showed a steep rise (41.4%) over the decade 198595 and 2 per cent over the quinquennial average of 199094, finally declined by 0.5 per cent, compared to the previous year. The highest incidence (8,935) constituting 44.2 per cent of the total cases were reported from Uttar Pradesh. The crime rate varied from a minimum of 0.2 in Bihar and Tripura to a maximum of 8.5 in Mizoram against the national average of 2.2.

Excise act

The incidence (1,14,355) under the Excise Act showed a steady rise with 7.7 per cent increase during the decade 1985-95, 18.2 per cent over the Q.A. of 1990-94 and 12 per cent over the previous year. Uttar Pradesh reported the highest incidence (22,739) with a share of 19.9 per cent to the total cases reported under this Act. The crime rate varied from a minimum of 0.2 in Arunachal Pradesh to a maximum of 345.8 in A and N Islands against the national average of 12.5.

Explosives and explosive substances act

The incidence (5,113) under the Explosives & Explosive Substances Act in 1995 showed an erratic trend with 51.6 per cent rise during the decade 1985-95, a fall of 16.9 per cent over the quinquennial average of 1990-94 and considerable decline of 10.2 per cent over the previous year. The highest incidence (1,316) constituting 25.7 per cent of the total cases were reported from Uttar Pradesh. The crime rate varied from a minimum of 0. 1 (in as many as. 5 States and a UT) to a maximum of 8.8 in Jammu and Kashmir.

Immoral traffic (Prevention) act

The incidence (8,447) under the Immoral Traffic (Prevention) Act in 1995 showed steady decline of 43 per cent during the decade 190-95, 36.3 per cent over the quinquennial average of 1990-94 and 16.6 per cent over the previous year. The State and UT-wise details of cases may be seen under the Chapter 'Crime Against Women'. The crime rate was the highest (8.8) in Tamil Nadu against the national average of 0.9.

Indian railways act

The incidence (32,105) under the Indian Railways Act though decreased by 1.1. per cent during the decade 1985-95, showed a rise of 4.7 per cent over the Q.A. of 1990-94 and 8.6 per cent over the previous year. Madhya Pradesh emerged as the major contributor (39.4%) where 12,644 such cases were registered. The crime rate too was the highest (17.5) in Madhya Pradesh against the national average of 3.5.

Registration of foreigners act

The incidence (1,611) under the Registration of Foreigners Act in 1995, decreased by 26 per cent over,, the quinquennial average of 1990-94 but increased substantially, by 9.1 per cent, compared to the previous year. The highest incidence (1,179) constituting 73.2 per cent of the total cases were reported from West Bengal.

Protection of civil rights act

The incidence under the Protection of Civil Right Act, in 1995 showed a considerable decline of 25.7. per cent over the quinquennial average of 1990-94 and nearly 30 percent (29.9) over the previous year. The State & UT-wise detailed statistics can be seen under the chapter: 'Crime Against Weaker Sections of Society (SCs/STs)'. The crime rate was the highest (2.5) in Pondicherry against the national average of 0.3.

Indian passport act

The incidence (775) under the Indian Passport Act in 1995

showed a mixed trend, with a decrease of 19.4% over the quinquennial average of 1990-94 and an increase of 2.5 per cent over the previous year. The highest incidence (443) constituting 57.2 per cent of the total cases were reported from Maharashtra.

Essential commodities act

The incidence (4,402) under the Essential Commodities Act in 1995, though increased by 6.5 per cent, over the previous year but when compared to the quinquennial average of 199094, indicated a considerable decrease (33%). The highest incidence (1,022) constituting 23.2 per cent of the total cases, were reported from West Bengal.

Terrorist and disruptive activities act

The incidence (1,304) under the Terrorist & Disruptive Activities Act in 1995 fell steeply, with decreases of 62.6 and 59 per cent over the quinquennial average of 1990-94 and over the previous year respectively. As in the past Jammu and Kashmir registered the bulk of such incidence (1,158) constituting 88.8 per cent as well as the highest crime rate (13.6), compared to the national average of 0.1.

Antiquity and art treasure act

The incidence (69) under the Antiquity & Art Treasure Act showed a steep rise of 127 per cent over the quinquennial average of 1990-94 but increased marginally from 66 in the previous year to 69 in this year.

Dowry prohibition act

'The incidence (2,814) under the Dowry Prohibition Act in 1995 showed an increasing trend with increases of 22.5 per cent and 3.9 per cent over the quinquennial average of 199094 and over 1994 respectively. Bihar registered the highest incidence (982) followed by Uttar Pradesh (653).

Together, these two States -accounted for 58.1 per cent of the total cases reported in the country. Bihar registered the highest crime rate (1-0) against the national average of 0.3.

One of the basic duties of the police is to prevent and detect crime, so that the citizens can enjoy their basic freedoms and human rights without the fear of crime. Although crime is endemic in any society and cannot be totally eliminated, it can be controlled if purposeful activities are directed at prevention in the first place and concerted efforts are made at detection. Prevention is a proactive strategy which comes into play before the crime strikes, whereas detection is a reactive step that Lakes place after the crime. To enable the police to achieve their task successfully for the benefit of society, the law gives them vast powers and has also laid down the procedures to be, followed. These have been further fine-tuned by judge-made laws, which are the Supreme Court judgements.

In simple terms, any activity proscribed by law is crime. Often, when we hear the tern) "crime", we automatically relate it to loss of property. Incidents of murder, rape, kidnapping, extortion etc., which take place during internal security situations, Communal riots and other serious law and order situations, are all crimes. It is the duty of the police and security forces to prevent these. For purposes of clarity, let us discuss, crime, prevention from two angles: preventing crime is disturbed areas and preventing crime in peaceful areas. At the outset, we would like to make it clear that there are no specific human rights standards or instruments directly dealing with this subject.

All the steps which are discussed herein, directly impinge, one way or the other, on the human rights of citizens. It is therefore necessary that, when implementing preventive measures, care should be taken not to violate basic freedoms and rights. For example, as part of preventive measures, it may be necessary to control the basic right of freedom of movement, the right to personal liberty and others. If care is taken to follow the ethics and legality, these can be done without affecting the dignity of the individual.

The basic purpose of deploying security forces in disturbed areas is to protect the lives and properties of the citizens from the depredations of lawless elements. To do this, the co-operation is needed, which will be forthcoming only when security forces respect the human rights of the people. Preventive steps would consist of the strategies of visibility, education and counselling. People living in disturbed areas are in a state of panic and fear. Security forces need to remove these fears and instill confidence in the people and this achieved through visibility.

Security forces should make their presence known to people through patrolling, establishing check-posts etc. They should also work out a detailed scheme to defend the public from the attacks of lawless elements. These plans are to be explained to the people and to make them realise that people are a part of these efforts, they should be given suitable roles in the scheme. The commanding officer or the unit commander should meet the people often for informal interactions, to know their perceptions of the danger and their level of confidence in the schemes.

People should receive education in the form of explanations about the goals of the lawless elements and their methodology. Often, security forces start with the assumption that the local people are not well disposed towards them and will not co-operate. This is far from the truth. It is quite likely that they are being forced, under threat, to co-operate with the unlawful elements. People should be educated about the modus operand of these elements and be given practical hints to safeguard themselves from the dangers of explosives, land mines etc. They should also be briefed about passing on information about any criminal occurrences taking place in the area. These steps, along with civil actions, will help the people co-operate with the security forces.

People in the affected areas are often ignorant of ways and methods to protect their own lives and properties. Through ongoing counselling, specific, simple and efficacious methods are to be thought of and passed on to the people. Individuals known to be sympathetic to lawless elements are to be spoken to and convinced about the need to preserve the democratic way of life and to dissociate from these elements. Security forces may also make preventive arrests, searches and seizures. These are to be done in accordance with the legal procedures elaborated in subsequent chapters. They should realise that one can achieve any difficult task without offending the dignity of a citizen.

Police should maintain visibility by undertaking extensive patrolling, particularly during nights. People should see that the police are around at all odd hours. Criminals, too, Would notice this and move away from the area. Station House officers and head constables should often meet the people of the area and have discussions with them about their fears and the efficacy of patrolling. People should be offered education about the need to take steps to prevent crimes from taking place. Even simple things like repairing a broken window, mending a fence, placing a light in the compound etc. go a long way towards preventing crime. Much of petty crime, like lifting articles from households, snatching of ornaments, cycle thefts etc., can be prevented if the people know how to prevent them. Police officers should frequently address the people and explain to them the need to take preventive steps themselves.

Legal Provisions

Chapter XI of the Code of Criminal Procedure 1973 gives the legal provisions for preventive action by the police.

Section 149. Police to prevent cognisable offence:

Every police officer may interpose for the purpose of preventing, and shall, to the best of his ability, prevent, the commission of any cognisable offence.

This section enables the police officers to intervene effectively in situations which may lead to the commission of a crime.

Section 150. Information of design to commit cognisable offences:

Every police officer receiving information of a design to commit any cognisable offence shall communicate such information to the police officer to whom he is subordinate, and to any other officer whose duty it is to prevent or take cognisance of the commission of any such offence,

This provision makes it obligatory to communicate information regarding the likelihood of commission of an offence to higher authorities, so that effective steps may be taken to prevent the same,

Section 152. Prevention of injury to public property :

A police officer may, of his own authority, interpose to prevent any injury attempted to be committed in his view to any public property, movable or immovable, or the removal or injury of any public landmark or buoy or other mark used for navigation.

Public property is the collective asset of society and is to be protected individuals often do not register complaint or pass on information about injury to public property, as it does not directly affect him. Hence the need for the police to intervene. Similarly, loss or damage to public landmarks or navigational aids will greatly inconvenience the people at large and are therefore to be prevented.

Section 153. Inspection of Weights and Measures :

(1) Any officer in charge of a police station may, without a warrant, enter any place within the limits of the station for the purpose of inspecting or searching of any weights and Measures or instruments for weighing used or kept therein, whenever he has reasons to believe that there are in such places any weights, measures or instruments for weighing which are false.

(2) If he finds in such place any weights, measures or instruments for weighing which are false, he may seize the same, and shall forthwith give information of such seizure to a magistrate having jurisdiction.

This section has beer provided to safeguard the interests of citizens in rural and semi-urban areas, who are generally duped by unscrupulous traders through the use of unauthorised and false weights and measures.

Section 151. Arrest to prevent the commission of cognisable offences :

(1) A police officer knowing of a design to commit any cognisable offence may arrest, without orders from the magistrate and without a warrant, the person so designing, if it appears to such officers that the commission of the offence cannot be otherwise prevented. This is the most important tool in the hands of police officers. It enables them to act quickly and decisively. This provision is often used to defuse explosive situations in the maintenance of order. Breach of peace is averted by removing troublesome elements from the scene.

Section 41(1)(b):

Any police officer may, without an order from a magistrate and without a warrant, arrest any person who has in his possession, without lawful excuse, the burden of proving which excuse shall lie on such person any implement of house-breaking;

This often takes place while the police are on patrol. They see a suspicious person and, on examination, find that he is in possession of a house-breaking implement. It is for him to prove why he is in possession of that and in those circumstances. This is an effective provision to prevent offences against property. In addition to these general provisions, specific legislations also have provisions to effect arrests to prevent the commission of a particular crime. There are also security sections under which individuals likely to commit breach of peace can, as a preventive measure, be asked to execute an undertaking not to do so by providing security.

Thus, the measures for preventing crime may marginally restrict the rights and freedoms of individuals in the larger interests of the society. The law provides, safeguards to ensure that these do not degenerate into absolute violations.

Human Rights ensure that the victims are:

- to be free from intimidation,
- to be informed about the availability of financial assistance and legal assistance,
- to get back stolen or other personal property which is no longer needed as evidence, and
- to a speedy investigation and trial of the case.

Compensation to Victims

Section 357 (1) of Criminal Procedure Code provides that

when a court imposes a sentence which includes a fine; the court may direct that the fine amount should be utilized:

(a) in defraying the expenses of prosecution

(b) in making payment in the loss caused to the victim

Section 357(3) of Criminal Procedure Code provides that the court can award compensation even in cases where fine does not form part of the sentence.

The Model Scheme for Victim-Assistance in India

Considering the present status of crime victims in India, the need to have a comprehensive victim-assistance policy is obvious and requires no reiteration. Acceptance of this policy should start with the recognition of certain basic rights of the victims, such as:

1) The Right to Protection from Criminal Victimisation

This is the right to know about the protective measures which a person may take to avoid possible victimisation.

It is for the law enforcement agencies to educate the public about crime prevention measures and also to take necessary steps to improve the community's self-protection ability.

2) The Right to Reparation for Consequences of Criminal Victimisation (physical injury, loss or trauma)

This right is aimed at ensuring physical, psychological, social and financial well-being of the victims. Consequently, the victims of crime should have

i) The right to have access to professional services and other support from the relevant agencies.

ii) The right to Government compensation for physical injury.

iii) The right to punish the offender through civil and criminal proceedings for the loss and damages suffered by the victim.

3) Rights Pertaining to the Agencies of Criminal Justice System

The victim must also have

i) The right to be informed about the procedures and practices of the criminal justice system in simple language.

ii) The right to information about the progress of investigation, arrest of the culprits, case status in the court etc.

iii) The right to fair treatment from the agencies of the criminal justice system.

iv) The right to privacy, dignity and respect.

v) The right to legal advice and assistance.

vi) The right to ask for a speedy disposal of the case.

vii) The right to have his recovered property returned early.

viii) The right to receive fair treatment when testifying in court.

ix) The right to protection from any intimidation, threat or aggression from the accused side.

The UN General Assembly Resolution 40/34 of 29.11.1985 lists the Basic Principles of Justice for Victims of Crime and Abuse of Power.

Declaration of Basic Principles of Justice for Victims of Crime and Abuse of Power

Recommended for adoption by the Seventh United Nations Congress on the Prevention of Crime and the Treatment of Offenders held at Milan from 26 August to

6 September, 1985 and adopted by General Assembly resolution 40/34 of 29 November, 1985

Victims of crime

1. "Victims" means persons who, individually or collectively, have suffered harm, including physical or mental injury, emotional suffering, economic loss or substantial impairment, of their fundamental rights, through acts or omissions that ' are in violation of criminal laws operative within Member States, including those laws prescribing criminal abuse of power,

2. A person may be considered a victim, under this Declaration, regardless of whether the perpetrator 'is identified, apprehended, prosecuted or convicted and regardless of the familiar relationship between the perpetrator and the victim.. The term "victim" also includes, where appropriate, the immediate family or dependants of the direct victim and persons who have suffered harm in intervening to assist victims in distress or to prevent victimization.

3. The provisions contained herein shall be applicable to all, without distinction of any kind, such as race, colour, sex, age, language, religion, nationality, political or other opinion, cultural beliefs or practices, property, birth or family status, ethnic or social origin, and disability.

4. Victims should be treated with compassion and respect for their dignity. They are entitled to access to the mechanisms of justice and to prompt redress, as provided for by national legislation, for the harm that they have suffered.

5. Judicial and administrative mechanisms should be established and strengthened where necessary to enable victims to obtain redress through formal or informal procedures that are expeditious, fair, inexpensive and

accessible. Victims should be informed of their rights in seeking redress through such mechanisms.

6. The responsiveness of judicial and administrative processes to the needs of victims should be facilitated by:

(a) Informing victims of their role and the scope, timing and progress of the proceedings and of the disposition of their cases, especially where serious crimes are involved and where they have requested such information;

(b) Allowing the views and concerns of victims to be presented and considered at appropriate stages of the proceedings where their personal interests are affected, without prejudice to the accused and consistent with the relevant national criminal justice system;

(c) Providing proper assistance to victims throughout the legal process;

(d) Taking measures to minimize inconvenience to victims, protect their privacy, when necessary, and ensure their safety, as well as that of their families and witnesses on their behalf, from intimidation and retaliation;

(e) Avoiding unnecessary delay in the disposition of cases and the execution of orders or decrees granting awards to victims.

7. Informal mechanisms for the resolution of disputes, including mediation, arbitration and customary justice or of practices, should be utilized where appropriate to facilitate concillation and redress for victims.

8. Offenders or third parties responsible for their behaviour should, where appropriate, make fair restitution to victims, their families or dependants. Such restitution should include the return or property or payment for the harm or loss suffered, reimbursement of expenses incurred as a result of the victimization, the provision of services and the restoration of rights.

9. Governments should review their practices, regulations and laws to consider restitution as an available sentencing option in criminal cases, in addition to other criminal sanctions.

10. In cases of substantial harm to the environment, restitution, if ordered, should include, as far as possible, restoration of the environment, reconstruction of the infrastructure, replacement of community facilities and reimbursement of the expenses of relocation, whenever Such harm results in the dislocation of a community.

11. Where public officials or other agents acting in an official or quasi-official capacity have violated national criminal laws, the victims should receive restitution from the State whose officials or agents were responsible for the harm inflicted. In cases where the Government under whose authority the victimizing act or omission occurred is no longer in existence, the State or Government successor in title should provide restitution to the victims.

12. When compensation is not fully available from the offender or other sources, States should endeavour to provide financial compensation to:

(a) Victims who have sustained significant bodily injury or impairment of physical or mental health as a result of serious crimes;

(b) The family, in particular dependants of persons who have died or become physically or mentally incapacitated as a result of such victimization.

13. The establishment, strengthening and expansion of national funds for compensation to victims should be encouraged. Where appropriate, other funds may also be established for this purpose, including in those cases where the State of which the victim is a national is not in a position to compensate the victim for the harm.

14. Victims should receive the necessary material, medical, psychological and social assistance through governmental, voluntary, community-based and indigenous means.

15. Victims should be informed of the availability of health and social services and other relevant assistance and be readily afforded access to them.

16. Police, justice, health, social service and other personnel concerned should receive training to sensitize them to the needs of victims, and guidelines to ensure proper and prompt aid.

17. In providing services and assistance to victims, attention should be given to those who have special needs because of the nature of the harm inflicted or because of factors such as those mentioned in paragraph 3 above.

Victims of abuse of power

18. "Victims" means persons who, individually or collectively, have Suffered harm, including physical or mental injury, emotional suffering, economic loss or substantial impairment of their fundamental rights, through acts or omissions that do not yet constitute violations of national criminal laws but of internationally recognized norms relating to human rights.

19. States should consider incorporating into the national law norms prescribing abuses of power and providing remedies to Victims of Such abuses. In particular, such remedies Should include restitution and/or compensation, and necessary material, medical, psychological and social assistance and support.

20. States should consider negotiating multilateral international treaties relating to victims, as defined in paragraph 18.

21. States should periodically review existing legislation and practices to ensure their responsiveness to changing

circumstances, enact and enforce, if necessary, legislation prescribing acts that constitute serious abuses of political or economic power, as well as promoting policies and mechanisms for the prevention of such acts, and should develop and make readily available appropriate rights and remedies for victims of such acts.

7
Statelessness and Mass Expulsions

Statelessness is not merely a legal problem. It is also a consequence of migrations, of movements of population, of forced exodus and of various forms of persecution. The frequency and growing magnitude of these problems in recent years explains, to a large extent, the renewed interest in statelessness, and particularly in de facto statelessness. De facto stateless people, as distinct from de jure stateless people, do theoretically have a nationality. But they have lost all real links with their country of origin and no longer have its protection, either because the country in question refuses to afford assistance and protection, or because the people in question have renounced it. Their situation is similar to that of refugees who, while keeping their nationality, no longer benefit from the effective protection of their State.

Stateless people are not, however, all refugees, and, conversely, refugees are not all stateless. In practice, the distinction between de jure and de facto statelessness is not always evident and this has sometimes led to the use of the terms 'de jure non-protected persons' and 'de facto non-protected persons', or 'technically stateless persons' and 'politically stateless people', in order to demonstrate the origin of non-protection. As de facto stateless persons, there are also those who have never had a nationality. In particular, the case of many Palestinians serves as illustration. There are also nomads and gypsies who live on the fringes of the nation state and who, as it were, embrace statelessness voluntarily. Their situation raises particular problems which the Council of Europe, for example, is trying to solve. Its recommendation of 1983 calls on States to retain certain criteria, such as the country of origin of immediate family or of frequent periods of residence, in order to facilitate their membership of a State and to allow them to travel freely.

From a humanitarian point of view, statelessness, whether de jure or de facto, is a major preoccupation. The stateless are part of those unwanted people who are refused right of entry to countries or who are turned back at borders according to political or economic circumstances. If they are taken in, they often live in uncertainty for many years. Statelessness is frequently transmitted from one generation to another. Nationality is not only the right to a passport and material advantages. It also confers upon the individual an identity and the sense of belonging to a community—elements without which a person remains vulnerable and uprooted. As a result of events during the inter-war years and the Second World War, the Universal Declaration of Human Rights proclaimed the right to a nationality as a fundamental human right. Article 15 states:

1. Everyone has the right to a nationality.
2. No-one shall be arbitrarily deprived of his nationality, nor denied the right to change his nationality.

But much effort is still required before this right is fully recognized. In recent decades, the international community became aware of the problem of stateless people at the same time as it was preoccupied with the fate of refugees. However, the two issues were dealt with separately by the United Nations. It is now becoming increasingly apparent that, in practice, the stateless are less protected than refugees. The 1954 Convention of the United Nations relating to the Status of Stateless Persons, formulated along the same lines as the 1951 Convention relating to the Status of Refugees, confers a special status on the stateless and guarantees them minimum standards of treatment.

Stateless persons are thus granted the same rights as nationals in certain areas: the right of access to courts of law, industrial and intellectual property, education, assistance and social security. For other rights and activities, they should be granted treatment no less favourable than generally accorded to aliens as regards movable and immovable property, the right of association, the right to engage in wage earning or unsalaried employment, the right to practise a liberal profession, the right to housing, education up to and beyond primary level, and freedom of movement. The Convention also requests States to issue to stateless persons identity papers and travel documents and to take measures to facilitate their assimilation and naturalization.

The treatment of stateless persons and refugees has many similarities. There are, however, certain differences which make statelessness a less advantageous situation than that of refugees. In the event of illegal entry or presence, only refugees are exempt from penalties. They are also guaranteed freedom from expulsion or forcible return to a country where they risk being persecuted. However, the 1954 Convention offers no more than a statutory arrangement for stateless persons. It does not offer a definitive solution. It does not look into the problem of nationality which is, after all, the only means to ensure true and lasting integration of the stateless into a national community. In this sense, the 1961 Convention on the Reduction of Statelessness took a step forward by attacking the problem at its source.

Stateless children should be granted the nationality of the State in whose territory they are born. This would avoid perpetuating statelessness from one generation to the next. If all countries were to conform to this principle, namely that of jus soli, there would be far fewer stateless persons. But this is hardly the case. Many countries apply the rule of jus sanguinis. They ensured that their own interests were preserved in the 1961 Convention. The co-existence of both principles weakens the efficacy of the Convention in relation to its avowed aim.

The Convention also seeks to avoid cases of statelessness which are the result of voluntary omission, of a change in civil status, of the stripping of nationality or of the transfer of territorial sovereignty. The Convention essentially ensures that no person shall lose his or her nationality without a guarantee of acquiring another. However, even here, the prerogatives of sovereignty have been assuaged, and exceptions introduced which largely reduce the scope of the principles in question. This is certainly the case of persons who may lose their nationality as a result of extended residence abroad.

Others may be deprived of nationality if, for example, they represent 'a serious threat' to the 'essential interests' of the State. These notions are not spelt out in more detail, and their Interpretation often results in injustice and arbitrary measures. De facto statelessness has been particularly overlooked in international conventions. Protection under the 1954 Convention is only aimed at people who have obtained status as stateless persons. Other than those who also have refugee status, and thereby enjoy more favourable conditions, the majority of de facto stateless persons are without protection. Even in war time when the number of refugees and stateless persons increases, the 1977 Geneva Protocols expressly qualify as protected persons only those stateless persons considered as such before the outbreak of hostilities, namely the de jure stateless.

A recommendation included in the Final Act of the Conference on the Status of Stateless Persons invites the Contracting States to extend the treatment accorded by the Convention to de facto stateless persons who have renounced the protection of their own State. Among the resolutions included in the Final Act of the Conference on the Reduction of Statelessness is one which recommends that persons who are stateless de facto should be treated as stateless dejure to enable them to acquire an effective nationality. But these are only recommendations which are in no way binding upon States.

Despite numerous compromises and concessions, the Conventions on Statelessness have not received the number of ratifications one might have hoped for: only 35 States have ratified the 1954 Convention and 13 that of 1961. To the weakness of standard-setting, one must add negligence by existing institutions. Stateless persons are almost alone therefore when facing the State. They frequently leave their country without any resources or valid identity papers. They may either be forcibly returned, or admitted temporarily and then rejected and escorted to the frontier. They may be mistreated—without any international organization offering assistance.

The Convention relating to the Status of Refugees III was able to benefit from the establishment of the Office of the United Nations High Commissioner for Refugees (UNHCR) which was entrusted with its supervision and application. UNHCR has the mandate to assist refugees, ensure their legal protection and follow up with the authorities of host countries. There are no such mechanisms for stateless persons. The 1961 Convention did foresee the establishment within the framework of the United Nations of a body to which persons claiming the benefit of the Convention might apply. UNHCR was so designated by the UN General Assembly (Resolution 3274 (XXIX) of 10 December 1974 and Resolution 31/36 of 30 November 1976). But no mention is made of UNHCR's competence with regard to the application of the 1954 Convention and to measures of assistance towards those who have not yet been deemed stateless persons.

Moreover, UNHCR, which could in practice go beyond conventional limits, has remained somewhat indifferent when it comes to the fate of the stateless. The term stateless person hardly ever appears in UNHCR publications—a fact which, together with the doctrinal vacuum in this particular area, only serves to heighten general indifference towards a problem which should, rather, inspire in human terms the same compassion as that shown to refugees.

The solutions provided so far by the international community with regard to the problem of statelessness have been found wanting and inefficient. They have been formulated more from the point of view of a State's prerogatives and sovereignty than of individual human rights. It is this imbalance which today requires correction through a new approach which takes into account the many dimensions of the problem. Action must be aimed at prevention and elimination. With regard to nationality, the law needs to be strengthened and better defined. The 1961 Convention does not express an international consensus. Few States (only 35 of them) participated in the Conference and only 13 have ratified the Convention. The elaboration of a new instrument might allow the emergence of a consensus and a new standard which, in any case, would serve to influence national legislation.

The 1961 Convention was a compromise between those countries which, in turn, supported either jus soli or jus sanguinis. Ideally, any future international instrument should go beyond compromises to a comprehensive approach to the elimination of statelessness. It would be advisable, for example, to adopt a single criterion for the acquisition of nationality: that of jus soli. The 1969 American Convention on Human Rights, for example, recognizes the right of any person to acquire the nationality of the State in whose territory he or she was born. The ability to deprive a citizen of nationality should be forbidden absolutely if it leads to statelessness. There are other measures that can be taken against those who go against national interests. A State should not turn away its own citizens, or ex-citizens who have no other nationality.

In the case of ceding of territory, States must ensure that the inhabitants do not become stateless. They might give the inhabitants, for example, the right to choose between the nationality of the successor or the predecessor State. The best way to eliminate statelessness is to allow stateless persons to acquire a nationality. States should envisage advantageous ways of naturalization and distinguish them from those usually offered to foreigners. In the event of a country of residence not granting its nationality to a stateless person, the United Nations should look into ways and means to resolve the problem. It is up to the United Nations to initiate and encourage the international community to be more sensitive to the problem of statelessness.

Mechanisms to protect and assist stateless persons should be established urgently. It is possible, for example, to envisage, through a protocol to the 1954 Convention, the-creation of a High Commissioner for Stateless Persons, However, it would be more appropriate to confer this task upon UNHCR. This would be a way not only of gaining from its experience in the field of protection, but of saving time, money and energy. UNHCR already has been given by the UN General Assembly the functions foreseen in the 1961 Convention. It should also monitor the application of the 1954 Convention.

The mandate of UNHCR is sufficiently flexible. In the same way that it is charged with the task of protecting refugees and displaced persons who do not fall under the definition of the 1951 Convention, it should be empowered to extend its activities to all stateless persons, de jure or de facto. It is important to recall in this connection that UNHCR has on-going activities not only in countries which are party to the Convention, but also in many which have not ratified it.

We believe it would be helpful if UNHCR could assume the following tasks.

— Promote the ratification of international Conventions relating to statelessness.

— Monitor the application of Conventions and report to the General Assembly on the state of application of Conventions and of its activities in favour of stateless persons.

— Collect all possible information concerning stateless persons, their number and whereabouts. The task should be all the easier, in that UNHCR already undertakes this for refugees and that within national administrations, it is often the same department which deals with refugees and stateless persons.

— Co-operate with governments with a view to improving the condition of stateless persons and reduce their number through the adoption of permanent solutions through appropriate inter-governmental agreements.

— Assist stateless persons in administrative matters and inform them of their rights.

— Raise public awareness of the problems of stateless persons and promote the reduction and elimination of statelessness.

— Include the needs of stateless persons in its public information and fund-raising activities.

The 1961 Convention foresees the jurisdiction of the Inter national Court of Justice in the event of disputes concerning the interpretation or application of the Convention. But the prerogative of seizing the Court is reserved for States. It would appear timely to set up an international authority to which stateless persons themselves could apply in order to uphold their rights. Nationality is not a simple affair of state. It is also a human right.

Statelessness is a source of political and socio-economic tension which affects the country of origin, the country of residence and neighbouring countries. Regional organizations should become more involved in the problem and contribute to its solution through initiatives adapted to local conditions. Regional mechanisms to control human rights could also be used to ensure respect for the right of every individual to a nationality and related rights such as that of choosing one's place of residence, of freely entering one's own country, or of not being expelled from it.

Despite the long history of mass expulsions, which have meant deprivation and death for hundreds of thousands of people and caused major social, economic and political upheavals, very little has been done at the international or even regional level to tackle the issue. There is no organization, either within or outside the United Nations system, with a specific mandate to deal with the problem. There has been no concerted attempt to formulate an international instrument or even a code of conduct to prevent or regulate mass expulsions. Although the expulsion of undesirable foreign individuals is considered to be within the sovereign legal prerogative of States, a number of jurists agree that mass expulsions of nationals or aliens can be considered unlawful under international law: they are arbitrary in their effect, they violate human rights, and cause unnecessary hardship to large numbers of innocent and vulnerable people. Of course, the governments which implement mass expulsions claim that they have a right to do so.

Economic justifications are commonly uppermost in official statements on this issue. Migrant workers from developing countries, perhaps the most regular victims of mass expulsions in recent years, are blamed for taking jobs that should be held by a country's own citizens. It is argued that migrant workers, especially those who enter a country in an irregular way, place undue pressure on public services in times of austerity, and aggravate balance of payments crises by sending remittances back to their own country.

Some migratory movements result in the establishment of settled alien communities. Business communities, sometimes termed 'middlemen minorities', have repeatedly been subject to expulsion. These communities commonly dominate the trading and commercial sector of their adopted country, and are set apart from the rest of the population by their race, religion or nationality. They usually retain an orientation towards their country of origin which, combined with their economic success, isolates them from the host community and renders them liable to charges of disloyalty and dishonesty. Other categories of migrants have been subject to expulsion in recent years, although not in such great numbers as migrant labourers and settled traders and entrepreneurs.

Groups of environmental refugees, forced to flee disasters such as floods, earthquakes, drought and famine, have occasionally been expelled from States which claim not to have the resources to care for large numbers of distressed foreigners. Even genuine refugees, victims of conflict or persecution, have been subject to mass expulsions from countries which regard them as an economic or political liability. In many recent cases of mass expulsion, economic justifications have been advanced by governments to disguise their real, political motives.

Four related sets of political motives for mass expulsion can be identified, in which both domestic and international considerations feature. First, expulsions result from a desire to rind convenient scapegoats for a government's policy failures. Second, they have been instigated during periods of political unrest, when minority groups represent a perceived threat to national security. Third, such minorities are vulnerable in the run-up to elections, when ruling parties attempt to maintain power by making dramatic populist gestures.

Finally, expulsions are used in the course of international disputes, to humiliate or create practical problems for rival States. But experience suggests that mass expulsions cause a great deal of needless suffering and seldom achieve their intended or stated objectives. In fact, they frequently prove to be counter-productive. Economic dislocation is common in the wake of large-scale expulsions. The departure of migrant workers can leave major gaps in the labour market without significantly reducing unemployment amongst nationals. The disruption of commerce may also occur, especially in countries where expelled minorities have special skills or play an important role in the trading or manufacturing sectors. Expulsions can easily provoke conflict between neighbouring States, impeding efforts to encourage regional co-operation. There is a constant danger that a State receiving large numbers of expellees will take reprisals, leading to a further deterioration of relations, increased spending on defence, and a greater risk of military conflict.

Receiving States are confronted with enormous problems on account of mass expulsions. In the short term, they have to arrange for the reception and rehabilitation of the expellees, who often arrive without resources and in a state of destitution. In the longer term, receiving States have to deal with the prospect of increased unemployment, pressure on public resources and competition for land. The return of disappointed and frustrated emigrants is also a source of social and political frictions, especially when they have been accustomed to a higher standard of living in another country. But it would be misleading to suggest that the consequences of mass expulsion are inevitably negative, especially in the longer term.

Critics of migrant labour systems have long argued that the skills and energy of migrant workers should be used productively at home rather than contributing to growth abroad. Although there is no specific international mechanism to deal with the problem of mass expulsions, it would not be desirable to establish a new office or to revise the mandate of an existing agency to fill the gap. However, it would be appropriate to designate an agency to forecast mass expulsions, monitor them and promote preventive measures. Despite its specific mandate and limited means, the United Nations Disaster Relief Office (UNDRO) has been considered the appropriate inter-governmental body in the United Nations system. Of course, other agencies—UNICEF, the World Food

Programme, the International Labour Office and the United Nations High Commissioner for Refugees—have an important role to play, as does the Red Cross and the voluntary agencies. Co-ordination between them and collective assistance to the designated body would be vital.

International legal responses must also be strengthened. The expulsion of nationals constitutes an unlawful act. As for foreign nationals, their mass expulsion, as distinguished from expulsion of individuals, should be subject to closer international scrutiny. The onus is clearly on the expelling State to avoid such action if possible, to justify the instigation of expulsions when they take place, and to give due regard to the human rights of the group targeted for expulsion. Some progress has recently been made in this direction.

Some forms of mass expulsion may prove difficult to eliminate. While States continue to make use of disappearances, detention without trial and torture, they are unlikely to eschew the relatively mild remedy of mass expulsions in their attempt to solve difficult political and economic problems. But like so many other forms of mass displacement, the conditions which lead States to implement mass expulsions do not spring up overnight. A government which pursues it laissezfaire immigration policy during a period of economic growth cannot expect large numbers of migrant workers to pack their bags and leave voluntarily as soon as recession sets in.

A country which benefits from the entrepreneurial activities of a minority group cannot expect to deprive that group of its economic and political influence states must therefore be sensitized to the need for foresight, long-term planning and due respect for the rights of minorities whether they be foreign or national. The international community must look for ways of anticipating and preventing mass expulsions. The United Nations system in particular has a major role to play.

We urge the international community to support the United Nations in this task by providing the assistance required for the victims of mass expulsions to be returned to and resettled in the receiving State in conditions of safety and dignity. We believe that the protection of people subjected to mass expulsions could be enhanced by developing a legal instrument or a set of principles governing their treatment. The 1986 Declaration of Principles of International Law on Mass Expulsion, of the International Law Association just mentioned, could provide a suitable starting point.

Migration has become a major issue in recent years for those concerned about international security or violence and peace. A growing body of literature discusses the new immigration in Europe and the reactions from governments and political groupings, especially right-wing parties and movements.' Other works have looked more closely into a particularly worrisome dimension of the interaction between nationals and foreigners: the increased and often spectacular incidence of racist personal violence.

The view that there is a connection between the number of asylum-seekers and the violence against migrants is one held in both halves of the established political spectrum. The most concrete manifestation of a link was provided by the Hoyerswerda and Rostock-Lichtenhagen attackers and the so-called 'normal citizens' who stood by and applauded them; and a certain section of the élite was only too ready to swallow the idea. After all—to put it in Hans Magnus Enzensberger's acerbic terms—you can't expect ordinary people having to face such a huge scale of immigrants residing in their neighbourhood to accept that burning children, strictly speaking, is not permissible.

The Chancellor declared that the unreasonable requirements resulting from immigration, not the 'unreasonable state of affairs resulting from the presence of people engaging in individual or organized man-hunts', constituted grounds for a possible state of emergency; the Minister of the Interior and other politicians in government expressed concern about Germany's reputation abroad.

The conservative interpretation of the link .between the asylum issue and violence against foreigners could be summed up as follows: Germany has an immigration problem but not an indigenous problem with violence or, alternatively, hostility to foreigners is a product of a dramatic influx of immigrants. Within the other half of the political spectrum, meanwhile, it has repeatedly been argued that it was only after the asylum issue was dramatized by politicians and the press that the attacks on hostels and asylum-seekers began.

In a nutshell, therefore, the opposing thesis runs: Germany has a problem with violence/neo-Fascism, but no fundamental immigration problems. We believe both interpretations are false. Both have more to do with German history than with the reality of present-day Germany; and it is probable that both actually contribute to the violence—through their own specific ways of denying reality, and through reciprocal polarization. The thesis that Germany has an immigration problem but does not, in principle, have a problem with violence—leaving aside the moral affront such a view constitutes in regard to the victims—can clearly be seen to be inadequate at the first empirical glance.

Attacks and other criminal offences are by no means directed solely against asylum-seekers, but also against German-born daughters, sons, and grandchildren of immigrants who have been residents for years and are de facto members of the indigenous working population; they are directed against tourists, Aussiedler (remigrants whose

German ancestors settled in Eastern Europe or Russia, or Germans from formerly German provinces in the East), disabled people, the homeless, homosexuals, and people who hold different political views.

Another reason why immigration cannot be the sole cause of the increase in acts of violence is the fact that hostility to foreigners also manifests itself in places where there is no real experience of 'foreigners', or where such experience is almost impossible. And even when situations of competition can be shown to exist, or when problems do arise from direct contact between cultures, the question still remains of why the response should take the form of acts of violence. We nonetheless start from the assumption that Germany does indeed have an immigration problem or at least did have one.

Even under more favourable conditions, a debate would still have to have been conducted about limiting immigration and applications for asylum. Having to conduct it in a context of arson and murder has been extremely difficult. In order to provide detailed corroboration for our assumptions, and to develop a more nuanced account of the link between the asylum debate and violence against foreigners, we shall begin by describing the different groups of offenders and by developing an explanatory model to account for the new violence. In a further section, we address the problem of immigration and asylum, and discuss the repercussions of the political debate on society. In the final section, we present the practical conclusions that can be drawn from our analysis.

One of the first major systematic empirical investigations into the offender group was that by the Trier-based sociologists Roland Eckert, Linda Steinmetz, Helmut Willems, and Stefanie Würtz. The Trier group analysed a total of 1398 police dossiers on anti-foreigner offences covering the period 1 January 1991 to 30 April 1992. The judgements in 53 cases involving a total of 148 individuals were also included in the analysis.

On the basis of the investigation, the following general observations may be made about the offenders:

— The overwhelming majority of offenders are youths or adolescents. More than a third (36.2%) are under 18, and about 90% are under 20; only 4.7% are over 30.

— The majority are male; the percentage of women or girls is only 3.7. One notable fact is that the proportion of girls increases as the age of the offenders goes down. All homicidal offences were committed by men.

— An overwhelming proportion of the offenders have a low or average level of schooling.

— The rate of unemployment amongst antiforeigner offenders is somewhat higher than amongst young people as a whole in Germany, but this is an important factor only for certain sub-categories of perpetrators.[5]

— A notable feature is the level of criminality amongst offenders. Previous police records for non-political offences exist for 47% of them, rising to 63% for those over 25 years of age.

Willems et al. identify four types of offenders with differing political attitudes and approaches to violence. Thus the hanger-on type does not have a pronounced right-wing or extreme rightwing world-view, and is not determinedly antiforeigner. Participation in acts of violence against foreigners is here a group-induced effect.

The hanger-on is sometimes a member of skinhead or Fascho youth groups, but more often simply belongs to groups of youths who get together in their spare time. Because of his basic social attitude, the hanger-on allows himself to be drawn into anti-foreigner activities. Major factors in this connection are pressure to conform, the compulsion to solidarity, and a feeling of comradeship—but also the desire not to be ousted from the group. The criminal youth (thug type) is generally somewhat older than the others and, at the time of the incident, already has a lengthy criminal record covering acts ranging from offences against property to grievous bodily harm. Typical features of his negative personal and professional career are: unfinished schooling; unemployment; family problems (alcoholic parents, divorce, experience of violence). These young people are action-oriented, aggressive, and inclined to violence.

As a rule, there is no markedly extreme right-wing political worldview lurking behind this inclination to violence, although anti-foreigner slogans are much in use within this group. They apparently serve to compensate for experiences of failure and to firm up the individual's own identity. The diffuse violence of this type of offender is by no means directed solely against 'foreigners'; it is aimed at any kind of victim—mostly people who rank as weak, or are perceived as such. The xenophobe or ethnocentrist is to be found mostly in the 'skinhead', 'hooligan', or 'Fascho' subcultures, but also figures in the various 'spare-time' gangs. Again, these offenders have no hard-and-fast extreme right-wing attitudes, and do not belong to extreme right-wing groups or parties.

Even though their xenophobic slogans and nationalist catchwords coincide to some extent with those of the organized extreme right, they cannot simply be lumped in with the latter. Their hostility to foreigners does not derive from any extreme right-wing ideology—it results rather from a diffuse feeling that 'Germans' are suffering disadvantage vis-a-vis 'foreigners', particularly asylum-seekers. In the case of this group, worries about the future and competition for scarce goods such as jobs, housing, and welfare benefits play an important role.

Finally, in the case of politically motivated, extreme right-wing or radical right-wing offenders, anti-foreigner violence is indeed the product of an extreme right-wing ideology. Offenders of this type have contact with, or are members of, extreme right-wing parties and groups; as a rule, they have also already been politically active in these circles.

In the debate about the causes of increasing attacks on groups of people marked out by offenders as foreign or odd, there is a wide range of differing theories or theorems on offer. It is generally agreed that these developments cannot be explained in terms of a single cause. The unofficial view that acts of violence are the clearly definable work of isolated criminal or misguided outsiders finds little support. The discussion at the social-science level generally proceeds on the assumption that the violence is an expression of critical trends within society as a whole.

One of the international mass media's first reactions to the violence in Hoyerswerda and Lichtenhagen was: Fascism is coming to life again in Germany. The French newspaper Le Monde, for example, published a cartoon of a large swastika made up entirely of tiny matchstick people. Behind this kind of explanatory model there often lies the notion of a persistence of Fascist structures in German society, temporarily masked but remaining present in latent form, in line with the quotation from Brecht: 'This womb is fruitful still'.

The explanation for an allegedly specifically German inclination to Fascism takes two forms: one accounts for it in terms of the peculiarities of German history, the German 'special path' into the modem world; the other derives it from German characteristics, from the German mentality. Key themes in the 'German special path' thesis are: failure of the Peasants' War in the 16th century and of the liberal-democratic revolution in the 19th century; late development of the middle class; and late achievement of German unity and nation-statehood. One feature regarded as corroborating this derivation is the fact that Fascism also rose to power in Italy, the other European state where national unity came very late, whereas in France and England, where bourgeois society emerged early on and where the nation-state was established at an early date, Fascist movements had no success.

The second explanation stresses the persistence of certain elements of mental make-up, in other words specifically German characteristics such as order, cleanliness, a fixation with authority, megalomania, and militarism. A more subtle variant of this explanatory approach is provided by recent psychoanalytical/ psychohistorical work which diagnoses the continuing but latent effects of concrete historical experiences of socialization - inadequate reflection on, and processing of, traditions, notably from the time of National Socialism.

The modernization approach focuses not so much on German history as on the trends present in all industrial societies. According to this approach - as expounded, for example, by Wilhelm Heitmeyer - right-wing extremism is a reaction typical of the 'loser' in the modernization process. The accelerated pace of development in modem industrial societies, so the argument goes, produces a constant degeneration of skills, puts social rankings and professional careers in doubt, and subjects a considerable section of the population to constant worries about decline in social status.

The unintelligibility of the social mechanisms by which success or failure is allotted, and the impossibility, in principle, of the individual's making any reliable plans as to the preconditions for his or her professional life career, result in a fundamental sense of insecurity. In such a climate of social anxiety, the extreme right's platform becomes a substitute for security. Its clichés used to interpret social reality offer a fourfold benefit:

— They provide simple interpretations of the social environment and the crises it manifests foreigners are taking our jobs and houses; they are the cause of the increase in crime and drug-addiction.

— They offer simple methods of removing the evil ('foreigners out!').

— They guarantee enhancement of the individual's own endangered social status.

— They provide an object of aggression that can be hated, or actually attacked, without moral scruple ('it's the foreigners' own fault; if they're persecuted, then that's only fitting punishment').

The thesis that xenophobic or extreme right-wing reactions result from collective deprivation does not presuppose any real impoverishment; the decisive factor, rather, is whether the social groups affected believe that, measured against their expectations and compared with other groups, they are disadvantaged in regard to the distribution of scarce benefits, such as job opportunities, housing, or social welfare. The frustrations produced by such comparisons then fix themselves on to the 'foreigners' who—either apparently or in reality—obtain the benefits to which these individuals believe themselves entitled. In his analysis of right-wing extremism amongst the young, Heitmeyer underlines the effect of the shift towards individualization associated with modernization.

The new opportunities for freedom which the indivdiualization of life opens up cannot be exploited by young people, and are instead, so he says, experienced as isolating and undermining. This feeling of powerlessness is reinforced by the breakdown of traditional milieus such as the family, the neighbourhood, the work-place, the trade union. This destruction of the social fabric of life, combined with the difficulty of formulating reliable prospects in regard to life and work in an individualized, atomized society, engender a need for clarity, certainty, and stability. Extreme right-wing groups seemingly offer an escape from this feeling of insecurity—by providing the opportunity to identify with a group, and by having recourse to so-called 'natural categories' such as race, nation, or masculinity. Acceptance of violence, says Heitmeyer, and the use of it, create the illusion of recaptured autonomy and power of action.

In an original essay on the subject, Eisenberg & Gronerneyer have combined elements of the classic analysis of Fascism with aspects of the modernization theory and developed them into a theory of the collapse of civilization. They distinguish three 'psycho-groups' amongst the young. The first, brought up in a traditionally authoritarian manner, has a tendency to Fascism. The second, the 'yuppie' group, exhibit more instrumental/ Machiavellian inclinations, that is to say they make their way in the world of performance and consumption using methods that range from the robust to the ruthless. However, the future, say the authors, belongs to the 'abandoned children' psycho-group, 'born amongst the concrete and later to be found stone in hand'. Their general unconnectedness is the reflection of a social and, above all, psychological/moral decivilization of bourgeois society.

The violence of the future will no longer be the product of the harshness and brutality of the old 'black pedagogy' but of the increasingly widespread coldness, the lack of attention and emotional nurturing. The classic entities through which socialization took place—notably the family as an emotional refuge from society—are declining in importance, and nothing constructive is taking their place: television is replacing parents as educators. 'Consumerism' as the most recent, contradictory form of capitalism is undermining not only external nature (viz. the ecological crisis), but also the inner natures of people; morality is breaking down, inhibitions are falling away. The media embody both aspects—consumerism and brutalization. What awaits us is not another 1933 but a ghetto revolution engendered by harshness.

The anger displayed by the new perpetrators of violence is not of Nazi but of narcissistic origin. And it is therefore directed, amongst others, at asylum-seekers, because they embody the possible reality of our society—real existing collapse. The borderline area between the social and the political system is also the focus of the political culture approach. This has a number of points in common with the explanatory model based on the notion of persisting traces of Fascism and 'authoritarian character'; in this case, however, the focal point of the analysis is not just German historical traditions, but also the specific conditions governing the political culture that prevails in the Federal Republic.

The term political culture is here used not in a normative or moral sense, as it is in everyday language or in the media, when there is talk of a 'decline in the political culture', meaning wrong behaviour or corruption by politicians. In the social sciences, political culture is used to describe the totality of attitudes, views, opinions, and behaviour of citizens in regard to the political system. This configuration of the subjective elements of politics determines the political climate and political consciousness of a society. It constitutes the seed-bed of social movements and thus also of right-wing extremism.

The extent to which the criminals in Hoyerswerda, Rostock, and Hünxe saw themselves as carrying out the will of a silent majority, and the extent to which politics and the media encouraged the violence by the way in which they tackled the asylum problem—both these, for example, are matters relating to Political culture. A notable difference may be observed here between the old and new Länder. In Rostock-Lichtenhagen, the young hooligans really did believe they were simply carrying out the wishes of a large number of spectators; that they were so doing was obvious from the applause and approval of the latter. There has been nothing comparable to this in the old Länder. Here, the arson attacks have so far been staged under cover of night, with a getaway car at the ready. But this does not mean that the violence in the west has not met with tacit approval. So far, however, it has remained secret, has not dared express itself openly.

Joachim Maaz traces the difference in the political culture in the two parts of Germany to the 'second dictatorship' experience in the former GDR. A major mechanism of GDR socialization was repression by the state, by the party. The least stirring of emancipation or autonomy was strictly suppressed. This has left traces, scars in the social character. At the same time, however, inadequacies in socialization were also contained by the repression, that is to say arrested, and the system provided social security and stability in cases of good conduct. The emancipation which the breakdown of the old order has brought is thoroughly contradictory.

The culture shock caused by reunification has led to a situation which we may, with Durkheim, characterize as 'anomic': it is no longer possible to live by the old norms and values, and not yet possible to do so by the new ones. And the internal assimilation of the new autonomy is taking place under (relatively) difficult external conditions. As a variation on the theme, Birgit Rommelspacher has introduced the concept of the dominance culture into the debate about right-wing extremism (Rommelspacher, 1992a and 1992b). She distances herself from interpretations of right-wing extremism as a way of coping with threat, and stresses that it is not primarily real problems such as impoverishment or social deprivation that lie behind the activation of extreme right-wing tendencies. What is involved, she claims, is rather the safeguarding of privileges and, where it comes to conflict, a process of 'expansive empowerment'. In the former GDR, says Rommelspacher, there is a 'racism born of weakness'. In order to cover up the shame provoked by self-devaluation, individuals identify that much more strongly with the nation.

The new nationalism in the western Länder, meanwhile, feeds on opposite kinds of motives. The establishment of the new political order brought a considerable narcissistic boost to the former FRG. The other side's defeat reflected the superiority of the Federal Republic's own political order and economic might. In the 'delirium of self-satisfaction', this superiority has constantly to be reconfirmed; disturbances in self-image produced - so an extrapolated interpretation might run - by disillusionment about the costs of unity and other critical developments, such as rising unemployment, have to be compensated for in a 'cycle of dominance' involving the devaluation of third parties.

The predominance of men amongst offenders—and also, incidentally, amongst the victims of violence—has prompted various authors to see youth violence as an expression of a masculinity cult or crisis of masculinity. Lothar Böhnisch and Reinhard Winter, for example, view extreme right-wing behaviour, with its high degree of acceptance of violence and its xenophobia, as displaying parallels with basic structures in the masculine approach to coping with life, being simply an exaggerated form of this (Böhnisch & Winter, 1993). In a patriarchy, men are integrated into a hegemonial culture which appears to be theirs, but which ultimately is not. The price for the power deriving from being a man is denial of access to one's own feelings and needs, to one's 'true self', which is distorted with attributes of external 'masculinity'.

The debasement of the female and of the weaker men is a stereotypical feature of this kind of shell-like masculinity. Where the basic structure of all-male clique-style groupings amongst the young develops within the context of daily experience of social and economic powerlessness, it constitutes a fertile breeding-ground for extreme right-wing tendencies. A variant of this theorem of instability in masculine status can be derived from the detailed empirical study of male milieus by Walter Hollstein. In his investigation, Hollstein starts from the assumption that the actual lives and experiences of men, particularly sexual relations, are undergoing major changes. These changes are reflected in the self-images of the men questioned.

Only in the lower classes does one still find unabashed pride in masculinity, but at the same time this group of men is the least satisfied in regard to the fulfilment of its life's goals. This double discrepancy between the established but outmoded male self-image and the changing/unsatisfactory external male world as diagnosed by Hollstein may constitute an important foundation for right-wing extremism and for violence. Both would be a means of compensating for crumbling masculinity.

Joachim Kersten also establishes a link between everyday patriarchy and male youth violence. Like Birgit Rommelspacher, he distances himself in his analysis from attributions of cause involving disintegration and lack of direction. Instead, he follows Robert W. Connell in seeing male youth violence as an expression of conflicts within 'hegemonial masculinity'. In this interpretation, the two aspects—predominantly male aberrant behaviour on the one hand and its control on the other—are seen as cultural practices for regulating the legitimate and illegitimate use of violence within public and private male domains. 'Good' hegemonial power extends to sexual precedence over women and the production of offspring, to dominance in areas where there is a legitimate use of violence as a means of controlling other (hostile) masculinity, and to the provision of material necessities/ control over production. The perverted masculine self-image that prevails amongst neighbourhood gangs, 'skins', and 'hooligans' falls back, so Kersten argues, in an altered form, on exactly the same functions of quasi-legitimate combativeness. Youth violence is thus ultimately characterizable as 'male-dominated aberrant behaviour' and contention over 'hegemonial masculinity'.

We do not wish, at this point, to put for-ward an alternative theory of our own. We believe the existing range of theories is quite sufficient and that, despite one or two internal contradictions, it is possible to tie them in with one another. The only reservation we have—not least because of the profile that emerges of the offenders—concerns those attempts at explanation that resort immediately to theories about Fascism or to Germany's special path. Even if one takes the political/ideological and organizational background of the New Right and extreme right wing in Germany seriously, one also has to take account of the historical changes that have occurred in the Federal Republic since World War II, and of similar problems in the domain of right-wing radicalism or hostility to foreigners in other countries.

Racist violence is a serious problem throughout Europe—'from Sweden to Italy, from Britain to Russia', and even countries with long liberal-democratic traditions, such as Sweden or The Netherlands, have seen an upsurge in violent offences against migrants and foreigners. Recourse to the familiar and easily comprehensible interpretative model based on Fascism and, in particular, German National Socialism, may distort analysis of the new violence rather than clarify it—even if we do continue to take into account the persisting effect of cultural and in particular psycho-historical factors. If we make a distinction between, on the one hand, the socio-psychological causes of the inclination to violence of what are mainly male youths, and, on the other, the direction in which this violence is aimed, it becomes clear that the theorems described above complement rather than exclude one another.

Official reaction to the new 1992/3 law on asylum followed general political predispositions: sighs of relief from the ruling parties and certain sections of the SPD; responses ranging from disappointment to outrage on the Left and amongst refugee organizations. 'The law on asylum lies in ruins, and with it the little bit of human dignity guaranteed by Article 1 and the little bit of legal recourse guaranteed by Article 19', wrote Viktor Pfaff, one of the leading lawyers involved in legal matters relating to foreigners and asylum in the Federal Republic, in an analysis for a leftist magazine. The heavyweight liberal press was not stinting in its criticism either. There was not much left, it said, of what was once the most liberal asylum legislation in the world.

Whatever the political evaluation, any social-scientific analysis will have to begin with the almost tautological observation that the kind of 'compromise on asylum' that has emerged is one that corresponds to the social balance of power and the ideological and party-political configuration in the Federal Republic as it existed at the time. All parties with political responsibility were under pressure to limit immigration. They also wanted to maintain the fiction, however, that they were still prepared to help genuine victims of persecution, even under the radically altered conditions. The decision as to whether Germany needs any immigration, and, if so, how much, is one that politicians have not yet confronted. And as far as the decision about how many refugees Germany was prepared to accept in future, no agreement was possible—though it must also be said that the old constitutional obligations prevented such a decision from being arrived at freely. The new law on asylum avoids this issue: possible avenues to a hypothetical decision-making process such as this have been drastically curtailed.

Real Existing Immigration Problems

Even an enlightened discussion about asylum is difficult because the problem is embedded in other controversial issues associated with immigration: the status of foreigners who have settled in Germany, and of those generations of immigrant families who were born here; the return of descendants of German settlers from eastern Europe and the CIS; illegal immigration; refugees from civil war. And the precise relationship of the asylum question to these topics is, in its turn, a disputed one.

Experts on migration agree that the Federal Republic has long since become an immigration country. The thesis that Germany is again in need of immigration in the medium term, for economic and demographic reasons, is also broadly established. However, as is shown by a glance at those states that view themselves as immigration countries, and pursue a policy of immigration, this kind of directed immigration would, in all probability, be highly selective, and indeed might have counterproductive effects (brain dram) from the point of view of development for the emigration countries. In view of the recession and growing mass unemployment, there is at present no likelihood of mustering any political majorities in favour of regulated labour migration into Germany—other than for seasonal or contractual work. All the more so since Aussiedler will continue for some years to encroach on the labour market, although their influx has now been brought under control through the imposition of limits on the numbers accepted annually. Because of the continuing crisis in the Third World, and because of the end of the East-West conflict, migratory movements have acquired a new historical quality; they are becoming a prime area of conflict in international relations.

As a consequence of the economic divide, and as a result of asymmetrical population growth, pressures to emigrate to the well-off industrialized countries are growing in the developing South, which has now been enlarged by the addition of various parts of the former Second World. The basic conflict consists in the fact that more people want to immigrate than the immigration countries are willing or able to take in. This, incidentally, applies across the whole world, with few exceptions: the number of states that feel overburdened by immigration is on the increase.

The only ultimately effective strategy and constructive alternative to an unsocial sealing off process that comes up frequently in discussions is that of tackling the causes of migratory movements. The industrial countries undoubtedly contribute in many ways to current migratory and fugitive movements—through the balance of power in the world economy, through the privileged exploitation of resources or by charging up regional conflicts through arms supplies. But even if there were a fundamental change of course and maximum political commitment, no more than marginal rectifications to the causes of migration could be expected. The fragmentation of the world and the global crises (overpopulation, underdevelopment, environmental destruction) have assumed such dramatic proportions that the repeated calls for the elimination of the causes of flight also amount to no more than a piece of 'ill-considered patter', as the German political scientist Gilbert Ziebura has termed it. The 'combined destabilization from within and without' render the notion of global freedom of movement illusory.

The problem affects both sides—the societies undergoing immigration and the immigrants themselves. Using the German example, Horst Afheldt has put forward impressive arguments to show that, given the current structural defects in economic development, a continuing high rate of immigration would present not only a political/psychological but also a material threat to democracy and the welfare state. Conversely, it is the case that the integration of those who have already come into the country, or are still to be accepted, can succeed only if immigration is limited.

The great majority of asylum-seekers come from countries where there is war or civil war, where ethnic minorities are discriminated against, or individuals/groups suffer political persecution. This remains the case even though in many instances—especially in Germany—an economic motive can be imputed for the request for asylum. The fact that asylum-seekers also make their way into the Federal Republic with the help of illegal organizations cannot be taken as automatically indicating 'abuse'. If someone is being persecuted, the help of an organization such as this can be their salvation.

On the other hand, it is clear that the illegal operators engage in a constant cat-and-mouse game with the German authorities in an attempt to circumvent the rules governing the asylum procedure, and generally do not care about the status of their clients or even their lives. But the attempt to distinguish between ,abuse' and 'use' of the asylum law distorts perception of the true problem. It is, for example, morally thoroughly dubious to refuse someone asylum because she or he is not being politically persecuted but is trying to flee intolerable living conditions —i.e. structural violence—simply on the grounds that this kind of violence kills them more slowly. This puts advocates of a liberal asylum policy before a dilemma.

As critics of restrictions on immigration, they rightly point out that even the old law on asylum was subject to considerable limitations, that many asylumseekers leave the country again, and that a country such as the Federal Republic would have no trouble at all coping with what, in comparison with the total population, is a tiny volume of immigration. Thus they argue, using the still comparatively low figures of the late 1980s. On the other hand they put forward sound arguments for an extension of the grounds of acceptance and for better provision for asylumseekers. The resultant problem that Germany would then necessarily become an even more attractive country for asylum is, however, not discussed.

Moreover, every analysis that used to stress the numerically insignificant burden to Germany, has, until the change in the asylum law, continually been overtaken by drastic increases in applications. Working out a non-cynical ethical stance on the asylum issue is harder than discussing ethical questions relating to apocalyptic nuclear threat, because any kind of restriction on asylum is inhuman. And yet there is a risk that the progressive camp will have to bid farewell to the spurious solutions with which it believed a German guarantee of an individual right to asylum for all victims of political persecution and a right of residence for the greatest possible number of refugees from civil war could be championed against a changed world situation and the partially fragmented social reality that now prevails in Germany. In addition to the approach of tackling the causes of flight, which we have already mentioned, these spurious solutions include the 'immigration laws' proposal or the so-called 'European option'. Even if the European Union succeeded in formulating a joint policy on immigration, this would not necessarily help those trying to enter a West European country. Quotas, e.g., would be reached very quickly at the beginning of each year, so the problems of entry via the asylum route or by illegal methods would automatically arise again. The as yet non-existent collective European solution to the asylum question will neither provide Germany with any significant relief nor be geared to a high standard of immigration.

Ultimately, asylum in cases of mass immigration can be assured only if there is a method that is acceptable from both the political and humanitarian point of view of making—and above all enforcing—decisions about who may stay and who must leave. The problems associated with accelerated processing of applications have been made very obvious by the new asylum law; and so has the consequence - the deportation of thousands every year. The real nub of the matter, however, is the question of the welfare state and the social contract. The Federal Republic of Germany could, in an emergency, accommodate and provide for millions of refugees in a relatively humane fashion. But for this to be possible, society would have to make available a significant proportion of its income, and this, it is clearly not willing to do.

The left-wing and liberal sections of the middle class would lose this fight against those of their compeers, who were unwilling to relinquish any of their prosperity, and, above all, against that third of society that has nothing left to give away of what, in a German context, is a very relative prosperity. And anyway there must be great doubts as to whether this kind of commitment is at all credible. Asking for housing of refugees is a simple matter if you do not have to compete for scarce and, most importantly, affordable accommodation. The section of Federal German society that is particularly liberal-minded by no means coincides with the group of Germans who have to bear the brunt of the processes of integration required by immigration.

Sibylle Tönnies has given a succinct account of the problem raised by the controversy about the new asylum law. She expressly excludes the question of whether the large number of asylum applications was not actually very justifiable, and whether it could not have been made even greater on humanitarian grounds. Instead, she points to the fact that the state could not enter into this debate with the population on the basis of guaranteed asylum for every individual because it really did not know whether the numbers involved were legion or not. It was therefore unable, says Tönnies, to give the population that feeling of security which the latter properly demands by virtue of the social contract. Even the most xenophile population imaginable would arrive at the limits of its tolerance if there were a general basic right to asylum. To this extent, the reproach directed at the majority of the SPD party in the Bundestag for its support of the new law, which required a two-thirds majority, has to be considerably modified. What is (and was) at issue is not just power—which the SPD still does not hold—but also democracy.

The observation which even many left-wing politicians have made to the effect that widespread feelings amongst the population cannot be ignored in the long term should not be precipitately dismissed as cheap populism. What lies behind it is, after all, the essentially banal political realization that asylum policy in particular depends on a minimum of approval amongst the indigenous population. Finally, as far as the issue of help or solidarity is concerned, even where the most progressive policy imaginable is in force, there will always be many people left who are not helped. And the question of how the resources which society is prepared to make available for the support of refugees can be used most effectively is one that is open to debate.

Another of the paradoxes associated with the asylum issue is that Germany can help more refugees if fewer of them go there. This observation would be cynical only if it were used as an excuse not to intervene; in economic terms, it is almost a commonplace. To care for refugees in many other countries would cost the Federal Republic—even if it assumed all the expenses—only a fraction of what it costs to accommodate them in Germany itself. And the United Nations provides far fewer resources for supporting 'real' refugees in the Third World than is spent in western Europe on economic refugees with no claim to asylum.

The debate about immigration and asylum in Germany has contributed in three ways to an aggravation of the problem and has also directly or indirectly fostered the various acts of violence and other attacks against foreigners. The clearest contribution is that made by the racist rhetoric of the New Right, with ramifications reaching into the conservative end of the political spectrum. In addition, migration and asylum are used by a section of the established parties as a scapegoat to offset social, political, or educational/psychological failings. But this kind of abuse of the asylum problem is not engaged in only by the political classes; it also has roots in the population. The scapegoat mechanism is a classic power technique for offsetting loss of legitimation. At the same time it provides ways for socially disoriented or marginalized groups to compensate for their situation; and it enables less disadvantaged strata of the population to rationalize defensive attitudes. The third factor that has helped aggravate the situation, however, stems from the polarized debate that has been going on for years between the broad political groupings, and in which they have laid the blame on each other for a situation whose proper analysis would have required them to abandon certain traditional denials of reality. These denials are propelled by powerful political fantasies or traditions—on the one hand, the nationalist, and, on the other, the internationalist tradition. As ideal-typical tendencies they are not entirely congruent with the two broad political camps, but their distribution across them varies significantly.

The national tradition is the cause of the stubborn refusal, particularly within CDU and CSU circles, to accept, or at least accommodate oneself to, the fact that Germany has long since become an immigration country. But even within the internationalist tradition—to which, in terms of basic principles, peace researchers generally feel much closer—denials of reality may also be found. Instead of there being even any thought of entering into a discussion about the competition for scarce benefits, the rhetoric about 'the boat being full' is often simply reversed and the xenophobia is countered with a xenophilia that refuses to acknowledge the genuine social conflicts and the organised and poverty-induced crime.

Social scientists of a psychological bent have repeatedly pointed out that both these tendencies—the one that makes bogeymen out of foreigners and the one that idealizes them—are linked to a disturbed relationship to one's own, and in this case also the German, identity. Might it be a case of proving who is the better German? Right-wingers are inclined to adhere to the monocultural nation-state, which no longer exists—and in the strict sense never existed, and left-wingers tend to cling to what is foreign, in order to have nothing more to do with the traditions in their own country. There will probably only be a chance of overcoming the nationalist tradition if the German Left for its part addresses the real existing problems of migration and asylum and draws the appropriate conclusions, instead of 'blithely continuing to lay claim to everything good, like tolerance, humanity, and internationalism'.

After all, the appeal for solidarity and multiculturality becomes implausible or ineffective if it excludes consideration of the difficulties involved in implementation, and if it does not take seriously the living conditions and anxieties of those on whose political support it remains dependent. Even enlightened interpretations of the migration and asylum problem have no chance of success with the well-meaning majority if they do not ensure that the latter's right to live within familiar economic, social, and psychological surroundings is also taken into account in analysis and political programming.

Medium-term preventive measures could include 'antagonistic co-operation' with young people inclined towards violence and xenophobia. A precondition for this would be avoiding too hasty negative categorizations: the problems and difficulties of these young people must be taken seriously. In the domain of political education, issues and methods would have to be redefined, with an eye to right-wing extremism and xenophobia. It is not sufficient constantly to develop new teaching models and convey new cognitive matter; it will also be necessary to reflect on the conditions in which teaming takes place and about internal social/emotional structures in school. Fostering the skill needed to resolve conflicts non-violently is not primarily an intellectual task. The media have a special responsibility as regards the reporting of events and the general violence that is on offer as part of entertainment. Agreements designed to avoid commercial competition for the best violent effects and greatest violence-appeal are long overdue.

The narcissistic disturbances, lack of empathy with victims, and inadequate social behaviour to which emotional shortcomings in overall socialization lead, occur amongst many children, not just amongst youths with an overt inclination to violence. To tackle these shortcomings, there is a need, amongst other things, for a social and family policy. Under the present overall economic and social conditions (breakdowns of the classic division of tabour and of old family structures), this means first and foremost a quantitative and qualitative improvement in nursery and all-day schooling.

A central element in any counterstrategy should be consideration of how the masculinity cult might be rectified, and how the experience and practice of masculinity might be influenced and politically modified. As to relations with immigrants who have settled in Germany, and with their descendants, the symbolic integration signalled by demonstrations and chains of candle-lights must be followed up by integration of a legally based material kind.

Relevant measures include the granting of naturalization after an established period of residence, making it easier to hold dual nationality, and the granting of more political rights, e.g. extending the right to vote in local elections to others besides EU citizens. In addition, the possibility of an anti-discrimination law should be discussed. As regards immigration, we consider the imposition of limits, including limits on the right to asylum, to be indispensable. We have furnished ample arguments in support of this view. At the same time, every attempt should be made to rectify the curtailments in the rule of law that have already occurred, and to put a stop to the 'structural violence' against foreigners that is practised by the administrative authorities. It would be deeply ironic if Germany succeeded in reducing the number of deaths among immigrants resulting from personal anti-foreigner violence to zero, only to see it replaced by an increasing number of suicides among asylumseekers resulting from that institutional violence. In addition, we argue for greater commitment on the part of Germany to worldwide aid to refugees and for a foreign policy that is more human rights-oriented as a whole.

8
Right to Self-Determination

The right to self-determination means that all the peoples have the right to determine, without any external interference, their political status and to pursue their economic, social and cultural development. This right, in fact, is a prerequisite to the enjoyment of all other rights. Though this right is so fundamental and natural, yet like all other rights, self-determination has its limits because its implication in breaking up countries is repugnant to international law and a threat to world peace and international order. This article seeks to examine the status of self-determination a human fight and discuss certain difficulties in realization of this fight in the existing international system based on sovereign states.

The universal declaration of Human Rights which was adopted by the United Nations General Assembly on 10th December 1948 does not mention self-determination specifically. The right of self-determination has, however, been recognised in many decisions of the United Nations organs; it has frequently been cited as the basis for action taken by those organs and it has been included among the human rights recognised and protected by the International Covenant on Economic, Social and Cultural

Rights as well as the International Covenant on Civil and Political Rights.

The General Assembly first recognized "The right of peoples and nations to self-determination" as a fundamental human right in Resolution 421D(V) of 4 December 1950 in which it called upon the Economic and Social Council and the Commission on Human Rights to make recommendations on ways and means to ensure the enjoyment of this right. The Assembly, in Resolution 545(VI) of 5 February 1952 decided to include in the international Covenant or Covenants on Human Rights an article on the right of all peoples and nations to self-determination in reaffirmation of the principle enunciated in the Charter of the United Nations.

In Resolution 637A(VII) of 16 December 1952, the General Assembly, recognizing that "the right of peoples and nations to self-determination is a pre-requisite to the full enjoyment of all fundamental human rights" and that "Every Member of the United Nations, in conform with the charter, should respect the maintenance of the right of self-determination in other States", adopted a series of recommendations on the subject, particularly for the peoples of Non-self-Governing and Trust territories. In Resolution 637C (VII), the General Assembly requested the Economic and Social Council to ask the Commission on Human Rights "to continue preparing recommendations concerning international respect for the right of peoples to self-determination. . . "

In Resolution 1514 (XV) of 14 December 1960, the General Assembly Solemnly proclaimed "the necessity of brining to a speedy and unconditional and colonialism in all its forms and manifestations and adopted the Declaration on the granting of. Independence to Colonial Countries and peoples. In another Resolution 2625 (XXV) of 24 October 1970,- the General Assembly adopted and proclaimed the Declaration on principles of International Law concerning friendly relations and cooperation among states. With regard to the principle of equal rights and self-determination of peoples, the declaration proclaims that:

> By virtue of the principles of equal rights and self-determination of peoples enshrined in the charter of the United Nations, all peoples have the right freely to determines, without external interference, their political status and to pursue their economic, social and cultural development and every state has the duty to respect this right in accordance with the provision of the charter.

It pas further provided that every state has the duty to promote through joint and separate action universal respect for and observance of human rights and fundamental freedoms in accordance with the charter. And that the establishment of a sovereign and independent state, the free Association or integration with an independent state or the emergence into any other political status freely determined by people constitute modes of implementing, the right to self-determination by the people.

In recent years, the General Assembly has repeatedly re-affirmed the right of self-determination, the denial of which, it views, would cause a serious impediment to the maintenance of international peace and security and the development of peaceful relations among nations. Thus, the inclusion of the principle of self-determination in the charter of the United Nations and repeated emphatic resolutions of General Assembly and its recognition and protection by the International Covenants on Human Rights, drafted to give effect to the Universal Declaration of Human Rights, elevate the status of self-determination from a mere principle to a recognized right of peoples and nations under International law. In short, it can be pointed out that the right of self-determination has become integral part of customary International law. Nations have expressed their consensus over in time and again through several international instruments and national policies and declarations.

The doctrine of national self-determination proved a very strong and effective force in the colonial era to arouse feelings of nationalism, The indigenous people fought their struggle against the colonial rulers for their right to rule and govern themselves. But this doctrine of self-determination, that continues in over own days poses a threat to the unity and integrity of several multi-nations sovereign states, Nationality in terms of common language, racial heritage, customs, religion, etc. is insufficient to explain the existing patterns of loyalty to contemporary nation-states.

A sense of nationality is subjective. The demand for self-determination generated in these states had aroused bitter conflicts may cause disintegration of several new states in the Third World. Even in Europe, where there is less of ethnic, linguistic, religious and cultural diversities, the doctrine proved very difficult to apply. The right to self-determination provides no clear basis for defining the territorial limits of a particular nationality and the problem becomes very difficult and complex when the peoples of the same community are living in more than one state," While they may have a population, they lack defined territorial base and leadership in effective control of the whole population.

Instead of national cohesion, unity, solidarity and settled order, there are often constant intra-groups righting and leadership struggle in these communities. In such chaotic conditions, it becomes all the more difficult to identify the 'national will'. In other words, it can be pointed out that the enjoyment of right of self-determination by all communities becomes difficult as hardly a few of them exhibit the classical attributes of a viable sovereign state. Other point for consideration is that the present international system is characterised with gross inequalities in terms of economic and military power. The right to self-determination could provide an instrument to the strong and powerful nations to destabilize the weak and smaller states to perpetuate their negemony. Economic' grievances and complaints about corruption and inefficient administration are wide-spread and are a major source of discontentment and tension in the modern nations.

The general dissatisfaction with the government and administration could be exploited by the outside agencies to encourage the centrifugal forces in any state. Further these activities of the states/powers can be legitimised with the doctrine of self-determination. Moreover, the application of this principle would result in the emergence of numerous small and weak states. It is very likely that being incapable to stand on their own feet, they would become dependent and puppets in the hands of great powers.

Another consideration is in context of the dilemma posed by often witnessed inconsistent behaviour of states in different situations. One can point out number of case situations in which the states had taken contradictory stand and applied double standards. For example, Pakistan had repeatedly demanded a plebiscite in Kashmir, while it denied the same to the Pakhtoons of North West Frontier Province. Pakistan accepted the verdict of the 'referendum' held in the Pakhtoon region under the aegis of a foreign government, but did not submit to the verdict of the Kashmiri people who had repeatedly cast their lot with the rest of India. That multi-linguistic and multi-ethnic countries like Pakistan and Iran had been vociferously supporting the so-called demand of the Kashmiri people for self-determination, while denying the same to the Baluch people. To push the right of self-determination in the name of region and organising insurgency will prove to disastrous for both, those who are organising it and those who are its victims.

In fact, for Pakistan and Iran, it will be like opening the Pandora's box. In short, it can be remarked that the right of self-determination is still vague and is being given conflicting interpretations by nations, according to their national interest and strategic considerations. Lastly, it can be pointed out that its context of a new emerging pattern of interdependence and global neighbourhood, to encourage sussionist forces in the name of self-determination will be detrimental and unreasonable. To say this does not mean that the right of self-determination does not have any place in the present international systems, rather it means that each case should be assessed objectively and on its own merit. The core or the basis of self-determination is that the government must rest on the consent of the people and that each government and the state machinery.

Right to Self-Determination

The demand of self-determination, is, unequivocally, ill-conceived and evil designed politically, socially, culturally, legally, because it is devoid of nationalism, national unity and integration. Rather, it odorous the sadistic attitude of separatism, secessionism, and seceding the territory of India that is called Bharat from the Union of States. Those who demand self-determination either do not realise the true perspective of self-determination, or, knowingly misleading the mischievous as well as ulterior motives.

The notion of self-determination as a human right has a strong emotional overtone as it has a long story behind it. It was formulated because of the effect of changing socio-economic-political relations as the response to threats brought about by aliens. The principle of self-determination of people gained world-wide importance between the two world wars. Between the wars self-determination was understood as a political principle which recognised right of people reiterating the principle of nationality.

In the Covenant of the League of Nations no express mention to self-determination was to be found. However, the Fourteen Points of President Wilson when implemented, a number of nations in Central and Eastern Europe gained independence; the term self-determination was used mainly to ethnic minorities living within the limits of a given territory inside a pre-existing state or empire during World War II. Two major aspects of self-determination were emphasised in the Atlantic Charter, viz., desire to see no territorial changes that do not accord with the freely expressed wishes of the peoples concerned respect the right of all people to choose the form of government under which they will live and they wish to see sovereign rights and self-government restored to those who have been forcibly deprived of them.

After the ceasing of the hostilities of World War II, the United Nations Charter assumed significance in the comity as well as polity of members of United Nations. One of the purpose of the United Nations as set out in Article 1 is "to develop friendly relations among nations based on respect for the principles of equal rights and self-determination of people . . .". Article 55 which deals with international economic and social co-operations reads : "With a view to the creation of conditions of' stability and well-being which are necessary for peaceful and friendly relations among nations based on respect for the principle of equal rights and self-determination of people . . . ". Article 73 of Chapter XI concerning "Declaration regarding

Non-Self Governing Territories" provides that "Members of the United Nations which have or assume responsibilities for the administration of territories whose people have not yet attained a full measure of self-government recognise the principle that the interests of the inhabitants of these territories are paramount ... and to this end ... to develop self-government". Article 76 of Chapter XII captioned as "International Trusteeship System" provided that "The basic objectives of the trusteeship . . . shall be to promote the political, economic, social and educational advancement of the inhabitants ; . and their progressive development towards self-government or independence as may be appropriate . . . Article 1 of International Covenants on Social and Cultural Economic Rights and Civil and Political Rights also recognise the right to self-determination.

The United Nations General Assembly mindful and conscious of its objectives made a Declaration on the granting of Independence to Colonial Countries and Peoples (Vide General Assembly Resolution 1514(XV) of 14 Dec. 1960) by "the recognising passionate yearling for freedom in all dependent peoples and the decisive role of such peoples in the attainment of their independence (from foreign rule or colony)", and "believing that the process of liberation is irresistible and irreversible and that, in order to avoid serious crises, an end must be put to colonialism and all practices of segregation and discrimination associated therewith", and declares that: "The subjection of the peoples to alien subjugation, domination and exploitation constitutes a denial of fundamental human rights, is contrary to the Charter of the United Nations and is an impediment to the promotion of world peace and co-operation.

All peoples have the right to self-determination; by virtue of that right they freely determine their political status and freely pursue their economic, social and cultural development. All States shall observe faithfully and strictly the provisions of the Charter of the United Nations, the Universal Declaration of Human Rights and the present Declaration on the basis of equality, non-interference in the internal affairs of all states, and respect for the sovereign rights of all peoples and their territorial integrity".

The above mentioned international instruments neatly demonstrate that right to self-determination is secured to the people under colonial rule, and according to the widely adopted present-day view only people under colonial rule have the right to self-determination, which involves accession to independent statehood, It does not matter how the population of such territory is ethically composed.

As soon as independent Statehood is reached, the territorial integrity of the country is protected against any attempt to destroy national unity, even if the given ethnic group is in this way brought under alien domination. Thus the right to self-determination is expressly related to colonial peoples. Interpretation of that kind can be inferred from Resolution VII of 11th May, 1968, adopted by International Conference on Human Rights; "The importance of the Universal Resolution of the right of people to self-determination and of the speedy granting of independence to colonial countries and peoples for the effective guarantee and observance of human rights".

The Conference called upon the General Assembly to draw up a specific programme for the granting of independence to territories under colonial rule and called upon the Security Council to resume consideration of the question of decolonization and expedite the granting of independence and self-determination of colonial peoples and countries. United Nations General Assembly Resolution 637-A/II declares that "the right of peoples and nations to self-determination is a prerequisite of the full enjoyment of all fundamental human rights" and recommended that United Nations Members "uphold the principle of self-determination of all peoples and nations".

The wider interpretation of the right to self-determination discerns the necessity to liquidate racial discrimination and apartheid in colonial and dependent territories and a total eradication of racial discrimination, apartheid and violation of the human rights of the people in colonial territories will be achieved most expeditiously by the faithful and complete implementation of United Nations Declaration. It may further discern that numerous Resolutions concerning the right to self-determination refer not only to peoples under colonial domination but also to peoples under alien domination. Case of South Africa and Palestinian peoples is a pointer in this perspective.

The right to self-determination mentioned in the international instruments asserts a right for peoples to be granted independence and create their own state for freely determining their political status and freely pursuing their economic, social and cultural development over natural resources. Not only people under colonial rule are entitled to it but also peoples under alien and racist domination. The General Assembly considered vide Resolution 2649/XXV that "the acquisition and retention of territory in contravention to the right of people of that territory of self-determination is inadmissible and a gross violation to the Charter". This wider concept of the right to self-determination is adopted in the provisions of the African Charter on Human and Peoples' Right..

The right to self-determination does not imply to secession for minorities groups living in an independent state, The right to self-determination relates to liberalization from external dependence from an other state. There cannot be right to self-determination (internal) which is political self-determination, and reducing the right of internal self-determination only to political self-determination is devoid of all canons of international instruments.

The State of Jammu & Kashmir was neither a colonial state nor under alien rule nor a trusteeship. It was a sovereign state under the rule of sovereign like other princely states, It joined the Union of India through the instrumentality of Instrument of Accession on 26th and 27th day of October, 1947. The Instrument of Accession was in conformity with the provisions of Indian Independence Act, 1947. It was same instrument as was signed by other princely states. Accession was confirmed by the Constituent Assembly of India by making Jammu and Kashmir as an integral part of Indian Union; Jammu and Kashmir Constituent Assembly 1954 and Jammu and Kashmir Constitution itself. By this act the people of the State of Jammu & Kashmir have freely and finally exercised their right to self-determination.

Obviously, neither the Constitution of India nor State Constitution makes any reference to right to self-determination. Since accession of the State with the Union of India Mr. Sheikh Mohammed Abdullah and his associates had been advocating for disaffiliation though they were participants as nominees and signatories to the Constitution of India. Their attitude was oscillating and this apostalize attitude culminated into a movement of secessionism which now seems to have taken the shape of Azadi or self-determination.

The Kashmiris only have been airing the voice of Azadi or self-determination. Question arises Azadi or self-determination from whom? Once self-government has been finally formulated within the basic structure of the Constitution of India then where is the question of further self-government or independence? As already explained above, there cannot be further self-government and internal independence because there is no canon of international law or national law to have a sovereign State within a Sovereign State. Even if we assume for a moment the issue of plebiscite, it would be in the right earnest to state that the people of Jammu & Kashmir once finally accepted the resolves of Constituent Assembly of India, Constituent Assembly of Jammu ana Kashmir, 1954, Constitutional Orders, 1954, 1966, etc., participated in elections, have had the fruits of national mainstream, cherished the fruits of 337 Central Laws since 1953, etc. have finally fearlessly and conscientiously exercised this right.

There is no question of further self-determination (internal). Kashmiris are emphasising for the fight to self-determination and such propaganda stirs whether Kashmiris (a few handful of an ethnic group) are the sole voice of the whole population of Jammu & Kashmir in this regard? Certainly not, Seeking self-determination by handful of few erratic means secessionism and seceding the territory of an integral part of the Union of India. In the words of Dr. B.R. Ambedkar that India is a Union of States and any demand for seceding any part of its territory is not permissible constitutionally, for that is against not only the basic structure of the Constitution of India but also against the spirit of Indian Nationalism.

9
Human Rights in a Caste Society

The provisions of human rights, termed as Fundamental Rights and Directive Principles, of State Policy contained in the Indian Constitution, are negated by the social and cultural rights deeply embedded in the caste system of this country. The country with more than 5000 sub-castes is divided, as if into smaller number of republics, each bound within its caste framework into a sectarian lot. The Western principles of liberalism as well as egalitarianism could not demolish the caste system, which stand as a monolithic monster and justifies every type of violation of human rights in the country. Some of these features may be analysed along historical, geographical, political, economic, legal as well as racial lines.

With the invasion of the Aryans the history and civilisation of the indigenous people of this country stood distorted. The various scriptures written by the Aryans distort the indigenous ideas of rights and responsibilities. The local natives were described as Asuras and demons and their subjection, extortion and extermination was justified. Victory and enslavement were won by force or fraud and killings were based on the principle of might being right. Although the killings were upheld as valid and normal, they were resorted to selectively. In fact, the process of colonization took a long time-many centuries.

The historical forces gave a code of conduct based on the Aryan system of values. The Vedas and Puranas gave way to Manusmriti, which was the high point that divided the population into racial and ethnic groups. The Manusmriti managed to perpetuate human slavery and adopted a double standard of co-option and exclusion. While suppressing the original inhabitants, it managed to keep them as serfs. It also could entrap through an elaborate code of conduct, both the human mind as well as human society. It stigmatized the locals as 'excluded', 'untouchables' and 'unseeables' and treated them as part of the cattle and vegetation.

Racial purity was intended to be maintained by endogamous marriages and social rejections. This gave rise to the description of the indigenous population as the 'other' or 'outsider' and a system of hierarchy was established in society, which resulted in what Ambedkar says, in the ascending scale of reverence and descending order of contempt.

The position of the untouchables or the Dalits or Bahujans, was based on a concocted philosophy and a diabolical theology. The doctrine of Karma and the theory of transmigration of soul was cunningly formulated to perpetuate inequality from birth to death and even afterwards. The mindset of the orthodox was put into a trap without any escape route for individual human beings. The concept of human rights was non-existent and its practice could never be dreamt of in such a socio-religious order. The entire contraption was perfected with such philosophical verbiage that while confounding the human mind it never let him get out of it.

The human psyche became a victim of contradiction and caste and religious acts were sacrosanct, beyond the limits of the civil society and State made laws. The above doctrinnaire approach to life and beyond gave rise to a set of political and economic institutions in the country. While there was internal colonialism within the nation, state inside a geographical territory, there were sub-nations within the nations and sub-humans within the human society. Just as the Shastras justified violation of human rights and wanton killings in wars or otherwise, the political and economic doctrines Justified expropriation and domination.

Wars were justified by theological arguments. The advice of Lord Krishna to Arjuna that he should wage war and even kill his cousin Duryodhana and his guru Dronacharya, was justified on the ground that it was not killing of brothers or relations as such but killing opponents who were already dead. Thus crime was justified on false notions of good and evil and right and wrong. Similarly, the case of Eklavya or the incident of 'Jatugriha Daha' where the 'outcastes' could be dispensed with showed rank manipulation of the shastras and the perversion of human values. This approach led to economic exploitation where caste and capital have supported each other and grown together making it difficult for the lower caste persons to penetrate, much less benefit, from development plans.

In other words, the 'outsider' is an outsider not only from the social, political and cultural arena, but also economic and wealth benefits. In fact wealth could accrue only to a limited group of people of certain high caste clans. Thus inequality and injustice became entrained into the system. This Is how today we see a forest dweller, who was a master of the land but now is landless and the so-called untouchable, assetless who lives only on manual labour wages. The concept and philosophy of human rights would be anathema; to such a society it is a dream which could never be realized. Since the illegal and extralegal system is supported by the spiritual and theological foundations, the constitutional and legal systems remain only in paper. Here is a case, where caste people practice apartheid and enjoy moral autonomy with impunity, and thus could not stand the scrutiny of any discerning rational human mind.

The most intriguing feature of the human rights violation in India is that the oppressor is invisible. There is no direct evidence of one or the other individual or caste that can be spotted and caught in the act of commission of the crime. There is however a pattern in the entire system which perpetrates crime, but the criminal cannot be identified and punished. This is because this violence has social approval and human rights violations have become part and have got the sanction of the political culture.

In fact the violations are based on caste and religious prejudices, organisational resources and institutional support and can never be prevented; at best they can only be alleviated. This imbroglio is explained by the failure of innumerable social reformers and many enlightened rulers in the past. The press, the police and even the judiciary acquiesce in the crimes. The violation of human rights in our country seems to have a pattern and is perhaps leading to a holocaust. The eminent historian of the German holocaust, Raul Hilberg, summed up the gradual development of holocaust in three stages. The first step began with Christianity's Ghettoisation of the Jews after failing to convert them. The second step involved the process of seeing the Jews as economic threat when the Jews emerged from the ghettos, but their assimilation in tile mainstream failed. The third step consisted of the "final solution", which was arrived at by the "scientific theory" about the Jews as racially inferior, and were a menace to the purity of Aryan blood. The Nazis when they arrived at this point in history did not discard the past. They built on it. They did not Jay the foundation, but they completed the superstructure. In fact they were ready administratively and psychologically to eliminate the Jews-millions of them were killed systematically and "scientifically".

A similar historical pattern seems to be emerging in the Indian scene today. The Dalits, Instead of following the dominant society like a sheep, thanks to their growing awareness about their own situation and efforts of an elite section, seems to be asserting today. This workshop itself is a sign of it. The orthodox elites of this country are not able to integrate them, because of a basic fallacy in the fundamentalist doctrine in which they are trapped. They, in fact, need to be liberated and not the Dalits or at best both need to be emancipated.

Since social and economic integration is becoming difficult because of the antithetical socio-economic interests, failure of land reforms, the on-going reckless economic liberalisation policy, the Dalits would always appear to be parasites in the Indian society and economy. They need separate and systematic treatment, but outside the caste hierarchy. They would soon appear to become a burden on the economic development of the country as globalisation proceeds, which will result. In the further pauperization of the poor. In fact, they would appear as a threat to the economy of the country and naturally the third step will be the "scientific solution", which may have to be resorted to by this dominant section. It will be of interest to note in this connection as to how and why the "final solution" was resorted to by the Nazis. The solution had the backing of the intellectuals in Germany. Today

'Hindutwa' has the backing of many scholars and the upper middle class elites of this country. They also stand by Indian history and culture, its philosophy and religious leaders, whose ideologies seem to be gaining in popularity. Take the case of our own Lord Jagannath's Puri Seer who justified Sati, and bars women from reciting the Vedas. The occasional spurt in violence or demolition of a mosque or a temple is a symptom of this deep rooted prejudice. The theory of cultural nationalism is akin to the Nazi approach of threat to the German society supposedly created by the Jews.

The Nazi doctrine was formulated by Joseph Arther Gonineau an eminent German thinker of his time in his publication, "Inequality of Human Race". Similarly Sir Framer Galtun, the British scientist invented eugenics. He derived from the Darwinian theory of Survival of the Fittest and argued that society should discourage breeding by those who are unfit either physically, mentally and socially in Germany. The theory of eugenics was carried by the Nazis to its logical conclusion. This was a welcome solution to the problem of racism. The scientific community manufactured gas chambers for eliminating the Jews.

The theories of inheritance of merit or intelligence, to the utter disregard of environment forces, seems to be engaging the attention of these scientists. The interpretation of Hindutwa in a different context by the Supreme Court has been a shot in the arm of the orthodox elites and also seems to be a pointer in the direction of social polarisation. It is therefore time the National Human Rights Commission took stock of the situation and initiated a movement for building counter theories through seminars, workshops and publications so as to neutralise or arrest the fast deteriorating situation. The only difference between the Nazi solution and the Indian solution will be that, while in Germany the police and the Army did the "Work" with the people assisting them; in India some people will commit genocide with others assisting them from the scene of action. The police inaction or wilful absence or non-registration of complaints when atrocities are committed against the Dalits is a case in point. The fact that atrocities are on the increase and that there is a pattern in them would predict doom for the Dalits, unless prevention is attempted in all seriousness.

10
Internal and External Conflicts

The nature of man—to acquire more and more wealth for the sake of luxurious living at the cost of others—remained the same. He became more ruthless in dealing with others. Enlargement of possession could be through war which became an "anicent business among men," "its beginnings are almost coincident with those of human race itself. But whatever the guise, one feature is striking and common. As soon as a state acquired the potential, it found an excuse to wage war against a weaker state.

The right of the individual bartered his life for promise of security and liberty. Neither the security not the liberty was his. Extension of Empires was the motive force for war. Man lost his freedom and rights by accepting his membership of a state. States are based on the principle of power. They serve the purpose of the powerful. The poor and powerless arc just the pawns. They are sacrificed. Erich Maria Remarque says: A word of command has made these silent figures our enemies; a word of command might transform them into our friends. Millions of men and women were put to sword, maimed and disabled in wars. When marauding Mughal soldiers trampled Aminabad (in Punjab) under the hoofs of their fierce horses Guru Nanak who witnessed the carnage, addressing their leader as Yama disguised as Babur, described: Terrible were the slaughter, Loud were the cries of the lamenters. If a strong man attacketh another who is equally strong; where is the grief in this, or whose is the grievances? But when a fierce tiger preys on the helpless cattle. The Herdsman must answer for it. Perturbed was Grotius when he asserted: Throughout the Christian world he observed a lack of restraint in relation to war, such as even barbarous races should be ashamed of. He observed that men rush to arms for slight causes, or no cause at all, and that when arms have once been taken up there is no longer any respect for law, divine or humane; it is as if, in accordance with a general decree, frenzy had openly been let loose for the committing of all crimes. When Might is Tight, the right is necessarily the privilege of the mighty few.

A Resolution unanimously adopted at the International Conference on Human Rights held at Tehran in the spring of 1968, whilst affirming that "peace is the underlying condition for the full observation of human rights and war is their negation", noted that armed conflicts continue to plague humanity and expressed the conviction that even during the period of armed conflict humanitarian principles must prevail. Is it not anomalous to speak of human rights in the context of war?

If one of the fundamental human rights is, as stated in Article 6 of the International Covenant on Civil and Political Rights, "the inherent right to life", is it unrealistic to speak of the protection of human rights in situations of violence aimed at the destruction of human life. In other words, as such even if no government can in practice renounce recourse to force, strict limits must be placed on its use both in peace and in war. Civil wars are not prohibited by international law. International law does, however, have something to say on participation by other states. The general rule is one of non-intervention. The General Assembly's Declaration on the Inadmissibility of Intervention in the Domestic Affairs of States and the Protection of their Independence and Sovereignty prohibits any state from intervening: "directly or indirectly, for any reason whatever, in the internal or external affairs of any other State.... no State shall organise, assist, forment, finance, incite or tolerate subversive, terrorist or armed activities directed towards the violent overthrow of the regime of another State, or interfere in civil strife in another State." State may, for a variety of political reasons, intervene to support the rebels, or alternatively, to support the established authorities.

Non-intervention is undoubtedly the best policy. The danger of intervention by a state in support of one party is that it will attract counter-intervention by another state in support of the other party and consequently an internal matter can escalate into an international law. The advent of nuclear weapons added a new dimension to the use of force. The first expression of protection for the individual involved in armed conflict was the 1864 Geneva Convention for the Amelioration of the condition of the Wounded and Sick of Armed Forces in the Field.

Contemporary humanitarian law is contained in the four 1949 Geneva Conventions and the two 1977 Protocols" thereto which are now regarded as customary international law. Sick, Wounded and shipwrecked military personnel are afforded protection by Conventions I and II, the third Convention sets out the minimum treatment to be afforded to prisoners of war, while the fourth articulates the protection of civilian persons (this represented an advance, in that, earlier protection to civilians had been relatively limited, being contained in the Hague Regulations and customary international law). The Geneva Conventions originally applied only to all international armed conflict situations, but this definition was extended in 1977 to include wars of "self-determination" and victims of "non-international armed conflicts". The latter builds on Article 3, which is common to all four conventions, and provides that certain minimum provisions apply in "armed conflict not of an international character." Specifically excluded are instances of "internal disturbances and tensions, such as riots, isolated and sporadic acts of violence and other acts of a similar nature.

Mention should also be made of the Convention for the Protection of Cultural Property in the event of Armed Conflict, adopted in 195413 which aims at protecting cultural objects and religious places, as well as objects designated vital to the survival of the civilian population—drinking water supplies, foodstuffs, agricultural areas for production thereof, and irrigation works.

M.V. Naidu, President, Canadian Peace Research and Education Association is justified in saying that when the lives of the citizens are threatened, or when the material bases for the existence of the people are being destroyed, or when the country's territories holding the citizens and those economic resources are being torn apart, or in a word, when the very security of a nation is in danger, then it may become necessary and justifiable for the government to disregard temporarily all other considerations, including the provision of civil rights and liberties of the citizens, while protecting the very existence of the state. Once national security is established, the civil liberties will have to be restored. More than the war, the could war brought out extreme antidemocratic sentiments. In the name of national security, reckless assaults on civil rights and liberties are launched. By definition, "civil war" is supposed to be "civil" and not "military", because it is supposed to be fought between civilian citizens of the same country, and not by the military forces of that country. However a massive civil conflict could end up as a war a full-fledged civil war. Whenever national emergencies arc declared and measures of national security are undertaken, civil liberties are the main sufferers.

National security measures may impinge upon ten basic civil rights and liberties:

1. Right to life and physical well-being.
2. Freedom of information and expression.
3. Freedom of assembly and association.
4. Right to equality before the law and equal protection of the law.
5. Right to due process (rule of law) or right against arbitrary government.
6. Freedom of conscience and belief.
7. Freedom of movement.
8. Right of property.
9. Political rights of voting, candidacy, and campaign.
10. Right against cruel and unusual punishment. 16

National Security can very well be maintained and strengthened without allowing civil rights and liberties been jeopardised. A militarily secure and strong nation is not necessarily a guarantor of individual freedoms. On the contrary, a militarily secure authoritarian regime may become more dictatorial by conceding less on democratic freedoms. Despite the instinct of conflict amongst the men all human activity in this world can be labelled a family on the ground that it appertains to this world as against the other worlds which may be unknown. All such activity legitimately can be described as family, as it takes place in this world. Recently at Nassau, the capital of Bahmas, during the Common-Wealth Parliamentary Association

Annual Conference, Himachal's former Chief Secretary and Speaker, Shri Thakur Sen Negi rightly emphasised: To a believer, all mankind is the progeny of the same Creator, Almighty God. To a Scientist mankind belongs to the same species of living beings, namely, the species Homo Sapiens.

Whatever the racial categorization, whatever the pigment of the skin, scratch the skin and the blood that oozes out invariably red. Theologically, the common Father God would not be such that He is not sensible. Cosmologically cannot be but rational. The very word cosmos denote order as distinguished from the older state chaos. Therefore, both ways the only sensible and logical culmination of Man's evolution would be a common brotherhood.

Boundaries between internal and external conflicts will have to redefined and more attention focused on internal armed conflicts. It will explore the reasons for this and emphasize the emergence of Identity conflicts as being of special significance. The search for identity appears to the Western Liberal as a problem of 'fundamentalism'. The challenge for the liberal paradigm would be how to engage in a constructive discourse which call accept a multi-ethnic, plural, global order. In other words, how does the peace research community and policy in general communicate to non-like-minded communities and address itself to internal wars and violence'? The demise of the Communist Utopia does not mean that problems have been shelved.

Accumulated historical problems will assume a new salience and intensity and it is likely that these conflicts will be more violent and intransigent. What we are witnessing today is an extremely volatile and fragile international environment. Global changes are not necessarily reflected in institutional changes in (tic stale system or within the international system. It is this disjuncture between the global changes, peoples' initiatives and the international institutions, whether they be the United Nations, the International Monetary Fund or the World Bank, which requires new global institutions to manage these concerns.

Armed Conflicts and Their Characteristics

Research on armed conflicts and their specificity may shed light on the types of conflicts we are witnessing today, and also give us an idea of emergent conflicts in the future. The 1988 SIPRI Yearbook identified 33 contemporary armed conflicts with armed conflict defined as a situation with over 1000 casualities. Thirty-two armed conflicts were recorded for 1989, According to these estimates the total number of armed conflicts seem to be on the decrease. But if we also consider armed conflicts listed as below 1000 casualities then we get a higher number of recorded conflicts. They suggest that the numbers have increased to about 75, and it is likely that more efficient reports would reveal that numbers would increase to about 150. Some interesting observations can be made based on the empirical data.

1. Most of the armed conflicts take place in the Third World countries.
2. The basic issues in the armed conflicts of 1989 were related to internal matters,
3. Inter-state conflicts are currently on the decline—perhaps for the moment. This has inspired the media and others to talk of a grand peace settlement,
4. In most of the conflicts which led to external intervention, either by the super-powers or by a major regional power, there have been military withdrawals or negotiations for phased withdrawals.
5. With regard to conflict management or resolution, the

UN Security Council has rarely been involved, in some cases the good offices of the UN Secretary General have prevailed, but most often conflict resolution has been the function of a big regional power. It is likely, however, that the. United Nations, and in particular the good offices of the Secretary General, will play a more active role in conflict resolution in the future.

6. In most cases, the internal conflicts have been fuelled by arms sales and military equipment to combatants, Arms have been provided not only by the super powers but also by some states in the Third World. Apart from arms their is evidence that chemical weapons are being used both by the state and by the guerilla.
7. There has been consistent and flagrant violation of human rights, and no respect for the Laws of War, Gross abuses of human rights are evident on the part of both the state and the guerilla movements. Civilians account for 74% of official deaths or almost 3 times as many military deaths.
8. In most cases, the conflicts have involved cross-border affiliations or networks, where a neighbouring state provides sanctuary as well as arms and training to the guerillas.
9. Many of the conflicts listed are identity conflicts, where granting substantial devolution of power or territorial autonomy would end most conflicts.

These propositions raise a range of new issues which may bring about a significant shift in the paradigm of conflict research and international relations. Firstly, there is the matter of building a sound comparative experience in internal. Conflict resolution. Here it is necessary to be able to identify the actors generally involved in internal conflicts—not only the state, but also factions within the state, ethnic groups or religious groups, particularly actors who are generally silent in the discourse. The Western liberal tradition has tended to ignore non-like-minded actors, particularly those belonging to fundamentalist religions or minority speaking languages.

Types of Internal Conflicts

We need to distinguish the various types of internal conflicts which generally result in serious or violent hostilities. From the data available on conflicts we may make the following classification with regard to internal conflicts:

1. Ideological conflicts, between the state and insurgent movements where the social inequality between classes is dominant,
2. Governance and authority conflicts, concerning the distribution of power and authority in society. Demands from the opposition are for regime changes and control over resources.
3. Racial conflicts, including the conflicts in South Africa and Namibia, as well as racial conflicts in the USA and Europe.
4. Environmental conflicts which are broadly resource-based conflicts, over land, water, the control of rivers and the protection of forests. There are two categories of environmental conflicts: environmental conflicts between mail and nature, and conflicts between states and population groups caused or exacerbated by environmental problems. Resolving them requires different approaches.
5. Identity conflicts where the dominant aspect is ethnic, religious, tribal or linguistic differences. Often these conflicts involve a mixture of identity and the search for security where the main contention concerns the devolution of power. This was the main type of war in 1987; such conflicts tire likely to increase. Identity

conflicts can he subdivided into territorial conflicts, ethnic and minority conflicts, religious assertions and struggles for self-determination.

Various linkages may exist between the conflicts so defined, or we may find a mixture of several. The above classification is, however, static and what is required is to conceptualize the various interrelations between them. It may well be that there are several types of conflicts which are waged simultaneously; or that a country faces two or more types of conflicts—for example, identity conflicts based oil the demand for autonomy, and governance and authority conflicts. For example, last year in Sri Lanka there were five armed conflicts waged simultaneously. In Colombia, there were several armed conflict being waged. In the Lebanon, several armed conflicts are being waged simultaneously. Given analytical problems in defining the specificity of these conflicts, some have preferred to term these internal conflicts as protracted social conflicts or intractable conflicts.

Identity Conflicts

Identity conflicts tire the most pervasive and the most violent. Identity is defined as an abiding sense of the self and of the relationship of the self to the world.

> Identity has been defined as an abiding sense of selfhood the core of which makes life predictable to ail individual. To have no ability to anticipate events is essentially to experience terror. Identity is conceived of as more than a psychological sense of self; it encompasses a sense that one is safe ill the world physically, psychologically, socially, even spiritually. Events which threaten to invalidate the core sense of identity will elicit defensive responses aimed at avoiding psychic and/or physical annihilation. Identity is postulated to operate in this way no(only in relation to interpersonal conflict but also in conflict between groups.

Little consensus exists in the literature regarding (tic terminology and basic concepts dealing with ethnicity. 'Ethnic group', 'minority', 'tribe', 'nation', 'nationality' are used by different authors in different ways, which of course leads to analytical confusion. Ethnicity is not a static concept but a dynamic one, in that ethnicity and ethnic boundaries can be continuously redefined, given certain factors.

Politicization of ethnicity is a long historical process, where a crucial factor is cent re/periphery interaction. Polarization does not seem to take place until a certain point has been passed: before this Point, there will normally be instances where conflict resolution could be achieved through compromise and accommodation. The reasons for the ethnic revival have been fairly clear identified.

A major reason for the ethnic revival is seen its the contradiction between state building and nation building, where the state, in its attempt to centralize resources, may come into conflict with the many nations who coexist within its borders. However, some such centre/periphery conflicts might well have been mediated through constitutional means (federalism) and other forms of devolution of power. The distinction between 'official nationalism' and 'imagined communities' has brought about theoretical rigour in understanding post-colonial Third World nationalism. Here some Third World states can be seen as artificial constructs not corrosponding to the many coexisting nationalities.

Imagined communities then are those which in turn create the myth of community as a strong force for identity. Considerable attention has been given to the tension between ethnicity and modernization. Here the argument has been that unreflected capitalism and modernization have created a sense of psychological deprivation (relative deprivation) which has led to a backlash in terms of a reawakening of fundamentalism. Development strategies may have unintended effects on interethnic relations.

Some scholars have advanced the concept of ethno-development, arguing that development theories must be sensitive to cultural pluralities. This is particularly relevant to development strategies which ignore minorities and where hegemonic elites and international donor agencies may concentrate on certain groups only. Many states have denied the existence of ethnic conflicts. In a recent study, Barsh evaluates the extent Io which international bodies responsible for the protection of human rights have recognised the significance of ethnic conflict as .1 destabilizing force in both developing and industrialized countries. The study concludes that a surprisingly large number of states refuse to acknowledge the possibility of ethnic divisions. Examples of such denial can be found in all regions, but most frequently in Asia and Africa, where the evidence suggests that the contemporary threat from ethnic conflict is also the greatest.

The role of the state is central to identity formations. The state creates and denies the identity of others. It is precisely here in this humans of nation building and state formation that ethnicity assumes particular salience. Together with the demands for democracy and participation, there are ethnic and religious minorities demanding greater autonomy, recognition and identity. These problems and tensions will be a major focus of attention in the years to come. The Third World, state formation will remain a complex problem, with concerns for general democracy, participation and demilitarization. Ethnic and religious claims will become more urgent and more clearly articulated. These tensions are likely to be further compounded by severe poverty and unemployment in many parts of the Third World. The demand for identity and culture will be located within the framework of increasing gaps between the elites and the poor, where their own language and culture may be the final focus of identity in a rapidly changing modernizing world to which the poor are denied access.

State violence and counter-violence serve to exacerbate cleavages. The violation of human tights, including extra-judicial killings or torture, has produced a vicious cycle of violence and terror. State violence has brought with it a sense of insecurity; this then acts as a strong force of mobilization which too often takes extra-parliamentary or militant forms, leading to armed conflicts. Further, in some cases, the misbehaviour of the armed forces and police—often ethnic armies has served to provoke guerilla behaviour. Further the monopoly of physical violence is no longer the sole property of the state. According to Weber, the modem state must be defined as the societal institution which lays claims on the legitimate monopoly of physical violence.

The essential attribute of the state creates the dilemma: on the one hand it has to protect its citizens against arbitrary violence of others, and for this purpose the state needs the monopoly on violence, or the means of using violence, respectively. On the other hand by this very monopoly the ruling group has the possibility to use violence for its own interests against the people, even arbitarily beyond accepted rules and laws. Other groups also have ready access to means of physical violence. These new actors tend to determine the direction of conflicts.

What is suggested here is that there is a global struggle for a redefinition of the state. The concept of the state and its role must be discussed within a changing global environment, where new actors and new initiatives challenge the ability of current state formations to resolve some of the most pressing problems of mankind, The 'multi-ethnic state' is an organizing concept which can accommodate ethnic claims and demands in all parts of the world. There is a growing awareness of the universality and complexity of ethnic problems and the need for concerned action to devise strategies, programmes and structures for managing ethnic conflicts. Some multi-ethnic states have worked out federal forms of devolution.

In the search for constitutional models there has been disagreement over unitary and federal efforts, and the extent of devolution and autonomy. There is a need to re-examine the role of constitutions and similar mechanisms for conflict management. Constitutions may, however, provide only dejure recognition. We need to identify cultural and social institutions within the countries concerne. There exist many mechanisms and religious and collective experiences which help to enhance cooperation and tolerance whilst respecting the positive aspects of ethnicity. They may be schools, places of common worship, trade unions or various informal community organizations. School curricula, particularly concerning the interpretation of the country's history, are important in the decommunalization of the mind. More studies are needed on the role of curricula, particularly their impact on young people in the formative years. In some cases, history books may have to be rewritten to recognize the multiethnic character of societies.

The role of the mass media is often crucial. Information, and the way it is handled, can exacerbate cleavages or help to enhance feelings of cooperation. All too often, disinformation campaigns and rumours serve to feed and excite tensions. The role of communications and information is an important aspect of research where more comparative knowledge is required.

Although significant changes have occured in the global situation there is a gap between the international institutions created during the post-war period and the new problems which are emerging. Much has been written about the role of the United Nations, and the role of the Secretary General in dispute settlement. Much has been said about the strengths and the limitations of the United Nations. An impressive record has been established in the operation of peacekeeping forces.

Equally impressive work has been done in mediation between states in many difficult circumstances. However, the mandate of the United Nations is basically to resolve disputes in the international arena. But what about violent internal conflicts which tend to destroy societies and cause untold human suffering? Would it be possible for the UN to revise its mandate regarding internal conflicts? Could it allow its good offices and its vast network of skills to be used to provide for timely intervention? Many proposals and recommendations have been made and the current conjuncture enables the UN to review its mandate in conflict resolution and peace making.

There is a consensus on the need for preventative action, early warning and prevention of violent conflicts. This work is still in its early stages but a new coalition is likely to emerge. There is also increased cooperation amongst networks, to create a wider forum for discussion on early warnings and conflict resolution. A very significant and import instrument in conflict transformation has been the role of elections. International attention and monitoring can be strenthened to facilitate and ensure periodic elections. In many cases, transformation can only be achieved by insisting on regular elections. Theoretical advances have been made concerning the role of third parties in conflict resolution, as well as in improving bargaining and negotiating strategies. New forms of conflict resolution have been suggested, from problem-solving approaches to professional facilitators. However, most of thes theoretical advances have been made within stable democracies with a consideration tradition in conflict management. Further, such studies tend to focus on what happens once parties are brought to the negotiations table, whereas the real problem is often how to identify the actors and what can be done to get people to negotiate at all.

Negotiations tend to imply equal partners, but domestic conflicts involving groups are often asymmetric or unequal conflicts between a powerful state and a weak opposition. Protracted social conflicts are generally not single issue situations. They inherit a past which acts as a heavy burden on the future.

11
Human Rights in Developing Countries

Historically, the struggle for human rights in the West has been, in the main, associated with the effort of the middle class to take over power from the feudal class. As such, the middle class had to seek, define and defend the political and civil space which it aspired and found. As a consequence, the struggle to establish and maintain Political and civil rights has become the main pursuit of the middle class especially amongst its members who have been strong believers of liberal democratic ideology.

In present-day world politics there are other compelling reasons, so the West argue, which make it necessary for human rights to be "universal values" hence to be adopted unquestionably by non-Westerners. By putting human rights on par with civil and political rights the rich and powerful Western nations hope to avoid the competition and challenges, in the economic, social and cultural spheres, from the non-Western nations, which, in turn, could lessen the threat from the increasingly economically successful non-Western nations to their privileged position. In other words, the advanced Western nations do not wish the struggle for economic development by the developing non-Western nations be equated by the latter with the struggle for human rights and human dignity. Indeed, many non-Western nations have declared openly that their economic struggle has been essentially a struggle for the right to exist in the wake of Western economic onslaught, domination and exploitation.

In fact, in spite of economic and social progress in various countries of Asia, a significant segment of Asia's population, for example, does not enjoy some of the most basic economic and social rights such as the right to adequate fair wages, to health, and to education. Urgent and equal attention to economic and social rights, besides human rights, of the poor Asians is needed because Asia is where the majority of the poor live.

If violation of economic rights is also seen as a violation of human rights, as has been argued by the non-Western nations, then the Western nations should be on trial too with human rights because the former see it as an attempt to curb their economic progress. This is done by putting the governments of the non-Western nations on trial for alleged violation of freedom of expression or freedom of assembly, which, in turn, will put the governments of the non-Western nations on the defensive. It violation of economic rights is also seen as violation of human rights, as has been argued by the non-Western nations, then the Western nations should be on trial, too. This is something that the West—its governments, intelligentsia, middle-class, and NGOs included— still fails to grasp.

The concept of human rights is synonymous, and narrowly so, with political and civil rights. So to them violation of human rights involved mainly detention without trial, disappearances, torture, extra judicial executions and capital punishment but not starvation of millions because of poverty and famine. Thus the human rights of hundreds of those being tortured and detained without trial seem to be more paramount in the Western liberal values than the rights of the starving millions to live and the social and economic rights of many millions more in the poverty stricken category.

Now and then, certain "cultural rights" like the right to speak one's language or practise one's religion is also included in the Western definition of human rights. As a result, economic and social rights have received much less emphasis than they deserve although for the vast majority of people in Asia, and for that matter, Africa and Latin America, it is those rights that matter most. In some parts of Asia, poverty is so severe that the poor have become trapped in contemporary forms of slavery such as bonded labour, child labour and child prostitution. In this context, it is interesting to observe how the West reacted to the 1989 Tiananmen tragedy in China. Since then China has been commonly dismissed by Western nations as having a poor human rights record. China may be weak on political and civil rights but very few in the West want to really recognise the tremendous achievements on economic and social rights in its efforts to feed, shelter and educate its millions.

In this sense the Western perception of human rights is inimical to the interests of the people of the Third World because the West sees human rights as revolving around the individual whereas in Asia, there is a strong notion of rights of the collective, the community and the nation. As argued by a prominent Malaysian social activist, Dr. Chandra Muzaffar, seen from the religious and cultural viewpoint, reducing human rights to civil and political rights, as the advanced Western nations have propagated, is tantamount to a terrible injustice. In any culture and religion, be it in Christianity, Islam, Buddhism, Hinduism or Judaism, the poor have preference. To ignore the rights of the poor is a moral crime. By any cultural standards, all persons, especially the poor, the needy and the destitute should have access to the basic necessities of food, clothing, shelter, education and health care, irrespective of age, sex, colour or religion. Every worker is also entitled to a fair recompensation for his or her work. For those who cannot look after themselves, permanently or temporarily, it is the responsibility of the community to provide them with all the necessary facilities.

The struggle for this basic human right, the right to exist, is the struggle which dominates the life of the majority of human beings in the world. The civil and political rights could only exist if this basic right to exist as human being has been fulfilled. This basic right to exist is universal in nature and continonsly shaped and conditioned by culture.

In cultural terms the human being exists as a wholistic entity. The rights of a person are therefore inter-related and interdependent. Human rights emerge, grow and develop in this cultural context. It is incorrect to privilege one set of rights over another. The life of a human being cannot be compartmentalised and this also applies to his rights. Besides, culturally, rights should not be separated from responsibilities. They are very much interwoven as clearly stated in any religion. Like the Universal Declaration of Human Rights, all religions and cultures, too, recognise the right to found a family, the right to privacy, the right of freedom of movement and residence, the right to use one's own language, the right to practise one's own culture and the right to freedom of religion.

However, one would argue that there is a yawning gap between ideal and reality in Muslim, Buddhist,

Christian and Hindu societies. But one may ask, which country in the modern world with a substantial Christian population has even tried to be minimally faithful to the life and mission of Jesus? Will the advanced Western nations help to bridge the gap between ideal and reality as far as democratic principles and human rights are concerned?

It is quite obvious that the proponents of civil and political rights, in the context of the New World Order, have no conception of the interconnectedness between human rights and responsibilities. Such a situation occurred because the New World Order itself has emerged from a civilization that has tried so hard to separate rights from responsibilities. A classic case study of this situation is in front of our eyes, in Europe itself; as found happening in the former Yugoslavia. While the advanced Western nations, the main players within the New World Order, are campaigning vigorously to the nations of Southeast Asia regarding the need to observe human rights in these countries, they have neglected their responsibility towards the 20000 Muslim women raped in Bosnia.

The best they have done thus far has been to provide food for these women and their community. This demonstrates the major flaw of the advanced Western nations, a flaw that once again exposes their hyprocritical attitudes towards freedom and human rights. While the United States and other Western nations become incensed and agitated over violations of human rights and undemocratic practices in some countries in Southeast Asia and in the rest of the Third World, they have shown no concern at all about the lack of democracy in international economic, political, cultural and intellectual relations. The undemocratic nature of the present international system, practised and supported by the New World Order, is an undeniable truth.

It is the cultural practice and weltanschauung of the Western nation not to want any democratic reforms to the international system. It is this system that allows them political and cultural dominance through the United Nations and some of its agencies. It is also a system that facilitates their military dominance of the world through an effective monopoly of high-tech weapons of mass destruction. It is a system that enables them to dominate and control the global economy through GATT, IMF and the World Bank. It is a system that allows them to control worldwide information flows thus controlling the weapon of mass mind control.

It is a system that promotes their culture to overwhelm and subougate other cultures -and in the process establishes their lifestyle as THE lifestyle of the world. It is a clear case of the majority submitting to the will of a minority. This is the cultural conditions within which the present vigorous campaigns on human rights conducted by the West all over the world has to be viewed and understood. It is a form of cultural conditioning by strong few on the weal many, to borrow a phrase from Wertheim the world renowned Dutch scholar.

The world conference on Human Rights in Vienna, in June, 1993, adopted unanimously the Vienna Declaration and Programme of Action. Indeed Vienna Declaration is not only a Declaration or enunciation of principles but also asserts a programme of action. It asserts that protection and promotion of human rights is the first responsibility of the government and calls for increased cooperation and coordination in support of human rights within the U.N. system. The Declaration emphatically states that all human rights are "Universal, indivisible and interrelated". It represents, in the words of Kevin Boyle ('Stocktaking on Human Rights'. 'Politics and Human Rights' edited by David Beetham) "an admittedly uneasy global consensus on core human rights principles and at least an outline of the priorities of action to implement that consensus". The Declaration stressed that economic and social rights are as important as civil and political rights. Disparity between two sets of rights was acknowledged by the U.N. Committee on Economic, Social and Cultural Rights itself in its statement to the Vienna World Conference. "The shocking reality is that despite the rhetoric, violations of civil and political rights continue to be treated as though they were far more serious, more patently intolerable than massive and direct denials of economic, social and cultural rights".

Indeed the acceptance at Vienna by the developed countries of the importance and validity of social and economic rights and interdependence of these rights with civil and political freedom represents a positive gain from the aftermath of the cold war. The concept of universality of human rights caused sharp differences of opinion among the States in the preparatory meetings and at the plenary sessions in Vienna. The head of the Chinese delegation, Lien Huapiu in his speech at the Vienna conference stated "one should not and cannot think the human rights standards and models of certain countries as the only proper ones and demand that all countries comply with them. It is neither realistic nor workable to make international economic assistance or even international cooperation conditional on them".

The political predominance of the group of countries which is temporary by nature cannot provide a license for the imposition of a set of guidelines and norms for the behaviour of the entire international community, especially since these states do not present an ideal, feasible or practical model in theory or practice, nor do they possess admirable pasts. Now the most strident challenge to the concept of Universality of human rights has come from the highly dynamic-growth countries of South East Asia. The nub of Asian criticism of Western concept of human rights is that developed countries of the West are seeking to impose Western values on non-western societies with different moral standards and social traditions-an act of moral and cultural imperialism, Further, the West is using human rights as a stalkinghorse to achieve economic domination over the poorer world.

While all governments should uphold human rights, each individual country should be allowed to interpret and implement the goal according to its own circumstances. It is, therefore, unfair for the West, whose concepts of human rights, developed over centuries within its political and historical context, to expect that unstable and undeveloped countries should guarantee a broad range of individual freedom like western countries. The problem of this sequential approach is that often it becomes an alibi for authoritarianism and justification for violation of human rights by the authorities. In contrast to this sequential approach to human rights, others argue for concurrency and state that human rights, particularly civil liberties, do not endanger social and economic development or undermine nation-building.

Protecting citizens from torture by State authorities or imprisonment without trial, permitting freedom of worship, are not incompatible with economic development. Indeed, preservation of these rights will strengthen the legitimacy of the government and encourage hard work among the people. Historical experience further shows that economic and social rights themselves cannot be guaranteed over time if people have no say over the formulation and implementation of those policies and denial of information over the effects of those policies. The Vienna Declaration tried to set at rest the debate between the primacy of civil and political rights on one hand and economic and social rights on the other. It categorically states that human rights are universal, indivisible, interdependent and interrelated. One of the criticisms voiced against Universal Declaration of Human Rights is that it lays greater emphasis on civil and political rights than on economic, social and cultural rights.

Conditions in Third World Countries

Looking at condition, prevailing in Third World countries one has to admit that poverty indeed is one of the most potent causes of the violation of human rights in these countries. Poverty undermines human dignity and without human dignity there is no human rights. The Supreme Court in India by an expansive interpretation of Article 21 of the Constitution has laid down that the right to life guaranteed by article 21 means "right to live with dignity which, inter-alia, means right to shelter, health etc." Justice Bhagwati speaking for the Supreme Court in the case of Francis Coralic Mullen has by an expansive interpretation of Article 21 of the Constitution incorporated the right to food, clothing and shelter in the expression "life" in Article 21 of the Constitution. Thus some of the social and economic rights of the Directive Principles have been judicially incorporated within the realm of Fundamental rights.

The fact that rich countries of the world accounting for 20 percent of its population consume 80 percent of the world's resources tells its own tale and highlights the need to put a sharper focus on social and economic rights. The sombre picture of poverty, ignorance and misery in most countries of Asia, Africa and Latin America, aggravated by gaps in distributional equity, cannot be accepted in a world order believing in tenets of liberalism. Three quarters of all humanity who live in the developing countries are weighed down by poverty and under-development.

Unfortunately, aid received from developed countries is often tied-aid to be spent in rich donor countries. Aid conditionalities also create problems. Sometimes clauses in aid conditions (bilateral and multilateral) make aid a function of political performance. Criteria for measuring performance are unclear, yet the threat of reductions/ interruptions/withdrawal remains. These uncertainties complicate the process of setting and attaining social objectives. Again not all donors set the same agenda. So recipient countries run the risk of satisfying some while upsetting others. There is a real need for donors to work among themselves to fix common conditions and criteria for measuring results.

It has been strongly maintained by the developing countries that there should be greater emphasis on development and that the right to development to which paramount consideration is to be given is not merely a moral but a legal right. This right is very much essential to maintain world peace which is the prime objective of the U.N. It is guaranteed by Articles 1(3) and 55 of the U N Charter. In this connection it may be mentioned that the Proclamation of Teheran issued after the International Conference on Human Rights held in Teheran in 1968 also emphasized the principle of indivisibility of human rights and pointed out that progress in this direction was dependent on sound and effective national and international policies of economic and social development".

The ideas of the Teheran Conference had a profound impact on the Declaration on Social Progress and Development adopted by the U.N. General Assembly in 1969 proclaiming that "international peace and security on the one hand and social progress and, economic development on the other are closely interdependent and influence each other and it is of cardinal importance to "accelerate social and economic progress everywhere, thus contributing to international peace and solidarity".

In the UN Commission on Human Rights there have been sharp differences on the question of realization of social, economic and cultural rights. At the 33rd Session of the Commission in 1977, it was decided to ask the Secretary General to undertake a comprehensive study of the right to development. This study published subsequently in 1979 stated that there is a substantial body of principles based on UN Charter and International Bill of Human Rights and reinforced by a range of Declarations and Resolutions which show the existence of a Human Right to Development in international law.

The General Assembly of the United Nations did finally adopt a Declaration on Right to Development after many years of preparation in 1986. The Declaration states that the right to development is "an inalienable" right by virtue of which every human person and all peoples are entitled to participate in and contribute to, and enjoy economic, social, cultural and political development in which all human rights and fundamental freedom can be fully realized". The Declaration goes on to mention that the "human person is the central subject of development and should be an active participant and beneficiary of the right to development".

Though the Right to Development has now become a catchword and repeatedly embodied in a number of UN documents, the Western world views this with some amount of scepticism. It fears that this will cast responsibility on the developed countries to contribute to uplifting the standards of developing countries. There will be obligation on the part of 'haves' to help the 'have-nots'. Thus emphasis on development will involve criticisms of developed Western countries because it is mainly on them the question of turning this right to reality lies. There is also the apprehension on the part of developed countries that over-emphasis on the Right to Development might divert attention of the Third World States as well as UN organization on the need to respect and protect political and civil rights.

Some developing countries, on the other hand, feel that there is not much point in placing emphasis on civil and political rights in a totally unequal world order. Civil and political rights are luxuries that can wait for higher level of economic development. From the technical and economic standpoint, as pointed out by David Beetham in an illuminating article ('what future of Economic and Social Rights?" a joint programme on the part of international Community and national governments to ensure that everybody's basic rights are met is an eminently practicable proposition.

Many studies like the World Bank study of Basic Needs published in 1981 and UNDP Human Developments Reports from 1990 onwards go to show that basic needs of everyone in the world can be guaranteed within a decade or so without any high cost to the taxpayers in the developed world. Though funds required for implementation of such vast programmes will be substantial in absolute terms, they are small when expressed as a percentage of the GNP of the developed economies. The World Bank study revealed that if developed Western countries were to fund about 50 percent of the cost, this will require only an increase in aid from 0.35 to 0.45 percent par annum of their GNP, if existing aids were progressively directed towards a basic needs programme.

However, the programme to meet basic needs, though feasible, may encounter many serious problems. The hard fact remains that prevalent international trade and financial system systematically favours the North at the expense of the South, especially those countries which are heavily dependent on the export of a few primary commodities.

Though there is an on-going furious debate over the effects of structural adjustment programmes, it can be said without fear of contradiction that they have failed to protect the poorest of the developing countries from the harmful side-effects of adjustment. Again, implementation of basic needs programme in developing countries is hampered by internal constraints. In many of these countries the privileged and entrenched groups remain more interested in prestige projects and military hardware than at meeting the basic needs of common people. A time has now come to press for making some social and economic rights enforceable in preference to the maximalist approach of covering all these rights.

The interim Constitution of South Africa has included within the ambit of fundamental rights the 'right to education', the right of a child to "security, basic nutrition and basic health". There is need for adoption of an Optional Protocol to International Covenant on Economic Social and Cultural Rights (ICESCR). There should be mechanism for monitoring violation of these rights and provisions for individual complaints. The Vienna Conference endorsed the work of the Commission on Human Rights and the Economic, Social and Cultural Rights Committee in drafting such an optional protocol to ESCER Covenant, which would make possible to lodge complaints about violations of these rights to the ESCER Committee.

In developing countries of Asia and Africa and Latin America there are massive violations of human rights of disadvantaged groups and marginalised sections of the society etc. There are outrageous violations of civil and political rights as well as social and economic rights. The state is often the major culprit, but in many instances civil society which in many places is feudal in its outlook and approach, is the perpetrator of these violations in connivance with the State administration.

However, despite these violations, the level of human rights consciousness because of grinding poverty and widespread illiteracy is low. Thus in developing societies, human rights movement have a transformative potential. They constitute challenges to vested interests and oppressive systems that deny basic rights to the common people. They are tools in the building of a good society where the basic rights and freedoms of the people will be safeguarded.

The subject of human rights is of perennial interest to humankind. Much has been written on the subject in all parts of the globe and the subject shall not cease to be discussed. The subject has been discussed more or less on a universalistic basis keeping into view the developments taking place in the West. Of course, these developments shall in any case form a part of any thinking on human rights.

However, what should essentially be stressed is the fact that the stream of thought conditioning the evolution of human rights in a particular country/era is reflective of the particular socio-economic conditions operative at the relevant time. This thought may in no case correspond to the one existing in other countries. For comparisons are obvious and may result in either romanticism or at worst distortions. The subject of human rights in developing countries should then be approached keeping in view their special socio-economic circumstances. This will help one to substantiate the theory and practice guiding the protection of human rights in developing countries. One must appreciate that these countries share some common characteristics, which helps to make generalized comments on human rights in these countries. The present paper purports to analyse

Evolution of Human Rights

A study down the memory lane of human rights reveals two parallel trends having evolved over the years, particularly in the European context. The first and foremost is the liberalist tradition advocated by philosophers like Locke and Bentham. Both of them advocated their philosophies as a reaction to the existing socio-political conditions, in which the individual human beings were subjected to extreme conditions of suppression by the state, whoever it was. They damned their predecessors who advocated extreme powers for the state, which was most often than not utilized against the individuals.

Both Bentham and Locke advocated liberty and freedom for individuals. This school of thought was much more popularly reflected in American and French Revolutions. Indeed these revolutions were largely successful in highlighting and protecting liberty and freedom of individuals. This individualistic approach to human rights resulted in a hierarchy of civil and political rights for individuals which has carried the day. Another significant consideration towards sustenance of individualistic approach to human rights in the west was the evolution of the economic system based on free enterprise and free competition.

The legal system advocated in this connection was the one of provide a body of predictable and ascertainable standards of behaviour allowing each economic factor to maintain a set of relatively safe expectations as to the conduct of other social actors. Such a legal system was necessary being a convenient device for permitting economic activities and consolidating and protecting the fruits of such action. A further consideration is that a large section of law in the West was the fruit of political struggles between contending groups. The first 'bills of rights' resulted from a continued bitterness between the kings and his barons for the former's arbitrary behaviour. The continued struggle between these competing forces resulted into constitutions, placing restraints on the powers of aristocracy and its feudal privileges. The evolution of human rights in such a circumstance became quiteessential for social progress and equilibrium.

Thirdly, with the gradual secularization of religion, mainly Christianity, there occurred a gradual erosion of the metaphysical components of religious tenets and their absorption into daily life as general more precepts. Resting on religious or ethical principles, legal rules acquired an extra-legal dimensions which strongly enhanced their value. Such a kind of theory was instrumental in evolution of a legal system and law which showed its commitment to uphold the dictates of individual rights based on the economic necessities of a laissez-faire system. Indeed the States showed a greater resilience towards human enhancement by minimalist interventions in the domain of individual rights.

In contradiction to the above school, Marxian concept about human rights puts emphasis on group (social) rights rather than individual rights. Dominated by the writings of Marx and the Fabian club particularly Laski, the argument runs that full realization of an individual's self is possible only within the context of a society. In as much as an individual should be concerned with his development, the society has an interest in facilitating the advancement of individuals. Because of the overwhelming responsibility of the state towards its subject, it is but natural that economic and social rights should have predominance over the individual ones.

In addition to above an account of the Modem rights theory must also be given. These theories have been developed either as a reaction to the earlier ones or as the refinements to the existing jurisprudence on human rights. Among them must be mentioned Rawls, Radbruch, Robert Nozik, Mcdougal and Dworkin. These theorists display a number of common characteristics. First, they are eclectic, benefiting from each other's insights so that it is imprecise to characterize their theories as simply utilitarian, natural rights, intuitive, behavioural, etc.

Secondly, modern theorist recognize and try to address, using various approaches, the tension between liberty and equality. Some do so through theories of resolution which try to show that these goals are reconcilable and achievable within the same social order. Some find the tension irreconcilable and seek to resolve the dilemma by ranking goals hierarchically. Others evolve refining theories which accept a relationship between liberty and equality characterized by shifting readjustments. Thirdly, most theorists acknowledge the need to construct an entire system of rights.

After the Second World War, many changes occurred on the world scenario. Amongst them arc the emergence of a large number of countries as independent nations, which were colonial domains of the West. Secondly, the emergence on the world scene of a large number of international organizations including primarily the United Nations and other allied organizations. Although the basic objective of the U.N. was to pursue the models of activities maintaining international peace and security, But over the years it undertook diverse activities in fulfilment of the objectives of an interdependent world. United Nations and its allied organizations have shown a remarkable interest in pursuing, though in a modest way the goal of protection of human rights at universal levels.

The worst kind of brutalization of human rights in the First and Second World War was the main motivating factor in pursuing the goals of protection of human rights in the post-war period. Although the relationship between the individual and the states was deemed to be the sole domain of the state, yet the international protection of individuals was either in the form of individual treaties as happened after Ist World War or through humanitarian intervention. Nevertheless the main plank of Allied powers included wider questions involving guarantee of human rights.

It was, therefore, deemed necessary that protection of human rights became one of the purposes of UN (Art, 1) and the charter has imposed obligations upon the member states to this end. Arts. 55 and 56 of the Charter imposes upon the United Nations and its member legal obligation to "promote" respect for and observance of human rights. The action taken by UN in this pursuit has taken several forms. A large number of declarations and treaties have been adopted mostly as a result of the work of UN Commission of Human Rights.

The extent to which such declarations and treaties have had or will have impact upon general protection of human rights in national countries is less clear. The United Nations acting mainly through the General Assembly and the Security Council, has sometimes acted to protect human rights by means other than the adoption of treaties and other documents. In pursuance of the implementation of the principle of 'respect for human rights and fundamental freedoms', the Human Rights Commission considered a preliminary draft of an international Bill of Rights prepared by a drafting committee in 1947. Because of difference of opinions as to its contents, the commission decided to draw up simultaneously a draft declaration, a draft convention and implementation.

In the process Universal Declaration of Human Rights (1948), Covenant on Civil and Political Rights (1966) and Covenant on Economic, Social and Cultural Rights (1967) were adopted. They together would from what is referred as 'International Bill of Human Rights'. The human rights as delimited in the above documents has been incorporated by many countries in their constitutions and other law, thus respecting the Universal application of human rights particularly an the field of civil and political rights. However, in economic, social and cultural rights, various states have no followed suit because of varying needs and models of socio-economic development.

The diverse Socio-cultural matrix of developing countries does not permit them to approach the promotion and protection of human right, in a thorough and unified way. Nor can they he guided by the Western style ideology and thinking on protection Of human rights. This is because of three reasons. The first being that incorporation of Western theories of human rights shall he a continuation of the Colonial heritage. Secondly, these countries being in a flux, (lie human rights a, determined and evolved by West shall he either Inappropriate or too rigid for these countries to adopt changing priorities. Thirdly, because of the politics of human rights practised by the ruling elites in these countries. They are united in their notion of governance and expediency of their rule which is often taken as a justification for derogation from the protection of human rights. It is indeed these views which are highly publicised at national and international levels.

As a matter of fact developing countries show a remarkable difference of cultures and socio-economic realities inter-se and intra-se. They also represent world's major religions and political ideologies like socialism, democracy or feudalism. At the same time they arc faced with tremendous problems of state building, economic reconstruction and regional, sub-regional and ethnic conflicts. These conflicts have grown to the extent so much so that even the foundation of the state as such is threatened.

There remains a sharp disagreement on the exact scope and nature of basic human rights, on the treatment of substantive human rights, economic issues and the methodology of protection of these human rights. More often than not the nature of conflict between liberty, equality and other competing values is easily discernible and in prone to many distortions, sometimes even hostility. This is again because of three reasons. Firstly, the primary aim is to strengthen the authority of the state and do not favour centrifugal tendencies which could benefit from full recognition of the rights and freedoms of individuals. Secondly, post-decolonization of purposes of economic development a strong government was needed for reconstruction and development.

The restriction of certain rights and liberties seemed inevitable. The economic and social rights had to be promoted at the expense of civil and political rights. Thirdly, because of peculiar social structure in these countries the government/leader had to exercise undisputed powers. The freedom authority dialectic operative in Western European tradition is alien to the cultures operating in developing countries. However, over the years three distinct legal systems have evolved in the group of developing countries. The first may be described as an absolutely autocratic state, which does not show any regard towards the promotion and protection of human rights. Being based on the tradition of ruler-ruled relationship, the ruler is deemed to be above law. In the process of amalgamation and furtherance of his rule, nothing stops him even if it would mean brutalization of certain minimum rights. This is particularly true in some Asian and African countries. The second category comprises of these countries with progressive regimes 'aiming at total or near total mobilization for rapid economic and social transformation and with de jure or de facto one party rule'. In theme countries one should find greater emphasis on social and economic transformation at such a pace that civil and political rights are 'qualified' to permit it. These countries have developed a highly mobilized social and political system geared to rapid economic and social system.

It is true that these countries have made immense strides in economic and social transformation. But over the years these countries have faced graver problems in terms of the challenge to the one party authority from groups and sub-groups, representing various shades of opinion and ideologies thus forcing the governments for tougher measures against these groups sometimes even nationalities even at the expense of human rights. Thus human rights violations have occurred because of threat to the social cohesion and economic progress.

The third group of countries constitute the countries having democratic rules and institutions with two or multi-party systems including India, Possessed with written constitutions and instruments of democracies, and a judiciary these countries are purportedly adherents to the theory of promotion and protection of human rights as enshrined in their constitutions. Of course, the written constitutions guarantee individual liberty, equality and freedom, yet the working of these countries have not shown praise worthy results. Of course, this is because of the fact that reality of socio-economic backwardness of huge populace is in their minds which puts a premium on the protection of human rights. Being pluralistic and having deeper social stratification of classes, there are no ideal solutions to the problem of promotion and protection of human rights. Being also faced with demands of large groups and sub-groups, a homogeneous approach to protection of human rights is neither tried nor can perhaps be achieved. Consequently very often in meeting such demands it is either the basic law which is violated or leads together unmanageable problems.

On any discourse on human rights, it is too often hurrying to consecrate a common standard of mankind for human rights. All throughout the world at all stages of history there seems to have been difficulties for evolving a concrete and particular theory and model for human rights. This is true for the developed West and shall be true for developing countries. Of course, the course of events in developed West has been too favourable for promotion and protection of human rights.

Nonetheless the developing countries are in chaos concerning the protection and implementation of human rights. Notwithstanding the core concern shown by international declarations and principles upon protection of human rights, it is difficult if not impossible, to arrive at a concept of human rights in developing countries, which is unanimously acceptable, nor is there is a common framework of action. It often happens that at any international action the developing countries are quick either to enter caveat/reservation or even if accepted are silently violating it. The disrespect shown to some of the international covenants on human rights is a growing recognition of the overestimation of the role of state and a positive threat of human rights.

Faced with immense under-development combined with foreign and colonial exploitation, poverty and illiteracy, the human rights are illusory to a large populace of these countries. In the process of pursuing socio-economic goals, the developing countries show a second rate respect to civil and political rights. Of course, it is true that present international economic system is largely responsible for under-developed conditions of poorer nations. In this connection it is instructive to refer to the efforts undertake by developing countries and UNCTAD to modify and change the conditions of international economic relations to the advantage of developing countries. It was presumed that equity in international relations could are percolats in the economies of developing countries.

Contrary to the expectations of developing countries, not only did the call for New International Order fail, but over the years new forms of economic dependency has been thrust upon developing countries by IMF, World Bank Sponsored structural adjustment programmes. These programmes have forced developing countries to change their economic policies. These policies have deeper implications for developing countries particularly their marginalised sections of populations. The net result of it is that potential for upliftment of human fights should be in danger. Needless to say that an unjust international order would be reflected in these states.

The tendencies of dehumanizing the human rights is writ large in developing countries. Whether in economic reorganization schemes/programmes or in a bourgeois administrative and institutional set up, the miserty of human rights has further been accentuated. The criminalization of politics and the lack of accountability has become the order of the day. The brutalization of the state power is reflected in the increase in number of state crimes, with little or slight confront from judiciary in terms of payment of compensation. The elites are becoming powerful enough to obstruct the ordinary course of rule of law, Rule of law is confined only to academics. The content of which has become defunct.

A situation of no return has reached in the politics of governance in developing countries. Apart from occasional outbursts from the judiciary, press, human rights activities, non-governmental organizations, there is no meaningful attempt to formulate a clear cut methodology for protection of human rights. An overall rethinking in this context is not only desirable but necessary also. It should be re-emphasized that the recognition, guarantee and effective protection of human fights of individuals and groups is of prime importance in maintaining the stability and cohesion in any society including developing countries.

No economic or social progress can be reached at the cost of violation of human rights, whatever they are. The promulgation and protection of human rights have to be consistent with the patterns and structures of authority and people aspirations as well as expectations. The role of human rights is to tune the administrative and judicial system and fortify rights and freedoms.

In any country with low level of literacy and underdevelopment, massive input is required for removing them. Of course, it is for the state to consider the required means and ways which should go a long way in reinforcing the importance of human rights. But along with it a massive effort is required to educate vast majority of people about the role of state and the incorporation of human rights in all models of human existence. This is an effort which has to be carried at all levels. This would help the lessen the overestimated role and authority of the state in developing countries.

Secondly, if the human rights have to he successfully implemented in a developing country, a free and independent judiciary to protect the rights is necessary. In India e.g. the judiciary particularly the higher judiciary has served the cause of human rights. However, there should be every effort to maintain and uphold the Rule of law in all its aspects. Moreover, the peoples' movement forsuccessful and judicious working, of the institutions of democracy has to be strengthened with more stress on the accountability of these institutions. That would indeed serve the cause of human rights in every society including the developing country.

Thirdly, there is every justification for more and more protection to marginalized person' in developing countries, Because over the years these 'marginalized persons' have been forced into an element of depravity, dehumanization and brutalization. If developing countries have to process and prosper they cannot do so with an open disregard to the necessities of these people. The governments have to be conscious of the plight of these classes.

Any economic rejuvenation plan must have an element of egalitarianism and protection of weaker sections at all levels, Because market can act as factor for allocation but cannot act as benefactor of the marginalized and deprived segments of population of developing countries. Lastly, it must be added that any developing country has its own difficulty in arriving at a consolidated thinking on the promotion and protection of human rights. This is because of very special kind of considerations in which a country is in. However, these difficulties must not be advocated as justification for abrogation of human rights.

Bibliography

Alston, 'Human Rights and Basic Needs'.

Antonio Cassese, *'The Self-Determination of Peoples'*, in Louis Henkin (ed.), The International Bill of Rights (New York, Columbia University Press, 1981). Both international covenants entered into force in 1976.

Antony G.N. Flew, 'Wants or Needs; Choices or Commands', in Fitzgerald, Human Needs and Politics.

Asborn Eide, *"Human Rights in World Society"*, Oslo. 1977.

Bhagwati, P.N. Human Rights in the Criminal Justice System 12 Indian Bar Review, 1985. Also *see* Mool Chand Sharma, Judicial Creativity and the Due Process Clause 12, Indian Bar Review, 1985.

Carter, J. L. Inaugural Address, 1977, quoted in, David P. Forsythe, *"Human Rights and World Politics"*. University of Nebraska Press, 1983.

Dr. Durga Das Basu, *Human Rights in Constitutional Law Practice*, Hell of India, Private Ltd. New Delhi, 1994.

For an overall survey of human rights situation *see*, K.P. Saksena, ed. *Human Rights: Perspective and Challenges in 1990s and Beyond* (New Delhi: Lancers Books, 1994).

For information on the special procedure of the ILO relating to freedom of association, *see* chap. XIV, section D (1) (h).

For texts, *see Human Rights: A Compilation of International Instruments*, UN Doc. ST/HR/1/Rev. 1 (1978). For a table of accessions to these instruments, ***see*** Human Rights International Instruments: Signatures, Ratifications, etc., UN Doc. ST/HR/4/Rev. 2 (1980).

Fouad Ajami, '*Human Rights and World Order Politics*', Alternatives, vol. 3 (1978).

Frank E. Krenz, "*The Refugee as a Subject of International Law*", International and Comp. Law Quarterly, Vol. 15, 1966.

Habermas, J. "*What is Universal Pragmatics?*," in Communication and the Evolution of Society, (trans. T. McCarthy, 1979) at 2-3.

Henkin, "Human Rights and 'Domestic Jurisdiction,'" in Buergenthal, ed., Human Rights, International Law, and the Helsinki Accord 21, (1977).

Human Rights and Social Justice-Foreword of book by Justice R. N. Bhagwati.

Jois, M.R., *Human Rights and Indian Value* (National Council of Teacher Education), Revised Edition, New Delhi, 1998.

Kemp, R. "*Planning, Public Hearings, and the Politics of Discourse*," in J. Forester, Critical Theory and Public Life (1985) at 182.

Kenneth E. Boulding, '*The Shadow of the Stationary State*', Daedalus, vol. 102 (1974).

Lawyers' Committee for International Human Rights, The Generals Give Back Uruguay (New York, 1985), P. 57; Weschler, A Miracle, a Universe; Inter-Church Committee on Human Rights in Latin America, Violations of Human Rights in Uruguay (Toronto, 1978); Weinstein, Uruguay.

Lawyers' Committee for International Human Rights, The Generals Give Back Uruguay.

Lawyers' Committee for International Human Rights, The Generals Give Back Uruguay (New York, 1985), P. 57; Weschler, A Miracle, a Universe, p. 112; Inter-Church Committee on Human Rights in Latin America, Violations of Human Rights in Uruguay (Toronto, 1978); Weinstein, Uruguay.

Myres S. Mc. Dongal, Harold D. Lasswell and Lung-Chu Chen, *Human Rights and World Public Order*, 1986 pp. 64-65.

Nagendra Singh, *India and International Law*, 10, (1969).

Official Records of the Economic and Social Council, Forty-second Session, Supplement No. 6 (E/4322 and Corr. 1).

Recommendation No. R(83) I of the Committee of Ministers to Member States of the Council of Europe on Stateless Nomads and Nomads of Undetermined Nationality, adopted on 22 Feb. 1983.

Richard Falk, '*Comparative Protection of Human Rights in Capitalist and Socialist Third World Countries*', Universal Human Rights, vol. I (1979), no. 2.

Roberta Cohen, "Human Rights Diplomacy: The Carter Administration and the Southern Cone," Human Rights Quarterly 4 (May 1982).

Sadruddin Aga Khan, "*Legal Problems Relating to Refugees and Displaced Persons*", Recueil Des Courts, Collected Courses of the Hague Academy of International Law, 1976, 1.

Saxena, J.N. "*Problems of Refugees in the Developing Countries and the Need for International Burden Sharing*", International Law in Transition, Essays in Memory of Judge Nagendra Singh, Lancers Pook, New Delhi, 1992.

See Autonio Cassese, International Law in a Divided World (1986).

See B. Malinowski, The Scientific Theory of Culture and Other Essays (Chapel Hill, NC, 1944), A. Maslow, '*A Theory of Human Motivation*', Psychological Review, vol. 50 (1943).

See Cot, 'Winning East-West in North-South', Foreign Policy, no. 46, (Spring 1982). -South: A Programme for Survival (London, Pan, 1980).

See Freedom of Association: Digest of Decisions of the Freedom of Association Committee of the Governing Body of the ILO. Third edition, ILO, 1985.

See generally McDougal *et al.* Human Rights and World Public Order (1986). *See* also Mani, U.S., Human Rights in Developing countries in Agarwala (ed.) New Horizon in International Law Developing countries.

See H. Gros Espiell, "*Evolving Concept of Human Rights*" in B.G. Ramachandran (ed.) Human Rights, 1979.

See Karl Joseph Partsch, Individuals in International Law, in: *Encyclopedia of Public International Law* (Amsterdam: Elsevier Science Publ., 1985).

See Rosalyn Higgins, *Conceptual Thinking About the Individual in International Law,* in: Falk, Kratochwill and Mendlovitz, ads., International La., A Contemporary Perspective (Colorado: Weetview Press, 1985).

See Sixth United Nations Congress on the Prevention of Crime and the Treatment of Offenders: Report prepared by the Secretariat (United Nations publication, Sales No. E.81.IV.4).

See the preamble and Article 4, 12(3), 188(3), 19(3), 21 and 22(2) of the Convenient, in Appendix B; also the Preamble and Article 4 of the Covenant on Economic, Social and Cultural Rights.

See, e.g., T. Donaldson, The Ethics of International Business. In advocating a "fairness-affordability" condition for all assertions of fundamental international rights, Donaldson asserts that purported basic human rights must satisfy a threshold criterion of affordability for potential duty-bearers.

See, Eugen Ehrlich, Fundamental Principles of the Sociology of Law (1962).

See, for example, Philip Alston, *'Human Rights and Basic Needs: A Critical Assessment'*, Revue des droits de l'homme, vol. 13 (1979).

See, for instance, Masami Ito, "The Problem of Human Rights in other Asian Traditions"; and Buddhist Traditions", *Human Rights Teaching* (UNESCO), vol. IV, 1985.

See, in particular, Article 21 of the Universal Declaration and Article 25 of the Covenant on Civil and Political Rights. These points have been discussed in detail in Chapter VI (Self Determination etc.).

See, the Convention on the Prevention and Punishment of Crime Against Internationally Protected Persons including Diplomatic Agents 1973, 131 L.M. 42 (!974); Misc. 19 (1975) Cmnd. 6176.

See, The International Bill of Human Rights (United Nations Publication, New York, 1978).

Seventh United Nations Congress on the Prevention of Crime and the Treatment of Offenders, Milan, 26 August-6 September 1985 (United Nations publication, Sales No. E.86.1V.1).

Seventh United Nations Congress on the Prevention of Crime and the Treatment of Offenders (United Nations publication, Sales No. E.86.IV.1).

Sixth United Nations Congress on the Prevention of Crime and the Treatment of Offenders, Caracas, 25 August-5 September 1980 (United Nations publication, Sales No. E.81.1VA).

The International Bill of Human Rights, *op. cit.*, pp. 10-20.

Thomas Buergenthal, *International Human Rights in a Nut Shell* (Minnesota: West Publ. Co., 1988).

Tom J. Farer (ed.), Toward a Humanitarian Diplomacy: A Primer for Policy (New York, New York University Press, 1980).

UNGA res.429 (V), 14 Dec.1950. The draft protocol on stateless persons also appears in Report of the Ad hoc Committee on Refugees and Stateless Persons, Second Session: UN doc.E/1850, Annex. II. The Committee had been renamed in the interim.

Weis, P., 'The International Status of Refugees and Stateless Persons,' (1956) Journal du droit international.

World Bank, *World Development Report*, 1980 (Washington, D.C., 1980).